WHAT THE BIBLE TEACHES

Contributors

ACTS
JAMES ANDERSON

James Anderson has served the Lord in the ministry of the Word and in gospel preaching for forty years throughout the United Kingdom. For most of this period he combined the demands of public service with a professional career and still found time to maintain an active interest in missionary activity and in the spread of the gospel to the villages of his native Ayrshire.

He is the author of the two well - received books *They Finished Their Course* and *They Finished Their Course In The Eighties* as well as of numerous tracts and booklets. For some years he was joint-editor of *Believer's Magazine*.

JAMES
GEORGE WAUGH

G.P. Waugh was born in Newarthill, Scotland, and saved in Annbank, Scotland, in 1937. Throughout a very demanding secular career, he has preached the gospel and ministered the Word extensively in Great Britain. With retirement, his ministry has taken him further afield to Australasia. He maintains a deep interest in the spread of the gospel abroad, having been associated with the Home and Foreign Mission Fund for many years

WHAT THE BIBLE TEACHES

with
Authorised Version
of
The Bible

IN ELEVEN VOLUMES
COVERING THE NEW TESTAMENT

VOLUME 9

JOHN RITCHIE LTD
KILMARNOCK, SCOTLAND

ISBN 0 946351 35 X

WHAT THE BIBLE TEACHES
Copyright © 1992 by John Ritchie Ltd.
40 Beansburn, Kilmarnock, Scotland

All rights reserved. No part of the publication may be reproduced, stored in a retrieval system, or transmitted in any form or by any other means – electronic, mechanical, photocopy, recording or otherwise – without the prior permission of the copyright owner.

Typeset at Newtext Composition, 465 Paisley Road, Glasgow.
Printed at The Bath Press, Avon.

CONTENTS

	Page
PREFACE	1
ACTS	
INTRODUCTION	3
OUTLINE	10
BIBLIOGRAPHY	6
TEXT AND EXPOSITION	13
ACTS AND JAMES	265
JAMES	271
INTRODUCTION	271
OUTLINE	273
BIBLIOGRAPHY	274
TEXT AND EXPOSITION	275

ABBREVIATIONS

AV	Authorised Version of King James Version 1611
JND	New Translation by J.N. Darby 1939
LXX	Septuagint Version of Old Testament
Mft	New Translation by James Moffatt 1922
NASB	New American Standard Bible 1960
NEB	New English Bible 1961
Nestle	Nestle (ed.) Novum Testamentum Graece
NIV	New International Version 1973
NT	New Testament
OT	Old Testament
Phps	New Testament in Modern English by J.B. Philips 1962
RSV	Revised Standard Version 1952
RV	Revised Version 1881
TR	Textus Receptus or Received Text
Wey	New Testament in Modern Speech by R.F. Weymouth 1929

PREFACE

They follow the noblest example who seek to open the Scriptures to others, for our Lord Himself did so for those two dejected disciples of Emmaus (Luke 24:32). Whether it is the evangelist "opening and alleging that Christ must needs have suffered and risen from the dead" (Acts 17:3) or the pastor-teacher "expounding ... in all the scriptures the things concerning himself" (Luke 24:27) or stimulating our hope "through the patience and comfort of the scriptures" (Rom 15:4), he serves well in thus giving attendance to the reading of the Scriptures (1 Tim 4:13).

It is of course of equal moment to recognise in the exercise of able men, the continued faithfulness of the risen Head in giving gifts to the Church, in spite of her unfaithfulness. How good to recognise that "the perfecting of the saints ... the work of the ministry ... the edifying of the body of Christ" need not be neglected. Every provision has been made to ensure the well-being of the people of God. And every opportunity should be taken by the minister of Christ and those to whom he ministers to ensure that the saints "grow up into him in all things which is the head, even Christ" (Eph 4:15).

At various times in the post-apostolic period, certain teachers have come to prominence, sometimes because they succumbed to error, sometimes because in faithfulness they paid the ultimate price for the truth they had bought and would not sell. Some generations had Calvin and Luther, others Darby and Kelly, but in every generation God's voice is heard. It is important that we hear His voice today and recognise that He does speak through His servants. The contributors to this series of commentaries are all highly-respected expositors among the churches of God. They labour in the Word in the English-speaking world and have been of blessing to many throughout their years of service.

The doctrinal standpoint of the commentaries is based upon the acceptance of the verbal and plenary inspiration of the Scriptures so that their inerrant and infallible teachings are the only rule of conscience. The impeccability of Christ, His virgin birth, vicarious death and bodily resurrection are indeed precious truths worthy of the christian's defence, and throughout the volumes of this series will be defended. Equally the Rapture will be presented as the Hope of the Church. Before the great Tribulation she will be raptured and God's prophetic programme will continue with Jacob's trouble, the public manifestation of Christ and the Millennium of blessing to a restored Israel and the innumerable Gentile multitude in a creation released from the bondage of corruption.

May the sound teaching of these commentaries be used by our God to the blessing of His people. May the searching of the Scriptures characterise all who read them.

The diligence of Mr. J.W. Ferguson and the late Professor J. Heading in proof-reading is gratefully acknowledged. Without such co-operation, the production of this commentary would not have been expedited so readily.

T. WILSON
K. STAPLEY

THE ACTS OF THE APOSTLES

Introduction

1. **General Observations**
2. **Authorship and Date**
3. **Title**
4. **Characteristics**
5. **Outline**
6. **Bibliography**

1. General Observations

The Acts of the Apostles is the first historical book written concerning the christian church. The opening words "The former treatise" (1:1) show that it is the continuation of the Gospel by Luke. Whereas this Gospel was the result of Luke's research into the origins of the gospel using eyewitnesses for his material (Luke 1:1-4), the latter part of the Acts of the Apostles contains much material of which Luke himself was an eyewitness.

The book records how eleven men (listed in 1:13), regarded by the Jewish leaders as uneducated and untrained in the academic schools of men, commenced to evangelise the known world; they were supplemented shortly afterwards by the new apostle Matthias, and later by the apostle Paul who spread the gospel further afield into Gentile territory. Others were, of course, involved; see 8:1; 11:19. In spite of their lack of academic qualifications, they did their work well, since the Spirit of God was guiding them and the Lord Jesus was "working with them" (Mark 16:20). The narrative begins in the great religious city of Jerusalem, and ends in the political capital of the ancient world, Rome, with other major cities such as Athens, Corinth and Ephesus visited in between.

One theme that is prominent throughout the book is that suggested in the advice given by the Jewish rabbi Gamaliel (5:34-39), who spoke about the inadvisability of fighting against God. Certainly men would try (Ps 2:2; Acts 4:27; Rev 17:14), but the resurrection and ascension of Christ prove that men cannot succeed against God's Christ, while the furtherance of the gospel shows that they cannot succeed against God's gospel nor against God's church, "for the gates of hell shall not prevail against it" (Matt 16:18).

If the inspiration for the Gospels derives from the coming of Christ into the world, then the inspiration for the Acts derives from the coming of the Spirit. These apostles, entrusted with the commencement of the evangelisation of the world, did so in the power of the risen Christ and also in the power of the newly-arrived Spirit of God, whose spectacular coming and immediate work form the great subject of ch.2.

The book is punctuated by a series of addresses given by Peter and Paul in the various places where they preached the gospel (2:14; 3:12; 10:34; 13:16; 17:22; 20:18; 22:1; 24:10; 26:2). These addresses were not well-prepared beforehand (as is the custom today), but were delivered impromptu, produced under the demands of the moment before the Jewish Sanhedrin, in Cornelius' home, in Jewish synagogues, before the Greek scholars and students on Mars' Hill in Athens, etc. Appropriate OT quotations and references are made to suit the particular types of audiences, giving us good examples of how to match our preaching to the backgrounds of our audiences. Not one of these addresses was a prepared sermon for an organised meeting, but each shows just how ready the hearts and minds of the first preachers were to present their message to every ready-made audience before which they stood.

The history that unfolds in the book is of a movement with a small beginning, and that spread out though not reaching the ends of the then-known earth. About one hundred and twenty people all of one nationality gathered in a single room in old Jerusalem in 1:15. The growth took place in spite of human opposition and their own weakness. Three thousand were added to their number in 2:41, though some of these may have been pilgrims visiting Jerusalem for the feast of Pentecost (but note that Peter was particularly addressing the "men of Judaea" and those "that dwell at Jerusalem" in v.14). Their number was about five thousand by the time 4:4 is reached. Next time Luke summarises the situation he uses no numbers: "believers were the more added to the Lord, multitudes both of men and women" (5:14); "when the number of the disciples was multiplied" (6:1); "the churches ... were multiplied" (9:31).

It must have been still more disconcerting to the Jewish leaders when "a great company of the priests were obedient to the faith" (6:7). Nor did persecution decrease the enthusiasm of the first Christians, for the blood of the martyrs has always proved to be the seed of the church. When persecution took place, it simply served God's purpose in scattering saints who promptly witnessed in the new areas to which they went (8:1; 11:19).

The most spectacular thing that God did was to arrest the chief persecutor, bringing him on to His side. Saul (later the apostle Paul) proved to be the most valuable capture, for he "laboured more abundantly than they all" (1 Cor 15:10). Through his labours, the gospel spread in ever-widening circles, and far from his Roman imprisonment at the end of the book being a tragedy it was a triumph: "the things which happened unto me have fallen out rather unto the furtherance of the gospel" (Phil 1:12; Acts 28:31).

By that time, the main cities of the ancient world, especially in Asia Minor, Macedonia and Greece, all had christian communities. And whereas the Acts concludes at that point, yet that was not the end of the ongoing story.

2. Authorship and Date

Like all the four Gospels, Acts is strictly an anonymous book. The writer has the distinction of having written two books without even once mentioning his own name (unlike all the Epistles, except that to the Hebrews and the three by John). The fact that the third Gospel and the Acts are addressed to the same honourable gentleman shows their common authorship. Whether Theophilus was the actual name of a person or of some particular "friend of God" (as the name means) with whom the author was acquainted, we do not know, but he was obviously a fellow-disciple of the Lord Jesus with a desire to know the authenticity of His story from first to last.

Since the second of these books to Theophilus is obviously a follow-on from the first, we could well call them the *First and Second Books of Luke*. His identity is hinted at by the use of the pronoun "we" in several passages of Acts. The first is in 16:10, when Paul was on the point of leaving Troas (the ancient city of Troy) to cross into Europe in response to the vision of a Macedonian appealing for help. The author has not included himself until that point, but joins Paul, Silas and Timothy on their journey into Europe. The author was obviously left behind in Philippi when Paul and his company left that city (cf. 16:10; 17:1, 10). Only when Paul and his company returned to Macedonia does Luke re-enter the story (20:5, 6). This would seem to indicate Luke's strong influence on the new church at Philippi. The author then returned to Troas in Asia, and seems to have been Paul's constant companion from then on, though at some stage he must have been in Galilee and Jerusalem gathering material from eye-witnesses for his Gospel. He may not have actually shared Paul's Caesarean imprisonment with him, but then neither did he literally share his Roman imprisonments (Col 4:14; 2 Tim 4:11). He was certainly Paul's companion on his protracted voyage to Rome (Acts 27:1, 4, 7), giving us a masterly eyewitness account of that journey with its unforgettable shipwreck. The use of the pronoun "we" continues even until Paul's arrival in Rome (28:16).

The only one of Paul's companions who fits these facts is Luke, mentioned in two of the first prison Epistles (Col 4:14; Philem 24). He is with Paul in Rome, and there seems to be no intention on his part of leaving him there alone, unlike some others. His personal attachment to Paul is stressed in the last Epistle that Paul wrote (2 Tim 4:11), so it is likely that what "the beloved physician" did for Paul during his second Roman imprisonment he also did for him during the first. It is from such internal evidence that a Lucan authorship is deduced for these two NT books. For further information on this subject, see the Introduction to *Luke* in this series *What the Bible Teaches*.

Another point that weighed heavily in this direction with the late Prof. Rendle Short was *The Medical Language of Luke*, to quote the title of Dr Hobert's book on the subject, of which Rendle Short was very fond. He quoted, "A close comparison of the language of the author with that of Hippocrates, Galen and Aretaeus shows that whoever wrote those two books was a medical man. He uses twenty-three technical medical expressions not found in other NT writers, four of which – diagnosis, thrombi, syndrome and dysentery – have been taken over into modern English". While Dr Hobert's book no longer carries the weight it once did, especially when compared with other Greek medical writers, what the author says about the medical language of the two books under consideration is still true.

The Acts comes to an abrupt end, leaving Paul in prison in Rome. The date of the writing of the book is not likely to be any later, therefore, than the prison Epistles which were written from the same address. The fact that the author describes the first part of that imprisonment demands a date as late as AD 63. (See the following table.)

We do not know why no third book was written, for rather obviously Paul had several years of further missionary activity. Equally it must be admitted that the Acts is anything but complete. For when we consider the long list of suffering experiences that Paul endured for the gospel's sake, as recorded in 2 Cor 11:23-33, we realise that the majority of them cannot be equated with any of the events described by Luke in the Acts. Moreover, not only does this book contain accounts of the work and journeys of only a few of the apostles, but it is obvious that it contains accounts of only some of the evangelistic exploits of the apostle Paul. For example, the Acts tells us of only three of his imprisonments, namely that in Philippi in ch.16, that in Caesarea in chs.23-26, and that in Rome in ch.28. Yet on his third missionary journey he writes about having been "in prisons more frequent" (2 Cor 11:23), although thus far only that in Philippi has been recorded by Luke. Again, Luke has written about only one occasion when Paul was shipwrecked, yet prior to that Paul has mentioned three such experiences in 2 Cor 11:25. Again, the Acts does not give us a single example of Paul being beaten with thirty-nine stripes by the Jews, yet he writes in 2 Cor 11:24 that he had been subjected to such beatings five times. This Epistle, 2 Corinthians, was one of his earlier letters, written in AD 57 during his third missionary journey, yet he lived for about a further twelve years. Has there ever been a life so full of purposeful adventure as his? But the Lord had said, "I will show him how great things he must suffer for my name's sake" (Acts 9:16).

The chronology of Acts is rather uncertain. The only events which may reasonably be fixed are the famine in Claudius Caesar's time (11:28); his expulsion of the Jews from Rome (18:2), and the taking up of the procuratorship by Porcius Festus (24:27). The exercise of fitting the events of the book into this framework is still difficult, and every year from AD 31 (proposed by Bengel) to AD 42 (proposed by Eusebius) has been suggested for Paul's conversion. Most scholars favour dates between AD 35 and AD 40. The largest number favour AD 37 or 38. If we accept this, the following table is likely to be reasonably accurate.

AD	37	Paul's conversion	Acts 9:1
	40	Paul's first visit to Jerusalem	9:26; Gal 1:18

42-44	Paul's first residence at Antioch	11:25-30
44	Paul's second visit to Jerusalem	11:30; 12:25
45-47	Paul's first missionary journey of 1100 miles	13:2; 14:26
47-51	Paul's second residence at Antioch	14:28
	Paul's third visit to Jerusalem	15:2-30; Gal 2:1-10
51, 53 or 54	Paul's second missionary journey of 2500 miles	15:36, 40; 18:22
53 or 54	Paul's fourth visit to Jerusalem	18:21-22
	Paul's third residence at Antioch	18:22-23
54-58	Paul's third missionary journey of 2800 miles	18:23; 21:15
58	Paul's fifth visit to Jerusalem	
	Paul's arrest and imprisonment at Caesarea	21:15; 23:35
60-61	Paul's voyage of 1800 miles and arrival in Rome	27:1; 28:16
63	Paul's release from prison	28:30
	Visits to Crete, Ephesus, Colosse, Macedonia, Corinth, Nicopolis, Dalmatia and Troas	1 & 2 Tim; Titus
66-68	Paul's martyrdom at Rome	2 Tim 4:6

(The reader will notice that other chronologies may give different dates.)

3. Title

Inspiration cannot be claimed for the actual titles of Bible books. One or two titles are obviously misleading, and *The Acts of the Apostles* is one such. After all, most of the apostles are named only in the list of people who met in the upper room in old Jerusalem (1:13). (Some Greek texts omit the word "apostles" in the title.) Once the story commences, Peter and John are prominent until ch.8; Peter alone in chs.10-11; and finally Paul alone for the rest of the book, apart from the conference in Jerusalem in ch. 15. All the apostles were alive except James, whose death is recorded in 12:2. As with the Gospels, only a sample of the work done is recorded in the book. The other apostles must have carried out their evangelism away from Luke's searchlight. Legend informs us of the directions in which some of them went. We must presume that the rest scattered and made their contributions to what was "preached to every creature which is under heaven" (Col 1:23).

The Second Book of Luke would indicate merely its authorship; *The Acts of Apostolic Men* would tell us only who were the chief participants; *The Acts of the Holy Spirit* would tell us who the prime mover was.

4. Characteristics

The book is obviously the first record of the spread of Christianity, and therefore of the christian church. While the author had not been an eyewitness of the events described in his Gospel, nor of the earlier events described in his second book, yet he was an eyewitness of many of the events described in the second half of his book.

Prominence is given to preaching, the means chosen by God to save those who believe (1 Cor 1:21). George Goodman, in his book *The Gospel We Preach* counted twenty-two sermons or speeches in the Acts. He states that nine of these were Peter's (1:15; 2:14; 3:12; 4:8; 5:24; 8:20; 10:34; 11:14; 15:7); nine were Paul's (13:16; 13:46; 14:13; 17:16; 20:18; 22:1; 24:10; 26:1; 28:25); the remainder came from Stephen (ch.7), Philip (ch.8), James (ch.15) and from Ananias (ch.9). For the different words used to describe their preaching, see Appendix 1.

Another characteristic of Acts is Luke's regular summaries of the progress of the gospel. (The same kind of summaries are also found in the earlier part of his Gospel.) In his Gospel, Luke has given summaries of the progress of the work of the Master; and in his history in the Acts we find the progress of the work of the apostles. Thus we may quote 6:7; 9:31; 12:24; 16:5; 19:20; 28:31. These summaries follow the actual descriptions of the particular progress made, as after Peter's preaching (2:42), and again in 4:4.

Another characteristic is the ascription of every major turning-point to the Holy Spirit. The starting point is the coming of the Spirit at Pentecost; the Spirit makes Philip the evangelist approach the Ethiopian eunuch (8:29); the Spirit moves Peter to accept Cornelius the Roman soldier (11:12); the Spirit instructs the church at Antioch to commend Paul and Barnabas to missionary work (13:2). As the late Dr. W. Barclay wrote in the introduction to his translation of the Acts, "In Acts every great man and every great movement is inspired and upheld by the Holy Spirit".

Luke draws more attention to earthly rulers than any other evangelist. In this respect he is the true historian. Having mentioned Caesar Augustus in his Gospel (the only evangelist to do so), along with the local ruler Cyrenius of Syria, he mentions both Herod and Pilate at the beginning (Luke 3:1) and at the end (Luke 23:1, 8). At the beginning of the Acts, he names the Jewish leaders Annas, Caiaphas, John and Alexander; at the end he adds both the local rulers Felix, Festus and Agrippa, as well as Augustus Caesar. (Augustus was really the second Roman Emperor; the word was as much a title as it was a name.) By this time, Tiberius (mentioned in Luke 3:1) and Claudius (Acts 18:2) had both resigned. It must be concluded, therefore, that the Augustus Caesar recorded in 25:21 was Nero, whose ill-repute is well known.

Far from any of these dignitaries hindering the Lord's work, they furthered it; not intentionally, of course, but in spite of their lack of goodwill. The Man whom they tried to eliminate during the period of the Gospels lives on; in spite of them, the movement which they also opposed in the Acts flourished.

There are a large number of resemblances between Luke's Gospel and the Acts.

In Luke the Lord is often at prayer; in Acts the church is often in prayer. "It is interesting to note that nowhere in the Gospel records do we find the disciples gathered for prayer ... It is only after the resurrection that the disciples are found in prayer" (Lloyd John Ogilvie).

The divine Person at work in the Gospel is the Saviour; the divine Person at work in the Acts is the Holy Spirit.

The promise of the Spirit in Luke 24 is repeated in Acts 1, and fulfilled in Acts 2.

The women in Luke 23, 24 are mentioned in Acts 1:14. Note the prominence that Luke gives to women, including widows, in his two books.

The last meeting-place of the disciples in Luke 24 is the great meeting-place in Acts 2, 3, 4 etc., that is, the courts of Herod's temple.

The birth of the Lord Jesus is the great subject of Luke 2; the birth of the church, which is His body, is the great subject of Acts 2.

Luke 2 shows salvation being provided; Acts 2 shows salvation being proclaimed.

Luke 1, 2 draw our attention to people waiting for the consolation of Israel; Acts 1 draws our attention to people waiting for the Comforter to come. The word for "wait" is the same in the original Greek.

Note temple scenes in both: Luke 1, 2, 14; Acts 3, etc. Note the hour of prayer in Luke 1:10 and Acts 3:1.

Luke 3 tells of a forty-day period in the life of the Lord Jesus preparatory to the commencement of His ministry that led to redemption being accomplished on the cross; Acts 1 tells of a forty-day period in the life of the Lord preparatory to His ascension to God's right hand for the work of intercession, and for the commencement of His work through the Holy Spirit.

The Gospel ends with the death of the Lord Jesus, which did not end His work but laid the foundation for its permanence and continuance; the Acts ends with the imprisonment of the apostle Paul, which did not end his work but fell out rather for the furtherance of the gospel.

Luke 1 tells us that the Gospel was written that Theophilus and we might know the certainty of those things in which we have been instructed; Acts 1:3 tells us about the infallibility of those things in which we have been instructed.

Luke commences with John baptising in water (3:3); Acts begins with the Lord baptising in the Spirit (1:5; 2:2-4).

Luke 1, 2 tell of the Lord's coming down; Acts 1 tells of Him being taken up to the throne of the universe, to God's right hand.

Luke 2 tells of a multitude of the heavenly host of angels announcing His arrival on earth; Acts 1 tells of two angels announcing His arrival back in heaven with the intimation that He is coming back again.

In Luke the highlights are miracles; in Acts the highlights are conversions, sometimes accompanied by miracles.

Luke emphasises Gentile blessing: Simeon in Luke 2:32; John Baptist in 3:6; the Lord in 4:24-27; the centurion's servant in 7:10; he mentions Samaritans three times; a Cyrenian carried the cross; "repentance and remission of sins" were to be preached among all nations (24:47). Acts 2:21 declares that "whosoever shall call on the name of the Lord shall be saved"; v.39 that the message was for "all that are afar off"; we read of Samaritans in ch.8; Cornelius in ch.10, and then the ever-widening circle of Gentiles reached through Paul's ministry.

Luke commences his Gospel with a reference to the event which Malachi had said in Mal 4:1, 5-6 would precede the day of the Lord; Acts begins with the quotation from Joel 2:28-32 which reported what would happen before the day of the Lord comes.

5. Outline

I.	The Ministry of the Risen Christ to His Disciples	1:1-1:11
	1. Waiting for the Spirit	1:1-1:8
	2. The Ascension of Christ	1:9-1:11
II.	The Witness in Jerusalem	1:12-7:60
	1. Peter and John	1:12-5:42
	2. Stephen	6:1-7:60
III.	The Witness in Judaea and Samaria	8:1-11:18
	1. The Scattered Church	8:1-8:4
	2. Philip the Evangelist	8:5-8:40
	3. The Greatest Jewish Conversion	9:1-9:31
	4. Peter Again	9:32-11:18
IV.	The Witness to the Uttermost Part of the Earth	11:19-28:31
	1. Antioch	11:19-11:30
	2. A Parenthesis: Herod and the First Apostolic Martyr	12:1-12:25
	3. Paul's First Missionary Journey	13:1-14:28
	4. The Apostolic Council	15:1-15:35
	5. Paul's Second Missionary Journey	15:36-18:22
	6. Paul's Third Missionary Journey	18:23-20:2
	7. Paul's Journey to Jerusalem	20:3-21:16
	8. Paul's Arrest and Witness	21:17-26:32
	9. Paul's Mission to Rome	27:1-28:31

6. Bibliography

Alexander, J.A. *The Acts of the Apostles*, Banner of Truth, 1963.
Blaiklock, E.M. *The Century of the New Testament*, I.V.F., 1962.
Blaiklock, E.M. *Cities of the New Testament*, P.&I., 1965; reprinted by Baker.
Bruce, F.F. *The Acts of the Apostles*, Tyndale Press, 1951.
Carter and Earle, *Commentary on the Bible (Acts)*, Oliphant, 1959.
Conybeare and Howson, *The Life and Epistles of St. Paul*, Longman, 1911.
Darby, J.N. *Meditations on the Acts of the Apostles*, Morrish.
Heading, J. *Acts*, Walterick Publishers, 1979.
Heading, J. *Dictionary of New Testament Churches*, 1984.
Kelly, W. *An Exposition of the Acts of the Apostles*, Hammond, 1952.
Longenecker, R.N. *Expositor's Bible Commentary* Vol. 9, P.&I.
Marshall, Howard, *Acts*, Tyndale IVP
Morgan, G. Campbell, *The Acts of the Apostles*, Fleming Revell, 1924.
Ramsay, Sir. W. *The Cities of St. Paul*, Hodder & Stoughton, 1907.
Stirling, J. *An Atlas of the Acts*, G. Philips & Son, 1960.
Wiersbe, W. *Be Dynamic: Acts 1-12*, Victor Books.
Wiersbe, W. *Be Daring : Acts 13-28*, Victor Books.

Text and Exposition

I. The Ministry of the Risen Christ to His Disciples (1:1-11)

1. Waiting for the Spirit
1:1-8

> v.1 "The former treatise have I made, O Theophilus, of all that Jesus began both to do and teach,
> v.2 Until the day in which he was taken up, after that he through the Holy Ghost had given commandments unto the apostles whom he had chosen:
> v.3 To whom also he shewed himself alive after his passion by many infallible proofs, being seen of them forty days, and speaking of the things pertaining to the kingdom of God:
> v.4 And, being assembled together with *them,* commanded them that they should not depart from Jerusalem, but wait for the promise of the Father, which, *saith he,* ye have heard of me.
> v.5 For John truly baptized with water; but ye shall be baptized with the Holy Ghost not many days hence.
> v.6 When they therefore were come together, they asked of him, saying, Lord, wilt thou at this time restore again the kingdom to Israel?
> v.7 And he said unto them, It is not for you to know the times or the seasons, which the Father hath put in his own power.
> v.8 But ye shall receive power, after that the Holy Ghost is come upon you: and ye shall be witnesses unto me both in Jerusalem, and in all Judæa, and in Samaria, and unto the uttermost part of the earth."

1-3 The contents of Luke's Gospel are implied in the words, "began both to do and teach". The work of the cross was completed, as indicated by the Lord's words, "It is finished," but after that He continued to work with His people (Mark 16:20). Thus the Lord's work continued throughout the Acts, the Spirit of God being the One through whom this work was done; "My Father worketh hitherto, and I work" (John 5:17). Note that Luke uses the name "Jesus", as used in historical contexts in the Gospels. Very rarely was He addressed directly by this name (Mark 10:47); the usual form of address was "Lord", though on rare occasions the Lord used the name "Jesus" of Himself (Acts 9:5; Rev 22:16).

No service for the Lord can be achieved spiritually without His "commandments".

Paul recalled these in Acts 26:16-19. These are not, of course, the commandments of the law, but for specific guidance in service, as well as that of love (John 13:34). These commandments were given "through the Holy Spirit", showing the absolute unity of the words of the Son and of the Spirit; He had received the Spirit without measure (John 3:34). Initially, these commandments were given just to "the apostles whom he had chosen"; after that, divine commandments are of general applicability: (i) their principles as found in the NT, and (ii) their practice as all believers seek the divine will for the nature and place of their service. Luke stresses that these apostles had been "chosen"; he had recorded this event in Luke 6:13; they had been sent out for service in 9:1, while later seventy others were chosen and sent forth (10:1). Of the choice of the apostles, the Lord had said, "Ye have not chosen me, but I have chosen you" (John 15:16). Today, believers should know the same thing, and be able to discern the divine choice in others, rejecting the claims of many in Christendom who speak and act contrary to the NT Scriptures.

We are told how long the Lord Jesus came and went among His disciples after His resurrection, and His appearances among them are described as constituting "many infallible proofs." These many infallible proofs comprise not only the actual appearances of the Saviour to His disciples, but also the simple things like talking and listening to them, and eating and drinking among them – perfectly ordinary, simple things in which only living people can engage. In the subsequent apostolic preaching, they did not use these ordinary things in their witness; rather they were eyewitnesses of His resurrection and they quoted the OT Scriptures to support the fact of the resurrection and ascension. Readers will be familiar with the many mentions of periods of forty days in the Bible. Luke in his Gospel draws our attention to the forty days at the beginning of the Lord's public ministry which demonstrated His sinlessness (Luke 3:2); now he relates the period of forty days which concluded His private ministry amongst His own, and which show that "death hath no more dominion over him" (Rom 6:9). Later in the Acts he quotes the three periods of forty years into which Stephen divided Moses' life (7:23, 36, 42).

Four times in ch.1 (vv.2, 9, 11, 22) Luke describes the ascension of Christ by the words "he was taken up", though elsewhere we read that He was "carried up" (Luke 24:51) and "received up" (1 Tim 3:16). The Holy Spirit did not come into the world until the Lord Jesus had been taken up, or until He had been glorified, to use the language of John 7:39. It is in consequence of the ascension of Christ, not of His resurrection, that the Holy Spirit takes His place in the world. As the Lord said, "If I go not away, the Comforter will not come unto you; but if I depart, I will send him unto you" (John 16:7).

4 "Being assembled together with them" was setting the pattern for the forthcoming local assemblies. He had already promised to be in the midst of those who gather in His Name (Matt 18:20), a feature seen again at the beginning of the upper room ministry when "he sat down with the twelve" (Matt 26:20).

"The promise of the Father, which ... ye have heard of me" relates to the Holy

Spirit who was shortly to be shed forth by the ascended Lord (Acts 2:33). Not that there had been no activity on the part of the Holy Spirit prior to this event. In his Gospel, Luke records the part played by the Spirit in the birth of Christ and in His public ministry, but here he implies that the upper room ministry of the Lord Jesus, recorded in John 14 (and also outside the room in chs.15-16), was also given through the Holy Spirit. In fact, the link in this context is with John's Gospel (14:16, 26; 15:26; 16:7, 13) rather than with Luke's. The occasion when the Spirit of God was promised to the disciples after the Lord's departure from this world was the overnight meeting in the upper room and afterwards. Some of God's promises have waited for centuries before being fulfilled, but others wait only for a short time; this one was to be fulfilled only seven weeks after it had been given. With any promise, "it was impossible for God to lie" (Heb 6:18).

It should not appear strange that the Lord Jesus told His disciples not to depart from Jerusalem. We can understand why He said that no prophet could perish out of Jerusalem (Luke 13:33). This place that God had chosen for sacrifice would be the place where the Jews would reject Him. He had to suffer outside the gate if the details of the sin offering were to be fulfilled (Heb 13:11; Lev 4-5); blood-guiltiness was to be attributed to the city outside of which His murdered body would be found (Deut 21:3). But was there any significance in Jerusalem being the place chosen for the descent of the Spirit? After all, the Lord had told the Samaritan woman that the time was arriving when true worship would be centred neither at Jerusalem nor at mount Gerizim (John 4:21).

One important fact to be noted is that the upper room where the promise of the Spirit was given was almost certainly the same room where the Spirit descended in Acts 2:1. This is indicated by the word "the" in "*the* upper room" in 1:13 (not "an upper room" as in the AV).

Since this was the city from which God's glory departed, literally in Ezek 11:22,23 from Solomon's temple prior to its destruction, and bodily in Acts 1:9 when the Lord ascended, then this must be the place to which the glory will return (Ezek 43:1-5). When the writer to the Hebrews is explaining the blessings of the new covenant in his final plea to the apparently undecided Jews, he says, "Ye are come unto mount Sion, and unto the city of the living God, the heavenly Jerusalem" (Heb 12:22). Again, the culmination of the whole Bible narrative is the emergence of a city-church, "the holy city, new Jerusalem, coming down from God out of heaven, prepared as a bride for her husband" (Rev 21:2). The literal city Jerusalem, although doomed to destruction, has become the symbol of the heavenly which shall never pass away.

Bible students know that the supremacy of Jerusalem in ecclesiastical things did not last. Long before Jerusalem was destroyed by Titus in AD 70, its leading role in the church had ceased; the centre of influence had changed to Antioch. But not even that city was permanent. Neither Jerusalem, Antioch, Rome nor any other city was to be a lasting centre or capital of the new creation that God was producing in the world through the Spirit and the gospel.

5 The Lord often mentioned John Baptist in His teaching, even after he had been beheaded (Matt 21:25), and after His resurrection the greatest of the prophets was not forgotten. So whereas v.4 describes the coming of the Spirit as the fulfilment of the promise of the Father (John 14-16), then v.5 describes this coming as the fulfilment of the preaching of John Baptist. The four Gospels tell us of John's preaching (Matt 3:11-12; Mark 1:8; Luke 3:16-17; John 1:33), but in the Acts, Luke records it twice (1:5; 19:3). John spoke of baptism, or immersion, in the Spirit, contrasting it with immersion in water that he practised. John forecast the day when the Holy Spirit would be not only on men but in them. The Lord foretold the day when the Holy Spirit would stay with men, not for a little while, but forever. The Holy Spirit would never again be given by measure to God's people, but in unlimited quantity. They were to be immersed in the Spirit of God, just as previously they had been immersed in water. Later, in the only reference to the subject in the Epistles (1 Cor 12:13), Paul explains that what happened in Acts 2:1-4 in fulfilment of John's preaching resulted in individuals from all kinds of backgrounds being formed into that wonderful new creation – the body of Christ, the church.

Note that John's reference to baptism with "fire" (Matt 3:11) has no connection with the tongues like "fire" in Acts 2:2. John's reference is to judgment, the burning up of the chaff with unquenchable fire; Acts 2:2 brings blessing, not judgment.

6-7 The apostles had been under the Lord's prophetic teaching many times before (Matt 13:40-50; Luke 12:36-40; 17:20-37; 21:5-36), but the apostles were still anxious to know the programme of events now that the Lord Jesus was about to depart from them into heaven. In spite of the Lord's previous teaching, their thoughts reverted to the restoration of "the kingdom to Israel", implying worldly thoughts rather than spiritual thoughts. The kingdom had been lost when Nebuchadnezzar had taken Jerusalem, after which the Jews had never been masters in their own land. The Romans had already taken the kingdom when the Lord was here. Luke in particular records the political aspirations of the Jews; there were those who looked for "redemption in Israel" when Anna substituted the Lord's Christ for political hopes (Luke 2:38); the Pharisees wanted to know "when the kingdom of God should come," namely when the Romans would be cast out (17:20); even the two on the Emmaus road trusted that the Lord "should have redeemed Israel" (24:21). So the apostles' thoughts were occupied with this subject rather than with the promised Holy Spirit and the spread of the gospel message. How quickly can the Lord's spiritual words be changed to those relating to political and social conditions! Thus their question, "Lord, wilt thou at this time restore again the kingdom to Israel?" The Lord immediately dismisses the thought, telling them that the secret is not for them. Details of the restoration are found in Dan 7; Rom 11; and the book of Revelation, but the hour is nowhere revealed. In any case, the rapture of the church must take place first.

The reference to "the times or the seasons" is not the only occurrence of the phrase in the NT. Paul uses it in 1 Thess 5:1. It appears that the new Christians in

Thessalonica had more knowledge of the subject than the apostles had here; simply because Paul had received this truth directly, after the Spirit had been given. (In the OT, similar expressions occur in Dan 2:21; 7:12; Eccles 3:1.)

God's prophetic programme is in view. Augustine and Trench seem to be agreed that "the times" are the durations of the periods of church history, whereas "the seasons" are the joints, the epoch-making events foreordained by God (see Acts 17:26). Augustine further describes the seasons: when all that has been slowly, and often without observation, ripening throughout long ages is mature, it comes to the birth in grand decisive events, which constitute at once the close of one period and the commencement of another. Such was the passing of the old Jewish dispensation; such will be the coming of the Lord in glory.

This seems to be complemented by Vine when he writes, "Broadly speaking *chronos* expresses the duration of a period; *kairos* stresses it as marked by certain features. Both the times (*chronos*), i.e. the lengths of the periods, and the seasons (*kairos*), epochs marked by certain events, have been kept by the Father within His own authority."

8 The Lord intimates that their immediate business is not to rule but to witness, and this business of witnessing was to be consequent upon their receiving power once the Holy Spirit came upon them. In this way, the Lord Jesus applies the truth of the Holy Spirit coming to His own.

It should be pointed out that while the word "power" appears twice in the AV of vv.7, 8 these are really two distinct words in the Greek text: the knowledge that God possesses concerning the future kingdom He is going to retain in His own authority (*exousia*), but He is about to endue His disciples with enabling power (*dunamis*) when the Spirit has arrived. The former word *exousia* is used in Matt 28:18, "All power is given unto me".

This enabling power (*dunamis*) is used elsewhere in the NT (e.g. Rom 8:1-4) for other purposes, but here it is given for witnessing. The first witness to the Lord Jesus introduced in the NT is John Baptist, but the word is used in Luke 24:48 to describe what the disciples were to be in connection with the resurrection of the Lord. Thereafter, the word is used about ten times in the Acts to describe what these new Christians were capable of doing.

In the realm of everyday things, anybody can be a witness. There are no barriers of age, class or colour; all that is required is that a person tells what he has seen and heard, that is, what he knows by experience. It is only because these first Christians had been witnesses that the message of the gospel was passed on, and by faith this is still the way in which it spreads. Thus the Lord prayed for those "which shall believe on me through their word" (John 17:20), and Paul wrote of a ladder of witnesses, "the things that thou hast heard of me among many witnesses, the same commit thou to faithful men, who shall be able to teach others also" (2 Tim 2:2).

The sphere of the original apostolic witness was to expand in ever-widening circles. It was to begin in Jerusalem, the city of the great King, the very place from which the Lord Jesus left them on His return to glory. It was to spread out to Judaea, the province surrounding Jerusalem, and then to Samaria, the province inhabited by people with whom pious Jews had no dealings (John 4:9). When the Lord sent out the twelve in Matt 10:5, He excluded Samaritan cities from their itinerary, though He refused to allow judgment to fall upon such cities and villages (Luke 9:52-56). But now that the christian age has dawned, there can be no such restriction. In fact, as the years passed, the witnesses operated to earth's remotest bounds. The phrase used to describe the outermost ring of those circles is the same as that used to describe the outermost boundary of the future kingdom of Messiah, "the uttermost parts of the earth" (Ps 2:8), indicating that the sphere of christian witness should be coextensive with the sphere of His future kingdom.

Notes

Angelic Activity in Acts: From 1:10 through to 27:23 the ministry of angels is mentioned at intervals in the Acts. They were visibly involved in the story as long as miracles were being displayed. By such means did God let His servants know that heaven was on their side. More generally, angels are "ministering spirits, sent forth to minister for them who shall be heirs of salvation" (Heb 1.14).

In 1:10 the two are called "men", but there is little doubt that they were angels. Their white apparel and where they came from indicate that. The Lord had already taught that He was going to return, both for His own (John 14:3) and as the Son of man in glory (Matt 24:30), but angels now repeated this truth. These angels were dressed like the young man in Mark 16:5. They appeared when the Lord was born, after He was tempted, and in the garden of Gethsemane. They awaited a summons that never came to rescue Him from the hands of men (Matt 26:53), and they announced His resurrection, ascension and coming again.

In 5:19; 12:7, 11 they opened prison doors for Peter. Paul never had this experience, but miracles were becoming less frequent in his time. God intervened miraculously for the deliverance of His servants, as in the earthquake in Philippi, but He did not always do so.

Stephen refers to the part angels played in the bringing of God's law to Israel (7:53), as does Paul in Gal 3:19. The mention of angels in Heb1 also refers to the OT. Whatever angels were involved in was heavenly in its objectives; hence the seriousness of the Jewish rejection of angelic activity, particularly by the Sadducees.

Philip twice received divine guidance in ch.8; first, an angel told him to go down to the desert road to meet the Ethiopian, although he does not seem to have told him the nature of his mission; then the Spirit of the Lord caught away Philip from the scene.

The story of Cornelius in ch.10 tells of an angel in a vision directing him to send messengers to Peter at Joppa, while Peter was alerted to their coming by a vision only. This was confirmed by the Holy Spirit (v.19). The next time Cornelius refers to his vision, he describes the messenger as a man in bright clothing (v.30). It is well to remember that Omnipotence has servants everywhere. The angel is also mentioned by Peter in 11:13.

As with miracles, the mention of angels becomes fewer as the book advances. The only mention in the second half of the book relates to the angel standing before Paul in the great storm and telling him that they would be shipwrecked, but that they would all be saved from drowning (27:23-25).

The other occasions when these heavenly beings occur are of a different nature. It was "an angel of the Lord" who smote Herod according to 12:23; in 6:15 Stephen's face is said to have been like the face of an angel (did it shine like Moses' face when he saw the glory of God?). Certainly this did not deter the Jews from stoning him to death. In 12:15 the believers responded "It is his angel", not believing Rhoda's testimony that Peter stood at the door.

2. The Ascension of Christ
1:9-11

v.9 "And when he had spoken these things, while they beheld, he was taken up; and a cloud received him out of their sight.

v.10 And while they looked stedfastly toward heaven as he went up, behold, two men stood by them in white apparel;

v.11 Which also said, Ye men of Galilee, why stand ye gazing up into heaven? this same Jesus, which is taken up from you into heaven, shall so come in like manner as ye have seen him go into heaven."

9 Luke now describes the final appearance of the risen Christ to His eleven apostles. The number of witnesses of this event was very restricted – certainly not the "five hundred brethren at once" who saw Him in resurrection (1 Cor 15:6). The inference from v.12 is that the ascension took place on the mount of Olives; in fact, Luke 24:50 shows that it took place at Bethany on the eastern slopes of the mount. While His disciples were still gathered around Him, listening to His last commandments, and while He blessed them, He began to rise towards heaven; natural restrictions do not apply to resurrection bodies. The disciples did not see Him asecend far, for "a cloud received him out of their sight." It was as if the Father came forth to meet the Son, and this meeting in the air was hidden from the apostles' gaze.

10 The ascension of the Lord was authenticated by His being received up visibly in a cloud and by an announcement to His disciples by two men in white apparel, evidently angels. Both emphasise the fact that He is in heaven. Clouds belong to the heavens, the atmospheric heavens; in the future day, He will appear in the "clouds of heaven" (Matt 24:30; 26:64), while angels are native inhabitants of heaven. Several biblical passages use the description "clouds of heaven", as well as the two just cited. One of the greatest of these is Dan 7:13, "I saw in the night visions, and behold, one like the Son of man came with the clouds of heaven, and came to the Ancient of days". Both Matthew and Mark, in their accounts of the Lord's trial before the Jewish Sanhedrin, quote Him as saying, "Hereafter shall ye see the Son of man sitting on the right hand of power, and coming in the clouds of heaven" (Matt 26:64;

Mark 14:62). Admittedly these are descriptions of His return in glory to claim His kingdom, while Acts 1:9 is the description of Him going into glory to receive His place at God's right hand in the bodily form of a Man glorified. Whether coming or going, He makes use of clouds, "Behold, he cometh with clouds; and every eye shall see him" (Rev 1:7; 14:14). Truly, by means of clouds, "we have a great high priest, that is passed into the heavens, Jesus the Son of God" (Heb 4:14).

Generally, clouds appear to hide God from the eyes of men, but they are still symbols of His presence. Note the thick cloud on the mount in Exod 19:16, and the pillar of cloud to lead the way in Exod 13:21. Thus at the ascension the recently-crucified Jesus is associated with a cloud, with all its past and future associations with Deity.

All this matches the appearance of these two men in white apparel. It was not unusual for angels to appear in such human guise: one such announced the Lord's resurrection (Mark 16:5); another appeared to Joshua as the captain of the armies of Israel (Josh 5:13-15); three visited Abraham to promise him a son (Gen 18:2). But the greatest message that angels in human form ever delivered was that the One who had been taken up in the clouds was coming back again.

11 The reason why two men in white apparel appeared was to authenticate their message; as the Lord had said, "the testimony of two men is true" (John 8:17), a feature that pervades the Scriptures.

The place from which the Lord was taken up is significant. Olivet had been the place of His tears (as for a different reason it had been a place of David's tears in 2 Sam 15:30). Three times the NT records that the Lord shed tears, each time on the mount of Olives. It was there that He wept over Jerusalem as He passed over the top of the mount to descend for His last Passover, and gazed down upon the city lying at His feet (Luke 19:41). It was on its eastern slopes that Bethany was situated, and in a tomb outside that village Lazarus was buried, and "Jesus wept" (John 11:35). On the western slopes there was a garden, the garden of Gethsemane in which He "offered up ... strong crying and tears unto him that was able to save him from death" (Heb 5:7). But the place of His tears became the place of His triumph; from the place where three times He shed tears, He was taken up into heaven.

Again, the place of His triumph was the place of the nation of Israel's disaster. Ezekiel the prophet saw a vision which was shortly to take place before Solomon's temple was destroyed. But this vision is also applicable to the Lord's ascension. The subject of Ezekiel's vision is God's chariot throne, and the prophet saw it moving reluctantly away from that wicked and rebellious people. In Ezek 10:18-19 the glory of the Lord, represented in that chariot throne, is seen leaving the city through the east gate. In 11:23 it is found right outside the city, standing on the mountain which is on its east side, namely the mount of Olives. That was the tragedy that explained the captivity of Ezekiel's generation – the departing glory. And that was what was happening to God's earthly people all over again with the withdrawal of their Messiah, prior to the destruction of Herod's temple by the Romans. The apostles had asked if He would restore the kingdom, but Calvary represented the rejection of that kingdom by the people, and thus once again God's glory in Christ was departing from the mountain on the east of the city.

But God has not cast off His people whom He foreknew, "this same Jesus ... shall so come in like manner as ye have seen him go into heaven". There has been much discussion as to whether this applies to the rapture or to the Lord's return in power and glory, but a verse like Zech 14:4 certainly suggests the latter, "his feet shall stand in that day upon the mount of Olives, which is before Jerusalem on the east, and the mount of Olives shall cleave in the midst thereof". The place of His tears has already been the place of His triumph, and it will again be the place of His future triumph.

II. The Witness in Jerusalem (1:12-7:60)

1. Peter and John
1:12-5:42

a. The First Prayer Meeting (1:12-14)

> v.12 "Then returned they unto Jerusalem from the mount called Olivet, which is from Jerusalem a sabbath day's journey.
> v.13 And when they were come in, they went up into an upper room, where abode both Peter, and James, and John, and Andrew, Philip, and Thomas, Bartholomew, and Matthew, James *the son* of Alphæus, and Simon Zelotes, and Judas *the brother* of James.
> v.14 These all continued with one accord in prayer and supplication, with the women, and Mary the mother of Jesus, and with his brethren."

12-14 The Master had instructed His disciples to wait in Jerusalem until they had received the promise of the Father. The return journey to Jerusalem is called "a sabbath day's journey". According to Jewish tradition, this is based on Num 35:5 and Josh 3:4, being two thousand cubits or six furlongs. But we can view it as the end of the relevance of the sabbath day for Christians, leading to the beginning of what is known as "the first day of the week" (Acts 20:7) or "the Lord's day" (Rev 1:10).

On their return from the mount of Olives, they again gathered in the upper room where the last Passover had been celebrated, and where the Lord's Supper had been instituted. What they were to wait for was still ten days in the future, though they did not know that number, in just the same way as we wait for the Lord's return at a time unknown to us. So they occupied the time in prayer and in other spiritual matters, as the Lord had said, "Occupy till I come" (Luke 19:13). We are told in v.13 that the remaining eleven apostles were present (the only time in the Acts where the names of eight of them are mentioned). Note that Peter's name comes first in every list of the apostles in the NT; this does not give him any pre-eminence, but he evidently had a kind of leadership granted him by the Lord. The "mother of Jesus" and His brethren were also there. This is the first indication that His brethren were now believers. As recently as the last feast of Tabernacles, only about eight months before, they did not believe in Him (John 7:5). But the events of the past months had changed that.

Those present numbered "about an hundred and twenty". That is why the Lord had originally provided a "large" upper room furnished (Luke 22:12). This size of room had not been necessary for the Passover, but the Lord was effectively providing for the needs of this larger group of believers after His ascension. The Lord's public ministry had extended over three and a half years, and there were one hundred and twenty people from Jerusalem present at this prayer meeting to prove how effective His ministry had been. That is not, of course, the grand total, for 1 Cor 15:6 tells us that over five hundred brethren at once saw the risen Christ during one of His appearances, no doubt in Galilee. This was surely quite a sizeable nucleus for the church which was so soon to commence.

One hundred and twenty is also the number of priests who functioned when Solomon's temple was dedicated (2 Chron 5:12). That represented the original grand total of the priesthood, and for the only time in their history they functioned together instead of "waiting by course". So when the new spiritual temple "not made with hands" was introduced in Acts 2, one hundred and twenty priests functioned together "with one accord".

b. Judas' Succcessor (1:15-26)

> v.15 "And in those days Peter stood up in the midst of the disciples, and said, (the number of names together were about an hundred and twenty,)
> v.16 Men *and* brethren, this scripture must needs have been fulfilled, which the Holy Ghost by the mouth of David spake before concerning Judas, which was guide to them that took Jesus.
> v.17 For he was numbered with us, and had obtained part of this ministry.
> v.18 Now this man purchased a field with the reward of iniquity; and falling headlong, he burst asunder in the midst, and all his bowels gushed out.
> v.19 And it was known unto all the dwellers at Jerusalem; insomuch as that field is called in their proper tongue, Aceldama, that is to say, The field of blood.
> v.20 For it is written in the book of Psalms, Let his habitation be desolate, and let no man dwell therein: and his bishoprick let another take.
> v.21 Wherefore of these men which have companied with us all the time that the Lord Jesus went in and out among us,
> v.22 Beginning from the baptism of John, unto that same day that he was taken up from us, must one be ordained to be a witness with us of his resurrection.
> v.23 And they appointed two, Joseph called Barsabas, who was surnamed Justus, and Matthias.
> v.24 And they prayed, and said, Thou, Lord, which knowest the hearts of all *men,* shew whether of these two thou hast chosen,

> v.25 That he may take part of this ministry and apostleship, from which Judas by transgression fell, that he might go to his own place.
> v.26 And they gave forth their lots; and the lot fell upon Matthias; and he was numbered with the eleven apostles."

15-20 During this prayer meeting, one of many which characterised the early days of the church (2:42; 4:24; 6:4; 12:5), Peter made the suggestion that a successor for Judas should be appointed, quoting scriptural support for this suggestion (Ps 69:25; 109:8), and claiming in v.16 that David spoke by the Holy Spirit. (The same claim is made for Ps 2 in 4:25.)

The fact that Judas' part in the events leading to the Lord's death had been prophesied in the OT put Judas into perspective. The Lord Himself had said that the Scriptures were thereby fulfilled (John 13:18). The disciples harboured no bitterness about one who, knowing the likely haunts of the Saviour (the garden of Gethsemane), took advantage of that knowledge and used it against the Master. The disciples realised that it was foreknown, and Peter and his friends accepted it. There was no bitterness, just acceptance.

The quotation in v.20 is a composite one, from Ps 69:25 and 109:8. But Ps 41:9 contains another, "mine own familiar friend, in whom I trusted, which did eat of my bread, hath lifted up his heel against me". A fourth quotation is found in Zech 11:13 relating to the thirty pieces of silver being cast down in the house of the Lord; this is quoted in Matt 27:7-10. The Lord Himself referred to such a quotation in His prayer (John 17:12).

While the Acts is a direct continuation of Luke's Gospel, and the mention of "the promise of the Father" constitutes a link with John's Gospel, the reference to the purchase of the field (v.18) provides a link with Matthew's Gospel. (The reader may be interested to refer to J. Heading's comments on Judas in the companion volume in this series.) Matthew alone tells of the price for which Judas sold the Lord, about his remorse when he realised that things had gone awfully wrong, and of him hanging himself. Luke takes up the narrative in v.18 and records the further mishap to his body.

The purchase of the field with the thirty pieces of silver is interesting; only Luke, with his usual precision, records the proper name of the potter's field once it was bought, "Aceldama, that is to say, The field of blood". May the Lord's body have found a grave in Judas' field had it not been for God's chosen servant Joseph of Arimathaea? Paupers and criminals may well have been buried there, but though "they appointed his grave with the wicked ... he was with the rich in his death" (Isa 53:9 RSV, JND). Is Luke, in quoting Peter, making a veiled reference to Isa 53:12, "he was numbered with the transgressors" (which in the normal course of events would have been followed by the transgressor's grave) when he notes that, in contrast, the traitor was "numbered with us" (v.17)?

It is interesting to note that three words of later significance in the church are used to describe Judas' functions: "ministry" (vv.17, 25) is the Greek word *diakonia*;

"bishoprick" (v.20) is the word translated "overseership"; in v.25 there is confirmation that Judas was an apostle (Matt 10:2; Luke 6:13) – his name always comes last in the apostolic lists in the Gospels.

Vv.18, 25 indicate the fates of Judas' body and soul. Jamieson, Fausset and Brown well describe "his own place" as follows: "A euphemistic or softened expression of the awful future of the traitor, implying not only destined habitation but congenial element." The apostle Paul in 2 Thess 2:3 gave the same title to the man of sin as the Lord Jesus gave to Judas in John17:12, namely, "the son of perdition". There is no further mention of Judas in the Bible.

21-26 It is not surprising that in v.24 the appointment of a successor to Judas was made a matter of prayer. Nor should we be surprised at the method chosen to decide who was to be the successor, namely, the giving forth of lots. Perhaps their simple acceptance of Prov 16:33, "The lot is cast into the lap; but the whole disposing thereof is of the Lord", decided for them the correctness of the procedure. There is little point in arguing that the method was wrong, on the grounds that the successful appointee is not mentioned again in the Acts and could not therefore have had divine approval, for eight of the apostles are not mentioned by name again either. In any case, the Holy Spirit was the One who made overseers in local churches (Acts 20:28), but the Holy Spirit had then not yet been given. The eleven apostles were therefore standing at the very end of the period of using OT methods, which would not continue into the era of the Holy Spirit. Lots were cast for the division of the land amongst the remaining seven tribes, and on three occasions it is stated that this procedure was "before the Lord" (Josh 18:6, 8, 10). The cities of the tribe of Levi were also chosen by lot (Josh 21:4). The idea of the Roman soldiers casting lots for the Lord's garments at the cross is the most objectionable use made of this practice, exactly as had been predicted by the Lord in Ps 22:18. Certainly it is not part of spiritual practice today now that the Holy Spirit has come.

The qualifications of the two men were particularly stringent, in just the same way as those of elders and servants are in local churches in 1 Tim 3. They had to have been with the Lord and His disciples right from the time of John's baptism up to the Lord's ascension. The Gospel records give no hint that there were any other men who had been so close to the Lord Jesus all the time. Peter reminded the group that "the Lord Jesus went in and out among us", no doubt "out" referring to His public ministry as in Matt 13:1-3 where "great multitudes" were gathered at the sea shore, and "in" referring to private ministry as in Matt 13:36 when He took only His disciples into the house for teaching purposes. Such a description is also made of Saul after his conversion (Acts 9:28), for evangelistic and ministerial activity.

Peter's speech here was counted by George Goodman as the first of those twenty-two addresses interspersed through Acts.

Certainly God knew the hearts of all men, and would therefore make the right choice as in David's case (1 Sam 16:7,12), and generally as stated in Heb 4:13. So a twelfth man joined the apostolic band. Although not named, he must have been among the apostles put in the common prison (Acts 5:18). Both Matthias and Joseph called Barsabas had been companions of the other apostles all the time that the Lord had been with them; this was a vital apostolic criterion – an apostle must have seen the Lord so as to be a qualified witness. "Am I not an apostle? ... have I not seen Jesus Christ our Lord?", wrote Paul (1 Cor 9:1).

c. *The Day of Pentecost (2:1-13)*

v.1 "And when the day of Pentecost was fully come, they were all with one accord in one place.
v.2 And suddenly there came a sound from heaven as of a rushing mighty wind, and it filled all the house where they were sitting.
v.3 And there appeared unto them cloven tongues like as of fire, and it sat upon each of them.
v.4 And they were all filled with the Holy Ghost, and began to speak with other tongues, as the Spirit gave them utterance.
v.5 And there were dwelling at Jerusalem Jews, devout men, out of every nation under heaven.
v.6 Now when this was noised abroad, the multitude came together, and were confounded, because that every man heard them speak in his own language.
v.7 And they were all amazed and marvelled, saying one to another, Behold, are not all these which speak Galilæans?
v.8 And how hear we every man in our own tongue, wherein we were born?
v.9 Parthians, and Medes, and Elamites, and the dwellers in Mesopotamia, and in Judæa, and Cappadocia, in Pontus, and Asia,
v.10 Phrygia, and Pamphylia, in Egypt, and in the parts of Libya about Cyrene, and strangers of Rome, Jews and proselytes,
v.11 Cretes and Arabians, we do hear them speak in our tongues the wonderful works of God.
v.12 And they were all amazed, and were in doubt, saying one to another, What meaneth this?
v.13 Others mocking said, These men are full of new wine."

The various meetings and objectives of ch.1 culminated in an event as spectacular as has ever happened in the world: the coming of the Holy Spirit for whom they were waiting. What took place stands in complete contrast to a previous major event in God's dealings with men, namely, the giving of the law as described in Exod 19 onwards. It is probable that both events took place on the same date though centuries apart. Ancient tradition suggests that the old covenant was enjoined some seven weeks after the crossing of the Red Sea by the children of Israel. Acts 2 deals with the fulfilment of the feast of Weeks, to give it its OT name (see Lev 23:15-21), or the feast of Pentecost, meaning fifty days, to give it its NT name.

The happy consequence of the latter was that about three thousand souls were saved out of the mass of people in Jerusalem at the time, whereas in the former about three thousand souls perished out of all the tribes of Israel, Levi excepted; compare Exod 32:28 with Acts 2:41. No wonder the apostle Paul called the former "the ministry of death", while he called the latter "the ministry of the Spirit" and "the ministry of righteousness" (2 Cor 3:7-8).

The new covenant was consecrated through the blood of the Lord Jesus (Luke 22:20), but here it is being inaugurated by the coming of the Spirit.

1 The day of Pentecost had fully come in a sense deeper than the mere expiry of the appointed fifty days. The peculiar form of the original (in the fulfilling of Pentecost) at least hints that the day long foreshadowed by the ancient feast of weeks was about to receive its complete fulfilment: Pentecost never shall be repeated. Luke here records the historical details, the narrative displaying the same factual simplicity which characterises the Gospels; their doctrinal import is clearly set out in 1 Cor 12:13 (see the companion volume by J. Hunter in loc).

"They were all with one accord in one place" when the Spirit fell upon them. This should describe any meeting of a local church. "All" does not imply partial attendance only (apart from special circumstances). Note how the words "all", "every man", "all the women", "every man and woman" appear in Exod 35, where we read of the command, collection and construction of the tabernacle. There is no insinuation that the gift of the Spirit was restricted to the twelve nor to some élite few; "all" is emphatic and includes the hundred and twenty (1:15). They were in one place not simply by prior arrangement but as having common bonds: begotten again unto a living hope by the resurrection. "With one accord" suggests a harmony of motivation and practice, keeping the "unity of the Spirit in the bond of peace" (Eph 4:3). "In one place" suggests the absence of denominationalism, the place being that chosen by the Lord as in Deut 12:5.

2 Initially, they heard a sound like a strong wind. Wind is one of the commonly-accepted symbols of the Holy Spirit in the OT; here, of course, it is not a mere symbol, but a reality. Since it filled the house, the implication is that the disciples were immersed in it, and hence this constituted the baptism in the Spirit. This divine act was very selective; it only filled the house, and was not operative on the outside. The manifestation of the dove was not used; in John 1:32, the Spirit was like a dove abiding solely upon the Son – here was unique selectivity. In Gen 8:6-12, the dove was in contrast with the raven; the latter was satisfied to stay outside the ark, but the dove returned to its unique abode until the waters of the flood had disappeared. Today the Spirit acts in the world (John 16:8-11), but He dwells only in believers.

3 The second symbol that appears in "tongues like as of fire" – not physical fire itself, but something very genuine as shown by the words "like as". This is not to be confused with the fire-baptism that John Baptist had linked with the baptism in the Spirit (Matt 3:11). We are not told exactly what it was that they saw and what sat upon each of them, since new divine manifestations cannot be expressed formally in words. It must not be thought that each tongue upon each disciple was "cloven"; rather the thought is that each tongue was divided upon all the disciples. If v.2 represents the baptism, then v.3 represents the particular gift that was distributed at that time. Other gifts were already possessed (Luke 9:1). For the tongues (languages) in v.4 cannot be separated from the tongues of fire in v.3; here was power in preaching in a new way.

The disciples would readily grasp the significance of these symbols, being quite familiar with OT scriptures which associate "his ministers" with wind and fire (Ps 104:4). Again, wind and fire are more than once linked with the movements of divine persons (see, for example, Pss 18:10; 104:3; Ezek 1:4), and the Lord Jesus had used this very symbol in His discourse with Nicodemus: "The wind bloweth where it listeth" (John 3:8).

4 Whereas they were immersed in the Spirit in v.2, yet in v.4 they were filled with the Spirit with a particular gift for particular service. While intimately associated in this passage it must not be assumed that being baptised in the Spirit and being filled with the Spirit are synonymous terms. Baptism was a once-for-all act, whereas believers were repeatedly filled with the Spirit, as can be verified by even a cursory reading of Acts (e.g. 4:31). Baptism in the Spirit was with a view to the forming of the body of Christ; filling with the Spirit is for service in the body of Christ. Here "they were all filled with the Holy Ghost, and began to speak with other tongues". It is a confusion of terms and misleading to speak of being put into the body of Christ at conversion. The human body is complete in all its members at birth; certainly it grows and matures but members are not added to it. So it is with the body of Christ: formed at Pentecost by the baptism of the Spirit, it will continue to grow and be edified until the close of the age.

In the companion volume on 1 Corinthians in this series, J. Hunter, writing on 1 Cor 12:13, comments:

"In (the power of) one Spirit were we all baptized into one body" by Christ. "Baptised" is in the aorist tense, which not only looks back to an act, but views the act in its completeness, as accomplished. This verb "baptised" refers, therefore, to Pentecost, and gives us the doctrinal explanation of that event. All references to this baptism have Pentecost in prospect (Matt 3:11; Mark 1:8; Luke 3:16; John1:33; Act 1:5) or in retrospect (Acts 11:15; 1 Cor 12:13) ... When Paul says "we" he has in view the whole Church in contrast to "ye" (v.27), referring to the local church. Do not the words of John the Baptist in the Gospels indicate that all whom he baptised in water would be baptised in the Spirit (Mark 1:8)? In the mind of God all Christians were seen to be baptised. It is essential to see that the Holy Spirit only came down once. His coming was unique and final. It was unique for it never happened before; it was final in that it will never happen again in that way. There was only one baptism of this kind ... Believers are not baptised in this way at conversion; they come into the good of what took place at Pentecost. There is no Scripture that states that believers are baptised in the Spirit at conversion. The words used of what takes place at conversion are indwelling, anointed, sealed, earnest, but not baptism. At the close of Acts 2, 3000 souls were saved and received the Holy Spirit without any outward evidence. There was no phenomenon. They were indwelt by the Spirit as we were indwelt, for no believer now has experience as in the early verses of Acts 2. This demonstrates that the experience of the 3000 at the close of the chapter is normal, and draws attention to the uniqueness and finality of the early verses. Nevertheless the 3000 now stood associated with the original baptised company in the Body of Christ. It was the same with us when we were converted. We entered into the benefits of the once-for-all out-pouring of the Holy Spirit.

5 The previous occasion when thousands of pilgrims had been in Jerusalem was only seven weeks before, at the feast of the Passover when the Lord Jesus had been crucified. They were "devout" since they were following the OT command, "Three times in the year all thy males shall appear before the Lord God" (Exod 23:17). At this next feast of Pentecost, things were quite different, but men were still "devout", or pious.

6-13 These Galilaean followers of Jesus of Nazareth (and no doubt other disciples from Jerusalem and Judaea) had suddenly acquired the ability to speak fluently the very dialects of all the different parts of the world from which the pilgrims had come. The believers realised that their newly-acquired gift had been given for evangelistic purposes, and with boldness they ventured outside the confines of the upper room in order to communicate the gospel message to other people. The rumour spread abroad, and the multitude quickly gathered around, asking for an explanation. (The multitude realised at the time that only Galileans were taking part in the testimony.) Note that the disciples did not engage in empty gossip. To utter ("utterance", v.4 AV) is the verb from which an English noun apophthegm is derived. An apophthegm is "a short cryptic remark containing some general or generally accepted truth" (Collins English Dictionary). This then was the ability to make weighty authoritative pronouncements, here concerning "the wonderful works of God". With these we may compare in content the prophetic utterances in the opening two chapters of Luke.

The pilgrims had come from fifteen different parts of the Roman Empire, and spoke about that number of different languages; yet they heard these Spirit-filled believers speaking in their own languages. There can be no support for the theory that the gift was a gift of hearing in the minds of these unbelievers rather than a gift of speaking by the believers. Some men were incredulous (no doubt those whose languages were not being spoken nearby when they were listening), so they easily attributed this strange phenomenon to drunkenness, a most unlikely cause at 9 o'clock in the morning.

Three different titles are used in the OT for the feast of Pentecost: the feast of weeks (e.g. Exod 34:22); the feast of harvest (Exod 23:16); and the day of the first fruits (Num 28:26). The first focuses, as does the term Pentecost, on the timing of the feast, the latter two on its significance. Three series of sacrifices were offered that day: the daily burnt offering morning and evening; the festive sacrifices prescribed for the day (Num 28:27-30); and those that accompanied the offering of the new meat offering (Lev 23:18f).

The offering of this new meat offering was the characteristic feature of the feast. It was "the firstfruits of wheat harvest" (Exod 34:22), just as the wave sheaf was the firstfruit (note the singular of the original) of barley harvest. Scripture itself attests that the offering of the wave sheaf was fulfilled in the resurrection of the Lord Jesus: "But now is Christ risen from the dead, and become the firstfruits of them that slept" (1 Cor 15:20). He is the firstfruit (it is again singular in the original) of that great harvest of redeemed ones from all ages who shall share the glory of His resurrection.

The two wave loaves may, therefore, have foreshadowed the infant church, the firstfruits of the glorious harvest which is being reaped throughout the present age. Brought out of the dwellings of the people (Lev 23:15), the "house where they were sitting", the new vessel of testimony (the two loaves) was waved before the Lord in the very courts of the temple on the day of Pentecost. In acknowledgement of the possible presence of sin, the loaves of the type were "baken with leaven".

Some are inclined to see in the two loaves the Jew and Gentile elements in the church, their oneness expressed in the fact that they comprises one offering. This is possible but unlikely for two reasons:
1. There were no believers from among the nations when the Spirit came.
2. The two discrete loaves, though forming a single offering, do not adequately symbolise the true oneness of the body.

Note

9-11 A Jewish translation of the NT, *The Authentic New Testament*, by Dr. Hugh Schonfield suggests that instead of regarding the list of places from which the pilgrims came as being fifteen in number, they were really twelve. A Jewish mind would appreciate the significance of such a number far more than a Gentile. His divisions are:
1. Parthians
2. Medes
3. Elamites
4. Natives of Mesopotamia
5. Edessa and Cappadocia
6. Pontus
7. Asia and Phrygia
8. Pamphylia
9. Egypt and the parts of Libia and Cyrene
10. Foreigners domiciled in Rome (both Jews and proselytes)
11. Cretes
12. Arabians

d. *Peter's Sermon (2:14-36)*

v.14 "But Peter, standing up with the eleven, lifted up his voice, and said unto them, Ye men of Judæa, and all *ye* that dwell at Jerusalem, be this known unto you, and hearken to my words:

v.15 For these are not drunken, as ye suppose, seeing it is *but* the third hour of the day.

v.16 But this is that which was spoken by the prophet Joel;

v.17 And it shall come to pass in the last days, saith God, I will pour out of my Spirit upon all flesh: and your sons and your daughters shall prophesy, and your young men shall see visions, and your old men shall dream dreams:

v.18 And on my servants and on my handmaidens I will pour out in those days of my Spirit; and they shall prophesy:

v.19 And I will shew wonders in heaven above, and signs in the earth beneath; blood, and fire, and vapour of smoke:

v.20 The sun shall be turned into darkness, and the moon into blood, before that great and notable day of the Lord come:

v.21 And it shall come to pass, *that* whosoever shall call on the name of the Lord shall be saved.

v.22 Ye men of Israel, hear these words; Jesus of Nazareth, a man approved of God among you by miracles and wonders and signs, which God did by him in the midst of you, as ye yourselves also know:

v.23 Him, being delivered by the determinate counsel and foreknowledge of God, ye have taken, and by wicked hands have crucified and slain:

v.24 Whom God hath raised up, having loosed the pains of death: because it was not possible that he should be holden of it.

v.25 For David speaketh concerning him, I foresaw the Lord always before my face, for he is on my right hand, that I should not be moved:

v.26 Therefore did my heart rejoice, and my tongue was glad; moreover also my flesh shall rest in hope:

v.27 Because thou wilt not leave my soul in hell, neither wilt thou suffer thine Holy One to see corruption.

v.28 Thou hast made known to me the ways of life; thou shalt make me full of joy with thy countenance.

v.29 Men *and* brethren, let me freely speak unto you of the patriarch David, that he is both dead and buried, and his sepulchre is with us unto this day.

v.30 Therefore being a prophet, and knowing that God has sworn with an oath to him, that of the fruit of his loins, according to the flesh, he would raise up Christ to sit on his throne;

v.31 He seeing this before spake of the resurrection of Christ, that his soul was not left in hell, neither his flesh did see corruption.

v.32 This Jesus hath God raised up, whereof we all are witnesses.

v.33 Therefore being by the right hand of God exalted, and having received of the Father the promise of the Holy Ghost, he hath shed forth this, which ye now see and hear.

v.34 For David is not ascended into the heavens: but he saith himself, The LORD said unto my Lord, Sit thou on my right hand,

v.35 Until I make thy foes thy footstool.

v.36 Therefore let all the house of Israel know assuredly, that God hath made that same Jesus, whom ye have crucified, both Lord and Christ."

14-16 Peter alone answers, and it appears that the apostles (including Matthias) stood as a group, as distinct from the rest of the one hundred and twenty disciples. Moreover, Peter addressed his sermon to men of Jerusalem and Judaea, rather than to the pilgrims from afar. He was not speaking in a language now, but in the common tongue of Jerusalem and Judaea (vv.14, 22). He only addressed them because he wanted to embrace those who by wicked hands had crucified and slain the Lord Jesus (v.23). No doubt others heard as well, since the message was given to "whosoever" (v.12).

The first question asked was, "What meaneth this?" Peter's reply was that of a transformed man. At the time of the previous feast he had been a coward who denied that he had any acquaintance with Jesus of Nazareth. Now, with ten other men who had also forsaken Him and fled, he stands up before this audience of thousands to explain what had happened to give them unprecedented courage and ability. Peter proceeds to claim that what they were experiencing, and his audience was witnessing, had been prophesied by the prophet Joel hundreds of years before. Note that Peter does not say that this prophecy was "fulfilled"; rather he uses the unique expression "this is that", suggesting in the context and quotation that there is a definite parallel, application and partial fulfilment.

17-21 During the Lord's ministry on earth, Peter showed a great ignorance of the OT, but after He opened "their understanding, that they might understand the scriptures" (Luke 24:45), and after the coming of the Spirit, Peter's knowledge of the OT was transformed. Thus in his sermon, he could easily quote from Joel and from three of the Psalms. Joel's prophecy described events in "the last days", a phrase in the NT that can describe the christian age, as well as that after the rapture. Thus "in the last days perilous times shall come" (2 Tim 3:1), while in "these last days" God has spoken to us by His Son (Heb 1:2). In such a quotation as this, we must ask whether the whole of the quotation applies to the present age, or whether some (or all) also applies to the period after the rapture. The answer must be found in Acts 2 itself. It was not true that there and then the Spirit of God was poured out upon "all" flesh; God was selective, and it referred to believers only. Certainly the scope of the prophecy was valid: both sexes – "your sons and your daughters"; the extremes of age groups – "your young men ... and your old men"; and even the servant class – "servants and ... handmaidens". Expositors have shown a wonderful imagination in trying to explain vv.19-20 in terms of events in the christian age, but the NT provides no authority for asserting that wonders in heaven, signs in the earth, blood, fire, vapour of smoke, the sun darkened, and the moon turned into blood, have any relevance to the present age. They remind us of events in the book of Revelation, after the rapture of the church (Rev 6:8-9; 16). These events are stated to take place "before that great and notable day of the Lord come", namely the day of judgment when the Lord comes in glory. Peter uses the quotation to link two vital truths for the time when he was preaching, (i) the pouring out of the Spirit, and (ii) "whosoever shall call on the name of the Lord shall be saved". These two truths characterise the day of Pentecost.

The time of that outpouring is also given, "*before* that great and notable day of the Lord come". Since the day of the Lord is a common OT name for the period introduced by divine judgment but culminating in Israel's day of bliss under Messiah's rule, this outpouring must precede that event. Hence it takes place at the beginning of the christian age, and also embraces the faithful remnant of Israel and the great number from all nations, kindreds, people and tongues who in the future will call on the name of the Lord. The disciples had anticipated the kingdom in a natural way ever since they had met Jesus of Nazareth; they had enquired about it when they had met Him after He had risen from the dead, though they had been told that still it was not yet in existence. Now they were learning that they were living in the age that immediately precedes it (but the centuries that would pass were not revealed to them). There also had been promised that they would be endued with power from on high; now they were experiencing this without delay.

The mention of visions and dreams (v.17) is of relevance in the Acts as means of guidance, and the miraculous wonders and signs done by the apostles confirmed and consolidated their testimony. The latter are called "powers of the world to come" in Hebrews, but the reference in Heb 2:5 does not necessarily commence just when the day of the Lord commences.

22 Transformed, and indeed inspired by the risen Christ and His blessed Spirit, Peter went on to tell what had happened to the Saviour during the seven weeks since the pilgrims were last in Jerusalem. The pattern of the address is similar to that of several addresses in the Acts. It tells about God's actions in the past, about what He is doing in the present, about what will happen in the future, and about what God requires of those who hear such addresses.

This address was quite spontaneous, yet geared to the background and circumstances of the audience. We must not think that the addresses in the Acts were well-prepared for organised audiences in conventional religious buildings. If we imitate them, it can be only in the realm of appropriateness. If the audience is Jewish, the address will include references to past dealings that God had with their nation; if Gentile, it will deal with the God of creation, avoiding obscure OT passages that few in an unsaved Gentile audience would understand. In the NT, the meeting-place was the place of public concourse, "the traffic lanes of humanity", whether the temple courts, a market place, a river-side, or Mars' Hill.

Four great acts of God through Jesus of Nazareth constitute the main points of the sermon. First, God approved Jesus by miracles and signs and wonders, the three different NT words used to describe the mighty works that Jesus did. Secondly, the death of Jesus was by God's plan and foreknowledge. Thirdly, God raised Him from the dead, and fourthly, God exalted Him to His own right hand. In all these situations, Peter cited his evidence, his witnesses, and they were there on the spot; plenty of evidence also existed in the OT Scriptures.

First, Peter recalled those amazing years when Jesus moved around the land in which they presently stood. Some years before, a member of their own Sanhedrin, Nicodemus, had confessed, "We know that thou art a teacher come from God: for no man can do these miracles that thou doest, except God be with him" (John 3:2). Peter now stresses the same point: the things that Jesus of Nazareth did indicated divine approval. The Lord Himself had expressed a similar thought, "My Father worketh hitherto, and I work" (John 5:17). Peter presses the point home when he adds, "as ye yourselves know". Some of those listening might easily have had friends and relatives who had benefited from His healing touch. How could they explain it, except by confessing that God was with Him (John 9:30-33) or by resorting to blasphemy (Matt 12:24)? What a contrast with the works of the evil one (Matt 7:22; 2 Thess 2:9-10; Rev 13:13-15).

23 But how does one explain His death if God was with Him? Those who had gathered around His cross had made much of this argument, "He trusted in God; let him deliver him now, if he will have him" (Matt 27:43). But, says Peter, He was "delivered by the determinate counsel and foreknowledge of God". The Revised Authorised Version renders this phrase as, "being delivered by the carefully planned intention and foreknowledge of God". In other words, God was involved in the death of the Lord Jesus. Harold St John described it as "a well-ordered crisis in the Godhead", but that did not absolve the Jews from blame. Peter reminds them of their part in the awful act, "ye have taken", "whom ye have crucified" (v.36), leading to these men being pricked in their heart (v.37). Other translations extend the thought in v.23 to show that the method adopted was to hand Him over to the lawless Gentiles (as in 3:13-14). Thus JND, following a slightly different Greek text, has, "ye, by the hand of lawless men, have crucified and slain", the lawless men being the Gentiles under Pilate. The Lord had predicted this in Luke 18:32.

24-29 The key note of most of the addresses in the Acts is, "God raised him from the dead", the thought of resurrection when God undid what men did (even in Athens Paul terminated his discourse on this note, Acts 17:31). We can never estimate "the pains of death" endured by the Saviour, but God loosed Him from them. The divine impossibilities in the NT form an interesting study, and v.24 contains one of them, "it was not possible that he should be holden of it (death)". On this vital point, Peter elaborates because this truth was so new to them. In order to let the Jews see that their own Scriptures were fully cognisant of the future resurrection of the Lord Jesus, Peter quotes his first of three Psalms at length (Ps 16:8-11), bringing out its implications afterwards

29-31 The preacher now interprets this Psalm, applying it to those very recent events and demonstrating that David was a prophet who was writing not about himself but about another, namely Jesus. The use in the Acts of this word "before" or its equivalent prefix is worthy of notice, David "before spake of the resurrection of Christ"; we shall consider this word "before" later.

Peter refers to the soul of the Lord Jesus as well as to His body when he deals with the subject of His death. It is easier to explain, "neither wilt thou suffer thine Holy One to see corruption" (v.27), than to explain satisfactorily, "thou wilt not leave my soul in hell".

"He descended into hell" is how the so-called apostles' creed understands the quotation, though how the millions upon millions of people who have recited this over the centuries have understood these words we are unable to assess. As frequently happens in quotations from the OT, in accordance with "when it (the Spirit of Christ) testified before hand the sufferings of Christ, and the glory that should follow" (1 Pet 1:11-12), the NT quotation is taken to mean far more than the OT original. However in both cases the separation between body and soul at death is taken for granted. They pass to distinct places: the body to the grave where generally it sees corruption (but "the sea"is mentioned in Rev 20:13), and the soul to the place called *Sheol* in OT times, this being the *Hades* in the NT, *Sheol* appears to be identical to the underworld, the land of the dead, in fact the grave in the broadest sense of the word. Naturally, without further explanation, our minds tend to recoil from the idea that our blessed Lord occupied the NT "hell" even for three days. We admit that different expositors explain the matter in different ways, and the present author can but present an explanation according to his own exercise.

We must examine other scriptures. Not only does our present passage tell us that He was in *Hades*, but several other NT passages use similar language. Rom 10:7 asks, "Who shall descend into the deep (or, abyss)? (that is, to bring up Christ again from the dead)". Apart from the deep or abyss being the place to which the demons that were cast out of Legion went (Luke 8:31), the word is translated "bottomless pit" in Rev 9:1; 20:1, 3, and is described as Satan's prison in v.2 of the latter chapter. Again, Eph 4:9 asserts, "he also descended first into the lower parts of the earth". The contrast in both of the above passages is that whereas the Lord's body was placed in the grave, His soul went lower still to the abyss, Sheol or Hades, a prison for other beings, specially for Satan's demons and later for Satan himself, but not for the Lord, who had the right and the ability to quit that prison.

Thus between His death and resurrection the Lord Jesus in soul visited some great depth. Certainly it was a spirit realm. Did He call it "paradise" in Luke 23:43? Certainly when He emerged it was in magnificent triumph, "he led captivity captive" (Eph 4:8); He destroyed "him that had the power of death, that is, the devil" and delivered "them who through fear of death were all their lifetime subject to bondage" (Heb 2:14-15).

Alford presents a distinct point of view, with important consequences, and other expositors concur. He writes, "The word 'paradise' became in Jewish theology the name for that part of *Hades*, the abode of the dead, where the souls of the righteous awaited the resurrection". 2 Cor 12:2, 4 equate paradise with "the third heaven". How can the two be reconciled? The suggestion is that the Lord did not only go to paradise, the upper part of *Hades*, but that He emptied that part of *Hades* of the souls of the righteous, transferring paradise to its new location. So He descended and then ascended. Not only was His soul not abandoned to *Sheol*, but neither were the souls of the righteous. Both *Hades* and paradise are intermediate. The ultimate destination of the redeemed is the Father's house; of all other occupants of *Sheol* or *Hades* it is the lake of fire; see Rev 20:10, 14."

Readers may find a third suggestion given by some expositors, but they are in the minority. They assert that the Lord never went to *Hades* at all; using Luke 23:46, "Father, into thy hands I commend my spirit", to imply that He returned to His Father's presence prior to His resurrection, returning so that body, soul and spirit should be manifest again in unity.

In v.30, Peter quotes from his second Psalm, namely Ps 132:11. There Solomon is rehearsing the life of David his father. "Of the fruit of thy body will I set upon thy throne" was looking forward to a living Christ and not a dead Christ, and hence the resurrection can be seen to apply as soon as the Lord died.

32-36 By way of conclusion, Peter stresses the resurrection and exaltation of "that same Jesus". After repeating, "This Jesus hath God raised up", he cites his witnesses, these being special witnesses, "not to all the people, but to witnesses chosen before of God, even to us" (Acts 10:41). "We all saw Him", is what he is asserting. And he proceeds to tell them where He is now: not now alive on earth, but enthroned by God in heaven at His right hand. To prove this from the Jews' own OT Scriptures, he cites his third Psalm, namely Ps 110, the most quoted Psalm in the NT. "Exalted", "ascended", "Lord", and "Christ" are words that Peter uses to describe where and what Jesus is now. More than that; He remains there until God makes all His foes His footstool, when He shall sit upon His own throne. To put it in Paul's words, He is "far above all" (Eph 1:21; 4:10). Peter impresses upon them the fact that the Person about whom he has been speaking is "that same Jesus", the One who had previously dwelt amongst men. The theme of the NT after Acts 2 is that Jesus Christ is Lord, Lord of all, Lord of lords. Confession of His Lordship is essential to salvation, and this confession is made by men speaking by the Holy Spirit (1 Cor 12:3). What unregenerate Jews denied that He was, God has made Him, Christ, namely Messiah or the Anointed One.

Consequent upon the exaltation of Jesus, Peter states that they had received the promise of the Holy Spirit. "This" was the evidence which they themselves had seen and heard. Note that in John 14:26, the Father would send the Holy Spirit, but in John 15:26 the Lord said that He would send the Spirit of truth from the Father. Here is intimate collaboration in the Godhead. In v.33, Peter states that "he hath shed forth this", having received the promised Holy Spirit from the Father. This transmission within the Godhead is something beyond our comprehension, but Peter's remark shows the consistency of the Lord's teaching.

Notes

17 "The day of the Lord" or "the last days" is mentioned frequently in the OT prophets from Isa 2:2 to Mal 4:5. Joel 2 is the only one quoted in the NT, and the actual name "day of the Lord" is mentioned only four times in the NT: Acts 2:20; 1 Thess 5:2; 2 Thess 2:2; 2 Pet 3:10.

Bible students are familiar with a series of usages of the words "day of ..." in the Scriptures. It always refers to a period of time during which a particular person is prominent. The chapter in which "the day of the Lord" first appears indicates its meaning clearly: "the Lord alone shall be exalted in that day" (Isa 2:11, 17). Its meaning is emphasised by another statement that appears twice in the same chapter, describing man taking shelter "for fear of the Lord, and for the glory of his majesty, when he ariseth to shake terribly the earth" (vv.19, 21).

"The day of the Lord" is not mentioned in the Gospels, but it must be equated with the period of the coming of the Son of man; see Matt 10:23; 13:41; 16:27-28; 19:28; 24:27, 30, 37, 39, 44; 25:13, 31; Mark 8:38; 13:26; 14:62; Luke 9:26; 12:40; 17:22, 24, 27, 30; 18:18; 21:27, 36, 69; John 1:51; 5:22, 27. All of these are direct references to Dan 7:9-14. The last phase of earthly rule will be entrusted to the Son of man, and the synoptic Gospels are full of references to this subject.

T.E. Wilson defines "the day of the Lord" in these terms: "It is a time of judgment on Israel and the nations. It includes the Great Tribulation, the battle of Armageddon, the Appearing of the Lord in glory and the millennial kingdom, with the final revolt at its end" (see the companion volume in this series on 1,2 Thessalonians).

The events mentioned in Joel 2 and Acts 2 were to take place "before that great and notable day of the Lord". Therefore earth still awaits that day. It would seem that the "last days" describe the culmination of God's dealings with man. Dispensationally God's dealings with man culminate in the day of grace which will be succeeded by divine intervention to put everything right. Historically this day will be when God at last terminates the times of the Gentiles, handing over all rule to the Man Christ Jesus. We are now living through the last chapter of the story before God takes up His great power and reigns. In these last days God has spoken to us in His Son (Heb 1:2). In these last days God has poured out His Spirit, and given capacities to humans that they never had before, enabling them to have freer communication with heaven and to draw from heaven's powers. In these last days, "whosoever shall call upon the name of the Lord shall be saved"; "in the last days perilous times shall come" (2 Tim 3:1); "there shall come in the last days scoffers" (2 Pet 3:3).

We have already commented on the few references to the day of the Lord in the NT letters, for it is a fact that "the day of the Lord" will dawn on earth. But Paul in particular is more concerned with a heavenly people. When he writes about the future, he is more inclined to use expressions such as "the day of our Lord Jesus Christ" (1 Cor 1:8); "the day of the Lord Jesus" (2 Cor 1:14); "the day of Jesus Christ" (Phil 1:16); "the day of Christ" (Phil 1:10; 2:16).

It is noteworthy that the theme of the day of Christ is not developed in Acts, where the earth is the scene of evangelistic activity. The progress of the gospel is uppermost. All other references to the prophetic future are to what will happen on earth. Thus "times of refreshing shall come from the presence of the Lord" (3:19) are for earth and for Israel. The idea of their obtaining relief when Jesus Christ shall be sent back to them should have been appealing. Stephen does not speak about the future, concentrating rather on where the Lord Jesus is now at God's right hand. Peter calls Him "the Judge of quick (living) and dead" (10:42). At Athens Paul states that God "hath appointed a day, in the which he will judge the world in righteousness" (17:31). This idea is found more times in the Psalms (Pss 9:8; 67:4; 72:4; 96:13; 98:9). The first statement in the Acts concerning the return of the Lord Jesus, "this same Jesus ... shall so come in like manner as ye have seen him go into heaven" (1:11) implies His return to earth, no doubt to the mount of Olives in accordance with Zech 14:4. But in Acts there are no references to the coming of the Lord for His church, that is, no mention of the rapture. There are more hints of that in John's Gospel than in the Acts. All other features of the day of grace are to be found here, but not the blessed hope.

23 In our main text, we have mentioned the "befores" in the Acts. These now deserve further consideration. The speakers are very anxious to prove that they are moving in the path of God's will. All that was happening was new in God's ways with men, but it was foreknown and prophesied.

In 1:16 Judas' betrayal of the Lord and subsequent events are said to have been spoken before by David. This must have removed any bitterness from the surviving apostles. They are learning that nothing happens by chance as far as God is concerned; it was all foreknown and also prophesied.

In 2:23 we are taken back into the eternal past. What happened to Jesus of Nazareth was planned in the divine counsels before time began on earth. The quotation from Ps 16 is from the LXX version. Hence, instead of "I have set the Lord before me", Peter quotes "I foresaw the Lord always before my face, for he is on my right hand, that I should not be moved". This version puts the passage more firmly into the prophetic field. The consequence is that David foresaw and spoke in advance about the resurrection of Christ (v.31). This means that Ps 16 is not only a breathing of David's confidence about his own personal resurrection, but a confident statement about that of Christ.

In his address to the Jewish people in 3:18, Peter repeats what he had said to his previous audience in ch.2: "those things with God before had showed by the mouth of all his prophets, that Christ should suffer, he hath so fulfilled". The previously-written OT does not just hint at the sufferings of Christ, but goes into considerable detail in the prophecies of many writers.

The claim that prophecy has been fulfilled appears three times in Peter's impromptu address in ch.3. V.20 also includes the prefix "before" in front of "preached" (it is one word in Greek, though other Greek texts have a different word "foreordained", followed by JND in his translation; "previously appointed" is another rendering). This constitutes the claim that Jesus is their Messiah. The final mention is in v.24, where Peter states that all the prophets (as in v.18) had prophesied about these days. They had forecast His sufferings, His Messiahship, and the day of opportunity brought to mankind as a result.

Samuel was the first of the prophets, and the only prophecy that can come into the reckoning is that of the faithful priest of 1 Sam 2:35. The bright light of such a day is found in Isaiah's acceptable year of the Lord (61:2), Jeremiah's new covenant (31:31) and Joel 2 as applied in Acts 2.

Peter's final statement of this nature was at the prayer meeting in Acts 4:28. The contrast between these confident Christians and the bewildered Jewish leaders is immense. Under threats from the authorities, they remind God that what the Gentiles and the Israelites (represented by the leaders Pontius Pilate and Herod) had done concerning Jesus was what God had "determined before to be done".

Suspicious Jewish Christians had to be convinced in Acts 15 that what was happening had all been planned and prophesied. James, the Lord's brother, settled the argument by claiming that Gentile blessing had been known to God from the beginning, or from eternity (v.18). Amos 9:11, 12 are quoted to support these other passages, proving that these days are in the purpose of God.

e. *The Response of the Audience (2:37-41)*

- v.37 "Now when they heard *this*, they were pricked in their heart, and said unto Peter and to the rest of the apostles, Men *and* brethren, what shall we do?
- v.38 Then Peter said unto them, Repent, and be baptized every one of you in the name of Jesus Christ for the remission of sins, and ye shall receive the gift of the Holy Ghost.
- v.39 For the promise is unto you, and to your children, and to all that are afar off, *even* as many as the Lord our God shall call.
- v.40 And with many other words did he testify and exhort, saying, Save yourselves from this untoward generation.
- v.41 Then they that gladly received his word were baptized: and the same day there were added *unto them* about three thousand souls."

37   There were those who felt uncomfortable about what they had just been told concerning their responsibility for the death of the Lord Jesus. The result was that they asked the second question in the chapter, "What shall we do?" This reminds us of similar questions, "Good Master, what shall I do to inherit eternal life?" (Luke 18:18); "Sirs, what must I do to be saved?" (Acts 16:30).

The men in Acts 2 were in a dilemma. After all, if one has made a mistake of that magnitude in crucifying the Lord of glory, one cannot undo it! But Peter had the answer, "Repent". This is not repentance in the general sense, but in the particular sense, relative to Jesus and their treatment of Him. They had cast Him out, but God had taken Him up; they had given Him the lowest place, even the death of the cross, but God had given Him the highest place at His right hand; they had condemned Him as though He were a common criminal, but God had vindicated Him completely.

They were also commanded to be baptised. Note that baptism was a command by an evangelist (10:48), as well as the exercise of an individual convert (8:36). Baptism was the evidence of repentance. While it resembles the baptism clearly associated with repentance preached by John (Mark 1:4), yet in Acts 2:38 it can scarcely be other than christian baptism since it was "in the name of Jesus Christ". It must be stated that the very word baptism means immersion and nothing else, in spite of religious tradition that has developed concerning this subject over the centuries. Repentance led to the remission of sins, and the subsequent baptism proved that they were gone, so that the new converts were now ready to receive the Holy Spirit as a gift – not in the initial spectacular way as in 2:2, but in the normal way. It cannot be overstressed that the Holy Spirit, like salvation, is a gift; He cannot be earned, or purchased, or merited. Simon of Samaria went wrong at this very point (8:18).

39 If Joel's prophecy had said that God's Spirit would be poured on *all* flesh, then such generality can be but millennial in character. Peter's reply declares that the promise of the Spirit is for Jews, their descendants, and "all that are afar off", implying that the promise is to all, but the reception is by converts only. Thus only those in Cornelius' house in Caesarea received the gift, not the whole city (10:45), and similarly to the restricted group in Ephesus (19:6).

40-41 And so the appeal and the promises continued. They were being challenged to dissociate themselves from that generation which had been guilty of crucifying Jesus of Nazareth. Baptism should have a separating influence, for it means that we do not "continue in sin" (Rom 6:1), neither do we continue to have friendship with those who remain His enemies. The reponse was massive. Any gladness would come after their repentance, not before; only His enemies, as unconverted, would rejoice (John 16:20). We should point out that the word "gladly" is omitted in many Greek texts and translations. But about three thousand in that audience responded, were baptised, and were added to the number of those who already believed. Thus there grew what the Lord Jesus said He would build, "I will build my church; and the gates of hell shall not prevail against it" (Matt 16:18). The word "hell" or "hades" stands in contrast to "living" in v.16.

Notes

38 Consider what the gospel message offered to its first hearers in the Acts.
Forgiveness of sins	2:38; 5:31; 10:43; 13:38; 26:18
Life	5:20; 11:18; 13:46,48
Salvation	2:21; 4:12; 11:14; 13:26,47; 15:11; 16:17,30; 28:28
Justification	13:39
An inheritance	20:32
Repentance (the condition for receiving the blessings of the gospel)	2:38; 3:19; 5:31; 8:22; 11:18; 17:30; 20:21

41 It is interesting to list the names given to the messages preached in the Acts.
"His words" (Peter's)	2:41
"The words of this life"	4:20

"Jesus Christ"	5:42
"The things concerning the kingdom of God"	8:12; 19:8; 20:25
"The word of the Lord"	8:25; 13:48, 49; 15:35, 36; 16:32
"Jesus"	8:35
"Christ ... the Son of God"	9:20
"The word of God"	11:1; 13:5, 44, 46; 17:13; 18:11; 19:20
"Words, whereby thou and all thy house shall be saved"	11:14
"The Lord Jesus"	11:20
"The word of this salvation"	13:26
"Glad tidings"	13:32
"The forgiveness of sins"	13:38
"The word of his grace"	14:3; 20:32
"The gospel"	14:7,21
"The word"	14:25; 16:6
"The way of God"	18:26
"The word of the Lord Jesus"	19:10
"The gospel of the grace of God"	20:24
"All the counsel of God"	20:25
"The kingdom of God"	28:23, 31

It is important to consider all the "progress reports" that occur in the Acts.

1. "The same day there were added unto them about three thousand souls" (2:41). The first gospel preaching in the church's history resulted in many being added to the saved of the Lord. Note that exact numbers are not given; the Spirit of inspiration was satisfied with the word "about", contrasting with the exact number "an hundred and fifty and three" in John 21:11.

2. "Many of them which heard the word believed; and the number of the men was about five thousand" (4:4). It would appear that these were in addition to the previous three thousand. It is also interesting to note that the word for "men" is not the generic *anthrōpos*, but *anēr*, indicating "male".

3. "And believers were the more added to the Lord, multitudes both of men and women" (5:14). This happened in spite of the setback caused by the sin of Ananias and Sapphira. No number is stated, just multitudes. Thus the progress so far is 3000 souls, 5000 males, and now multitudes of men and women.

4. "The number of the disciples was multiplied"; "the word of God increased; and the number of the disciples multiplied in Jerusalem greatly; and a great company of the priests were obedient to the faith" (6:1, 7). The language indicates tremendous progress. No doubt the meaning is that the effect of the word has increased, but Luke uses the word "multiplied" for the first time to indicate the progress, rather than the word "added". In fact, the adverb "greatly" enhances the word "multiplied". One group, the priests, is singled out for special mention.

5. "Then had the churches rest throughout all Judaea and Galilee and Samaria, and were edified; and walking in the fear of the Lord, and in the comfort of the Holy Ghost,

were multiplied" (9:31). The background is persecution, which did not diminish the work of God so as to produce reduction. The word "multiplied" is again used, but this time not of believers, but of the churches. No wonder Jewish leaders had wondered "whereunto this would grow" (5:24). (Note: in other Greek texts and translations the plural "churches" is replaced by the singular form "church".)

6. "But the word of God grew and multiplied" (12:24). This comes at the end of the incidents involving Herod, which culminated in his death. The contrast is highlighted in the hymn, "While mortals rise and perish, God endures unchanging on". The Greek word translated "grew" is the same as the one translated "increased" in 6:7. For the third time "multiplied" is used, but differently from the previous occasions. Disciples were multiplied in 6:1,7; the church was multiplied in 9:31; now it is the Word multiplying.

7. "And so were the churches established in the faith, and increased in number daily" (16:5). The progress reports are becoming fewer. But then the scope of the preachers is becoming wider. All the previous reports were about progress in a small part of the world. Expansion is taking place. In chs.2 and 4 the daily increase was of believers, but now there is a daily increase of churches.

If we take a world view, this progress has continued until now.

f. The First Church (2:42-47)

v.42 "And they continued stedfastly in the apostles' doctrine and fellowship, and in breaking of bread, and in prayers.
v.43 And fear came upon every soul: and many wonders and signs were done by the apostles.
v.44 And all that believed were together, and had all things common;
v.45 And sold their possessions and goods, and parted them to all *men*, as every man had need.
v.46 And they, continuing daily with one accord in the temple, and breaking bread from house to house, did eat their meat with gladness and singleness of heart.
v.47 Praising God, and having favour with all the people. And the Lord added to the church daily such as should be saved."

In certain important Greek manuscripts, the actual word "church" does not appear in this passage (v.47). In spite of this, it is obvious that what had come into existence was the church. All of us were born before we were given our names, and so it was with the living organism known as the church. The English word is now a misnomer, since people usually apply it to a building, whereas in the NT the Greek word *ekklēsia* never means a building. Unfortunately, nowhere the is the AV weaker in its translation of the Scriptures than in ecclesiastical terminology; this was deliberate at the dictates of King James I, lest established church order should be undermined. The preferable translation is JND's "assembly", or the NEB's reversion to Tyndale's "congregation", though now-a-days this word can be misunderstood.

42 Conversion and baptism were only the beginning for these first Christians, and this should be so for every Christian. It is always necessary to continue. The round of activities in which they continued is given in v.42, and they may be traced through the rest of the Acts and the Epistles. The four features of church activity in the verse are neither continuous nor parallel, but they embrace a lot though not everything. They constitute a quadrilateral.

A.M.S. Gooding has suggested that "the apostles' doctrine (teaching)" comprised fifty per cent teaching from the OT, twenty-five per cent of the oral teaching given to the apostles by the Lord, and twenty-five per cent new revelation given by the NT apostles and prophets through the Holy Spirit before the completion of the canon of Holy Scripture. We consider the details of this teaching later, at the end of our comments in v.42.

The word "fellowship" did not have a technical meaning. It simply indicated the company that the early Christians kept. In a hostile world, especially because of the Jewish element in it, they were continually in each other's company. From a spiritual point of view, it is usually dangerous when this ceases to be so, and when like Demas he "loved this present world" (2 Tim 4:10). The practical aspects of fellowship will be seen as we proceed through the Acts.

The "breaking of bread" was the act of commemoration left them by their Lord just a few hours before He was crucified. It was the means chosen by Him whereby they would constantly remember Him; it was always collective, and it was obviously frequent. Paul later received this from the Lord, and he called it "the Lord's supper" (1 Cor 11:20, 23). Another example in the Acts is 20:7, taking place in Troas.

The church began in a prayer meeting, and an examination of the early chapters of the Acts shows that it continued with prayer meetings. It almost seems to have been continuous, as for example when some would give themselves "continually to prayer" (6:4, 6). When any member was imprisoned and released, that member knew that he would find the church in session at a prayer meeting, regardless of the time of day (12:5, 12).

Regarding "the apostles' doctrine" it is interesting now to collect together from the addresses in the Acts what the apostles believed about God and the Lord Jesus, about the gospel, the church and the future.

What the apostles believed about God. The apostles and the first converts would believe that He was the God of Abraham, Isaac and Jacob, with all the powers attributed to Him in the OT. Stephen's address in ch.7 makes this clear. They believed that He was the God so recently revealed to them by His Son, the Lord Jesus. Often in the great addresses which punctuate the Acts we find that what they believed about God is unfolded by illustration.

The prefix *pro*, found some seven times in the earlier chapters of Acts, cannot be ignored. Each occurrence indicates something of the foreknowledge of God, which is an essential feature of omnipotence. This is necessitated by the predictive element of Scripture of which there are two examples in these early chapters: the first regarding Judas' treachery (1:16), the second the resurrection (2:31).

The greatest example of divine foreknowledge stated in the Acts concerns the Lord Jesus: His death, burial, resurrection and ascension. Thus Peter says in 2:23, "Him, being delivered by the determinate counsel and foreknowledge of God". The Revised Authorised Version gives the rendering, "the carefully planned intention and foreknowledge"; Schonfield's *Authentic New Testament* gives, "God's deliberate intention and foreknowledge"; J.B. Phillips gives, "the predetermined plan and foreknowledge". Never in the history of the world has anything gone according to plan like the death of the Lord Jesus, and that plan was God's, not man's. Well might James say, "Known unto God are all his works from the beginning of the world" (15:18).

The same event is described in Ps 2, according to 4:27, 28, "Of a truth against thy holy child Jesus, whom thou hast anointed, both Herod, and Pontius Pilate, with the Gentiles, and the people of Israel, were gathered together, for to do whatsoever thy hand and thy counsel determined before to be done."

If any event is proclaimed in these great speeches of Acts with greater emphasis, it is the resurrection of that same great Person. In 2:21 Peter has said that David "before spake of the resurrection of Christ" (Ps 16:10); Peter has said the same in 3:18, "those things, which God had showed by the mouth of all his prophets, that Christ should suffer, he hath so fulfilled". And the apostle Paul adds his similar testimony in 13:27-37, "they that dwell at Jerusalem, and their rulers, because they knew him not, nor yet the voices of the prophets which are read every sabbath day, they have fulfilled them in condemning him ... And when they had fulfilled all that was written of him, they took him down from the tree."

His betrayal, His trial, His crucifixion, His resurrection and His ascension, all known to God, were prophesied in the OT Scriptures and literally fulfilled in the environs of Jerusalem. Pss 1, 16, 110, 118, 132 are all cited.

But the purpose of God did not extend only to all the experiences of the Lord Jesus. This God is still the God of the Jew; moreover, revelations from these same addresses show that He is indeed the God of the Gentiles also.

The speech in question is that given by Paul on Mars' Hill in ancient Athens. Paul says that God has "made of one blood all nations of men for to dwell on all the face of the earth, and hath determined the times before appointed, and the bounds of their habitation" (17:26). Other translations of this vital verse are: "He has determined their pre-appointed times and the boundaries of their habitation" (Revised AV); "From one man He made every nation of men, that they should inhabit the whole earth; and He determined the times set for them and the exact places where they should live" (NIV); "He determined allotted periods and the boundaries of their habitation" (RSV). (Only an examination of the Greek text will show why such translations differ so much from the AV). He is not only the God of the nations, but He is also the God of history. This fact rests on Moses' statement to the nation of Israel, "the Most High divided to the nations their inheritance ... he separated the sons of Adam, he set the bounds of the people according to the number of the children of Israel" (Deut 32:8).

Tracing back still further in time, it becomes apparent that the God of the apostles was not only the God of Israel and of the nations, but He was also the God of creation. Those who prayed in Acts 4:24 said, "Lord, thou art God, which hast made heaven, and earth, and the sea, and all that in them is". Paul uses this theme in his address to the people of Lystra, "turn ... unto the living God, which made heaven, and earth, and the sea, and all things that are therein ... he did good, and gave us rain from heaven, and fruitful seasons, filling our hearts with food and gladness" (14:15,17). Paul is stressing to a heathen audience that a living God cannot be represented by dead idols which are worthless and less than nothing. When such people tried to recognise Paul and Barnabas as gods, the apostle could not preach the gospel, but relied solely upon the message of the living God of creation.

Again, this theme is Paul's starting point in his address to the Athenian scholars, "God ... made the world and all things therein" (17:24).

What the apostles believed about the Lord Jesus. Whatever the doubts that the apostles still had entertained about their Master when He was crucified, they have all vanished when the preaching described in the Acts takes place. They have accepted that their Master was not crucified because He could not avoid it. It was not the treachery of Judas, nor the sentence of Pilate that caused Him to be crucified, but God's purpose. Paul argues in 17:1-3 that the Scriptures taught that Christ must needs have suffered and risen from the dead, and that Jesus whom he preached to the Thessalonians was Christ. They certainly believed that their Master had risen from the dead, and was alive. This fact was their inspiration and power in their testimony of the gospel.

The apostles had actually witnessed the Lord's ascension. They claimed that the heavens must receive Him; both Stephen and Saul of Tarsus saw Him in His elevated position. In 10:36, Peter declared that He is Lord of all.

Apart from where He is now, the apostles believed that a great future awaited their Master. They believed that He was to have a kingdom, but they did not know when. They had been assured by angels that He was coming back again. They believed that He would restore not only Israel to their rightful place in their own land, but that He would restore all things (3:19). The apostle Paul went further, and declared that His coming again would be for the whole world, confirming a considerably repeated statement from the Psalms that He will "judge the world in righteousness" (17:31).

What the apostles believed about the gospel. What they preached is frequently called the "word of God" and the "word of the Lord", but in 13:26 Paul calls it the "word of salvation". The demon-possessed girl in Philippi kept on describing the preachers as "the servants of the most high God, which show unto us the way of salvation" (16:17). The angel of the Lord told Peter to go and tell the people gathered in the temple courts "all the words of this life". Paul called it "the word of his (God's) grace" (20:32).

The apostles generally called on their audiences to repent, which indicated that previously such men had been on the wrong road. Paul urged "repentance toward God, and faith toward our Lord Jesus Christ" (20:21). True repentance is always accompanied by faith, and genuine faith presupposes repentance. In Peter's early preaching to the Jews, repentance was not so much for sins in general, as for a wrong attitude towards God's Son, the Lord Jesus, whom they had caused to be crucified. The message of the gospel is not so much the sin-question as the Son-question. Certainly the person who believes in the Lord Jesus should not follow a life that continues in sin (Rom 6:1).

In 13:39 Paul mentions the truth of justification which he was to expound in Romans and Galatians. Those justified had received forgiveness of sins – and that apart from the law of Moses. It was the stand that he took on this truth that brought him endless problems with the Jewish world, both inside and outside the church. Forgiveness of sins as a free offer from God through Christ is mentioned three times in Acts, namely 5:31; 13:38; 26:18. The first offer was made in Jerusalem, and the last one in Rome.

The gospel not only deals with the past of those who believe in Jesus; Paul twice speaks about the inheritance of those who are sanctified by faith (20:32; 26:18).

While none of the truths of the Spirit of God is particularly expounded in the Acts, yet the fact of the Spirit's place in the lives of believers is indicated many times. "Did ye receive the Holy Spirit when ye believed?" (19:2 RV), was Paul's question to the disciples in Ephesus. The Spirit "fell" on those gathered in Cornelius' house (10:44), to indicate the acceptance of the Gentiles by God, as well as to guarantee their future with God.

Then, as now, that same gospel is the only means of blessing for mankind, for "Neither is there salvation is any other" (4:12); "And his name through faith in his name" is what makes any man whole (3:16).

What the apostles believed about the church. What Peter understood by the keys of the kingdom (Matt 16:19) can only be conjectured, but he is undoubtedly using them in the Acts. Only later does Paul write of the builders of God's temple (1 Cor 3:10ff), but what was being done in the Acts resulted in local churches being formed.

Although the church as the body of Christ is an exclusively NT revelation, these first preachers were happy to find some typical allusions in the OT. Both Stephen and Paul spoke of God desiring a temple that was not made with hands. This condemnation of the existing and soon-to-be-destroyed temple of Herod provided a contrast to what was being built spiritually as they both spoke.

Stephen asserted that while the tabernacle gave place to the temple, yet an earthly temple was forever inadequate for God. This is developed by James at the council of Jerusalem in ch.15. In fact, he claimed that a successor to "the tabernacle of David" was to be built in accordance with Amos 9:11-12, and that this would embrace the Gentiles being brought into blessing such as Paul and Barnabas had been experiencing. Note that "the tabernacle of David" can only be the tent erected on mount Zion to receive the ark in 1 Chron 16:1, and not Moses' tabernacle which was still at Gibeon, and arkless in the early years of Solomon's reign (2 Chron 1:3-4).

No matter what detail they did not know, these three brethren knew that a new concept was developing before their very eyes during the initial years of their ministry. As far as the apostles among them were concerned, no doubt they recalled their Master's words, "believe me, the hour cometh, when ye shall neither in this mountain (Gerizim), nor yet at Jerusalem, worship the Father ... the hour cometh, and now is, when the true worshippers shall worship the Father in spirit and in truth" (John 4:21, 23). Or again from the same Gospel, "Other sheep I have, which are not of this fold: them also I must bring, and they shall hear my voice; and there shall be one fold (lit. flock), and one shepherd" (10:16).

A Person, not a place; a flock, not a fold; a spiritual house, not a physical temple – these are what the apostles associated with the church.

What the apostles believed about the kingdom of God. It must not be assumed that the kingdom and the church are mutually exclusive. Admittedly, the Gospels mention the kingdom very frequently, and the church epistles seldom; but it must not be overlooked that while the growth of the church is the chief subject of the Acts, yet the kingdom of God is mentioned seven times (1:3; 8:12; 14:22; 19:8; 20:25; 28:23, 31).

The truth is that the kingdom neither began nor ended with the earthly life of the Lord Jesus. It acquired a more spiritual meaning by His coming. After His resurrection, He spoke about His kingdom, but never about His church explicitly. Philip and Paul both preached the kingdom of God, and just as their converts formed part of the church, so they were also in the kingdom. The kingdom contains the church. Some of the minor prophets speak about the *house* of the kingdom where the king and his courtiers dwelt. This may be a fair analogy of the relationship between the church and the kingdom. The former is in the latter. The former has a closer relationship to its living Head; the latter is in relationship to the King, and eventually sharing administration with Him. During the church age, to Paul the kingdom was moral in its concept, "the kingdom of God is not meat and drink; but righteousness, and peace, and joy in the Holy Ghost" (Rom 14:17).

Philip preached the kingdom of God and helped to form local churches of God in Samaria (8:12). Paul did likewise in Lystra (14:22), Ephesus (19:8; 20:25) and Rome (18:23, 31).

43 Several times notice is taken of the impact of these events on ordinary people, namely, fear. Obviously everything was attributed to the working of God among the disciples. The same effect was produced on the Philistines by the bringing of the ark of the covenant into the camp of Israel, "And the Philistines were afraid" (1 Sam 4:7). At mount Sinai Moses said "I exceedingly fear and quake" (Heb 12:21). Jacob experienced the same effect, "he was afraid and said, How dreadful is this place! This is none other but the house of God" (Gen 28:17). It was the effect that Paul expected should be produced on unsaved visitors to the gatherings of the Corinthian church just because God was there when gifts were properly exercised (1 Cor 14:24-25). It was the effect produced on everybody both inside and outside the church in Acts 5:11 when Ananias and Sapphira were judged by God.

Doubtless the fear was produced not only because these Galilaean disciples could speak in other languages, but also because of the miracles of healing performed just as their Master had done. The phenomenon of miracles which began with the Lord's public ministry continued well through the first century of the christian era. Peter had proclaimed earlier in the chapter that God's approval of Jesus of Nazareth had been expressed by miracles (v.22). Describing later what happened in those early days, Mark 16:20 records that the Lord was "working with them, and confirming the word with signs following". Similarly, Heb 2:4 says, "God also bearing them witness, both with signs and wonders, and with divers miracles, and gifts of the Holy Ghost, according to his own will".

This confirmation is sometimes expressed with a general description of miracles, as in 2:43, and sometimes with the reader's attention focussed on a specific miracle, as in 3:7-11.

44-45 Another characteristic of the early church that we would find hard to imitate was their community of goods. It appears that the apostles did not encourage them to adopt this attitude to material things, but they did accept it. They obviously felt that they could hold nothing back from Him who had given His all to them. Whereas ch.2 describes their attitude to their own possessions and goods, yet chs.4-5 give us specific examples. 2 Cor 8:13, 14 give a more developed arrangement when local churches are to be found everywhere, the context being that of the churches of the Gentiles sending a substantial gift to the poor saints in Jerusalem: "I mean not that other men be eased, and ye burdened: but by an equality, that now at this time your abundance may be a supply for their want, that their abundance also may be a supply for your want: that there may be equality". The first church in Jerusalem had community of goods, although, as 5:4 shows, there was no necessity to do so.

Enthusiasm can have its dangers, but even more dangerous is the opposite spirit of apathy. The flush of first love can make even Christians do things the outworking of which cannot be foreseen (for after a few years the growing lack of possessions helped to cause the great dearth in Judaea recorded in 11:29), but the cold, calculating response to the greatest story in the world, that of the gospel, is reprehensible in the extreme.

Christians, like their Lord, are to be characterised by giving. Some have given away all that they have possessed, others have kept as much as they could. The question of future reward enters here, but possessions, whether small or large, when kept should be held for the Lord's use. For example, one cannot entertain the Lord's servants without a home!

46 The birth-place of the church was the upstairs room in Jerusalem where the

Lord had celebrated the last Passover with His disciples, and where He had instituted the Lord's Supper. With the addition of three thousand souls to the one hundred and twenty, this room was obviously far too small to accommodate the whole Jerusalem church. It is interesting to note where they moved to – the temple courts. What more appropriate place was there! What more suitable place for testimony! These early chapters mention this meeting-place several times. But the use of their own homes is also prominent. They were to be found consorting in the temple courts, but their common meals were served in each other's houses. These two kinds of premises are mentioned again in 5:42.

47 Luke's Gospel ends with the followers of the Lord Jesus continually in the temple praising and blessing God, because of the risen and ascended Christ. This first episode of Acts finds them praising God because of the descent of the Spirit and the formation of the church. Again, as in the Gospels, the common people reacted differently from the Jewish authorities. The latter were very hostile, but the former favoured the Saviour's followers.

As already pointed out, ch.2 ends with the first of Luke's summaries, "the Lord added to the church daily such as should be saved". The sudden change from "God" to "the Lord" is surely intended to attribute the daily increase in numbers to the personal activity of the risen Head Himself. The words in the AV "such as should be saved" may appear to be awkward. But few Greek versions of the Scriptures support the translation that the salvation of these believers was planned in advance. The present participle passive identifies "added" as those who were being saved. Neither does the word *ekklēsia* (church) appear in this verse in some Greek manuscripts; it then appears for the first time in 5:11.

Notes

The importance of Acts 2 in the record of God's dealings with men cannot be overestimated. To recapitulate, the giving of the Spirit was:

a. The fulfilment of the promise of the Father (John 14-16), given some seven weeks before.

b. The fulfilment of the preaching of John Baptist in the opening chapters of the four Gospels, dating back some three and a half years.

c. The partial fulfilment of the prophecy of Joel 2, given several centuries before. This will have a complete future fulfilment when God's earthly people Israel shall have this tremendous experience.

d. The antitype of the even older feast of Weeks (Lev 23:15-21), when two loaves were offered before the Lord. The offering of the firstfruits prefigured the resurrection of the Lord Jesus with its promise of a glorious harvest. Pentecost, after the grain harvest had been gathered in, threshed, milled and baked, foretold the final outcome of that harvest. It may be that the two loaves indicate the incorporation of Jew and Gentile in the blessing of God.

e. The establishment of a new temple, not made with hands, to replace the one made with hands, whose destruction less than forty years ahead had been prophesied by the Lord Jesus in Matt 24:2.

f. The inauguration of a new covenant in contrast to the old one of Exod 19 which had been tried and found wanting, nobody ever being justified under its terms.

g. The reversal of the judgment of Gen 11:7-9, under which mankind was divided through language difficulties, whereas the pilgrims in Jerusalem understood the preachers who spoke to them in their own languages. It was not God's will that this particular gift should be perpetuated to the present day, hence over the centuries thousands of missionaries have had to learn difficult languages in order to testify to natives the gospel of the grace of God.

g. *The Lame Man Healed (3:1-11)*

v.1 "Now Peter and John went up together into the temple at the hour of prayer, *being* the ninth *hour*.
v.2 And a certain man lame from his mother's womb was carried, whom they laid daily at the gate of the temple which is called Beautiful, to ask alms of them that entered into the temple;
v.3 Who seeing Peter and John about to go into the temple asked an alms.
v.4 And Peter, fastening his eyes upon him with John, said, Look on us.
v.5 And he gave heed unto them, expecting to receive something of them.
v.6 Then Peter said, Silver and gold have I none; but such as I have give I thee: In the name of Jesus Christ of Nazareth rise up and walk.
v.7 And he took him by the right hand, and lifted *him* up: and immediately his feet and ankle bones received strength.
v.8 And he leaping up stood, and walked, and entered with them into the temple, walking, and leaping, and praising God.
v.9 And all the people saw him walking and praising God:
v.10 And they knew that it was he which sat for alms at the Beautiful gate of the temple: and they were filled with wonder and amazement at that which had happened unto him.
v.11 And as the lame man which was healed held Peter and John, all the people ran together unto them in the porch that is called Solomon's, greatly wondering."

1-8 The second episode in the Acts, like the first, occupies two chapters. It begins with the first specific miracle of the post-ascension era, namely, the healing of a lame beggar who was over forty years of age (4:22), at one of the temple gates. It must have been a degrading sight to have the "house of prayer for all nations" surrounded by beggars. If God had really been resident among His people as of old, and if Christ had been accepted by His people, then this degrading sight would never have occurred, since the house of God would have been holy. As it was, outside at the gates there were beggars, while inside the courts there were thieves (Matt 21:13). Hence the Lord Jesus spoke of it as "your house" (Matt 23:38), declaring that it would be left desolate to them, in contrast to "my house" in Isa 56:7.

This lame man, over forty years old (4:22), was laid daily at this gate, and the implication must be that he was often there when the Lord Jesus entered the temple courts for teaching during His last week. Yet he was not healed by the Lord; the time of healing, the time of salvation, is in the divine hands. Some are saved early in life as was Timothy, others at the end as was the thief on the cross. Evangelists must not be discouraged when there appears to be a dearth of blessing in spite of their faithful endeavours; they must anticipate blessing in the future, perhaps after many days.

Nine o'clock in the morning, the hour of prayer, was the time of the morning sacrifice, the time for the offering up of incense and for the trimming of the lamps (Exod 30:7). Zacharias, as a faithful priest, engaged in such activity (Luke 1:8-10), though we cannot imagine that Peter and John went into the temple courts to interest themselves in any Jewish ritual. Penniless apostles were accosted by a penniless beggar, but with them were wealth and power resident in Jesus' name, such as no unregenerate Jew ever conceived of. Redemption comes not through silver and gold (1 Pet 1:18), but there are spiritual counterparts that correspond to "gold, silver, precious stones" that every believer should possess (1 Cor 3:12). Certainly Peter and John would not offer "wood, hay, stubble", for these could accomplish no work for the Lord. It should be pointed out that divinely-accomplished miracles were instantaneous, complete and lasting; any copy (and men are quite willing to copy when possible, as in Matt 7:22) is not genuine.

A few observations at this point on Bible miracles will be helpful. Bible teachers have pointed out that at various periods in history God has given exceptional displays of His power by miracles of a spectacular nature. The first period extended from the exodus out of Egypt until Israel entered into the land of promise. The second embraced the years of the ministries of Elijah and Elisha, while the third extended from the commencement of the Lord's public ministry until about the close of the Acts. All miracles were divine endorsements of His people and His servants. They were also confirmation of the Lord's personal presence with His servants (Heb 2:4), and they will be prominent when God's King comes, whereas previously they had been spasmodic.

Before He returned to heaven, the Lord told His apostles, "Verily, verily, I say unto you, He that believeth on me, the works that I do shall he do also; and greater works than these shall he do; because I go unto my Father" (John 14:12). What He had given them the power to do before His death they would continue to do afterwards.

The apostle Paul calls these "the signs of an apostle" (2 Cor 12:12). The writer to the Hebrews calls them "the powers of the world to come" (6:5), while Isaiah had promised that these would be in evidence when Messiah came. In Matt 8:17 the Lord's miracles are therefore said to have been in fulfilment of Isa 53:4, and in Luke 4:18-20 to have been in fulfilment of Isa 61:1-2. Certainly John Baptist was reassured as to His being the Messiah when he was told the wonderful works that He was doing (Luke 7:18-22).

In 2:22 Peter claims that the Lord was approved by God among the Jews by miracles (*dunamis*), that is, evidences of divine power; by wonders (*teras*), that is, what describes their effect on the beholders; and by signs (*sēmeion*), that is, what points to the greatness of the Person in whose name they were wrought. This is the name given to all the miracles recorded as wrought by the Lord in John's Gospel. They were signs or pointers to the fact that He was the Son of God (20:30-31). The words "wonders and signs"are used in Acts 2:43 to describe the mighty works of the apostles after they had received the Holy Spirit.

The first specific miracle mentioned was the healing of the lame beggar by Peter at the temple gate. A second general statement is made in 5:12; the miracle-workers were again the apostles, and the words used to describe them are the same as in 2:43, "signs and wonders". There follows a list of the kinds of people who were healed (vv.15, 16); the people's expectations were so high that they wanted at least Peter's shadow to fall on them.

Stephen is the next person who is said to have worked "great wonders and miracles" (6:8). (Actually the same two Greek words appearing in 2:43 and 5:12 are used.) Philip, like Stephen, one of the seven "deacons", is found working signs ("miracles" AV) in 8:6, followed by a list of the kind of things that he was doing (v.7). This was doubtless the power coveted by Simon Magus. If people came to the Lord for loaves and fishes (John 6:26), there were others who came only for healing, or in the extreme case to receive the ability to pass on the Holy Spirit to others (Acts 8:19).

The second and third specific miracles recorded were performed by Peter at Lystra and Joppa in 9:34, 40. The latter is the first raising from the dead in the Acts.

The first mention of miracles in the ministry of Paul and Barnabas appears in the description of their visit to Iconium in 14:3, where the words used are again "signs and wonders". There follow the first specific miracle performed by Paul, the healing of a cripple (14:10), and then the raising of Eutychus from the dead (20:9-10). There is a strong parallelism between Paul's first two miracles and the two by Peter recorded in ch.9, the healing of a cripple and the raising of a dead person.

The most spectacular story of miracle-working in Paul's experience took place at Ephesus; Luke calls them special or unusual miracles (19:11). They were unusual in that articles of clothing from Paul's body could heal infirmities. Imitations were tried by unregenerate Jews with disastrous results. Strangers to the Saviour cannot presume to use the power of Jesus' name. Sons of Sceva, like Jannes and Jambres (2 Tim 3:8), can go only so far in the spirit realm.

The fewness of miracles towards the end of the book is quite remarkable. Did God use them sparingly? Though we must recall that Paul wrote of "the working of miracles" to the Corinthians towards the end of his third journey (1 Cor 12:10). There is however no record of them in most of the places to which Paul went preaching the gospel. Paul's prison doors were not opened as Peter's were in the earlier chapters of the book.

The only miracles after ch.20 were those performed by Paul on the island of Melita (28:3-9). Miracles were not used to remove Paul's own infirmities nor those of Timothy. Paul resorted to prayer so that his thorn in the flesh might or might not be removed according to the Lord's will (2 Cor 12:7-9).

9-11 Naturally the news of the miracle, attested by the presence of the new companion for the apostles, drew a crowd. The reality of the miracle was not denied by the Pharisees (4:14), as had been the miracle performed by the Lord Jesus on the blind man previously (John 9:18). Thus the opportunity was too good for the apostles to miss – a ready-made audience, anxious to have an explanation of such a notable miracle. Their business was to take every opportunity of telling people about the Lord Jesus, and evangelists today can testify of ready-made audiences often provided by the Lord. Thus there follows the third of Peter's addresses.

h. Peter's Third Address (3:12-26)

v.12 "And when Peter saw *it*, he answered unto the people, Ye men of Israel, why marvel ye at this? or why look ye so earnestly on us, as though by our own power or holiness we had made this man to walk?

v.13 The God of Abraham, and of Isaac, and of Jacob; the God of our fathers, hath glorified his Son Jesus; whom ye delivered up, and denied him in the presence of Pilate, when he was determined to let *him* go.

v.14 But ye denied the Holy One and the Just, and desired a murderer to be granted unto you;

v.15 And killed the Prince of life, whom God hath raised from the dead; whereof we are witnesses.

v.16 And his name through faith in his name hath made this man strong, whom ye see and know: yea, the faith which is by him hath given him this perfect soundness in the presence of you all.

v.17 And now, brethren, I wot that through ignorance ye did *it*, as *did* also your rulers.

v.18 But those things, which God before had shewed by the mouth of all his prophets, that Christ should suffer, he hath so fulfilled.

v.19 Repent ye therefore, and be converted, that your sins may be blotted out, when the times of refreshing shall come from the presence of the Lord;

v.20 And he shall send Jesus Christ, which before was preached unto you:

v.21 Whom the heaven must receive until the times of restitution of all things, which God hath spoken by the mouth of all his holy prophets since the world began.

v.22 For Moses truly said unto the fathers, A prophet shall the Lord your God raise up unto you of your brethren, like unto me; him shall ye hear in all things whatsoever he shall say unto you.

v.23 And it shall come to pass, *that* every soul, which will not hear that prophet, shall be destroyed from among the people.

v.24 Yea, and all the prophets from Samuel and those that follow after, as many as have spoken, have likewise foretold of these days.

v.25 Ye are the children of the prophets, and of the covenant which God made with our fathers, saying unto Abraham, And in thy seed shall all the kindreds of the earth be blessed.

v.26 Unto you first God, having raised up his Son Jesus, sent him to bless you, in turning away every one of you from his iniquities."

12 Peter "answered" his audience's unspoken question; he knew by their outward looks and actions what their question was. How could two Galilaean fishermen enable a man never before able to walk, to become now capable of doing so? He confessed that it was certainly not through their own power nor through their own godliness. "Without me ye can do nothing", the Lord had said (John 15:5), and this applies to all spiritual work for the Lord. The true testimony of all servants should be, "I can do all things through Christ which strengtheneth me" (Phil 4:13). Otherwise the flesh tries through lack of faith, and fails in its hoped-for objectives (Matt 17:19-21).

13 Peter makes much of the common ground that existed between them and their Jewish audience, the common ground being the OT Scriptures, not its development into tradition, doctrine and ceremony by their theologians over the years. Peter's God was the same as that confessed by the Jews; they all went back to the "God of Abraham, and of Isaac, and of Jacob", a title that increased threefold in Genesis and Exodus as these three fathers came and departed from the scene in the OT. Here Peter is anxious immediately to insist that Jesus is God's Son (*pais*; see note on 3:26). The address hinges upon three mentions of the word "presence", at least in the AV. Peter recalls: (i) what had taken place in the *presence* of Pilate a few weeks ago; (ii) what had happened that very day in the *presence* of them all (v.16); and (iii) what would come from the *presence* of the Lord, if only they would repent (v.19).

For the only time in his sermons and writings, Peter uses a verb reminiscent of John's Gospel to describe the sequel to the Lord's crucifixion: God "glorified" Him (John 16:14; 17:1); though using a noun, he later wrote, "the glory that should follow" (1 Pet 1:11). The language is designed to emphasise, as in the previous sermon, that God did the opposite of what they did. They betrayed Jesus and they disowned Him, but God glorified Him. Twice Peter emphasises that they disowned Him. The guilt was entirely theirs; he attaches no blame to Pilate, who had made up his mind that Jesus ought not to be executed, since he confessed that he could find no fault in Him. However, ultimately Pilate unjustly "delivered Jesus to their will" (Luke 23:25) because the voices of the chief priests prevailed, and this Roman governor in the coming day of judgment will have to answer before God for his unjust deed.

14 Not only is there a contrast between what God and what these men had done, but there is also a contrast between the Man of God's choice and the man whom they chose. The Lord Jesus was "the holy One and the Just", whereas Barabbas was a murderer. The world reached a crisis on that day of the Lord's trial. The opportunity arose to reverse the whole course of human history, though the Jews did not, of course, know this fact. The Man who came to give was rejected in place of the man who came to take; the Man who came to save was rejected in preference to the man who came to kill; the Man who was the great peacemaker was rejected in favour of the revolutionary. Their very title and name show the difference. The Lord was the

Son of His Father; the name Barabbas means "son of father" – the Lord's character could be traced to that of the eternal Father, while that of Barabbas could be traced back to his original father, Adam, for by man sin entered into the world (Rom 5:12).

15 Again, the heinousness of their crime is stressed; they killed the Author of life. (This refers to the Jews' responsibility in the crucifixion, for the Lord had taught in John 10:18 that no man would take His life from Him, since He would lay it down by Himself.) He who had raised other people from the dead, and had prevented many from dying of various diseases, was actually killed by them. What a contradiction they had engaged in. But God reversed their action by raising Him from the dead. Just as they had rejected Him as King, claiming Caesar only as king, and as they had mocked Him as the King of the Jews, so God will reverse such actions in that day when His Son will be set as King on His holy hill of Zion. How Peter delighted to stress in his sermons that God raised from the dead Him whom they had crucified. He wanted them to feel their guilt, and the reason for his delight was the fact, as in ch.2, that the apostles had all been witnesses of the manifestations of their risen Lord.

16 Peter now changes his subject to what had taken place in the presence of them all that very day, for the miracle had been a very public one, unlike, for example, that of the raising of Jairus' daughter. The power that had made the lame man able to walk was the power of Jesus' name. Admittedly He was no longer physically present, but the power of His name was as great as His physical presence had been. The man whom they saw and knew had been made strong and given complete healing through faith in Jesus' name. Vv.3-6 appear to suggest that the faith was on Peter's part, not on the man's part, since he was merely thinking of financial gain. This is quite unlike what Paul would later do in Lystra, where the apostle perceived that a cripple "had faith to be healed" (Acts 14:19). In the work of the gospel, there must be faith both on the part of the evangelist and on the part of the one evangelised. In any case, Peter stresses that faith as well as the power derives from the Lord.

17-18 But only v.16 is occupied with the miracle; Peter now reverts to the people's responsibility. He attributes their sin to ignorance, both on their part and on the part of their rulers. Paul effectively stated the same thing in Antioch in Acts 13:27; the people at Jerusalem and their rulers "knew him not". Both Peter and Paul show that the sufferings of Christ had all been described in detail by the prophets. Peter had learned this from the Lord in Luke 24:44-45, and later he wrote about his subject in 1 Pet 1:11. In other words. God fulfilled what He had foretold. Three times in the TR this verb *prokatangellō* is used in the NT; twice in this address (vv.18, 24) and once by Stephen (7:52); it means to "tell thoroughly in advance". (Some Greek manuscripts use a different verb in 3:24.)

19 As in 2:38, Peter's call is now to "Repent", so that sins may be blotted out. This goes beyond the OT concept of sins being covered through atonement; rather, the full work of Christ is implied, as David aspired after in Ps 51:9, "blot out all mine iniquities". In consequence, they could receive there and then times of refreshing from the presence of the Lord. There was no possibility of the Lord being sent back to them immediately, that they might receive a second chance of accepting Him nationally. The ways of God were moving on inexorably. In the OT, God had long promised His people times of refreshing once their Messiah had come. Joel 2 is only one OT passage that promised such times. Other passages are: "There shall be showers of blessing" (Ezek 34:26); "I will pour water on him that is thirsty" (Isa 44:3). These OT passages obviously describe the coming of the Spirit; the new church had just experienced what God had promised Israel.

20-21 Not that the nation would never see Jesus their Messiah again. God would send the Redeemer to Zion, but meanwhile the heavens must receive Him; the Forerunner has entered in (Heb 6:20), now seated "on the right hand of the throne of the Majesty in the heavens" (8:1). To state clearly the time when they would see the Lord Jesus again, Peter points forward to "the times of restitution of all things". It is not normal to express the truth of the coming of the Messiah in this way. Previously Peter, like the writer to the Hebrews, had stated that He would be there in the heavens until His enemies would be made His footstool, but there he treats the subject more positively. The phrase "until the times of restitution of all things" is a description of the future reign of Christ. It implies the principle of restitution or restoration to which Moses' law paid such attention in Exod 22. It is then that the kingdom will be restored to Israel in fulfilment of the answer to the apostles' question in Acts 1:6. It is then that the related question of Elias coming and restoring all things will be fulfilled (Mark 9:12). When God's King reigns, everything that is out of place in the world will be restored to its proper place. Israel and all the nations will be back where they belong. Every principle of good and evil will be where it belongs, namely, truth on the throne and wrong on the scaffold. Peter adds that God had been speaking about this golden age by all the holy prophets since the world began, although he realised that there had also been false prophets among the people (2 Pet 2:1; Jer 5:31).

22-24 Peter goes on to claim that the Lord Jesus was the prophet of whom Moses spoke in Deut 18:15, 19. John Baptist had been questioned about this "prophet" in John's Gospel, while others had considered the Lord to be this Prophet (1:21; 6:14; 7:40). Here for the first time is the assertion, by Peter, that Jesus was that Prophet. Moses had forecast that two very differing attitudes could be adopted towards that Prophet when He came: submission or opposition, resulting in blessing or destruction. Opposition is what Peter warned his audience against in the temple courts in Jerusalem that day. These days of privilege and responsibility had been the constant testimony of Samuel, the first of the prophets, and of all those who had followed him in the prophetic line, whether their actual testimony is recorded in the OT or not.

25-26 Acts commences, as does Matthew's Gospel, with a determined attempt to prove to hearers in the one, and readers in the other, that there is continuity between God's ways in the OT and in the NT. Peter insists that all that has recently happened is the fulfilling of the ancient promises, and that people who are the children (strictly "sons") both of the prophets and of the covenant made with Abraham ought to listen in their own interests. By "sons" of the prophets Peter seems to have implied, not any connection by lineage, but a connection deriving from responsibility to adhere to their message from God. Moreover, in our v.25, the apostle anticipates God's blessing being extended to all the nations of the earth when he quotes Gen 22:18, though he recognised that the offer must first go to Israel. Both Paul and Peter realised that there was the same divine preference and order: "to the Jew first, and also to the Greek" (Rom 1:16). However, a great deal of prejudice had to be broken down before the way was clear for first century gospel preachers to give their message to Gentile audiences, and this applied to Peter as well (Acts 10:9-16, 28).

In v.26 the word "Son" is used; strictly another word occurs in the Greek text. This is the second of four occasions (3:13, 26; 4:27, 30) when Peter uses an unusual word to describe the Lord Jesus, *pais*, meaning "child" or "servant". It is borrowed from the prophecy of Isaiah, and denotes Jesus as the great Servant-Son of Jehovah, in whom all Messianic hopes and predictions are fulfilled. No wonder the temple officers were "grieved" (Acts 4:1). Thus for the third time, Peter asserts that the Saviour's mission was to turn people away from their sins and iniquities.

i. The First Imprisonment (4:1-22)

v.1 "And as they spake unto the people, the priests, and the captain of the temple, and the Sadducees, came upon them,

v.2 Being grieved that they taught the people, and preached through Jesus the resurrection from the dead.

v.3 And they laid hands on them, and put *them* in hold unto the next day: for it was now eventide.

v.4 Howbeit many of them which heard the word believed; and the number of the men was about five thousand.

v.5 And it came to pass on the morrow, that their rulers, and elders, and scribes,

v.6 And Annas the high priest, and Caiaphas, and John, and Alexander, and as many as were of the kindred of the high priest, were gathered together at Jerusalem.

v.7 And when they had set them in the midst, they asked, By what power, or by what name, have ye done this?

v.8 Then Peter, filled with the Holy Ghost, said unto them, Ye rulers of the people, and elders of Israel,

v.9 If we this day be examined of the good deed done to the impotent man, by what means he is made whole;

v.10 Be it known unto you all, and to all the people of Israel, that by the name of Jesus Christ of Nazareth, whom ye crucified, whom God raised from the dead, *even* by him doth this man stand here before you whole.

v.11 This is the stone which was set at nought of you builders, which is become the head of the corner.
v.12 Neither is there salvation in any other: for there is none other name under heaven given among men, whereby we must be saved.
v.13 Now when they saw the boldness of Peter and John, and perceived that they were unlearned and ignorant men, they marvelled; and they took knowledge of them, that they had been with Jesus.
v.14 And beholding the man which was healed standing with them, they could say nothing against it.
v.15 But when they had commanded them to go aside out of the council, they conferred among themselves,
v.16 Saying, What shall we do to these men? for that indeed a notable miracle hath been done by them *is* manifest to all them that dwell in Jerusalem; and we cannot deny *it*.
v.17 But that it spread no further among the people, let us straitly threaten them, that they speak henceforth to no man in this name.
v.18 And they called them, and commanded them not to speak at all nor teach in the name of Jesus.
v.19 But Peter and John answered and said unto them, Whether it be right in the sight of God to hearken unto you more than unto God, judge ye.
v.20 For we cannot but speak the things which we have seen and heard.
v.21 So when they had further threatened them, they let them go, finding nothing how they might punish them, because of the people: for all *men* glorified God for that which was done.
v.22 For the man was above forty years old, on whom this miracle of healing was shewed."

1-3 The second unplanned open-air meeting of the Acts, just described in ch.3, was suddenly interrupted by the arrival of a deputation from the Sanhedrin, partly composed of the Sadducees who did not believe in resurrection. Their religious anger was to be directed against those who were preaching this subject. (Other interrupted meetings can be found in 10:44; 20:9.) Peter's preaching must have lasted for a considerable time, from the ninth hour until eventide, so the message recorded in ch.3 can but form a small part of what he said altogether. So this deputation arrested Peter and John, and detained them overnight, the first of many occasions when these first preachers were imprisoned simply for preaching the gospel. Many subsequent preachers, in many parts of the world, have experienced the same injustice. It was obviously intended to bring them before a meeting of the full Sanhedrin in the morning. What the Lord had suffered before the Sanhedrin at His trial, two of His followers were now to experience in a lesser measure and with less drastic results. The Lord's prediction in John 16:2 had not yet reached its fulfilment.

4 The second progress report follows, "many of them which heard the word believed; and the number of the men was about five thousand", in spite of this open injustice by the Sanhedrin. So the followers of the crucified and risen Lord Jesus increased; one hundred and twenty, three thousand, five thousand (the word "about" being used in all cases). No numbers are given again, until we read of the 144000 sealed and the great multitude that could not be numbered from all nations in Rev 7:4, 9.

5-7   The Sanhedrin assembled the next morning to confront the two Galilaean fishermen who had the effrontery to espouse and proclaim the cause of the recently-executed Jesus of Nazareth. These two apostles were the ones who had been in the courtyard of the high priest's palace when the Lord had appeared before this council; John had been brave, but Peter had left fearful and weeping. The names of the leaders are given; some were the very men implicated in the intrigues which resulted in the Saviour being crucified. The question that they asked of the two prisoners (v.7) was virtually the same as they had related to the crowd which had gathered following the healing of the lame man the day before: the name and the power by which the event had happened. No doubt these leaders had had a verbal report of Peter's words, and were not satisfied.

8-12   For the second time in this book, the filling with the Spirit is mentioned. As filled with the Spirit in 2:4, they had all been able to speak in various languages. In 13:9 Paul had been able to discern a child of the devil and an enemy of all unrighteousness. Now in 4:8 before the Sanhedrin, Peter is bold enough not to be overawed by those men who recently had been responsible for the death of his Lord. Hence in vv.8-12 he enters upon another short discourse on his favourite subject, the good news about the Lord Jesus. He asserts that the good deed done to the impotent man was entirely owing to "Jesus Christ of Nazareth". He no longer places the responsibility for His death upon the people in general as in ch.2, but upon the Sanhedrin, "whom ye crucified", immediately followed by "whom God raised from the dead". In his previous message he concentrated on Deut 18, telling his audience who Jesus was, namely "that prophet"; this time he takes as his OT text Ps 118:22. This Psalm deals prophetically with the sufferings of Christ and the glory that should follow. The Lord Jesus is that stone in the Psalm; Peter had heard the Lord Himself speaking about this verse, so knew that it referred to Him directly (Matt 21:42). This stone had been cast aside time after time by the religious leaders who, seen as the temple-builders, could find no place for Him. Now at last He is declared to be the headstone of the corner, the very foundation of all that God is building. Moreover, Peter concludes by asserting that nobody else at all can take His place as the Saviour of their nation. He presses strongly the importance of the Person whom they had missed acknowledging, and he insists that there is no alternative. Not only did physical salvation come to the lame man through that one name under heaven, but the spiritual salvation of all also depends solely upon that name.

This Psalm is one of the three OT passages quoted by the Lord Jesus during His last week on earth, all three of which are quoted again in the early chapters of Acts as having been fulfilled.

1. As already mentioned, Ps 118 is quoted in the Lord's application of the parable of the vineyard (Matt 21:42); see also Mark 12:10,11; Luke 20:17. Peter obviously rejoices in the fulfilment of this prophecy, for he quotes it again in 1 Pet 2:7, linking it with other OT prophecies which present Messiah as a stone.

2. In Matt 22:44 the Lord quotes Ps 110:1, describing Himself as David's Son and David's Lord. Mark 12:35-37 records the same incident, as does Luke 20:41-44. This Psalm is quoted by Peter in Acts 2:34-35 as descriptive of the exaltation of the Lord Jesus.

3. The third OT passage referred to by the Lord in the shadow of His cross is Dan 7:13, "behold, one like the Son of man came with the clouds of heaven". The Lord refers to this in Matt 26:44 when He was on trial before the Jewish Sanhedrin. He said, "I say unto you, Hereafter shall ye see the Son of man sitting on the right hand of power, and coming in the clouds of heaven". Mark 14:62 is almost identical, while Luke 22:69 records, "Hereafter shall the Son of man sit on the right hand of the power of God". This prophetic statement had been fulfilled by the time of Stephen's martyrdom, when he said, "Behold, I see the heavens opened, and the Son of man standing on the right hand of God" (Acts 7:56) – standing as if He were about to intervene.

13-17 The Sanhedrin was bewildered. Previously, the Jews, not knowing that the Lord's doctrine was really the Father's doctrine, had considered Him as "having never learned" (John 7:15-16). Now these two prisoners were counted as "unlearned and ignorant men". That is to say, they had not passed through the theological schools of the day, as had Paul in his preconverted years, having been brought up at the feet of Gamaliel. Today, they would be counted as "uneducated laymen", though many evangelists and teachers of the Scriptures far exceed spiritually men who have only received naturally the academic teachings of men. The Sanhedrin knew that Peter and John had been associates of Jesus, and the formerly-lame man was bold enough to stand with them before the council. So they needed time to consider the problem privately, and hence they ordered the two apostles out while they went into private session. It was impossible to deny that a striking miracle had taken place, but they did not want news of it spread abroad, since it was so clearly connected with the person of Jesus.

18-22 Calling the apostles back into their presence, they ordered them not to speak or teach "in the name of Jesus". Peter and John made no such promise, insisting that they must tell what they had seen and heard. In other words, they had to be faithful witnesses. Later, Peter wrote as a general principle, "Submit ... to every ordinance of man for the Lord's sake: whether it be to the king, as supreme: or unto governors, as unto them that are sent by him for the punishment of evildoers, and for the praise of them that do well" (1 Pet 2:13-14). See also Paul's words on the subject in Rom 13:1-5. Moreover, Peter wrote about being happy for suffering for righteousness' sake, not being afraid of the terror of men (1 Pet 3:14-15), being ready to answer every man who "asketh you a reason of the hope that is in you with meekness and fear".
Certainly in the present incident, there could be no question of meeting the

demands of the Sanhedrin. Peter's reply was quite forthright, "Whether it be right in the sight of God to hearken unto you more than unto God, judge ye" (v.19). The Lord had told them to go into all the world and preach the gospel, commencing at Jerusalem; here were unbelieving human rulers telling them not to do so. If a lower authority (in this case the Sanhedrin) countermands the orders of a higher (in this case God), then the Christian's duty is clear. Not that one should go out of one's way to cause unnecessary trouble! If permission is needed to hold an open-air meeting in a particular place, then obviously that permission should be sought.

There are two examples of this principle in Daniel. In both cases, the consequences were far worse than in Acts 4, but God delivered His four servants on account of their faithfulness.

1. Shadrach, Meshach and Abed-nego refused to disobey the Ten Commandments by worshipping Nebuchadnezzar's golden image (ch.3).

2. Daniel himself refused to obey an edict of Darius, that he should not pray to God for thirty days (ch.6).

Peter stated his case in Acts 5:29, "We ought to obey God rather than man" when there was a conflict of commands.

Notes

The Sanhedrin and its Meetings in the NT

The word Sanhedrin (*sunedrion*, "a council") was "the term used by the rabbis both for the supreme council and court in Jerusalem of 71 members, and for the lesser tribunals of 23. In the NT the Sanhedrin was a body dominated by the high priest and aristocratic Sadducees" (H.L. Ellison in *The New International Dictionary of the Christian Church*; Paternoster, 1975).

In approximately three months around the crucifixion of the Lord Jesus there were some nine meetings of the Sanhedrin, all seeking to terminate the work of the Lord both before and after His cross.

First Meeting. Following the raising of Lazarus (John 11:47), "Then gathered the chief priests and the Pharisees a council, and said, What do we?".

Second Meeting. As Jesus and His disciples arrived at Jerusalem for the last passover, "Then assembled together the chief priests, and the scribes, and the elders of the people, unto the palace of the high priest, who was called Caiaphas, and consulted that they might take Jesus by subtilty, and kill him" (Matt 26:2-5; Luke 22:2).

Third Meeting. During the hours of darkness of the passover day, again in the palace of the high priest, "they that had laid hold on Jesus led him away to Caiaphas the high priest, where the scribes and the elders were assembled ... Now the chief priests, and elders, and all the council, sought false witness" (Matt 26:57-59; Mark 14:53; Luke 22:54).

Fourth Meeting. "As soon as it was day, the elders of the people and the chief priests and the scribes came together, and led him into their council" (Luke 22:66; Matt 27:1; Mark 15:1).

Fifth Meeting. "Pilate ... called together the chief priests and the rulers of the people" (Luke 23:13). Note that the second to the fifth meetings took place in less than twenty-four hours; the third to the fifth meetings must have taken place in less than twelve hours.

Sixth Meeting. On the resurrection morning, "some of the watch came into the city, and showed unto the chief priests all the things that were done. And when they were assembled with the elders, and had taken counsel, they gave large money to the soldiers" (Matt 28:11-12). This meeting shows the consternation of the Sanhedrin when they feared that Jesus was alive in spite of His crucifixion.

Seventh Meeting. A day or two after Pentecost, the morning after the healing of the lame beggar at the Beautiful Gate of the temple, their concern was to stop the spreading of the message of the gospel concerning Jesus, "their rulers, and elders, and scribes, and Annas the high priest, and Caiaphas ... were gathered together at Jerusalem" (Acts 4:5-6,15-16).

Eighth Meeting. A short time after the previous meeting, the new movement continued to make progress, resulting in the second imprisonment, this time of all the apostles. Thus "the high priest came, and they that were with him, and called the council together, and all the senate of the children of Israel" (Acts 5:21). Expositors explain the word "senate" in various ways, perhaps consisting of all the Jewish elders whether they were members of the Sanhedrin or not.

Ninth Meeting. A short time later, in order to deal with Stephen, "they stirred up the people, and the elders, and the scribes, and came upon him, and caught him, and brought him to the council" (Acts 6:12-15).

Later, Paul appeared before the Sanhedrin (23:1), consisting of the high priest, Pharisees and Sadducees. A few days afterwards, some of the council descended to Caesarea to accuse Paul before the governor Felix (24:1).

j. The Continuous Prayer Meeting (4:23-37)

v.23 "And being let go, they went to their own company, and reported all that the chief priests and elders had said unto them.
v.24 And when they heard that, they lifted up their voice to God with one accord, and said, Lord, thou *art* God, which hast made heaven, and earth, and the sea, and all that in them is:
v.25 Who by the mouth of thy servant David hast said, Why did the heathen rage, and the people imagine vain things?
v.26 The kings of the earth stood up, and the rulers were gathered together against the Lord, and against his Christ.
v.27 For of a truth against thy holy child Jesus, whom thou hast anointed, both Herod, and Pontius Pilate, with the Gentiles, and the people of Israel, were gathered together,
v.28 For to do whatsoever thy hand and thy counsel determined before to be done.
v.29 And now, Lord, behold their threatenings: and grant unto thy servants, that with all boldness they may speak thy word,
v.30 By stretching forth thine hand to heal; and that signs and wonders may be done by the name of thy holy child Jesus.
v.31 And when they had prayed, the place was shaken where they were assembled together; and they were all filled with the Holy Ghost, and they spake the word of God with boldness.
v.32 And the multitude of them that believed were of one heart and one soul: neither said any *of them* that aught of the things which he possessed was his own; but they had all things common.
v.33 And with great power gave the apostles witness of the resurrection of the Lord Jesus: and great grace was upon them all.
v.34 Neither was there any among them that lacked: for as many as were possessors of lands or houses sold them, and brought the prices of the things that were sold,
v.35 And laid *them* down at the apostles' feet: and distribution was made unto every man according as he had need.
v.36 And Joses, who by the apostles was surnamed Barnabas, (which is, being interpreted, The son of consolation,) a Levite, *and* of the country of Cyprus,
v.37 Having land, sold *it*, and brought the money, and laid *it* at the apostles' feet."

23-24 Released by the authorities, the two apostles had no doubt as to where they should go. It was to the local church, and it appears that this was almost in continuous session. (See 12:12 where again Peter knew where to go when released once more from prison.) The preachers went to their own people, always a good company for a Christian, and reported what the Sanhedrin had said. For the first time we have the actual words of one of their prayers. This occurs many times in the OT, and sometimes in the experience of the Lord Jesus when He was present on earth, such as John 17. Moreover, this is the fourth of five times where it is stated that they were acting "with one accord". Unity is half the conquest of the battle when a great venture is under way. No wonder Satan was anxious to undermine this unity and as soon as possible, and that from within (5:3).

We must not think that there is a prescribed formula for prayer. But note in John 17 the first few verses are devoted to the Son recognising the person of the Father, and then He prays for the apostles and for those who would believe afterwards. There could be no idle words in His prayer, nor an arbitrary use of divine names interminably repeated. It is the same in Acts 4:24-30. They were addressing a great God in heaven, in view of the service that He had given them on earth. First they addressed Him as the Creator God, and used divine names and titles very sparingly throughout. What power was possessed by Him who created the heavens, the earth, the seas, and all that is found in all three! So often the believer's concept of God and His power is far too small, but not so with these first Christians.

25-28 Secondly, they recalled that He was the God of prophecy, the One who by His Spirit caused His servants to speak and write about events before they happened. For the second time inspiration is claimed in the Acts for an OT passage, and we are told the name of the otherwise unknown author of Ps 2, namely David. This Psalm is essentially millennial in character, and the primary application of the people, kings and rulers acting together against the Lord and His anointed One is found in Rev 17:14 where the kings and the beast have one mind to "make war with the Lamb". The whole of the Acts also tells us about men trying to fight against God, as Gamaliel warned in 5:39. But clearly the local church in Jerusalem was referring to a third event, the greatest example of all on that subject, as indicated by the names Herod and Pontius Pilate. The subject described is the trial and crucifixion of the Lord Jesus, when there was a confederacy of the strangest of associates, namely, the Gentiles and the people of Israel, with the two quarrelling rulers Herod and Pontius Pilate, all taking counsel together against God and His Christ.

It had been the intention of these evil men to rid themselves of all the restraint that God imposes upon mankind, but what they planned (feeling that they were completely free from the will of God) actually fulfilled the divine purpose rather than their's. The Greek word translated "determined before" (*proorizō*) is elsewhere translated "predestinated" four times in the NT. These earthly rulers were the instruments of a higher hand than their's; had they only known, they were doing God's will. However they are responsible for their evil motives and deeds. "Surely the wrath of men shall praise thee" (Ps 76:10).

It is interesting to note the words for "servant" used in this prayer. Twice the word *pais* is used to describe the Lord (vv.27, 30; also in 3:12, 26 where the word "Son" is used in the AV). In this prayer, the word is translated "child", though other translations used the word "servant". This highlights and contrasts the word used in the prayer to describe themselves, *doulos*, "slaves" (v.29). Nowhere else in the Acts do the apostles use this lowly word to describe themselves, though Paul uses it of himself and Timothy in Phil 1:1. May it not have been deliberately chosen here to throw up their appreciation of their Lord in contrast with themselves?

29-31 This God of creation and Controller of nations and rulers is now asked to take note of the threatenings of authority, and to give the preachers boldness to proclaim His word. They did not ask for guidance when they already had His command to preach. We ought not to ask God either to change His mind to free us from obligations, or to repeat His command as though its first issue had been faulty. It is His right to command, and ours to obey. But when obedience may lead to danger, then it is appropriate to ask Him for boldness.

This Greek word *parrēsia* is again translated "boldness" in Heb 10:19 and "confidence" in 1 John 4:17. In all three situations, a person may well feel overawed and afraid, but there are three difficult situations where a child of God need not be afraid, but rather should experience boldness, by invitation, grace or by prayer. One may be apprehensive about entering the holiest of all, the innermost shrine or the antitype of the OT tabernacle and temple, especially considering that only one man alive at any one time, the high priest, had that right throughout the whole of OT times. But now every believer in the Lord Jesus is informed of a wide open door into that divine presence, along with a standing invitation to enter at any time. What a boldness is this, when the OT high priest could enter only once a year, and "not without blood" (Heb 9:7).

Looking to the future, the apostle John informs us that believers in the Lord Jesus have boldness in the day of judgment.

> "Bold shall we stand in that great day
> For who ought to our charge shall lay"

And thirdly in Acts 4:31 the apostles display this same boldness, but it is for witness contrary to the commands of the hostile authorities. This word "boldness" is used three times in this passage. It is used first in v.13 to describe how the two apostles behaved before the Sanhedrin after spending a night in custody. Their boldness stemmed from the fact that they knew so much about the Lord Jesus, far more than the Sanhedrin knew on a purely natural level. It appears that v.13 really means that the rulers recognised that these two had been with the followers of Jesus, but that they had fled when He was arrested. What they did not recognise was that the boldness which had taken the place of their former cowardice derived from their belief that the risen Lord was with them, and that they were empowered by the Holy Spirit.

The second mention of the word is in v.29 where they ask God to grant them boldness to do what the authorities were forbidding them to do. Their original boldness was because of their connection with the Lord Jesus, but now they are still asking God for boldness. The third occurrence of the word is in v.31, where in the power of the Spirit of God they spoke the word with boldness. A connection with the Godhead ensures that a believer is sufficient for anything to which he is called.

V.30 gives the second occasion in the book when many miracles were performed by the apostles, confirmation of the fact that God was with them; it was the divine answer to the rulers' hostility. The God, who has shaken in the past and who will yet shake the earth in the future (Heb 12:26), now shakes the building in which the believers are gathered. The divine answer included a collective filling with the Holy Spirit as in 2:4, to be distinguished from the once-for-all baptism in the Spirit. An individual filling for Peter for a special occasion has already been mentioned in v.8; so as far as the record is concerned this is now the third time that Peter has had the experience of being filled with the Spirit. The repetition of this fact obviously shows that it is not a continuous state, and in the Acts it is not the result of a command as in Eph 5:18, but a divine movement not dissimilar to that whereby the Scriptures were inspired when holy men of old were borne along by the Holy Spirit (2 Pet 1:21).

32-35 There is a strong similarity between 4:32-37 and 2:44-47. The oneness that existed among the believers extended to community of goods. However, ch.4 goes further than ch.2, by telling of individuals selling their possessions and putting the proceeds into the common purse. Two examples are given, one illustrating the best of motives (4:36-37) and one the worst (5:1-11).

The word "great" is prominent in this paragraph, "great power ... great grace" (v.33), and we may also mention "great fear" (5:11). The power is the result of being filled with the Spirit; the grace is not so much a demonstration of what they had freely received from God, as of their response in showing grace to others; the fear has been mentioned already in 2:43, the respect for God which was the result of the demonstration of His presence and power.

36-37 The supreme example of unselfish giving is now introduced in the early history of the church: Barnabas, the first convert actually named in the story. Joses was his preconversion name, but the apostles gave him another which was obviously expressive of his role in the early church, "The son of consolation". He was a Levite, but very different from the one appearing in the Lord's parable of the Good Samaritan. Here was a Levite now separated from the ritualistic temple system in Jerusalem. The fact that he belonged to Cyprus probably indicates why the first port of call of the first little missionary group (13:4) was that island in the eastern Mediterranean. It would be a strange Christian who did not take the gospel to his own people first.

It appears that Barnabas already had christian connections, for Mark the evangelist is described as being "sister's son to Barnabas" (Col 4:10). It was, therefore, in his sister's house that the church met in Jerusalem (Acts 12:12). Such a home was invaluable, since practically all the apostles belonged to Galilee and initially would not have had homes in Jerusalem. Barnabas is the, only man described by Luke in Acts as a "good" man (11:24); the first evidence of his goodness was his generosity in giving the entire proceeds of his patrimony for the benefit of the church, laying the proceeds at the feet of the apostles. Later money was sent to the "elders" of the church at Jerusalem (11:30). Barnabas was used by the Lord to convince the church at Jerusalem of the reality of the conversion of Saul (9:27).

Notes

Meeting-places of the Early Church

Most writers, whatever their ecclesiastical connections, are agreed that the Greek word *ekklēsia* never meant a building. Thus J. Heading writes, "In the NT this Greek word is never used of a building, and it is a great achievement of the powers of darkness, influencing the very thinking of people through the mistaken meaning of words, to direct attention to buildings rather than to the redeemed people of the Lord." An author of quite a different persuasion, W. Barclay, writes, "It is worth noting that in all the NT the word 'church' is never used to describe a 'building'. It always describes a body of men and women who have given their hearts to God."

But nevertheless there were places where the first believers met. Firstly there was the upper room in Jerusalem. The Greek text of 1:13 actually should be translated "they went up into *the* upper room". This is traditionally believed to have been the home of John Mark's mother in the city. That being so, it was the place where the last Passover was celebrated, the place where the Lord's Supper was instituted, and one of the places where the risen Lord appeared to His disciples. It was the scene of the prayer meeting described in Acts 1, for it was a "large" room (Luke 22:12). Again, it was the place where the disciples were when the baptism in the Spirit took place, and was, therefore, the birthplace of the church.

The addition of about three thousand believers to their ranks clearly made this upper room inadequate, so the disciples seem to have begun to meet in Solomon's porch in the temple in the city. This is mentioned in 2:46 and 5:12. Outwardly, it may appear that they were now taking temple-ground, but they were really in an outside place relative to it. When in Jerusalem, the Lord Jesus "walked in the temple in Solomon's porch" (John 10:23), and used the temple courts for teaching (Luke 21:37); but He had no formal contact with the ritual perpetuated by the priests at the altar and inside the temple building itself.

In the various places throughout the old Roman Empire where such churches grew up, often the local churches would meet in the homes of the believers. No such example is mentioned in the Acts (though 16:40 in Philippi may suggest this), but there are at least five such examples elsewhere in the NT (Rom 16:3-5, 23; 1 Cor 16:19; Col 4:15; Philem 2).

k. *Ananias and Sapphira (5:1-16)*

    v.1   "But a certain man named Ananias, with Sapphira his wife, sold a possession.
    v.2   And kept back *part* of the price, his wife also being privy *to it*, and brought a certain part, and laid *it* at the apostles' feet.

WHAT THE BIBLE TEACHES / ACTS 5   67

v.3   But Peter said, Ananias, why hath Satan filled thine heart to lie to the Holy Ghost, and to keep back *part* of the price of the land?

v.4   Whiles it remained, was it not thine own? and after it was sold, was it not in thine own power? why hast thou conceived this thing in thine heart? thou hast not lied unto men, but unto God.

v.5   And Ananias hearing these words fell down, and gave up the ghost: and great fear came on all them that heard these things.

v.6   And the young men arose, wound him up, and carried *him* out, and buried *him*.

v.7   And it was about the space of three hours after, when his wife, not knowing what was done, came in.

v.8   And Peter answered unto her, Tell me whether ye sold the land for so much? And she said, Yea, for so much.

v.9   Then Peter said unto her, How is it that ye have agreed together to tempt the Spirit of the Lord? behold, the feet of them which have buried thy husband *are* at the door, and shall carry thee out.

v.10 Then fell she down straightway at his feet, and yielded up the ghost: and the young men came in, and found her dead, and, carrying *her* forth, buried *her* by her husband.

v.11 And great fear came upon all the church, and upon as many as heard these things.

v.12 And by the hands of the apostles were many signs and wonders wrought among the people; (and they were all with one accord in Solomon's porch.

v.13 And of the rest durst no man join himself to them: but the people magnified them.

v.14 And believers were the more added to the Lord, multitudes both of men and women.)

v.15 Insomuch that they brought forth the sick into the streets, and laid *them* on beds and couches, that at the least the shadow of Peter passing by might overshadow some of them.

v.16 There came also a multitude *out* of the cities round about unto Jerusalem, bringing sick folks, and them which were vexed with unclean spirits: and they were healed every one."

1-2 The chapter division that occurs here interrupts the narrative, for in ch.5 we are given the second example of a seemingly kindhearted couple selling their goods with the apparent aim of handing over the proceeds of the sale to the church, again at "the apostles' feet". While their aim was to receive the same approbation that Barnabas had obtained, they were not willing to pay the price that Barnabas paid. In fact, the story stands in complete contrast to that in ch.4, for whereas there we have believers filled with the Spirit, in ch.5 we have a couple whose hearts were filled with Satan (v.3).

We must not think that the first church was perfect; it was composed of humans like ourselves with all their failings, and they had a lot to learn from the apostles. Two successive chapters tell of problems in the church, and both were caused by money. In the midst of such an atmosphere of rejoicing brought about by the resurrection of Christ and the coming of the Spirit of God, there were those who either allowed material things to take first place or who murmured when things did not appear to go smoothly. Luke is the writer who draws attention to financial matters more than other NT writers; for example, Luke 1:53; 3:14; 6:24; 7:41; 9:3; 10:4, 35; 12:16, 33; 14:28; 15:8, 12; 16:2, 19; 18:22; 19:8, 13-27; 20:25; 21:1-4; 22:5, 36; Acts 8:18; 20:33-35.

3-4 Peter's words mean that nobody was obliged to sell his property, and even if he did there was no obligation to hand over all the proceeds to the church. The sin of Ananias and Sapphira was that, having sold their possession, they *pretended* to hand over all the proceeds. (This is the first of three men called Ananias in the Acts, two of whom were professing Christians. The man in 5:1 was a hindrance to God's testimony; that in 9:10 was a great help, while in 23:1 we have a cruel and merciless high priest.) Peter charged Ananias with lying to the Holy Spirit; evidently Peter possessed the gift of "discerning of spirits" (1 Cor 11:10). A believer may not sin *directly* against the Lord Jesus or against the Holy Spirit; compare David's confession. "Against thee, thee only, have I sinned" (Ps 51:4). But sinning against the brethren is tantamount to sinning against Christ in 1 Cor 8:12, and sinning against the apostles and the church by telling lies in Acts 4:3 is equivalent to sinning against the Holy Spirit.

5-10 Summary judgment was administered by God against Ananias, and three hours later against his wife Sapphira, when she arrived at the meeting of the church and repeated the lie. Right from the commencement of the church, God indicated that He was in control even when grace reigned. (This should be compared with the commencement of the tabernacle system and the death of the priests Nadab and Abihu who died before the Lord in Lev 10:1-2; again God indicated that He was in control when law reigned.) Judgment by death is not entirely unknown in the NT. It happened again in the days of the Corinthian church (1 Cor 11:30), because they were using the two emblems at the Lord's Supper in unworthy ways that were not connected with remembrance and worship. It is a lasting principle in Holy Scripture that "he that will (that is, wishes to) love life, and see good days, let him refrain his tongue from evil, and his lips that they speak no guile" (1 Pet 3:10-12), quoted from Ps 34:12-16. There have always been Christians fit for heaven, but not fit for testimony on earth. It is clear that the "young men" sometimes had unpleasant tasks to do; they were called "devout men" at Stephen's burial (8:2).

11 As with the miracles that were being performed (2:43), so with this judgment; fear came upon every soul, both within and outside the church. Such is the price of having the divine presence; it imposes standards that cannot be regarded lightly.

12 The story of Ananias and Sapphira is an unhappy interlude; v.12 sees the resumption of the spiritual story. Such incidents, caused by human failure, have been only too common in church history. They should always be only hiccoughs. The onward march of the testimony must be continued in spite of all; godly leaders should ensure that this is so. V.12 records the third cluster of miracles performed by the apostles. Divine power cannot be hindered by His people's sin, provided that this sin has been put away and the lesson learned and provided that spiritual men remain through whom the power can flow (in this case the apostles).

13-16 By this time, the church is found with a new meeting-place, Solomon's porch in the temple precincts. Obviously the upper room was far too small for the number of believers. Solomon's porch is mentioned in John 10:23 as the place in Herod's temple where Jewish leaders sought to stone the Lord. "He came unto his own (things), and his own (people) received him not" (John 1:11). Solomon's porch was the part of the temple courts where the second large open air meeting in the Acts took place as the crowds surrounded the apostles after the healing of the lame man (3:11). This special porch then becomes the place where Christians in general gathered in church capacity (5:12). The church had no secrets, even when meeting in a public place. Those who were not of them were deterred from nominal adherence by God's presence. The old temple was doomed. Within forty years it was to be destroyed, but the infant church was meeting in the temple precincts, and was eventually to acquire the new name "temple", always in the Epistles meaning the inner sanctuary rather than the general precincts. (Two different Greek words demand this distinction.)

V.14 represents the third of Luke's summaries or progress reports about the spread of the gospel. No number is given to the increase as in 2:41 and 4:4, but the word "multitudes" is introduced. This is all the more amazing in view of the first reported troubles of the church in the opening paragraph of the chapter. This progress report is followed by a remarkable description of the effect that these miracles had on the population. Firstly, people were so desperate to contact the leader Peter that they were anxious that at least his shadow should fall on their sick, and, secondly, people from neighbouring cities brought their sick into Jerusalem for healing. Whether the passing shadow of Peter had any healing virtue is not definitely stated, but it does bear testimony to the remarkable power in evidence among the apostles. In this connection, we may form our own opinion as to the meaning of "they were healed *every one*".

l. *The Second Imprisonment (5:17-28)*

> v.17 "Then the high priest rose up, and all they that were with him, (which is the sect of the Sadducees,) and were filled with indignation,
> v.18 And laid their hands on the apostles, and put them in the common prison.
> v.19 But the angel of the Lord by night opened the prison doors, and brought them forth, and said,
> v.20 Go, stand and speak in the temple to the people all the words of this life.

v.21 And when they heard *that*, they entered into the temple early in the morning, and taught. But the high priest came, and they that were with him, and called the council together, and all the senate of the children of Israel, and sent to the prison to have them brought.

v.22 But when the officers came, and found them not in the prison, they returned, and told,

v.23 Saying, The prison truly found we shut with all safety, and the keepers standing without before the doors: but when we had opened we found no man within.

v.24 Now when the high priest and the captain of the temple and the chief priests heard these things, they doubted of them whereunto this would grow.

v.25 Then came one and told them, saying, Behold, the men whom ye put in prison are standing in the temple, and teaching the people.

v.26 Then went the captain with the officers, and brought them without violence: for they feared the people, lest they should have been stoned.

v.27 And when they had brought them, they set *them* before the council: and the high priest asked them,

v.28 Saying, Did not we straitly command you that ye should not teach in this name? and, behold, ye have filled Jerusalem with your doctrine, and intend to bring this man's blood upon us."

17-19 The first imprisonment had not removed the apostles' zeal, while the continuation of miracles in the power of Jesus' name irritated the authorities, so on this second occasion all the apostles found themselves in prison. This time they were released by divine intervention through the angel of the Lord, the first of five occasions when angelic activity is mentioned, mainly for the protection of God's servants, but also for their guidance. (See 8:26; 10:3, 22; 12:7-11; 12:23; 27:23.)

20 The escaped prisoners neither went into hiding (as in John 20:19), nor scattered in all directions to make recapture difficult. Rather they obeyed the angel's instructions to return to the temple court to proclaim "all the words of this life" (v.20). What a lovely name for the message of the gospel! Several modern translations of the Scriptures, especially of the paraphrase type, insert the word "new" before "life", but this word does not appear in the original Greek manuscripts. Admittedly the idea is there, since resurrection life, the very life of God, was new, and was offered by these Galilaean preachers.

21 The sect of the Sadducees from which the Jewish Sanhedrin was largely drawn must have been baffled with this confronation both with life after death and with angels, neither of which they acknowledged (23:8). To faith this seems a small thing; if one angel could open the stone-door of a grave, then another could open a prison door. It is obvious that we are still dealing with a period of history when the word preached was being confirmed by signs, including divine intervention for the opening of prison doors. God's power is still able to do this, but He does not choose to do so now that the apostolic days are past. We have already considered the many meetings of the Sanhedrin that were taking place during those days. They had met in emergency session a few weeks previously to rid themselves of the Leader of these disciples, obviously with no success, and now they are convening frequently to deal with the newly-found zeal of these disciples. How tragic it is to witness the convulsions of unbelief! Jesus Christ was alive, whether they believed it or not. What His servants offered their hearers was life, whether or not the rulers would embrace it.

22-26 Having imprisoned the apostles, the Sanhedrin met in order to examine them. The officers who were sent to fetch them from prison for trial found a strange situation: the guard was on duty; the door was shut; everything seemed to be in order; but the cells were empty. While they were reporting this bewildering state of affairs, the report came that the escaped prisoners were standing in the temple "teaching the people". Rather hestitantly, the captain and the officers went to re-arrest the preachers, apprehensive lest the crowd should stone them as the Sanhedrin would stone Stephen shortly afterwards.

27-28 What a tribute from hostile authorities to faithful followers of the Lord Jesus, "ye have filled Jerusalem with your doctrine". The charge that they had disobeyed an order was met with, "We ought to obey God rather than men" (v.29). How could these preachers resist the opportunity of repeating once more how their God had intervened so remarkably in the matter of Jesus of Nazareth by raising Him from the dead?

m.   *Peter's Fourth Address (5:29-42)*

- v.29 "Then Peter and the *other* apostles answered and said, We ought to obey God rather than men.
- v.30 The God of our fathers raised up Jesus, whom ye slew and hanged on a tree.
- v.31 Him hath God exalted with his right hand *to be* a Prince and a Saviour, for to give repentance to Israel, and forgiveness of sins.
- v.32 And we are his witnesses of these things; and *so is* also the Holy Ghost, whom God hath given to them that obey him.
- v.33 When they heard *that*, they were cut *to the heart*, and took counsel to slay them.
- v.34 Then stood there up one in the council, a Pharisee, named Gamaliel, a doctor of the law, had in reputation among all the people, and commanded to put the apostles forth a little space;
- v.35 And said unto them, Ye men of Israel, take heed to yourselves what ye intend to do as touching these men.
- v.36 For before these days rose up Theudas, boasting himself to be somebody; to whom a number of men, about four hundred, joined themselves: who was slain; and all, as many as obeyed him, were scattered, and brought to nought.

v.37 After this man rose up Judas of Galilee in the days of the taxing, and drew away much people after him: he also perished; and all, *even* as many as obeyed him, were dispersed.
v.38 And now I say unto you, Refrain from these men, and let them alone: for if this counsel or this work be of men, it will come to nought:
v.39 But if it be of God, ye cannot overthrow it; lest haply ye be found even to fight against God.
v.40 And to him they agreed: and when they had called the apostles, and beaten *them*, they commanded that they should not speak in the name of Jesus, and let them go.
v.41 And they departed from the presence of the council, rejoicing that they were counted worthy to suffer shame for his name.
v.42 And daily in the temple, and in every house, they ceased not to teach and preach Jesus Christ."

29-32 The actual address is given in vv.29-32, while the consequences appear in the rest of ch.5. Peter's fourth address was brief (the other apostles were also involved), but covers the essentials with remarkable succinctness; it commences with "obey" and ends with "obey". Perhaps this is a summary of the totality of the address. The starting point was God's reversal of what they had done when they slew the Lord Jesus. Peter always made much of the resurrection of the Saviour, but this was not the end of the story; He is exalted to God's right hand – an obvious reference to Ps 110:1. "Prince" is another new title accorded to the Lord. It is elsewhere translated "author" (Heb 12:2) and "captain" (Heb 2:10); it indicates a ruler or leader. *Sotēr*, a Saviour, is now also used to describe the Lord Jesus for the first time in the Acts, this being the fourth time in the NT. Peter has now called Jesus by the titles Lord, Christ, Prince and Saviour; are we too slow in giving Him such honours? Each title has its own significance in the contexts of preaching, prayer and worship, but we should not be too technical, restricting either titles or the number of them when they occur in the Scriptures. But we should use them reverently and appropriately.

For the third time, Peter deals with repentance; only that can bring forgiveness or remission of sins. This is the second time that he has said that this is the result of acknowledging the Lord Jesus. Again he stresses that his story is not a second-hand one; the other disciples are also witnesses of what he claims. The Holy Spirit is also a witness both to what the Saviour has done and to where He is now. (The Holy Spirit as a witness is not mentioned again in the Acts, but the idea also occurs in Rom 8:16; Heb 10:15; 1 John 5:6.)

33-39 The Sanhedrin was obviously increasingly angered by the growing confidence and strength of language of these "unlearned and ignorant men" (4:13). It was their intention to send them the way of their Lord, had not Gamaliel intervened. He was one of the minority Pharisees on the Sanhedrin, tutor of Saul who has not yet appeared in the record (22:3). Gamaliel was held in high honour, and after he died it was stated that there was no more reverence for the law and that purity and abstinence died out at the same time. Before sentence was passed, he insisted upon a secret session, during which he warned the Sanhedrin about the dangerous course that they might pursue. He recalled two incidents from their nation's troubled history in which risings had petered out. The motives of Theudas and Judas were probably as much for self-aggrandisement as for national liberation. The four hundred who followed Theudas were scattered, while the many people who followed Judas (about the time when the Lord was born) were dispersed, and Judas was slain. Employing human wisdom only, Gamaliel suggested that this christian movement would suffer the same fate if it were of human origin, but if it were of divine origin then it would be very serious to oppose it. God used Gamaliel, of course, to achieve His will.

Thus Gamaliel poses the idea of fighting against God, perhaps even thinking of Ps 2:1-5. In spite of all the opposition to the Saviour by the Pharisees in the Gospels, it is they who seem to have had some common sense towards the Christians in the Acts, in contrast to the Sadducees. Some of the Pharisees later believed, though with a faith mixed with the law (15:5), while they took Paul's side in 23:9 in similar circumstances when he deliberately mentioned the resurrection. They even seemed better than the philosophers of Athens (17:32)!

The fact that one cannot fight against God is one of the great lessons of the Acts. The wrath of man was made to praise God through the cross-work of the Lord Jesus. Persecution was soon to spread the gospel message rather than stem its progress (8:1; 11:19), thus forming the base, Antioch, from which Paul's missionary journeys would radiate. It was proved time and again that the gates of hades could not prevail against His church. Even Paul, in prison at the end of the book, demonstrated that the things that had happened to him had fallen out for the furtherance of the gospel (Phil 1:12). One cannot fight against God!

40-42 The apostles were beaten, an almost inevitable result of being arrested in those days (see Paul's own testimony to this fact in 2 Cor 11:23-25), and were again ordered not to preach the gospel. Not to accept this prohibition would mean further persecution, but they had no intention of remaining silent. The temple courts were used for public testimony, while "every house" was used for more private teaching (the Lord used both places for His teaching).

2. Stephen
6:1-7:60

a. *The Second Financial Problem of the Church (6:1-7)*

v.1   "And in those days, when the number of the disciples was multiplied, there arose a murmuring of the Grecians against the Hebrews, because their widows were neglected in the daily ministration.

v.2   Then the twelve called the multitude of the disciples *unto them*, and said, It is not reason that we should leave the word of God, and serve tables.

v.3 Wherefore, brethren, look ye out among you seven men of honest report, full of the Holy Ghost and wisdom, whom we may appoint over this business.
v.4 But we will give ourselves continually to prayer, and to the ministry of the word.
v.5 And the saying pleased the whole multitude: and they chose Stephen, a man full of faith and of the Holy Ghost, and Philip, and Prochorus, and Nicanor, and Timon, and Parmenas, and Nicolas a proselyte of Antioch:
v.6 Whom they set before the apostles: and when they had prayed, they laid *their* hands on them.
v.7 And the word of God increased; and the number of the disciples multiplied in Jerusalem greatly; and a great company of the priests were obedient to the faith."

1 Following immediately upon this further expansion, the church at Jerusalem encountered a second problem. Again it concerned money. If the problem in ch.5 was one of giving, then the problem in ch.6 concerned receiving. The "Grecians" were Jewish believers using the Greek language, while the "Hebrews" were Jewish believers using the Aramaic language. One of the uses to which the church's generosity was devoted was the support of widows. In this respect the church was simply following the example of its God. Some twenty-eight times in the OT widows are mentioned as being the subject of God's special interest, or the care of them by men is commended. Luke is particularly attentive to widows in his writings, as he mentions them five times in his first book, and writes of two groups of them in his second (6:1; 9:39). Paul too regards the lone widow in the church as a believer meriting special financial consideration (1 Tim 5:3).

2 The apostles accepted the complaint, but declined to undertake the task of supervising the financial distribution themselves. Paul's later participation in arranging relief for poor saints at Jerusalem (Rom 15:26; 1 Cor 16:1; 2 Cor 8-9) indicates that what was decided in Acts 6 was not taken as a complete precedent, for Paul as an apostle did engage in such work. It is sometimes asserted by expositors and by paragraph titles in older Bibles that seven "deacons" were appointed. The word *diakonos* ("deacon") is not mentioned as a noun in the chapter at all, but its verbal form "serve" is found in v.2 There is no basis for the idea that deacon service is always of the administrative nature indicated in this chapter. Further examination of the use of the word throughout the NT will show that it has a very broad scope, including many forms of christian service, both material and spiritual, by men and women, including the Lord, the apostles, Paul and Timothy. In fact, the root of the word is found in the word "ministry" in v.4. And moreover, service of a spiritual nature awaited two of those who were selected as the first deacons (or "ministers").

3-5 Even for service of a non-spiritual nature, the church should require high standards. The first requirement of any believer who has to handle the Lord's money is so much higher than that required even by a worldly institution, that is, honesty. Seven men were chosen (there should be always two or more) so that their work could be seen openly as honest by the church membership. It is equally essential that such men should be spiritual, "full of the Holy Spirit". This should never be taken as a requirement only for preachers; it is a requirement for any believer handling anything in the work of an assembly. The third requisite in a situation where servants may be accused of bias is wisdom. In such administrative matters, the church chose the men who would engage in the work (as in 2 Cor 8:4, 19), but in matters relating to spiritual gift, the choice was that of the Lord. Note in v.5 that "full of faith" was an added qualification. Thus a brother may have banking experience, but this by itself does not justify his being an assembly treasurer! A brother may be a secular teacher, but this does not justify his being a teacher in the assembly. A brother may be an able secular administrator, but this does not justify his being an elder in an assembly.

6   For the first time in the NT the laying on of hands is mentioned. It was a common practice in OT times with special reference to animal sacrifices, and in that connection it indicated the identification of the offerer with his offering. This meaning was carried over into the NT. Laying on of hands, whether by apostles in Acts 6, by the prophets and teachers in Acts 13:3, or by elders in 1 Tim 4:14, indicated their complete identification with the work to be done by those on whom hands were laid.

To counteract the alleged bias on the part of the previous distributors of the church's largesse, all seven of these servants with a new duty were of Hellenistic origin, judging from their names. Only two of these, Stephen and Philip, are mentioned again in the Acts, Philip even as late as 21:8.

7   This early murmuring in the NT, being a parallel to that which was such a plague to the Israelites in the OT as they started on their desert journey (Exod 16:2; 17:3), was a further hiccough in the onward progress of the church. Having described it, Luke gives yet another of his summaries, "the word of God increased; and the number of the disciples multiplied in Jerusalem greatly". Has Luke deliberately changed his descriptive word from "added" to "multiplied"? This latter word certainly indicates a much faster rate of progress.

John's Gospel has indicated that the new faith had made inroads into the ranks of the Pharisees (12:42), though without outward confession. Now Luke records that it was also making inroads into the ranks of the priests. Only by reading the Epistle to the Hebrews can we appreciate that, far from losing anything by becoming Christians, these converted priests were gaining everything. The system which they had been brought up to value was soon to be destroyed at the hands of the future Roman Emperor Titus when Herod's temple was destroyed, and meanwhile these priests (and the Jews as well) were gaining a new priesthood, the High Priest being the Lord Jesus Himself, with a heavenly sanctuary and spiritual sacrifices, none of which can ever pass away.

b. Stephen Accused (6:8-15)

- v.8 "And Stephen, full of faith and power, did great wonders and miracles among the people.
- v.9 Then there arose certain of the synagogue, which is called *the synagogue* of the Libertines, and Cyrenians, and Alexandrians, and of them of Cilicia and of Asia, disputing with Stephen.
- v.10 And they were not able to resist the wisdom and the spirit by which he spake.
- v.11 Then they suborned men, which said, We have heard him speak blasphemous words against Moses, and *against* God.
- v.12 And they stirred up the people, and the elders, and the scribes, and came upon *him*, and caught him, and brought *him* to the council.
- v.13 And set up false witnesses, which said, This man ceaseth not to speak blasphemous words against this holy place, and the law:
- v.14 For we have heard him say, that this Jesus of Nazareth shall destroy this place, and shall change the customs which Moses delivered us.
- v.15 And all that sat in the council, looking stedfastly on him, saw his face as it had been the face of an angel."

8 This third summary of the great progress made by the gospel at the hands or by the mouths of these early Christians is followed by the mention of a third group of miracles, performed not by an apostle but by Stephen. The tribute to him is steadily built up by Luke. The requirement of these first church treasurers was that they were to be "full of the Holy Ghost and wisdom". Then we are told that Stephen was "full of faith and of the Holy Ghost", followed by the statement that he was "full of faith and power". Yet he had a very short period of service compared with most servants of the Lord, for he, not an apostle, was the first martyr (though many others quickly followed as stated by Paul in 26:10).

9 The opposition to Stephen was led by a particular synagogue in Jerusalem, the synagogue of the Libertines (there was a large number of synagogues in Jerusalem at that time). The suggestion has been made that this synagogue belonged to freed slaves, their residential origins being two places in Africa and two in Asia. *The International Bible Dictionary* suggests that they were probably Jews who had been taken captive by the Romans, freed, and then allowed to settle in Jerusalem in such numbers that they built their own synagogue.

10-14 As had his Saviour's accusers some months before, so now these Libertines found it impossible to achieve their purpose relative to Stephen through normal channels, and so they resorted to subterfuge. The third meeting of the Jewish Sanhedrin in the Acts, all of which were emergency meetings, was summoned to hear allegations against the Lord's servant brought by false witnesses. Both in the Lord's case and in Stephen's, we recall Ps 35:11, "False witnesses did rise up; they laid to my charge things that I knew not". Stephen was charged, as was the Lord, with blasphemy against the Jews' holy place and the law of Moses (Matt 26:61; John 19:7). The garbled charges were that the Lord Jesus would destroy their temple and change their rites which they had learned from Moses. How right they were without realising it! We are not told in these verses exactly what Stephen had said, but the Lord had prophesied in Matt 24:2 that the temple would be destroyed, and Paul had taught that Christ would have died in vain, had the law remained (Gal 2:16, 21).

These two subjects form the main argument of Stephen's address to the council in ch.7. He places the whole subject of "this place" in perspective, showing what God's original and ultimate plans for His dwelling-place were, and how much their forebears had opposed Moses from the very beginning. The climax of his condemnation of his own nation was reached when he condemned them first for the persecution of the prophets (compare the parable of the vineyard), and then for the rejection of that law which had been given to them through angels. (This is the first of three occasions in the NT when the giving of the law is associated with angels: Acts 7:53; Gal 3:19; Heb 2:2.)

15 Luke elevates Stephen's part in the story of God's dealings with Israel by indicating that he was the recipient of a vision of glory, as Abraham had been according to 7:2, and as Moses had been according to 7:31-34. As heaven opened, the glory of God and Jesus glorified at God's right hand met the eyes of God's faithful witness (7:55).

Clearly, Stephen demonstrated the calm peace of Christ even before the Sanhedrin, and this is described as if his face "had been the face of an angel", a fact that must have been galling to the Sadducees who did not believe in angels. No doubt the subsequent address was given by Stephen in the light of Matt 10:20, "For it is not ye that speak, but the Spirit of your Father which speaketh in you".

c. *Stephen's Defence (7:1-60)*

> v.1 "Then said the high priest, Are these things so?
> v.2 And he said, Men, brethren, and fathers, hearken; The God of glory appeared unto our father Abraham, when he was in Mesopotamia, before he dwelt in Charran,
> v.3 And said unto him, Get thee out of thy country, and from thy kindred, and come into the land which I shall shew thee.
> v.4 Then came he out of the land of the Chaldæans, and dwelt in Charran: and from thence, when his father was dead, he removed him into this land, wherein ye now dwell.
> v.5 And he gave him none inheritance in it, no, not *so much as* to set his foot on: yet he promised that he would give it to him for a possession, and to his seed after him, when *as yet* he had no child.
> v.6 And God spake on this wise, That his seed should sojourn in a strange land; and that they should bring them into bondage, and entreat *them* evil four hundred years.
> v.7 And the nation to whom they shall be in bondage will I judge, said God: and after that shall they come forth, and serve me in this place.

v.8   And he gave him the covenant of circumcision: and so *Abraham* begat Isaac, and circumcised him the eighth day; and Isaac *begat* Jacob; and Jacob *begat* the twelve patriarchs.
v.9   And the patriarchs, moved with envy, sold Joseph into Egypt: but God was with him.
v.10 And delivered him out of all his afflictions, and gave him favour and wisdom in the sight of Pharaoh king of Egypt; and he made him governor over Egypt and all his house.
v.11 Now there came a dearth over all the land of Egypt and Chanaan, and great affliction: and our fathers found no sustenance.
v.12 But when Jacob heard that there was corn in Egypt, he sent out our fathers first.
v.13 And at the second *time* Joseph was made known to his brethren; and Joseph's kindred was made known unto Pharaoh.
v.14 Then sent Joseph, and called his father Jacob to *him*, and all his kindred, threescore and fifteen souls.
v.15 So Jacob went down into Egypt, and died, he, and our fathers,
v.16 And were carried over into Sychem, and laid in the sepulchre that Abraham bought for a sum of money of the sons of Emmor *the father* of Sychem.
v.17 But when the time of the promise drew nigh, which God had sworn to Abraham, the people grew and multiplied in Egypt,
v.18 Till another king arose, which knew not Joseph.
v.19 The same dealt subtilly with our kindred, and evil entreated our fathers, so that they cast out their young children, to the end they might not live.
v.20 In which time Moses was born, and was exceeding fair, and nourished up in his father's house three months:
v.21 And when he was cast out, Pharaoh's daughter took him up, and nourished him for her own son.
v.22 And Moses was learned in all the wisdom of the Egyptians, and was mighty in words and in deeds.
v.23 And when he was full forty years old, it came into his heart to visit his brethren the children of Israel.
v.24 And seeing one *of them* suffer wrong, he defended *him*, and avenged him that was oppressed, and smote the Egyptian:
v.25 For he supposed his brethren would have understood how that God by his hand would deliver them: but they understood not.
v.26 And the next day he shewed himself unto them as they strove, and would have set them at one again, saying, Sirs, ye are brethren; why do ye wrong one to another?
v.27 But he that did his neighbour wrong thrust him away, saying, Who made thee a ruler and a judge over us?
v.28 Wilt thou kill me, as thou diddest the Egyptian yesterday?
v.29 Then fled Moses at this saying, and was a stranger in the land of Madian, where he begat two sons.
v.30 And when forty years were expired, there appeared to him in the wilderness of mount Sina an angel of the Lord in a flame of fire in a bush.
v.31 When Moses saw *it*, he wondered at the sight: and as he drew near to behold *it*, the voice of the Lord came unto him,

v.32	*Saying,* I *am* the God of thy fathers, the God of Abraham, and the God of Isaac, and the God of Jacob. Then Moses trembled, and durst not behold.
v.33	Then said the Lord to him, Put off thy shoes from thy feet: for the place where thou standest is holy ground.
v.34	I have seen, I have seen the affliction of my people which is in Egypt, and I have heard their groaning, and am come down to deliver them. And now come, I will send thee into Egypt.
v.35	This Moses whom they refused, saying, Who made thee a ruler and a judge? the same did God send *to be* a ruler and a deliverer by the hand of the angel which appeared to him in the bush.
v.36	He brought them out, after that he had shewed wonders and signs in the land of Egypt, and in the Red sea, and in the wilderness forty years.
v.37	This is that Moses, which said unto the children of Israel, A prophet shall the Lord your God raise up unto you of your brethren, like unto me; him shall ye hear.
v.38	This is he, that was in the church in the wilderness with the angel which spake to him in the mount Sina, and *with* our fathers: who received the lively oracles to give unto us:
v.39	To whom our fathers would not obey, but thrust *him* from them, and in their hearts turned back again into Egypt.
v.40	Saying unto Aaron, Make us gods to go before us: for *as for* this Moses, which brought us out of the land of Egypt, we wot not what is become of him.
v.41	And they made a calf in those days, and offered sacrifice unto the idol, and rejoiced in the works of their own hands.
v.42	Then God turned, and gave them up to worship the host of heaven; as it is written in the book of the prophets, O ye house of Israel, have ye offered to me slain beasts and sacrifices *by the space of* forty years in the wilderness?
v.43	Yea, ye took up the tabernacle of Moloch, and the star of your god Remphan, figures which ye made to worship them: and I will carry you away beyond Babylon.
v.44	Our fathers had the tabernacle of witness in the wilderness, as he had appointed, speaking unto Moses, that he should make it according to the fashion that he had seen.
v.45	Which also our fathers that came after brought in with Jesus into the possession of the Gentiles, whom God drave out before the face of our fathers, unto the days of David;
v.46	Who found favour before God, and desired to find a tabernacle for the God of Jacob.
v.47	But Solomon built him an house.
v.48	Howbeit the most High dwelleth not in temples made with hands; as saith the prophet,
v.49	Heaven *is* my throne, and earth *is* my footstool: what house will ye build me? saith the Lord: or what *is* the place of my rest?
v.50	Hath not my hand made all these things?
v.51	Ye stiffnecked and uncircumcised in heart and ears, ye do always resist the Holy Ghost: as your fathers *did,* so *do* ye.
v.52	Which of the prophets have not your fathers persecuted? and they have slain them which shewed before of the coming of the Just One; of whom ye have been now the betrayers and murderers:

v.53 Who have received the law by the disposition of angels, and have not kept *it*.
v.54 When they heard these things, they were cut to the heart, and they gnashed on him with *their* teeth.
v.55 But he, being full of the Holy Ghost, looked up stedfastly into heaven, and saw the glory of God, and Jesus standing on the right hand of God.
v.56 And said, Behold, I see the heavens opened, and the Son of man standing on the right hand of God.
v.57 Then they cried out with a loud voice, and stopped their ears, and ran upon him with one accord,
v.58 And cast *him* out of the city, and stoned *him*: and the witnesses laid down their clothes at a young man's feet, whose name was Saul.
v.59 And they stoned Stephen, calling upon *God*, and saying, Lord Jesus, receive my spirit.
v.60 And he kneeled down, and cried with a loud voice, Lord, lay not this sin to their charge. And when he had said this, he fell asleep."

Outside the historical narrative of chs.6,7, Stephen is mentioned only three times in the NT (8:2; 11:19; 22:20 by Paul), but this grasp of God's purpose and his likeness to Christ are greater than that of most. His whole story can be summed up under three headings:

6:1-7   The Church in problems and Stephen emerging.
6:8-15   The Church in persecution and Stephen enlarging.
7:1-60   The Church in purpose and prophecy and Stephen expounding.

Owing to space limitations, we are unable to comment in detail upon every OT reference made by Stephen in his great discourse in ch.7, but we offer the reader the following observations and notes.

1-50 Stephen's defence, as Bible scholars have called it, follows the familiar pattern for Jewish audiences, namely that of recalling their nation's history. But recognisable threads run through the address, since Stephen was not just recalling various odd events in their history; there was purpose in his selection of material, leading up to the climax at the end.

The most important thread centres on the words "this place" (v.7), and God's purpose for Abraham was connected with this. The quotation in v.7 is a composite one, consisting of two parts: "that nation, whom they shall serve, will I judge" (Gen 15:14) and "When thou hast brought forth the people out of Egypt, ye shall serve God upon this mountain" (Exod 3:12). Then Moses is said to be "in the church in the wilderness" (v.38); this is the only time in the NT that the Greek word *ekklēsia* is used to describe God's earthly people. The nation had the tabernacle in the wilderness, and we are reminded in v.44 that it had been made according to the pattern that Moses had seen. This had been God's original commandment to Moses in Exod 25:9, and it is even quoted in Heb 8:5 where the tabernacle is described as "the example and shadow of heavenly things". We cannot over-emphasise the way in which the heavenly dwelling-place of God was to be represented temporarily by material structures on earth. Stephen then draws David into the story, with his desire to find "a tabernacle for the God of Jacob" (v.45), though it was Solomon who ultimately was permitted to build the house (v.46). These were wellknown historical facts that the Sanhedrin could not contradict, but it is then that Stephen displays his understanding of God's purpose by quoting from Isa 66:1, stressing that the most High does not and cannot dwell "in temples made with hands". Though not mentioning the NT church directly, Stephen obviously has this in mind, in keeping with Paul's later words, "Know ye not that ye are the temple of God?" (1 Cor 2:16); "ye are the temple of the living God" (2 Cor 6:16); "an holy temple in the Lord" (Eph 2:21). The church is not an earthly building or institution, but a heavenly one; it is "not of this building" (Heb 9:11). Paul repeated the same truth when he addressed the idolatrous Athenian scholars in 17:24, "God ... dwelleth not in temples made with hands".

The burden of the Acts is that for converted Jews the old had passed away and that the new has come for converts. (Jewish recipients of Galatians and Hebrews appear to have lost this truth, by desiring to return to law and ceremony.) Stephen's accusers alleged that he had said that Jesus of Nazareth would destroy "this place", that is, Herod's temple, the ultimate successor to the temple that Solomon built and that was destroyed by Nebuchadnezzar. Whatever Stephen's actual words had been, he was virtually admitting that their place was to be destroyed or superseded; "Behold, your house is left unto you desolate", said the Lord, stressing the word "your" (Matt 23:38). How much of NT truth revolves around the destruction of the old temple and the building of the new that is not made with hands.

It is interesting to note that what Stephen's accusers alleged may have referred to what the Lord Jesus said in John 2:19, "Destroy this temple, and in three days I will raise it up". In his customary helpful way, John explains that the Lord was speaking of the temple of His body (v.21). Although the disciples did not remember this until after His resurrection, yet unbelievers could readily quote this statement (partially altered so as to suggest that the Lord would destroy Herod's temple) at the end of His life below (Matt 26:61; 27:40). Jamieson, Faussett and Brown go further, and suggest: "By its resurrection the true temple of God on earth was reared up, of which the stone one was just a shadow; so that the allusion is not quite exclusively to Himself, but takes in that Temple of which He is the foundation, and all believers are the living stones".

All of this may have been in Stephen's mind when, at the conclusion of his address, he saw the glory of God (v.55), not in the tabernacles or temples on earth (there were three of each in the Scriptures), but associated with Jesus standing at the right hand of God. The glory which departed from the mount on the east side of the city in ch.1 is seen in the face of the rejected Christ in heaven. The fact that Stephen saw the Lord "standing" and not sitting suggests firstly that there was an immediate welcome awaiting him in heaven, and secondly that the Lord was almost ready to intervene on behalf of His faithful servant.

We draw attention to a second thread that runs through Stephen's address. But first notice the historical subdivisions in this address:

vv.2-16   The fathers: Abraham, Isaac, Jacob, Joseph.
vv.17-44   Moses.
vv.45-50   David and Solomon.

After commencing with Abraham, who is the starting point of most narrations of the story of God's earthly people, Stephen proceeds to recall the lives of Joseph and Moses in detail, the object being to lead up to the backsliding of Israel and their resistance of the Holy Spirit (v.51).

Joseph, Moses and the Lord Jesus each came from a palace on behalf of God's people, but all three were rejected by the very people whom they came to help. However, this rejection by the people did not thwart God's purpose; it was actually used as God's means whereby Joseph, Moses and the Lord Jesus reached their positions of glory. The basic theme of the Acts is that man cannot fight against God by rejecting His servants, since God will actually take man's wrath and make it praise Him.

In Joseph's case envious brothers tried to prevent the fulfilment of his dream, which portrayed them falling down and worshipping him. They doubtless regarded his dream as indicating that one day he would be the ruler of their petty tribe. They decided to prevent that by selling him as a slave into Egypt (v.9). Unknowingly they sent him to the sphere of his future glory, as the deputy ruler of the premier world power. Eventually they had to come to Egypt to beg for corn, and that from Joseph. They became totally dependent upon him, and moved down into Egypt as God had prophesised in Gen 15:13. Far from preventing Joseph's dream being fulfilled, they helped to fulfil it.

In Moses' case, he appeared when the time came for the people's exodus from Egypt. He was brought up in Pharaoh's palace as the son of the king's daughter. The succession ran in the female line in Egypt, but Moses chose to identify himself with the nation of slaves rather than with the ruling class. He chose to suffer affliction with the people of God, than to enjoy the pleasures of sin for a season; esteeming the reproach of Christ greater riches than the treasures in Egypt" (Heb 11:25-26). However, his grace was not appreciated, and he was refused by the people (Acts 7:35). But that was not the end of the story; deliverance from Egypt was to be attained only through one man, the man whom the people had rejected forty years before. The ruler and the judge whom they refused was the one whom God sent to be a ruler and a deliverer. Again, a man, a council or a nation cannot fight against God with any success.

It is Stephen who breaks up the life of Moses into three parts, each lasting forty years.

1. The original forty years' life that he spent in Egypt (v.23).
2. The forty years that he spent in Midian (v.30).
3. The forty years that he led the nation through the wilderness (vv.36, 42).

51-55 It almost appears that Stephen cut short his address. The whole story was so self-evident and frustrating to the Sanhedrin, namely that of a continuous rejection of God by a continuous rejection of His servants. Stephen concludes by castigating his own nation in a way that even Peter never did. Some commentators remark upon an underlying tone placatory of the Roman authorities which, they say, is to be found in the Acts. If this is so, then it is not evident in Stephen's defence, unless flaying the Jewish leaders would please the Romans (not that Stephen had such an intention). He accuses them of persistent resistance to the messengers of God, culminating in their rejection of "the Just One". (This title for the Saviour is found only in the Acts, and is used three times, each by a different speaker, 3:14; 7:52; 22:14.)

Their attitude to the law of Moses shows that they did not have respect either for him or for the customs that he had delivered. They had not only betrayed and murdered their Messiah, but they had not kept Moses' law given to them through angels. The Lord accused the Jews of this in John 7:19, and their self-satisfaction went back to Abraham (John 8:33-40). Their attitude to the prophets had been to persecute and slay those who had shown beforehand the coming of the Messiah; He had shown this in the parable of the vineyard (Matt 21:35-36), and even more openly He had accused the Pharisees effectively of partaking of the blood of the prophets (Matt 23:30-33). Admittedly, we do not read often in the OT of the death of the prophets, but we recall Heb 11:37, "they were stoned ... were slain with the sword", these being the ones through whom God "spake in time past unto the fathers" (Heb 1:1). Men do the same today, not physically, but with lives filled with indifference and pleasures that provide no time to listen to the gospel message or to be interested in it.

56-60 As the anger of the Sanhedrin boiled over, it was exacerbated by Stephen's testimony that he could look right into an open heaven and see Jesus, whom they had cast out and ensured that He was crucified a few weeks previously, standing at the right hand of God. There is divine readiness in heaven for all eventualities, as when the heavens were opened to Ezekiel and he saw visions of God (Ezek 1:1). Stephen calls Him by the title "Son of man", identifying Him with the great vision in Dan 7:13. The Lord usually referred to Himself by this title in the Gospels, and in particular to His glory and coming in the clouds of heaven, and that before this same Jewish Sanhedrin (Matt 26:64). Stephen's claim before this same Sanhedrin was the keystone in their examination of the Lord Jesus. The high priest interrupted the Lord, and condemned Him for blasphemy because of His statement (Matt 26:64-65; Mark 14:62-64; Luke 22:69-71), though at that time they could not take His life according to a Roman ruling. But now in Stephen's case, this ruling had been lifted, so they interrupt him and cast him out of the city, there to stone him to death.

In the Gospels, the title "Son of man" could indicate sympathy unto salvation (Luke 9:56; 19:10), and also judgment to come (Matt 24:37-39). Similarly here, the Lord's posture as "standing" suggests both aspects, that of sympathy and of judgment. The sight of the Lord's glory later brought Saul of Tarsus to his knees, but Stephen's testimony of this sight brought the Sanhedrin-mob to its feet to stone him to death. Stoning was a judicial act, being one of the most painful forms of public execution, but not nearly so prolonged as death by crucifixion. However, it was no more the end of the story than was the death of his Lord and Master those months before. The Lord was raised, and altered the whole course of history; Saul was converted, and he too was used by God to alter the whole course of history.

The chapter ends (v.58) with the first mention of Saul, chief of sinners, who later became the greatest pioneer missionary. This was followed by Stephen's final prayer, "Lord, lay not this sin to their charge". Augustine suggested that there was a link between the two: "If Stephen had not prayed, the church would not have had Paul".

Notes

1. The similarities between Stephen and the Lord Jesus are remarkable, reminding us of 1 Pet 2:21, "that ye should follow his steps".
    a. Both were charged with blasphemy: the Lord in Matt 26:65; Mark 16:64; Stephen in Acts 6:11.
    b. Both had false witnesses brought to testify against them: the Lord in Matt 26:60; Mark 14:56-57; Stephen in Acts 6:13.
    c. Both spoke of the Son of man in glory: the Lord in Matt 26:64; Mark 14:62; Luke 22:69; Stephen in Acts 7:56.
    d. Both died outside the city of Jerusalem with all the significance that Heb 13:13 attaches to that.
    e. Each asked God for forgiveness for his national executioners: the Lord in Luke 23:34; Stephen in Acts 7:60.
    f. The consequences of the public execution of each were far-reaching: the Savour providing salvation for all who will believe; Stephen's death involving the conversion of Saul of Tarsus (Acts 7:58; 22:20).
    g. Both were buried by the godly, although victims of public executions were normally buried in paupers' or criminals' graves. Joseph of Arimathaea obtained special permission from Pilate (John 19:38) to take away the Lord's body from being buried with the wicked, that He might be with the rich man in His death. Acts 8:2 suggests that devout men recovered Stephen's body for decent burial.

The big difference is that the Lord Jesus dismissed His spirit (John 19:30) because no man could take His life from Him while Stephen asked God to receive his departing spirit (Acts 7:59). Also while the Lord was finishing the work that God had given Him to do, Stephen fell asleep (Acts 7:60). While the latter is certainly not as spectacular as what the Lord was doing, it does introduce a new concept. This is the first time in the NT that death for the believer is described as falling asleep (as far as the body is concerned). (It is used of one OT character only in the Acts, David, 13:36.) What a change the resurrection of Christ has made to His people! It has transformed death into a sleep as far as the body is concerned, and this shall be wakened on the resurrection morning.

William Prentice suggests that ch.7 shows how a Christian ought to die, while the story of Saul in ch.9 shows how a Christian ought to live.

2. Problems in Stephen's Defence.

In this connection, the reader is referred to the book *The Acts of the Apostles* by J. A. Alexander, published by Banner of Truth.

The problems are these:

a. In v.4 useful information is given about Abraham that is found nowhere in Genesis. Stephen suggests that Charan (Haran in the OT) was the half-way house for Abraham until his father died, after which he completed the journey that the glory of God had called him to undertake. It was geographically half-way (north-westwards) between Ur and the land of Canaan.

b. In v.16 there appears to be confusion between Abraham and Jacob, between Gen 23:16 and 33:19.

c. The number of Jacob's descendants is given as seventy-five (v.14), whereas both Exod 1:5 and Deut 10:22 make the number seventy, and Gen 46:26 makes it sixty-six. The Dead Sea Scrolls and the LXX give the number of souls who went down into Egypt as seventy-five in both Gen 46:26 and Exod 1:5, leaving only Deut 10:22 with the number seventy. Many NT problems created by quotations from the OT are resolved if it is remembered that the Greek LXX was a frequent source of information.

d. Historical sequence is not adhered to relative to the Exodus. Obviously it came after the signs and wonders shown in Egypt, rather than those shown in the Desert of Sinai, or those shown in the occupation of the land of promise.

e. The quotation from Amos 5:25 etc, is suggested to apply to the desert journey rather than to several centuries later in the land. Their idolatry did not start in the wilderness except for the golden calf. Amos describes the captivity of Israel as taking them beyond Damascus, but Stephen changes this to "beyond Babylon". Amos lived in view of the captivity of the Northern Kingdom; Stephen wants to take in both.

Bible critics have made much of these problems. Francis W. Newman mentioned the discrepancy between Abraham and Jacob (v.16) in his book *Phases of Faith*. John Nelson Darby, featured in that book as "the Irish Clergyman", replied in his book *The Irrationalism of Infidelity*, and his explanation of the confusion is worth quoting at length:

"That there is a difficulty in this passage (7:16), is beyond a doubt; and some mistake difficult for us now to solve. There is a name which is inexactly connected with an historical fact in the OT. It is also one of those difficulties long since discussed. But to call in question inspiration because of it, is to put what an error in copying would produce, in competition with all the moral and spiritual evidence of Divine power, manifest in the whole contents of the book itself, and in its effects in the world for ages. It is so falsely measuring the intrinsic importance of evidence, and the character of proof, that the person rejecting the Scriptures because of it would prove nothing but his own incompetency to measure evidence. A book two thousand years old, has a mistake in a sentence, which the omission of a word entirely rectifies, without changing anything – a word very likely to creep in. And this is used to discredit what bears the largest, fullest, strongest, positive proofs of every kind, of being the testimony of God; and has produced, and does produce, effects which nothing but the testimony of God could do.

The objection is this – Abraham is said, as the passage stands, to have bought the place of the sepulchre of the sons of Emor. It was Jacob, if the sons of Emmor be rightly here, not Abraham who did so. The solution of it is, in one sense, exceedingly easy. The only question is, Is it really the true one? The word 'Abraham' being left out, all difficulty disappears, 'Jacob died, as did also our fathers, and were carried over to Sychem, and placed in the sepulchre which he bought', etc. Now Joseph *was* buried there; and Jerome states, that Paula saw the sepulchres of the rest; and Wetstein quotes Syncellus and two Jewish writers to the same purpose. The omission of Abraham is given credit to by this – that one uncial MS, ancient and of good authority, has an addition here which gives strong ground to suppose Abraham to be an interpolation.

I would lead the attention of my reader to another point here. Let him read Stephen's speech; and he will find a very brief, but most perfect and complete summary for application to the consciences of the Jews, of the history of the patriarchs from Abraham to the end of Joseph's history; a summary which supposes the most perfect and accurate knowledge possible of the details of the history; a man thoroughly master of the whole account given in Genesis, and carrying it in his mind, as all perfectly well-known, so as to give, in few words, the whole moral bearing of all its parts. It would have been impossible for any one, leaving aside inspiration (and if inspired the question is at an end), for any one not perfectly familiar with every part of it, to have given such an abridgment of the history; but it would have been equally impossible for a person so informed, and master of his subject, to have made such a mistake; because the facts were connected with most interesting points in Jewish history, which made the deepest impression on their memory, and connected themselves with their earliest and strongest associations, and are in the history itself too entirely distinct, and accompanied with far too great a detail of different circumstances, to allow of the supposition of any confusion of mind between the two. The supposition, therefore, that Stephen confounded the two is in every point of view, the most improbable solution of any one that can be made. This, it is true, is nothing for a sceptic; because he gains his point by it, or at least raises a doubt. That his reasoning is very absurd is no matter to him; because if he can produce a doubt, faith is at an end. Hence he uses arguments which would be absolutely unreasonable in any human inquiry, and at once rejected. Now I am bold to say, that nothing can be more unreasonable than that an author, who could have produced such a summary of the patriarchal history as Acts 7, should make the blunder supposed to be made in verse 16. The mere literal authority would lead to correct it, by leaving out Abraham; but the internal evidence would lead me, I confess, to believe "the sons of Emmor the father of Sychem" interpolated; and it would run this: "In the sepulchre which Abraham bought for a sum of money". I would add, that the Peschito Syriac reads the verbs in the singular – "Jacob died as also our fathers, and was carried over to Sychem, and laid in the tomb which Abraham bought for a sum of money." The point seems to be, that he had it when Israel was not in possession of the land, Sychem being mentioned as showing God's title over the whole land; for it was now the seat of Samaritanism, a point in Stephen's speech of moment, as was his showing that the best and most blessed of their ancestors had nothing there at all but what they bought, were still pilgrims and strangers as the saints now were becoming, through the Jews' rejection of Messiah, and the Holy Ghost's testimony in Stephen's own person. It is the whole tenor and bearing of Stephen's speech – the rejection of the lawgiver whom God sent as a deliverer, and the delivering to the Gentiles of Him who was their preserver of life, and hence the stranger's place for the true-hearted; Solomon's temple itself being rejected by the testimony of their own prophets. Some one, seeing "Sychem, where Jacob was carried over," added the "Emmor father of Sychem" and left "Abraham" in the text.

In result, it is fully confessed that a difficulty exists in the text as it stands.

The reason assigned for it by the infidel is the most improbable of any, humanly speaking.

We are not in possession of means to correct with certainty the mistake that exists.

There is a very probable way of accounting for it, without doing any violence whatever to the text as it stands, when one word is omitted, or if the last words naming the persons are omitted; for the account of the transaction, if either be, is perfectly exact: the mistake is in the name only.

This last remark is material; namely, that it is a mistake which a transcriber might make, or a marginal reference to a name introduce: no moral error, no mistake, even in the facts, setting aside the name, exists. The teaching of the Holy Ghost in the passage is in no way in question, otherwise than in the insertion of a name."

In spite of the argument in the above lengthy quotation, the present author ventures to make a different suggestion, bearing in mind the distinction between the fact that words spoken by men were *not necessarily divinely inspired*, but that the recording of such words was *divinely inspired*. Therefore from a human point of view (which is not out of place here) it is worth remembering that the speaker was giving an unprepared address in a very critical situation without any hope of verifying his facts beforehand, however excellent a memory he might have had. Bible history *is not necessarily inspired*, but its *inclusion in Scripture is inspired of God*. When Paul called the high priest Ananias a whited wall in 23:3, it could not be claimed that he was inspired to be so unlike his Lord. Satan's words in Job 1-2 were not inspired, but their retention in Scripture certainly is.

There were many statements made by Judah's kings recorded in Chronicles which could not possibly have been inspired, but we never doubt that their preservation in Scripture is the work of the Holy Spirit. "All scripture is given by inspiration of God" (2 Tim 3:16), and some readers may prefer this as an explanation of the difficulty in Stephen's speech. It is best not to be too dogmatic when believers have different suggestions, though we reject entirely the ideas of unbelieving critics.

3. A New Era "not made with hands"; cf. Heb 9:11

"True worshippers shall worship the Father in spirit and in truth" (John 4:23)

Acts 6-7: Jerusalem	Acts 17: Athens	Acts 19: Ephesus
Stephen and the Jews	Paul and the Cultured	Paul and the Heathen
"We have heard him (Stephen) speak...against Moses, and against God" (6:11). "This man ceaseth not to speak blasphemous words against this holy place, and the law: for we have heard him say, that this Jesus of Nazareth shall destroy this place, and shall change the customs which Moses delivered us" (6:13-14) "The most High dwelleth not in temples made with hands; as saith the prophet, Heaven is my throne, and earth is my footstool: what house will ye build me?...or what is the place of my rest? (7:48-50). To the Jewish world. the OT quotation is addressed that they might realise that they have no temple now, for ...	"God that made the world and all things therein seeing that he is Lord of heaven and earth, dwelleth not in temples made with hands; neither is worshipped with men's hands, as though he needed anything, seeing he giveth to all life, and breath, and all things" (17:24-25). To the cultured world is addressed a quotation from certain of their own poets (v. 28). that they might realise that they have no altar "TO THE UNKNOWN GOD" on Mars' hills now, for ...	"This Paul hath persuaded...saying that they be no gods, which are made with hands" (19:26). Cf. 14:11-18. The heathen world must realise that there is to be no worship in the temple of Diana now, although it was one of the seven wonders of the ancient world, for ...
neither in Jerusalem	*nor yet in this mountain*	*nor in this city*
"True worshippers shall worship the Father in spirit and in truth" (John 4:23)		

God did visit the nations to take out them a people for His name. Men could neither prevent the destruction or decay of what was made with hands nor prevent the building of the new "not made with hands" (see 15:14).

III. The Witness in Judaea and Samaria (8:1-11:18)

1. The Scattered Church
8:1-4

> v.1 "And Saul was consenting unto his death. And at that time there was a great persecution against the church which was at Jerusalem; and they were all scattered abroad throughout the regions of Judæa and Samaria, except the apostles.
> v.2 And devout men carried Stephen *to his burial*, and made great lamentation over him.
> v.3 As for Saul, he made havoc of the church, entering into every house, and haling men and women committed *them* to prison.
> v.4 Therefore they that were scattered abroad went every where preaching the word."

1-2 Strictly speaking, the chapter division interrupts the flow of the narrative. Saul is seen emerging as the chief persecutor of the infant church. What happened to Stephen was just the prelude. For the second time in the book, the large group of Christians in Jerusalem is called "the church" (5:11 if the word in 2:47 is omitted). It was to become the object of the attention of a young man, Saul of Tarsus.

The result of that persecution was that, while the church leaders, the apostles, remained in Jerusalem, the saints were scattered. Naturally, they scattered to the nearest places in their land, Judaea and Samaria, though ultimately they found their way to "Phenice, and Cyprus, and Antioch" (11:19), which involved long distances. These two districts had been last mentioned in 1:8. That verse, a statement from the lips of the Lord Jesus, had described the expanding areas of their future witness. However, the months were passing, and they had taken no steps to extend their witness to those other areas. Strictly, one cannot open doors of testimony without divine leading (as Paul in 13:2-4; although he knew that this would be the will of the Lord as he had been told in 26:17). So what they could not do voluntarily was forced on them by Saul's persecution. The wrath of man was again made to praise God. This is another example of the fact that men cannot fight against God with success.

The fleeing Christians did not go into hiding; they did not lie low. Rather they went everywhere preaching the Word, this being the means that the Lord used and uses to propagate the seed (1 Cor 1:18, 23; 2:3). The blood of the martyrs has frequently been the seed of the church, and the scattering of believers has equally frequently resulted in the spreading of the gospel.

3-4 In 2:46 houses were the scene of the church's fellowship; in 5:42 houses were the scene of the church's witness, but here in 8:3 houses were the places from which Saul sought to eradicate Christianity. Although we have the promise that God will remember sins and iniquities no more (Heb 10:17), yet Paul could never forget his past sinful activity. To the Sanhedrin he said, "I persecuted this way unto the death, binding and delivering into prisons both men and women" (22:4); to king Agrippa he said, "many of the saints did I shut up in prison ... they were put to death ... I punished them oft ... compelled them to blaspheme; and being exceedingly mad against them, I persecuted them even unto strange cities" (26:10-11); to the Corinthians he wrote, "I am the least of the apostles, that am not meet to be called an apostle, because I persecuted the church of God" (1 Cor 15:9); to Timothy he wrote, "who was before a blasphemer, and a persecutor, and injurious: but I obtained mercy" (1 Tim 1:13).

2. Philip the Evangelist
   8:5-40

a. In Samaria (8:5-25)

v.5 "Then Philip went down to the city of Samaria, and preached Christ unto them.
v.6 And the people with one accord gave heed unto those things which Philip spake, hearing and seeing the miracles which he did.
v.7 For unclean spirits, crying with loud voice, came out of many that were possessed *with them*: and many taken with palsies, and that were lame, were healed.
v.8 And there was great joy in that city.
v.9 But there was a certain man, called Simon, which beforetime in the same city used sorcery, and bewitched the people of Samaria, giving out that himself was some great one:
v.10 To whom they all gave heed, from the least to the greatest, saying, This man is the great power of God.
v.11 And to him they had regard, because that of long time he had bewitched them with sorceries.
v.12 But when they believed Philip preaching the things concerning the kingdom of God, and the name of Jesus Christ, they were baptized, both men and women.
v.13 Then Simon himself believed also: and when he was baptized, he continued with Philip, and wondered, beholding the miracles and signs which were done.
v.14 Now when the apostles which were at Jerusalem heard that Samaria had received the word of God, they sent unto them Peter and John:
v.15 Who, when they were come down, prayed for them, that they might receive the Holy Ghost:
v.16 (For as yet he was fallen upon none of them: only they were baptized in the name of the Lord Jesus.)
v.17 Then laid they *their* hands on them, and they received the Holy Ghost.
v.18 And when Simon saw that through laying on of the apostles' hands the Holy Ghost was given, he offered them money.
v.19 Saying, Give me also this power, that on whomsoever I lay hands, he may receive the Holy Ghost.
v.20 But Peter said unto him, Thy money perish with thee, because thou hast thought that the gift of God may be purchased with money.

v.21 Thou hast neither part nor lot in this matter: for thy heart is not right in the sight of God.
v.22 Repent therefore of this thy wickedness, and pray God, if perhaps the thought of thine heart may be forgiven thee.
v.23 For I perceive that thou art in the gall of bitterness, and *in* the bond of iniquity.
v.24 Then answered Simon, and said, Pray ye to the Lord for me, that none of these things which ye have spoken come upon me.
v.25 And they, when they had testified and preached the word of the Lord, returned to Jerusalem, and preached the gospel in many villages of the Samaritans."

5-8 The first of the scattered Christians to be named is Philip. He was first mentioned as one of the seven men entrusted with the distribution to widows from the church funds. That was a short-lived responsibility, for now driven from Jerusalem he exercises his gift as an evangelist. It is clear from 6:3,5 that the seven men were already gifted prior to their selection to deal with financial matters, and that they continued to exercise their gifts during the period of their administrative task (as did Stephen in 6:8). Truly, the Lord gave "some, evangelists" (Eph 4:11). The scenes of Philip's evangelistic activities are two in number: the populous city of Samaria and then the solitude of a desert road. Both kinds of places still call for the attention of evangelists today, leading to many converts or to few. In 8:40, Philip "came to Caesarea", and he was still there with his four daughters after Paul's three missionary journeys were over, and known as "Philip the evangelist" (21:8).

Samaria often occurs in the OT. In NT times, Samaria was forbidden territory for those whom the Lord sent out in Matt 10:5; both His mission and their mission was "to the lost sheep of the house of Israel" (10:6; 15:24). But His mission was not one of judgment, even if the Samaritans would not receive Him; He would not allow James and John to attempt to bring down fire from heaven to consume them (Luke 9:51-56), for He had come to save men's lives and not to destroy them. John 4:1-42 provides an example of the Lord's mercy upon the Samaritans, who also shared the Jewish hope of a coming Messiah. The Lord had announced to the woman at the well that He was the Messiah (4:26); she had told the men of her city that this was the Christ, known as the Saviour of the world (vv.29, 42). Now Philip "preached Christ unto them".

The response was remarkable. This fourth notice of miracles being wrought is connected with Philip's preaching in Samaria (the preaching came first – the people heard; the miracles came second – the people saw). The apostles, especially Peter, practised miracles; Stephen did in 6:8; and now Philip is also recorded as having practised them. It was a spiritual gift (1 Cor 12:10) granted to some in the early church. The people were released from spiritual and physical bondage, and this caused the "great joy" in the city.

9-21 The NT does not describe ideal conditions, and even today christian workers are sometimes perplexed by spurious conversions. To all appearances, such so-called "converts" seem to be genuine for a season, and it is then upsetting when they prove not to be so. The story of Simon should offer consolation, since the evangelist Philip was deceived for a time, though Peter saw through this deception as one who possessed the gift of "discerning of spirits" (1 Cor 12:10). "The prince of the power of the air" was busy at several pagan places when the gospel was preached. It was sorcery here in Samaria and also in Cyprus (13:6); it was divination in Philippi (16:16), and evil spirits in Ephesus (19:15).

Simon was able to convince the people that he was "some great one", and people of all ages and status believed that he was "the great power of God"; this had lasted for a "long time". That Philip could make any impression upon the people of such a city shows that the purpose of God and the power of the Spirit were present; Philip's message concerning Christ and the kingdom of God, together with the miracles that he performed were recognised as genuine, contrasting with the magic of Simon. He can be regarded as a type of the coming man of sin, claiming to be God, and effecting "power and signs and lying wonders" (2 Thess 2:4, 9), whom men will own because they will not receive the love of the truth to be saved.

The power of God was such that both men and women believed and were baptised in the name of the Lord Jesus (vv.12, 16). This is always the scriptural order, as in Corinth later (18:8). To reverse the order, and to baptise infants regardless of the fact that only few are saved (Matt 7:14; 1 Cor 1:26), is to disregard entirely the Scriptures of truth. Today, tradition often appears to be the truth to those whose minds are taught error in this matter. The fact that Simon was baptised suggests that the reality of his faith was not sufficiently enquired into, since obviously large numbers were concerned, and Philip appears to have been alone in this work. In 2:41, three thousand were baptised, though then there were many available to ascertain the reality of their faith. With no long gap between a confession of faith and baptism, we may ask (with no hope of an answer), Did one or two slip through the net? Today, baptism usually takes place some time after a confession of faith, and in much smaller numbers in local assemblies, so more care can be exercised, but even then, alas, some drift back to the world after baptism. In Simon's case, the motive for his profession seems to have been a fear of losing his influence; he still wanted to be great rather than humbling himself. In their baptism, his former devotees were proclaiming their allegiance to a new Lord, so Simon as a leader was abandoned completely. To avoid being left behind, he therefore "believed also" and was baptised; the end of the record shows the state in which he actually found himself. He waited for an opportunity to exercise his pre-eminence again, and this was not long in coming.

When the news of the Samaritans receiving the word of God reached the apostles in Jerusalem, Peter and John came down (Jerusalem was always "up", and all the country around was "down" – see 18:22; 21:15), evidently to be of apostolic help, since Philip was not an apostle. They recognised immediately that the new baptised converts did not possess the Holy Spirit. This was an important matter, since in 2:38 Peter had plainly stated that "ye shall receive the gift of the Holy Ghost", for the promise was unto all. When the three thousand and five thousand were converted, no reference is made regarding apostolic intervention for them to receive the Holy Spirit. Pentecost occurred once for the original Jewish believers, and there was no repetition of the rushing mighty wind and tongues like as of fire. The Lord had sent the Holy Spirit from the Father, and subsequent believers received Him without these outward manifestations and apostolic intervention.

But the Samaritans were clearly different; Peter and John (but not Philip or anyone else) prayed for them, so that they should also receive the Holy Spirit, and He was received through the laying on of the apostolic hands. The Samaritans now became as the Jewish believers before them. A pattern is not being established here, since no apostles exist today to do such a thing. The case is not the norm, but arises because of the special relationship that existed between the Jews and the Samaritans. As a nation, the Samaritans cut themselves off from the Jews, both to the south in Judaea and Jerusalem, and to the north in Galilee. There were no dealings between Jews and Samaritans. But amongst believers, this separation was not to be maintained. Samaritan worship was to be abandoned, and the new worship deriving from Jerusalem was to be received – that is, worship in spirit and in truth. This had to be appreciated, and so Peter and John were really sent by the Lord from Jerusalem, so that the Samaritan believers could see the origin, not only of the new preaching and baptism, but also of the reception of the Spirit. Without this, the Samaritans could immediately have formed a "denomination", and a division in the early church would have been formed.

In v.18, the implication is that none of the Samaritans received the gift to impart the Holy Spirit, else Simon may well have been one of many with this capacity. Thus Simon realised that only the apostles could impart the Spirit (without any understanding as to why this should have been so in Samaria), and was determined that he should lead the Samaritan believers just as he had done in their pre-conversion spiritist days. By attempting to buy the ability to impart the Holy Spirit, he earned the apostolic rebuke that establishes a vital principle for all blessings received from the Lord, "Thy money perish with thee, because thou hast thought that the gift of God may be purchased with money. Thou has neither part nor lot in this matter: for thy heart is not right in the sight of God" (vv.20-21).

22-24 The whole event shows that Simon could not have been a real Christian. His money was to go to destruction (perdition, damnation) along with him. He had no saving-faith in the elementary terms of the gospel of free grace. He had neither share nor inheritance in it. His heart was not right in the sight of God, and he was poisoned by bitterness and bound by iniquity. There is no conclusion to the story. "Repent ... perhaps" (v.22) almost suggest that repentance was no longer possible, particularly when v.24 shows that Simon was not capable of prayer. This may well be an example of the Lord's words in Matt 12:31-32, "blasphemy against the Holy Ghost shall not be forgiven unto men ... but whosoever speaketh against the Holy Ghost, it shall not be forgiven him, neither in this world, neither in the world to come".

Simon's profession was obviously one of convenience. He reminds us of some of the kinds of ground in the parable of the sower, and that he was one of the tares that were planted amongst the wheat. His baptism guarantees nothing, showing that even first century preachers of the calibre of Philip could be deceived. Today, no one can guarantee that converts will prove genuine. If we refused to baptise lest they do not, then we should never baptise any. There is a hesitancy that is too cautious, just as there is a forwardness that is too rash.

25 One of the sidelights of the story is that the two apostles took the opportunity of preaching the gospel in many villages on their way back to Jerusalem. They had lost the desire of James and John to attempt to bring down fire from heaven upon the Samaritans. If Peter had any reserve in the matter, this was put on one side in view of what his eyes had seen of the work of Philip. His prejudices would require to be broken down again later, before an actual Gentile could hear the gospel from his lips in a Gentile home (ch.10).

b. *The First African Responds to the Gospel (8:26-40)*

- v.26 "And the angel of the Lord spake unto Philip, saying, Arise, and go toward the south unto the way that goeth down from Jerusalem unto Gaza, which is desert.
- v.27 And he arose and went: and, behold, a man of Ethiopia, an eunuch of great authority under Candace queen of the Ethiopians, who had the charge of all her treasure, and had come to Jerusalem for to worship,
- v.28 Was returning, and sitting in his chariot read Esaias the prophet.
- v.29 Then the Spirit said unto Philip, Go near, and join thyself to this chariot.
- v.30 And Philip ran thither to *him,* and heard him read the prophet Esaias, and said, Understandest thou what thou readest?
- v.31 And he said, How can I, except some man should guide me? And he desired Philip that he would come up and sit with him.
- v.32 The place of the scripture which he read was this, He was led as a sheep to the slaughter; and like a lamb dumb before his shearer, so opened he not his mouth;
- v.33 In his humiliation his judgment was taken away: and who shall declare his generation? for his life is taken from the earth.
- v.34 And the eunuch answered Philip, and said, I pray thee, of whom speaketh the prophet this? of himself, or of some other man?
- v.35 Then Philip opened his mouth, and began at the same scripture, and preached unto him Jesus.
- v.36 And as they went on *their* way, they came unto a certain water: and the eunuch said, See, *here is* water; what doth hinder me to be baptized?
- v.37 And Philip said, If thou believest with all thine heart, thou mayest. And he answered and said, I believe that Jesus Christ is the Son of God.
- v.38 And he commanded the chariot to stand still: and they went down both into the water, both Philip and the eunuch: and he baptized him.

v.39 And when they were come up out of the water, the Spirit of the Lord caught away Philip, that the eunuch saw him no more: and he went on his way rejoicing.

v.40 But Philip was found at Azotus: and passing through he preached in all the cities, till he came to Cæsarea."

26 From this campaign of outstanding success in Samaria, Philip was instructed by the angel of the Lord to go south beyond Jerusalem, where he would meet a disappointed pilgrim. The journey would have been about sixty miles. Philip, bearer of a Greek name, is to pave the way for the breach of a second barrier to the spread of the gospel. In the first part of ch.8 he takes the gospel to a non-Jewish province of Canaan; in the second he takes it to a man from a different continent altogether. Divine guidance is important for all the Lord's servants, and sometimes it runs contrary to natural reasoning. The angel required Philip to leave a flourishing work with many conversions for a desert place with little prospect of meeting anybody. There is no record that he called at Jerusalem on the way, and there was obviously no attempt to consult with the apostles there. The preacher's orders came from heaven and not from an earthly headquarters. The same happened in Acts 10:20; 17:9. On the other hand, sometimes guidance in service does come from the suggestions or requests of other believers, as when Peter was called to Joppa (9:38), and when Paul sent Timothy on various missions (1 Thess 3:1). Neither are results, though counted in scores, a criterion by which to determine whether to continue to preach in a particular place, though clearly such spiritual results caused Paul to remain in Ephesus for some time (1 Cor 16:8-9). Thus several kinds of guidance were granted to first-century preachers, and this is shown clearly in the NT, though the concept of a central headquarters from which guidance is sought is completely absent. Believers ignore these fundamental principles to their great loss.

27-35 Ethiopia was a country lying to the south of Egypt, and is often mentioned in the OT. It was settled by the descendants of Cush, and even Moses married "an Ethiopian woman" (Num 12:1). As Philip stood at the side of the caravan highway that linked Asia with Africa, a chariot rumbled along occupied by an "eunuch of great authority under Candace queen of the Ethiopians, who had charge of all her treasure". We may understand him as the "Chancellor of the Exchequer" of Ethiopia. He was a seeking pilgrim, a would-be proselyte, and this is not surprising since Jewish religion and culture had spread to Egypt and Ethiopia. He was returning from his pilgrimage to Jerusalem (perhaps for a feast day) empty-hearted (like those worshippers at the feast of tabernacles in John 7). He could not participate actively in Jewish rites, because of his race and because of his physical condition. But he was not returning empty-handed, for somehow at Jerusalem he had acquired a copy, or at least part, of Isaiah's prophecy. He had reached what we know as ch.53 in his reading, when the evangelist approached to ask if he understood what he had been reading aloud, perhaps to a companion in the chariot with him. Thus the first recorded sermon on

Isa 53 was preached, and the disappointed pilgrim's hopes were realised, after his visit to Jerusalem but not during it. Even by being a spectactor of Jewish rites, he could not learn by those means the gospel of the Lord Jesus.

Obviously Philip grasped clearly the meaning of the OT Scriptures, else he would have been a poor preacher indeed. How he gained his knowledge we are not told, but he must have sat under the ministry of the apostles, and they had heard the Lord speaking of "all things ... written in the law of Moses, and in the prophets, and in the psalms, *concerning me*" (Luke 24:4). This enabled Philip to preach "Jesus". Isa 53 features many times in the NT as referring to the Lord Jesus (John 12:38; Rom 10:16; Matt 8:17; 27:57, 60; Mark 15:28). Evangelists must be prepared to use any relevant part of the Scriptures that may be necessary in any personal contact with the unsaved and ignorant.

Note that the Lord "opened ... not his mouth" as the Lamb (v.32), but Philip "opened his mouth" as the evangelist (v.35).

36-38 We are not told what knowledge the eunuch had of baptism prior to his meeting with Philip, but we believe that Philip would teach not only the way of salvation through Jesus the Lamb of God, but also what the Lord expected of new converts. Hence the readiness of the eunuch to be baptised at the first available moment. In his heart of hearts, the man had become a Christian, and immediately asked for baptism when he asw enough water by the side of the desert road to suit the purpose. The two important conditions for baptism are here clearly stated: a sufficiency of water for immersion, and a belief in the heart that "Jesus Christ is the Son of God". We admit that v.37 does not occur in certain Greek manuscripts, and hence it is omitted in modern translations. Thus JND omits it in his translation, though he includes it in his footnotes. In any case, the contents of v.37 are in harmony with other Scriptures, and are implied in what immediately precedes and follows. It would appear that Philip was going to make absolutely certain that he was not going to baptise another Simon as in Samaria. The two conditions, enough water and faith, are the only conditions for baptism.

39-40 With his mission fulfilled, Philip was miraculously caught away by the Spirit of God (note Ezek 8:3), while the rejoicing eunuch continued on his way home to Africa. (Ethiopean tradition asserts that the eunuch became the first evangelist in his home country.)

It is generally agreed that baptism is incumbent on a believer whether or not there is a local church with which he can be identified. Baptism is one of the first outward manifestations of salvation, and in all NT examples we find that it precedes reception into a local church.

The Spirit did not take Philip far, since Azotus is not far to the north of Gaza. In fact, Philip retraced his steps to Samaria along the Palestinian coastline, preaching in every city from Azotus to Caesarea, and the list must have included Joppa, and perhaps Lydda a few miles inland. The mention of Caesarea is arresting, and emphasises the significance of the divine intervention in the events of ch.10. Although Philip was there, it was not he who was chosen by the Lord to introduce the Gentiles to the faith; rather Peter and others were called there for this purpose, and Cornelius heard the gospel from Peter's lips.

3. The Greatest Jewish Conversion
9:1-31

v.1 "And Saul, yet breathing out threatenings and slaughter against the disciples of the Lord, went unto the high priest,

v.2 And desired of him letters to Damascus to the synagogues, that if he found any of this way, whether they were men or women, he might bring them bound unto Jerusalem.

v.3 And as he journeyed, he came near Damascus: and suddenly there shined round about him a light from heaven:

v.4 And he fell to the earth, and heard a voice saying unto him, Saul, Saul, why persecutest thou me?

v.5 And he said, Who art thou, Lord? And the Lord said, I am Jesus whom thou persecutest: *it is* hard for thee to kick against the pricks.

v.6 And he trembling and astonished said, Lord, what wilt thou have me to do? And the Lord *said* unto him, Arise, and go into the city, and it shall be told thee what thou must do.

v.7 And the men which journeyed with him stood speechless, hearing a voice, but seeing no man.

v.8 And Saul arose from the earth; and when his eyes were opened, he saw no man: but they led him by the hand, and brought *him* into Damascus.

v.9 And he was three days without sight, and neither did eat nor drink.

v.10 And there was a certain disciple at Damascus, named Ananias; and to him said the Lord in a vision, Ananias. And he said, Behold, I *am here*, Lord.

v.11 And the Lord *said* unto him, Arise, and go into the street which is called Straight, and inquire in the house of Judas for *one* called Saul, of Tarsus: for, behold, he prayeth,

v.12 And hath seen in a vision a man named Ananias coming in, and putting *his* hand on him, that he might receive his sight.

v.13 Then Ananias answered, Lord, I have heard by many of this man, how much evil he hath done to thy saints at Jerusalem:

v.14 And here he hath authority from the chief priests to bind all that call on thy name.

v.15 But the Lord said unto him, Go thy way: for he is a chosen vessel unto me, to bear my name before the Gentiles, and kings, and the children of Israel:

v.16 For I will shew him how great things he must suffer for my name's sake.

v.17 And Ananias went his way, and entered into the house; and putting his hands on him said, Brother Saul, the Lord, *even* Jesus, that appeared unto thee in the way as thou camest, hath sent me, that thou mightest receive thy sight, and be filled with the Holy Ghost.

v.18 And immediately there fell from his eyes as it had been scales: and he received sight forthwith, and arose, and was baptized.
v.19 And when he had received meat, he was strengthened. Then was Saul certain days with the disciples which were at Damascus.
v.20 And straightway he preached Christ in the synagogues, that he is the Son of God.
v.21 But all that heard *him* were amazed, and said; Is not this he that destroyed them which called on this name in Jerusalem, and came hither for that intent, that he might bring them bound unto the chief priests?
v.22 But Saul increased the more in strength, and confounded the Jews which dwelt at Damascus, proving that this is very Christ.
v.23 And after that many days were fulfilled, the Jews took counsel to kill him:
v.24 But their laying await was known of Saul. And they watched the gates day and night to kill him.
v.25 Then the disciples took him by night, and let *him* down by the wall in a basket.
v.26 And when Saul was come to Jerusalem, he assayed to join himself to the disciples: but they were all afraid of him, and believed not that he was a disciple.
v.27 But Barnabas took him, and brought *him* to the apostles, and declared unto them how he had seen the Lord in the way, and that he had spoken to him, and how he had preached boldly at Damascus in the name of Jesus.
v.28 And he was with them coming in and going out at Jerusalem.
v.29 And he spake boldly in the name of the Lord Jesus, and disputed against the Grecians: but they went about to slay him.
v.30 *Which* when the brethren knew, they brought him down to Cæsarea, and sent him forth to Tarsus.
v.31 Then had the churches rest throughout all Judæa and Galilee and Samaria, and were edified; and walking in the fear of the Lord, and in the comfort of the Holy Ghost, were multiplied."

It has often been pointed out that in three successive chapters of the Acts three representative men were won for Christ. This movement of faith in the risen and glorified Christ was not going to be a small local one in Jerusalem. Ch.8 presents a native of Africa becoming a Christian; ch.9 a native of Asia; and ch.10 a native of Europe. No other continents were known to exist at that time. If Acts 2 saw the confusion of tongues (caused by God in Gen 11:7 because of man's rebellion against Himself) overcome by those possessing the gift of speaking other languages granted by the Holy Spirit, as multitudes listened to "the wonderful works of God," then Acts 8-10 sees the distinction of continents and colours (again, see Gen 11:8) obliterated relative to the gospel of Christ.

The Asiatic/Jewish representative was the greatest sinner of them all (1 Tim 1:15). The Ethiopian and the Roman were seekers; those who seek would find, said the Lord, but the Jew was an opponent of all that Christ stood for. The story of Saul of Tarsus is broken by ch.8 (8:3 effectively joins on to 9:1). At the beginning of ch.9

he was still filled with indignation against Jesus of Nazareth, and was upset that his persecution had merely spread the movement that he was anxious to destroy. In v.2 believers in the Lord Jesus are referred to as people of "this way" for the first time. Nobody had a greater purpose in life than they, and nobody knew better where they were going. Sir Robert Anderson chose the designation as the title for one of his books. In it he explains that the expression indicates "a certain mode of life and conduct" (Lange), or "a definite and progressive direction of the inner and outer life of man" (Canon Cooke). He continues: "On the apostles' lips it meant the true faith and a right life. And its occurrences in the Acts (9:2; 18:25, 26; 19:9, 23; 22:4; 24:14, 22) give proof not only that it was in common use, but that it was a phrase of the disciples' own choosing" (pp.5-6).

1-2 The only "strange" city (26:1) (although in the plural in this verse) mentioned in connection with Saul's campaign of harassing Christians is Damascus. He needed the authority of the high priest to carry out his objectives (a fact recalled by Paul in 22:5), and this stands in contrast to his appearing before the high priest in 23:2. But he did not reach Damascus as an unbeliever standing up for the rites, doctrine and manner of life of the pure Jewish religion, but as a subdued and reformed man. The story should encourage us not only to love our enemies and to pray for those who despitefully use us, but also to seek the conversion of our bitterest opponents. God arrested the man who did more than any other to stamp out Christianity, and brought him to His side. And nobody did more than he to spread the faith which once he tried to destroy, for he "laboured more abundantly than they all" (1 Cor 15:10). The story of his conversion is told three times in the Acts, first a straightforward account by the historian Luke, and then two personal accounts by Paul of the events that took place, together with further details (chs.22,26). In other words, the details of this event never left his mind after many years' missionary service, and he was ready to repeat them when necessary, even before his enemies.

The conversion of Saul of Tarsus, while lying in the middle of three significant ones, is the most spectacular in that there was no human instrument at all. It is also called a "pattern" conversion in 1Tim1:16. In other words, if God could save Saul, then He can save anybody thus sunk into sin. It also teaches that what the great convert did with his life afterwards all converts should do. It is significant that the expression *A Damascus road experience* has entered the English language as a synonym for a conversion experience.

Saul has first appeared as a participant in the stoning of Stephen: the witnesses laid their clothing at his feet. They were false witnesses (6:13), but Deut 17:5-7 laid the onus of casting the first stones on them. Luke tells us that he was consenting to Stephen's death (8:1), which language Paul uses about himself (22:20). The language may be stronger than the English suggests, for in the second narration of his conversion story Paul says, in effect, "I gave my voice or vote against the saints" (26:10), that is, as a member of the Sanhedrin he voted in favour of Christians being put to death for their faith.

If we collect the statements made, both by Luke and by Paul, we obtain a complete picture of what Paul meant when he said that he was "exceedingly mad against them" (26:11). First he participated in Stephen's martyrdom, and then he joined in the great persecution against the Jerusalem church, making havoc of it and engaging in house-searches for the believers, as the result of which many fled, happily taking their faith with them. Paul himself confesses in 26:11 that punishment took place in "every synagogue", suggesting that the believers were not meeting in the synagogues but that they were taken there for punishment. He was no half-hearted persecutor, and he did not care whether they were men or women; they were all taken to prison.

Threats and murder ("threatenings and slaughter") in 9:1 were in his programme. It was not only Stephen's death of which he approved, but those of many others (26:10). He visited other places apart from Damascus for the same purpose; arresting these early Christians, Saul took them in chains to Jerusalem, there to let the chief priests decide their fate. And all the time he was a very religious man, yet a terrible fanatic. Our world has many such men who break all the rules of their moral code in their determination to pursue their own blind prejudice. Later Paul wrote about the lack of any connection between the Jewish knowledge of the law and their keeping of it (Rom 2:19-24). The Lord had warned, "the time cometh, that whosoever killeth you will think that he doeth God service ... because they have not known the Father, nor me" (John 16:2-3). In other words, bring God into the matter when one separates doctrine from practice, and this will justify turning evil into good!

1 Tim 1 contains two lists of kinds of sinners. The first are all moral: lawless and disobedient, ungodly and sinners, unholy and profane, muderers of father and of mothers, manslayers, whoremongers, those that defile themselves with mankind, liars, perjured persons (vv.9-10). No doubt Saul was not guilty of any of the sins of these kinds of men, yet he learned that that did not leave him blameless. The second list is his own description of himself, "I ... was before a blasphemer, and a persecutor, and injurious" (v.13).

3-9 The persecution that he had initiated in other "strange cities" was to be repeated at Damascus, but Saul was arrested by the Man in glory whom he was really persecuting. He believed that Jesus was dead, that His body had been buried secretly by His disciples (Matt 28:15), and now Saul discovers that this same Jesus is not only alive, but that He is in heaven. The enormity of his sin reached his conscience when he realised that all his hatred and hostility had been directed, not just at Christians, but at their Lord who was very much alive in heaven.

This light that shone round about Saul was the brightest light ever to appear over the earth; later Paul described it as "above the brightness of the sun" (26:13); this recalls the transfiguration description of the Lord, "his face did shine as the sun" (Matt 17:22). This was not just a "glory cloud", but in 22:14 it is recorded that Saul actually saw the Just One.

In v.4, it is interesting to note that the risen Lord addressed Saul by his name twice, "Saul, Saul". This is the seventh and last such double-naming of an individual in the Bible, and in most cases the double-naming of such individuals resulted in a major turning-point in their lives. It was to:

1. Abraham in Gen 22:11, regarding the sacrifice of Isaac his son.
2. Jacob in Gen 46:2 when he was ordered to go into Egypt, obviously thinking that it was the wrong thing to do.
3. Moses in Exod 3:4, commissioning him to return to Egypt to commence his mission, at the time when he was living in the desert with no thought of returning.
4. Samuel in 1 Sam 3:10, conveying to him secrets about Israel's future which more or less gave him a status in Israel far beyond that of a Levitical priest.
5. Martha in the NT addressed twice by the Lord in Luke 10:41.
6. Peter addressed twice by the Lord as "Simon, Simon" in Luke 22:31.
7. Saul addressed twice by the Lord on the Damascus road.

There are of course other repetitions of proper names apart from individuals, such as "Jerusalem, Jerusalem" in Matt 23:37. Exceptionally, the Lord will be called "Lord, Lord" in Matt 7:22, and we recall the solemn verse Matt 27:46.

Saul's first question was, "Who art thou, Lord?". Saul knew immediately, and this shows that the Spirit was already working in his heart, for "no man can say that Jesus is the Lord, but by the Holy Ghost" (1 Cor 12:3). The answer was the name that he had detested, "I am Jesus"; it is exceptional for the Lord to use this name directly of Himself (see Rev 22:16). The statement, "it is hard for thee to kick against the pricks" is not found in some Greek manuscripts, but it was definitely spoken by the Lord for Paul recalls it in 26:14. Saul's second question was, "Lord, what wilt thou have me to do?" (This too is missing from some Greek manuscripts, but it was definitely asked since Paul recalls it in 22:10). The new convert was asking for his marching orders to service. Never was a sudden conversion more complete. For most of us there is a delay between conversion and commitment, but for Saul of Tarsus they were simultaneous. The story is an excellent illustration of the conditions for conversion that the apostle himself states in Rom 10:9. He confessed Jesus as Lord, and obviously immediately believed in his heart that God had raised Him from the dead, and that he was now saved. And he never forgot that day.

In v.6 there is recorded only a few words of the Lord Jesus, that Saul should go into Damascus, there to receive instructions as to what he should do. But Paul recollected in 26:16-18 the fact that the Lord, even at that early stage, provided information about the scope of his future service. He would become a witness to the Gentiles, and later in Jerusalem the Lord told him that the Jews would not receive his testimony concerning Himself (22:18), the fact that he would be sent to the Gentiles being repeated. But note that Saul awaited the divine call as to when he should first go to the Gentiles, after many years of preparation and service (13:2).

Saul was blind, as if to ensure that he realised the tremendous effect that the sight of divine glory could cause upon a human being. He was changed morally, physically and spiritually by that sight, and the blindness would perhaps show him that he was now blind to Judaism as a valid religion. It is strange to realise that here was a convert, being led by unconverted men to the place of God's choice, Damascus. How different from 17:15, where "they that conducted Paul" were no doubt believers.

10-12 Saul arrived in Damascus a very different man from what he had intended. An angel guided Philip to the eunuch in ch.8, but visions directed Ananias in ch.9, and Peter in ch.10 to the objects of spiritual need. Note that two of these involved "double-visions". In ch.9, both Ananias and Saul had visions; in ch.10 both Peter and Cornelius had visions; God's method of working in different hearts dovetailed to achieve His purposes. Neither Ananias nor Peter was keen to go at first, since they feared the consequences. Both natural fears and deep-seated prejudices can make a believer reluctant to respond to divine guidance. But of Saul, the Lord said to Ananias, "he prayeth". Perhaps this activity in which Saul was engaged made Ananias (obviously a common name, since this is the second man bearing this name that has so far occurred in the Acts) much more willing to respond to the divine leading. Divinely-recognised prayer is the last thing that one would have expected of a proud Pharisee (Matt 6:5; Luke 18:11-12); yet prayer is the beginning of many spiritual exercises at all times after conversion. Let no one suggest that a man of prayer is not also a man of action, for Paul was both. In busy days and long journeys, and in times of imprisonment, Paul was a man of constant thanksgiving and prayer, "without ceasing I make mention of you always in my prayers" (Rom 1:9), as Nehemiah had done before him "day and night" (Neh 1:6).

13-14 In his answer to the Lord, Ananias used the name "saints" for the early believers, this being the first time the name occurs in Acts. It means "holy ones", not because of how they conducted themselves in their daily lives, but because of what the Lord Jesus had done for them. They were given a name used largely in the OT for priests and angels. Moreover, it was not a name only for selected believers, but for all. Why some believers are reluctant to use it when it is such a common designation in the NT is hard to understand. The traditional and popular concept of using the word "saint" in the name of most so-called church buildings is completely unscriptural, as is the practice of designating only some special religious men of the past by the title "saint". It is quite wrong ever to use the word "saint" as a title. In this respect, as in many other cases, believers should learn to use scriptural language, and not that of tradition and common usage. Paul loves to use the designation, and virtually always uses it to describe all the Christians to whom he wrote his NT letters. Practically it means "sanctified" or "set apart" ones. Thus priests and angels were suitable to be used by God, and so also should believers be today.

Ananias' words to the Lord show that he and many others knew that Saul was coming to Damascus, and the reason for his coming, together with his authority for his evil activity. News had travelled in front of Saul, no doubt causing much distress to the Lord's people.

15-16 Ananias received a personal revelation from God concerning Saul of Tarsus: He had an outstanding future of service for him. He was not only chosen to be a Christian, he was chosen to be a vessel that God could us. As he came to understand this himself, Paul later wrote, "God ... separated me from my mother's womb, and called me by his grace" (Gal 1:15). To Timothy he wrote, "he counted me faithful, putting me into the ministry (into service)" (1 Tim 1:12). The chief of sinners was to become the chief of servants, and the bondservant of all (Matt 20:27). This new convert would ultimately know what it meant to have "the care of all the churches" before his heart (2 Cor 11:28).

The word "vessel" is an interesting one, describing a person whom God wants to use. The apostle came to love the idea; used at the beginning of his converted life, the word was also used at the end, "he shall be a vessel unto honour, sanctified, and meet for the master's use, and prepared unto every good work" (2 Tim 2:20-21). God expects His vessels to be "of gold and of silver", those whom He can trust in His service. The principles behind the divine choice are clearly not restricted to Paul; His choice should impart to every believer a tremendous sense of security and of purpose. Purpose is particularly evident in the life of service of the apostle to the Gentiles.

While Paul regularly gave the Jews precedence in his preaching (13:14; 14:1; 17:1, 10; 18:4; 19:8), yet they are mentioned last to Ananias; in fact, this was Paul's strategy to reach the Gentiles, for "the gospel of the uncircumcision was committed" to him (Gal 2:7). Thus to Ananias are mentioned the Gentiles as the people before whom Paul would carry the Lord's name. Then "kings", such as king Agrippa (26:1-2) and Nero in Rome (2 Tim 4:16-17). "How great things he must suffer for my name's sake" is nowhere better illustrated that in verses such as 1 Cor 4:9-13 and 2 Cor 11:23-33. He would suffer in greater measure than did the converts whom Saul originally caused to suffer. Though he were saved, yet he could never completely shake off the past when God's gracious hands of discipline were upon him, and the same may be said of king David previously, when the sword would never depart from his house (2 Sam 12:10).

17 With such an explanation of God's purpose, all sense of fear must have been banished from Ananias' mind. The way in which he addressed the blinded Saul is incomparable: "Brother Saul". One of the first probable victims of the intended persecution greets as brother the man who was to have led the persecution. What can a relationship with Jesus Christ not do in leaping over the barriers of suspicion, hatred and everything else? (Note that the use of "brethren" in the Acts does not always imply a christian relationship – the context must decide. Thus in 2:37 and 13:15 the word is one of Jewish relationship only, but in 11:1 a christian relationship is implied.) Ananias used the title "Lord" and name "Jesus"; the former had been used by Saul and the latter by the Lord on the Damascus road (v.5). It is important to note that Ananias had been instructed to lay his hands on Saul "that he might receive his sight" (v.12), and v.18 demonstrates this fact. This disciple evidently had the God-given power to accomplish miracles under divine instruction. It is not stated that

Saul being "filled with the Holy Ghost" was a result of this laying on of hands. He already possessed the Spirit when he called Jesus "Lord". This filling was for service with power and courage. And Saul rapidly used this new filling by the Spirit for testimony.

18-19 Having recovered his sight, Saul's first act was to be baptised. Even so, he waited longer than any other convert mentioned in the Acts, no doubt caused by the particular circumstances in which he found himself. Contrast this with the Philippian jailor, who was promptly baptised after his unexpected conversion (16:31-33). Saul was strengthened physically in v.19, and spiritually in v.22. And he immediately did what is proper for all new disciples: he attached himself to the disciples in Damascus who loved the same Lord. The synagogue as a place of religious concourse (as distinct from testimony) was for him now at an end. He had come to Damascus intending to bind the believers, but instead he bound himself to them in christian love and fellowship. He knew the right company for those who own the Lord; he became one of them (Col 4:9, 12).

20-22 Yet he sought out the Jews in their various synagogues in Damascus that he might preach to them that Jesus was the Son of God. His knowledge of the OT would be partially illuminated by the new revelation that he had received, and by the fact that, like other early followers of the Lord Jesus, he was filled with the Holy Spirit (v.17). So there was consternation about Saul among two classes of people in Damascus:

1. The Christians, because he joined them instead of persecuting them.

2. The Jews, because he preached to them the message that previously he had wanted to stamp out.

In v.22, the message is slightly different; here Saul proved that Jesus "is very Christ", having "increased the more in strength". It was now no longer only preaching (as in v.20), but "proving", namely from the Jewish OT Scriptures. It may well be that between v.20 and v.22 Saul went into Arabia, and returned to Damascus (Gal 1:17), there having learned in quietness and by revelation the new meaning of the OT Scriptires that enabled him afterwards to use them as a basis of all proof concerning the Christ.

23-25 We do not know how long Saul stayed in Damascus, but eventually ("after … many days") it became too dangerous for him. His suffering commenced in the first place where he ever preached the gospel. From the human point of view, his being let down the wall of Damascus was the first of many narrow escapes; here, the plot was due to the Jews. But when he recalled the event in 2 Cor 11:32-33, the plot was due to "the governor under Aretas the king" being desirous to take Saul, so it appears that this was a joint military-religious plot against God's new servant. But when Saul escaped from the town by night in a basket, it is obvious that the early disciples and preachers did not presume on divine protection, however bad the circumstances. If He chose to deliver them, Amen; but they did not take unnecessary risks. Even the Lord Himself did not use the resources of His personal deity to meet the needs of His stainless humanity, and likewise His servants, although endowed with the gift of healing, never used it upon or for themselves. Yet after many experiences, the apostle Paul could later write, "who delivered us from so great a death, and doth deliver: in whom we trust that he will yet deliver us" (2 Cor 1:10).

26 Saul returned to Jerusalem a new man, and as such he chose again a new company. Instead of reporting on the success or otherwise of his mission to Damascus to the high priest who had commissioned him, he reported to the believers whom he had previously persecuted "unto the death". Naturally they were afraid, and "believed not that he was a disciple". It appears that after 8:1, where all the believers except the apostles had been scattered from Jerusalem, some had returned or else there had been further converts, so as to establish a local church there again. News had reached Damascus prior to his arrival there (vv.13-14), but apparently not in the reverse direction. Under such circumstances, strong persuasion would be necessary to convince the Jerusalem church that Saul was now a believer bold in faith and testimony. So they would not receive him, unlike many years later when Paul could exhort others to receive new converts (Philem12).

27-30 So Barnabas appears again. Always a "good man", he testified of Saul's conversion and subsequent service. How he obtained his information we are not told, but the Jerusalem church trusted him completely, and acted upon what he told them of Saul's experience in three statements:

1. Saul saw the Lord on the way to Damascus.

2. The Lord had spoken to Saul.

3. Saul had preached boldly at Damascus in the name of Jesus.

Such a personal commendation did not require a letter to confirm it, though letters are preferable when no personal commendation is available. The writing of a letter is no cold and formal piece of assembly business, but the product of spiritual exercise on the part of the writers who should write carefully and honestly (18:27). A believer asking for a letter of commendation should ensure that his life and service merit a "good report", otherwise there is nothing to write about.

As at Damascus, so at Jerusalem – Saul completely identified himself with his fellow-Christians. Happy is the believer who behaves likewise wherever he lives. As he was "coming in and going out", he was following in the footsteps of his Lord

(1:21), "coming in" referring to the spiritual activity of the local church, and "going out" referring to his testimony outside among the Jews. Just as he had preached boldly at Damascus, so he spoke boldly at Jerusalem in the name of the Lord Jesus. We are not told of converts, rather of hostility. In fact, the Lord had told him, "they will not receive thy testimony concerning me", and He instructed him to depart from Jerusalem (22:18-21). As in Damascus, so in Jerusalem; the Jews "went about to slay him". The result was that Saul had to make his second escape, this time back to his birthplace via Caesarea.

31 We now have the fourth of Luke's summaries, this time concerning the "churches" or "church" for some Greek manuscripts have the word in the singular and not in the plural. (See 1 Cor 15:9; Gal 1:13, where the singular "church" is used to describe every local church where Saul's persecution reached.) Later, local churches are recognised, particularly throughout Paul's missionary journeys and letters, but here the oneness of the church is emphasised.

Thus persecution temporarily ceased, and for the third time Luke uses the word "multiplied", though not of individual believers but of the church. Rest was granted throughout the three regions named by the Lord in 1:8, Judaea, Galilee and Samaria. There was reverence for the Lord, comfort by the Holy Spirit, and there was edification by the Scriptures, by the apostles, and by divinely-raised-up teachers.

The Greek word rendered in this verse by "edified" is always translated in the Gospels as "built" or "builded". It never recovers its *physical* connotation in the NT, continuing to be translated "edified" or "built" in a *spiritual* sense. This is in accord with the change from God dwelling amongst His people in a material building in the OT to His dwelling in the spiritual house which is the church in the NT.

The fear of man was temporarily suspended with the conversion and departure of Saul; the fear of the Lord (not fright but reverential awe) was the paramount fear of those first believers. The subjective work of the Holy Spirit is now mentioned for the first time: His comfort. This is the basic meaning of the word "Comforter". Until now in the Acts He has empowered the believers in their witness; now He is said to be comforting or encouraging them.

Notes

The Church
> The Gospel by Matthew is the only one in which the word "church" occurs. The verse 16:18 contains the Lord's own foretelling about His intention to build it. The only other occurrence is in 18:17, a local company being envisaged, where believers have fellowship the one with the other, but where problems inevitably arise.
>
> The church spoken about by the Lord came into existence after His ascension without human planning. Christians will not hesitate to say that it was formed in Acts 2, although the actual word *ekklēsia* is not found in some Greek MSS of 2:47. But that is

the company to which the name is definitely given in 5:11; 8:1, etc. Such companies of believers were designated by the same name wherever the gospel was preached, and they were gathered together by divine leading – the will of man should give place to the leading of the Lord both then and now when a new convert, exercised by the Scriptures, sees the necessity of joining a local church. The Lord adds, not a new believer. The choice is that of the Lord; obedience is that of the new convert after baptism.

This is the kind of group that began to meet in Jerusalem after the day of Pentecost. The same word is used to describe groups of converts who, as summoned by God, met in the various places where the gospel was preached, with people believing on the Lord Jesus. These local churches were not branches of some central church; rather, the preaching of the gospel and the planting of local churches took place together, evangelists being used until ministers of the word of God could come among them as in Antioch (11:20, 23, 26). It is sweet to think that there were churches in those very places of Judaea and Galilee where the Lord Jesus had lived and preached among men. No details are given anywhere in the NT as to how or when these were formed.

The church at Antioch is identified in 11:26; 13:1; 14:27. Between these last two references, Paul's first missionary journey took place, covering a number of places around the north-eastern part of the Mediterranean area. Luke's description of the return journey says, "they ... ordained them elders in every church" (14:23). Syria and Cilicia were not included in this first missionary journey, but they were areas throughout which there were other churches which Paul and Silas later "confirmed" (15:41).

4. Peter Again
9:32-11:18

a. At Lydda and Joppa (9:32-43)

v.32 "And it came to pass, as Peter passed throughout all *quarters,* he came down also to the saints which dwelt at Lydda.
v.33 And there he found a certain man named Æneas, which had kept his bed eight years, and was sick of the palsy.
v.34 And Peter said unto him, Æneas, Jesus Christ maketh thee whole: arise, and make thy bed. And he arose immediately.
v.35 And all that dwelt at Lydda and Saron saw him, and turned to the Lord.
v.36 Now there was at Joppa a certain disciple named Tabitha, which by interpretation is called Dorcas: this woman was full of good works and almsdeeds which she did.
v.37 And it came to pass in those days, that she was sick, and died: whom when they had washed, they laid *her* in an upper chamber.
v.38 And forasmuch as Lydda was nigh to Joppa, and the disciples had heard that Peter was there, they sent unto him two men, desiring *him* that he would not delay to come to them.
v.39 Then Peter arose and went with them. When he was come, they brought him into the upper chamber: and all the widows stood by him weeping, and shewing the coats and garments which Dorcas made, while she was with them.

v.40 But Peter put them all forth, and kneeled down, and prayed; and turning *him* to the body said, Tabitha, arise. And she opened her eyes: and when she saw Peter, she sat up.
v.41 And he gave her *his* hand, and lifted her up, and when he had called the saints and widows, presented her alive.
v.42 And it was known throughout all Joppa; and many believed in the Lord.
v.43 And it came to pass, that he tarried many days in Joppa with one Simon a tanner."

Because of space limitations, comments on historical passages can from now on only be brief. Having introduced us to Saul, Luke leaves him at Tarsus for a period of several years, where we presume that God prepared him for his future ministry. He then focuses attention on the missionary exploits of Peter until ch.12, bearing in mind that in the record he had left Jerusalem only once (for Samaria). God was arranging Peter's circumstances, so that he should be in the right place for his next important evangelistic exploit in Caesarea.

32-35 Peter had returned to Jerusalem after his visit to Samaria (8:25). The more settled conditions noted in 9:31 then found him engaged in an extensive itinerant ministry: he "passed through all quarters", as he had done previously for three years with the Lord during His years of service on earth. The places named lay between Jerusalem and the coast westwards, whereas his first journey out of Jerusalem had been northwards to Samaria. Obviously there were saints in those places before Peter visited them, possibly the fruit of Philip's preaching from Azotus to Caesarea. Not only was God's work strengthened in the local churches as a result of Peter's visit, but it was also confirmed by signs following, as here in Lydda. This is the second specific miracle recorded in the Acts (as distinct from a general statement as in 8:6), and like the first in ch.3 it was performed by Peter on a paralysed man. The contrast between forty years and eight years is remarkable, showing that age is no barrier to God's working of salvation in a soul. The effect of the miracle was a considerable turning to the Lord in this one place Lydda; in fact "all" in Lydda and Saron turned to the Lord, although this was faith based on sight. This involvement of whole cities is unique in the NT, but we may quote Nineveh in the OT (Jon 3:10). The word "turned" is used seven times in Acts to describe conversion, and it is used also by Paul in 1 Thess 1:9, "ye turned to God from idols".

36-37 Meanwhile an emergency arose in the coastal town of Joppa further along the same road. A much-loved sister named Dorcas sickened and died. Previous chapters have described how the early believers helped each other with the financial proceeds of the sale of their houses and lands. Dorcas had ministered to poor widows, in particular with the work of her hands, "coats and garments". Luke has drawn attention to some five widows in his Gospel; now he is drawing attention to a second group of widows in the Acts. The name of Dorcas has become appellative of sisters characterised by practical good words; the testimony that she had among the widows of Joppa is generally reproduced wherever Christians are full of good works and almsdeeds. Paul wrote of widows, "Well reported of for good works", followed by a suitable list (1 Tim 5:10).

38 Peter went even further than the Lord had done when Jairus' daughter was raised; then He took only five into the room with Himself (Mark 5:37, 40), but here Peter went in alone. This reminds us of Elijah and Elisha (1 Kings 18:19; 2 Kings 4:33), and the contrast with the raising of Lazarus amidst a large company of the Jews (John 11:45). Just as the Lord had done when Lazarus had died, Peter prayed, although he could not claim the same intimacy with the Father as the Saviour had. Just as the Lord addressed personally those whom He raised from the dead, so Peter called Dorcas by her name personally. At Peter's command, she opened her eyes and then his hand lifted her up; divine healing and raising always resulted in a complete cure.

43-43 The consequence of the raising of Dorcas from the dead was similar to that which followed the healing of Aeneas, "many (not "all" in this case) believed in the Lord". Peter stayed in Joppa "for many days", evidently for evangelistic and ministerial service. God had a major task for him to do before he returned to Jerusalem.

Note

38 Peter, with the gift of raising the dead, was asked and invited to go to Joppa. It was not Peter's exercise, but that of the disciples in Joppa. The same applies to other forms of service; Paul's ability in teaching the word of God (11:25-26) was similarly recognised, and he was invited.

b.   *The Conversion of Cornelius (10:1-48)*

v.1   "There was a certain man in Cæsarea called Cornelius, a centurion of the band called the Italian *band,*
v.2   A devout *man,* and one that feared God with all his house, which gave much alms to the people, and prayed to God alway.
v.3   He saw in a vision evidently about the ninth hour of the day an angel of God coming in to him, and saying unto him, Cornelius.
v.4   And when he looked on him, he was afraid, and said, What is it, Lord? And he said unto him, Thy prayers and thine alms are come up for a memorial before God.
v.5   And now send men to Joppa, and call for *one* Simon, whose surname is Peter:
v.6   He lodgeth with one Simon a tanner, whose house is by the sea side: he shall tell thee what thou oughtest to do.
v.7   And when the angel which spake unto Cornelius was departed, he called two of his household servants, and a devout soldier of them that waited on him continually;

v.8	And when he had declared all *these* things unto them, he sent them to Joppa.
v.9	On the morrow, as they went on their journey, and drew nigh unto the city, Peter went up upon the housetop to pray about the sixth hour:
v.10	And he became very hungry, and would have eaten: but while they made ready, he fell into a trance,
v.11	And saw heaven opened, and a certain vessel descending unto him, as it had been a great sheet knit at the four corners, and let down to the earth:
v.12	Wherein were all manner of fourfooted beasts of the earth, and wild beasts, and creeping things, and fowls of the air.
v.13	And there came a voice to him, Rise, Peter; kill, and eat.
v.14	But Peter said, Not so, Lord; for I have never eaten any thing that is common or unclean.
v.15	And the voice *spake* unto him again the second time, What God hath cleansed, *that* call not thou common.
v.16	This was done thrice: and the vessel was received up again into heaven.
v.17	Now while Peter doubted in himself what this vision which he had seen should mean, behold, the men which were sent from Cornelius had made inquiry for Simon's house, and stood before the gate,
v.18	And called, and asked whether Simon, which was surnamed Peter, were lodged there.
v.19	While Peter thought on the vision, the Spirit said unto him, Behold, three men seek thee.
v.20	Arise therefore, and get thee down, and go with them, doubting nothing: for I have sent them.
v.21	Then Peter went down to the men which were sent unto him from Cornelius; and said, Behold, I am he whom ye seek: what *is* the cause wherefore ye are come?
v.22	And they said, Cornelius the centurion, a just man, and one that feareth God, and of good report among all the nation of the Jews, was warned from God by an holy angel to send for thee into his house, and to hear words of thee.
v.23	Then called he them in, and lodged *them.* And on the morrow Peter went away with them, and certain brethren from Joppa accompanied him.
v.24	And the morrow after they entered into Cæsarea. And Cornelius waited for them, and had called together his kinsmen and near friends.
v.25	And as Peter was coming in, Cornelius met him, and fell down at his feet, and worshipped *him.*
v.26	But Peter took him up, saying, Stand up; I myself also am a man.
v.27	And as he talked with him, he went in, and found many that were come together.
v.28	And he said unto them, Ye know how that it is an unlawful thing for a man that is a Jew to keep company, or come unto one of another nation; but God hath shewed me that I should not call any man common or unclean.
v.29	Therefore came I *unto you* without gainsaying, as soon as I was sent for: I ask therefore for what intent ye have sent for me?

v.30 And Cornelius said, Four days, ago I was fasting until this hour; and at the ninth hour I prayed in my house, and, behold, a man stood before me in bright clothing,
v.31 And said, Cornelius, thy prayer is heard, and thine alms are had in remembrance in the sight of God.
v.32 Send therefore to Joppa, and call hither Simon, whose surname is Peter; he is lodged in the house of *one* Simon a tanner by the sea side; who, when he cometh, shall speak unto thee.
v.33 Immediately therefore I sent to thee; and thou hast well done that thou art come. Now therefore are we all here present before God, to hear all things that are commanded thee of God.
v.34 Then Peter opened *his* mouth, and said, Of a truth I perceive that God is no respecter of persons:
v.35 But in every nation he that feareth him, and worketh righteousness, is accepted with him.
v.36 The word which *God* sent unto the children of Israel, preaching peace by Jesus Christ: (he is Lord of all:)
v.37 That word, *I say,* ye know, which was published throughout all Judæa, and began from Galilee, after the baptism which John preached;
v.38 How God anointed Jesus of Nazareth with the Holy Ghost and with power: who went about doing good, and healing all that were oppressed of the devil; for God was with him.
v.39 And we are witnesses of all things which he did both in the land of the Jews, and in Jerusalem; whom they slew and hanged on a tree:
v.40 Him God raised up the third day, and shewed him openly;
v.41 Not to all the people, but unto witnesses chosen before of God, *even* to us, who did eat and drink with him after he rose from the dead.
v.42 And he commanded us to preach unto the people, and to testify that it is he which was ordained of God *to be* the Judge of quick and dead.
v.43 To him give all the prophets witness, that through his name whosoever believeth in him shall receive remission of sins.
v.44 While Peter yet spake these words, the Holy Ghost fell on all them which heard the word.
v.45 And they of the circumcision which believed were astonished, as many as came with Peter, because that on the Gentiles also was poured out the gift of the Holy Ghost.
v.46 For they heard them speak with tongues, and magnify God. Then answered Peter,
v.47 Can any man forbid water, that these should not be baptized, which have received the Holy Ghost as well as we?
v.48 And he commanded them to be baptized in the name of the Lord. Then prayed they him to tarry certain days."

1-8 The story of Peter from 9:32 to 10:48 constitutes the only record of one of his missionary journeys in this book. Ch.9 presents him resident for a time in Joppa, some thirty miles south along the Mediterranean coast from Caesarea, the administrative Roman capital of the district, including Jerusalem.

A centurion was not a particularly high-ranking officer in the Roman army. In spite of the fact that the Jews staged rebellions against them (see 5:36-37), some were influenced by their religion, and some of them had benefitted from the healing powers of the Saviour (Matt 8:5-13; Luke 7:1-10).

Cornelius was obviously a God-fearer and very charitable. Such was his belief in God, that he was at prayer. Family and servants were alike God-fearing. Lovers of the gospel know that good works and devotions do not save, although they are not to be condemned, particularly when the people concerned have not heard the gospel message. Individuals in two successive chapters of Acts practised them: Dorcas because she was a believer, and Cornelius in spite of the fact that he was not. However, Cornelius' piety and prayers attracted divine attention. He is like Job in the OT, living according to the light given, in accordance with Rom 2:10-11. But the light of creation and that of Judaism have been overtaken by the light of the glorious gospel of Christ – "the glory that excelleth" (2 Cor 3:10). So God takes pity on the sincere Roman who in no sense is rejecting the gospel message, and in a miraculous fashion arranges for him to hear the gospel of Christ, knowing the results beforehand.

9-23 The circumstances were dramatic! A sincere God-fearer is living some thirty miles from the leading apostle. With the benefit of hindsight we can see that Peter was in Joppa *both* for the sake of raising Dorcas from the dead *and* for the sake of pointing Cornelius to the Saviour. But Peter is far more prejudiced than the cultured Saul of Tarsus. He took one step forward in the direction of God's "whosoever" when he went down to Samaria in ch.8. He was obviously taking another step forward when he took up residence in Simon the tanner's house in Joppa. Now he is to take a gaint leap forward in ch.10. He is to learn that "God is no respecter of persons: but in every nation he that feareth him, and worketh righteousness, is accepted with him" (vv.34-35). Nevertheless, subsequently Peter remained the apostle to the Jews (Gal 2:8).

First God spoke to Cornelius through an angelic vision. The centurion's use of the title "Lord" shows that the Holy Spirit was already working in his heart. He was given instructions as to where to find a man who would have a message for him, "what thou oughtest to do" (v.6). In Peter's message, there is only one thing that the men had to "do", namely, "believe". Three men were therefore sent to Joppa for Peter, the two "household servants" being in the plural as a mark of confirmation of their errand.

The next day Peter received his instructions, also by a vision (but under different circumstances, for great hunger affected him physically, and for a little time he was no longer in mental contact with the world around him). God used the method of a great sheet with unclean animals (according to the law), and a voice from heaven.

God often informs the two parties about His intentions. Thus in ch.9, both Saul and Ananias were informed independently. In 13:2, the prophets and teachers were informed, whereas Saul had been informed in 26:17. This was not necessarily always so; in 18:27 Apollos had his own exercise, but the believers in Achaia were informed by Aquila and Priscilla. Personal and uncorroborated claims to have received divine guidance are sometimes suspect, particularly when there may be a self-spirit of boastfulness and elevation above many who do not receive such calls.

Peter's reserve about breaking the Mosaic law's rules about uncleanness was challenged three times in the vision. The origin of the vision was "heaven" (v.16), yet his disobedient response was, "Not so, Lord", standing in sharp contrast to Saul's obedient response in 9:6, "Lord, what wilt thou have me to do?" In both cases, whether obedient or disobedient, the title "Lord" was used. How can we call Jesus Lord, and not do the things that He says? The thrice-given vision followed by the direction of the Spirit (v.19) and the arrival of the three messengers from Cornelius, caused Peter to agree to go. The double journey could not be accomplished in one day, perhaps on foot, so they stayed overnight. Here we have three Gentiles staying in a Jewish home, while later seven Jews entered into a Roman house. The number of witnesses for the great event to follow is being multiplied. This special event must not be done in a corner, for later Peter had to convince the apostles and brethren at Jerusalem and in Judaea (11:1-2).

(It is interesting to note that in the two great conversion stories in Acts 9 and 10, God provided those involved with addresses to visit. In 9:11, Ananias was told to call at Judas' house, Straight St., Damascus, where Saul was staying. In 10:5-6, Cornelius was told to send men to find Peter care of Simon the tanner, at his house by the seaside.) Everything was done so specifically, finally producing Peter's response, "What was I, that I could withstand God?" (11:17). In other words, the Lord knows the house and its contents of each believer.

24-33 Anticipating the coming of the Lord's servant whose name he had received from the angel, Cornelius was not content with a private audience. His prayers had been heard, but he was not going to be selfish; v.6 states that Peter shall tell *thee*, but in the event "many ... were come together". In v.28, Peter was very honest, and first stated his prejudices which he now realised could not be maintained. It was against the law for a Jew to company with or visit anybody from another nation, but now he was discovering the greatest lesson of Acts 10, "God is no respecter of persons". This statement is found more than half a dozen times in Scripture, but it was never as absolutely true as here. In judgments, there was to be no respect of persons; there was to be absolute fairness, with no bias. But here Peter is learning that the middle wall of partition has been broken down (Eph 2:13-18); the enmity has been abolished. The address which follows ends on a high note that should thrill the soul of every saint, "whosoever believeth in him shall receive remission of sins" (v.43). Later Peter described this experience in 15:7, "God made choice among us, that the Gentiles by my mouth hear the word of the gospel, and believe"; "God ... put no difference between us and them, purifying their hearts by faith" (v.9).

Peter's fifth address was delivered, not in a christian meeting room, but in a private house to a ready-gathered audience. It was obviously not the first house meeting in Palestine, but it was the first in a Gentile home.

34-43 The audience had obviously been in Palestine long enough to know the story, at least in the days of the flesh of the Lord Jesus. Peter was there to explain to them the significance of that story, starting with what they already knew of the story. To preach "over the heads" of the people is not true gospel preaching at all. Like all recountings of it, God's part in it is stressed: God is no respecter of persons; God anointed Jesus of Nazareth with the Holy Spirit for service: God was with Him; God raised Him from the dead; God chose the witnesses; God had appointed Him to be the Judge of the living and the dead. Readers can easily find in the Gospels supporting statements that prove these facts. The Saviour's command to His servants was to preach to the people; God's command to the world is to repent. It may not generally serve any purpose to tell Gentiles what the Jewish OT had to say in advance of this story (except a passing reference to the prophets in the v.43) but the audience was probably composed of potential proselytes. Such, like Lydia later, seem to have been easier to persuade than intransigent Jews that Jesus fulfilled all Jewish hopes.

It is interesting to note that Peter called the cross "a tree" (v.39). This was his personal way of speaking about it. Perhaps his later role as apostle to the Jews makes this more appropriate. Paul preferred to use the word "cross". They both meant the same, but their personal descriptive words had particular significance to the people among whom they worked. The burden of the gospel message must be the same for everyone, but the presentation of it must take into account the nature of the audience. Peter's Jewish mind would link the tree with Deut 21:23 and the consequent curse (though he was speaking to Gentiles here). Paul's Gentile audiences would largely be ignorant of that association unless they had come under Jewish influence. So he preferred to refer to the "cross" with all its associations for the Roman world. Only slaves and the worst of criminals were crucified. Either way, the Lord's deep humiliation is involved.

And Peter does not condemn good works. In fact, he stresses how much the "Lord of all" practised them. However, they are not the grounds of salvation, even though they are highly commendable. How much poorer the world would be for the lack of them. But the requirement of Peter's preaching is stressed, "whosoever believeth in him shall receive remission of sins".

44-48 Clearly, Peter had not yet concluded his address; this is an example of an "interrupted meeting". It is also clear that all believed at the same moment, as soon as "remission of sins" by faith was mentioned. (Compare this with the abrupt ending of Paul's address in Athens, as soon as he mentioned the subject of the Lord's resurrection, 17:31.) No evangelist would mind a new convert interrupting his address, but when an infidel does so it can be particularly awkward.

While Peter was still speaking, the Holy Spirit fell "on all them which heard the word". Some have suggested that the word "all" includes the Jews with Peter, and even Peter himself, but this is most improbable since they already possessed the Holy Spirit. Some have called this a "second Pentecost", but again this is more improbable, since the Spirit was given once according to promise – not half the Spirit at one time and the other half an another time (we speak reverently). The Spirit was always available after Pentecost, and all new converts were baptised into the one Spirit. It was unusual for a special manifestation of the Spirit to be made (only four times in the Acts). The thousands of other converts in Jerusalem experienced the "usual" possession of the Spirit, affecting the character of the convert, his moral and spiritual fruit, as well as spiritual gifts and power for life and service. The original three and five thousand converts in Jerusalem were thus endued, as was promised in 2:28, but no longer was there any rushing mighty wind and no cloven tongues like as of fire. That happened once, and that at Pentecost when the Spirit was sent from heaven. Later, Peter related that these Gentile converts were "baptised with the Holy Ghost", and that God had given them "the like gift as he did unto us" (11:16-17). The Spirit was already present for the baptism to take place.

The evidence of believing in the christian age is the reception of the Holy Spirit, with the great changes that this effects. The proof of Gentile conversion was seen, not in the inward working of the Spirit, but in the outward expression of the Spirit's presence. This was necessary under such new circumstances. The blessings of what had happened on the day of Pentecost in Acts 2 now became the portion of this group of Cornelius and his friends. No wonder Peter's six Jewish friends were astonished at an event so unexpected, but they could neither doubt not deny what had happened. They would be with Peter to substantiate his claims in Jerusalem that the Gentiles had been converted and that the Spirit had been received (11:12). Such believers could not even attempt to justify any denial or rejection of what God had done. Certainly those in Jerusalem believed this testimony (11:18). But had the Spirit not been manifested openly upon the Gentiles, no tangible proof could have been conveyed back to Jerusalem that conversion had really been effected. Today, many evangelists can sadly wonder whether a "confession of faith" is genuine because of any lack of evidence subsequently in the person's life and spiritual interests.

Certainly what took place in Cornelius' house was reminiscent of Pentecost in a certain manner, but it was not a repetition of Pentecost, firstly for the Jews and secondly for the Gentiles. The Holy Spirit (already given) fell (v.44); the Holy Spirit was poured out as a gift (v.45); the Holy Spirit was received (v.47). The reason why Peter knew that this had occurred is because of the word "For" commencing v.46, namely because of one particular outwardly manifest gift. This is the second example of speaking in languages in the Acts, but it does not seem to have had the same immediate purpose as the first in ch.2. Originally in ch.2, this gift had been received in a house, but it had been used as a sign to those who did not believe, being used outside the house, and enabling the visitors to Jerusalem to hear "the wonderful works of God" in their languages; the original purpose in Acts 10:46 was to "magnify God". What they did with their gift outside the house we are not told. It is not likely that there were pilgrims to Caesarea from outside the area who would need testimony in their own languages; Jerusalem was the place of pilgrimage, the city of the great King, the place which God had chosen to place His name there.

Ch.2 saw the birth of the church; ch.10 proved that the Gentiles had been admitted on equal terms to that same church, and that they were fellow-members of the same body.

The reception of the Spirit preceded water baptism, and was not the result of the laying on of Peter's hands after baptism as in the case of Samaria; the former is the pattern for the present age. Where distinctions occur in the NT, there is always a specific reason for them.

Note that the exercise for baptism did not come from Cornelius (as in the case of the Ethiopian eunuch). Rather, baptism was a command from the evangelist Peter, and there was no resistance to this on Cornelius' part. No doubt evangelists today do not issue such commands because there is no immediate outward affect of the presence of the Spirit of God in a new convert. Note also that the evangelist did not disappear as soon as he had gained converts; he tarried for "certain days", evidently to engage in a teaching ministry. Did not the Lord Jesus tarry in Sychar for two days after the people recognised Him as "the Saviour of the world" (John 4:40, 43)? Yet now Peter was going to be questioned for his actions, but the Gentile world had been invaded by the gospel of Christ.

c. Repentance Granted to Gentiles (11:1-18)

v.1 "And the apostles and brethren that were in Judæa heard that the Gentiles had also received the word of God.

v.2 And when Peter was come up to Jerusalem, they that were of the circumcision contended with him.

v.3 Saying, Thou wentest in to men uncircumcised, and didst eat with them.

v.4 But Peter rehearsed *the matter* from the beginning, and expounded *it* by order unto them, saying,

v.5 I was in the city of Joppa praying: and in a trance I saw a vision, A certain vessel descend, as it had been a great sheet, let down from heaven by four corners; and it came even to me:

v.6 Upon the which when I had fastened mine eyes, I considered, and saw fourfooted beasts of the earth, and wild beasts, and creeping things, and fowls of the air.

v.7 And I heard a voice saying unto me, Arise, Peter; slay and eat.

v.8 But I said, Not so, Lord: for nothing common or unclean hath at any time entered into my mouth.

v.9 But the voice answered me again from heaven, What God hath cleansed, *that* call not thou common.

v.10 And this was done three times: and all were drawn up again into heaven.

v.11 And, behold, immediately there were three men already come unto the house where I was, sent from Cæsarea unto me.

v.12 And the Spirit bade me go with them, nothing doubting. Moreover these six brethren accompanied me and we entered into the man's house:

v.13 And he shewed us how he had seen an angel in his house, which stood and said unto him, Send men to Joppa, and call for Simon, whose surname is Peter;

v.14 Who shall tell thee words, whereby thou and all thy house shall be saved.

v.15 And as I began to speak, the Holy Ghost fell on them, as on us at the beginning.
v.16 Then remembered I the word of the Lord, how that he said, John indeed baptized with water; but ye shall be baptized with the Holy Ghost.
v.17 Forasmuch then as God gave them the like gift as *he did* unto us, who believed on the Lord Jesus Christ; what was I, that I could withstand God?
v.18 When they heard these things, they held their peace and glorified God, saying, Then hath God also to the Gentiles granted repentance unto life."

We can make but few comments on this paragraph, important as it is, since we have Peter repeating what had happened in Joppa and in Caesarea (11:5-17).

1-18 On his return to Jerusalem, Peter was challenged for having eaten with uncircumcised Gentiles. "They ... of the circumsision" are Jews who had believed (see 10:45), but evidently they were as prejudiced as Peter had been. There is the added suggestion here that they were beginning to crystallise into a party who looked on circumcision (and other legal rites) as indispensible obligations. Happily they were prepared to listen as Peter related the salient facts of his visit, culminating in the Holy Spirit falling on the company assembled in Cornelius' home.

Thus ends the fourth section of the Acts – on the high-water mark as far as the Gentiles are concerned, that God had granted to Gentile sinners repentance unto life.

Peter's defence of his actions with respect to Cornelius can be summarised as follows:

1. Three times God had spoken to him in a vision of the great sheet full of unclean animals. "A threefold cord is not quickly broken" (Eccl 4:12). (The number of "threes" in Peter's life is remarkable, and the reader can search them out.) Similarly, young Samuel had received a threefold call to his mission, another major departure in God's way with His people (1 Sam 3).
2. His evidence could be corroborated by the six men who had accompanied him from Joppa to Caesarea (v.12). The use of the word "these" suggests that all these six men accompanied him later to Jerusalem.
3. The Spirit had expressly bidden him to go "nothing doubting". This verb means to differ, either with others or with oneself. "Nothing" may imply not being at all hesitant, or, not making unwarranted distinctions between Jew and Gentile, an allusion to the lesson intended by the vision.
4. The greatest evidence of all was the falling of the Holy Spirit on the audience (v.15). In a sense this was the final seal. See 2 Cor 1:2; Eph 1:13; 4:30.
5. It was God who had given them "the like gift" (literally, the equal gift), not Peter who, conscious of his nothingness, recoiled from even the suggestion of forbidding or hindering Him (v.17).

The verdict of the Jewish believers upon hearing this testimony from one whom they could trust was, "Then hath God also to the Gentiles granted repentance unto life" (v.18). No doubt devout Jews would be amazed at God's willingness to grant them life on such simple terms as faith. The meeting seems to have ended harmoniously, but unhappily it was not the end of the controversy, for Judaisers plagued the work of the apostle Paul as long as he lived and preached.

Acts 8, 9 & 10

	Name of New Convert	Colour	Race	Home Continent	Agent of Conversion	Where it Happened	Agent Guided by
Acts 8	Ethiopian Eunuch	Black	Ham	Africa	Philip	Gaza – S. Palestine	Angel of the Lord
Acts 9	Saul	Yellow	Shem	Asia	Jesus	Damascus – N. Palestine	God (Gal 1:15)
Acts 10	Cornelius	White	Japheth	Europe	Peter	Joppa – C. Palestine	Vision

All three were baptised, the Ethiopian and Cornelius immediately, and Saul three days after his conversion.

If Acts 2 shows the partial demolition of the language barriers created at Babel in Gen 9. Then Acts 8, 9 and 10 show the ignoring of racial barriers in the church. These conversions are harbingers of the hymn. "Elect from every nation, Yet one o'er all the earth".

See Pages 120 & 121 for an Analysis of Peter's Addresses

IV. The Witness to the Uttermost Part of the Earth (11:19-28:31)

1. *Antioch*
    11:19-31

    v.19 "Now they which were scattered abroad upon the presecution that arose about Stephen travelled as far as Phenice, and Cyprus, and Antioch, preaching the word to none but unto the Jews only.

    v.20 And some of them were men of Cyprus and Cyrene, which, when they were come to Antioch, spake unto the Grecians, preaching the Lord Jesus.

    v.21 And the hand of the Lord was with them: and a great number believed, and turned unto the Lord.

    v.22 Then tidings of these things came unto the ears of the church which was in Jerusalem: and they sent forth Barnabas, that he should go as far as Antioch.

    v.23 Who, when he came, and had seen the grace of God, was glad, and exhorted them all, that with purpose of heart they would cleave unto the Lord.

    v.24 For he was a good man, and full of the Holy Ghost and of faith: and much people was added unto the Lord.

    v.25 Then departed Barnabas to Tarsus, for to seek Saul:

> v.26 And when he had found him, he brought him unto Antioch. And it came to pass, that a whole year they assembled themselves with the church, and taught much people. And the disciples were called Christians first in Antioch.
> v.27 And in these days came prophets from Jerusalem unto Antioch.
> v.28 And there stood up one of them named Agabus, and signified by the Spirit that there should be great dearth throughout all the world: which came to pass in the days of Claudius Cæsar.
> v.29 Then the disciples, every man according to his ability, determined to send relief unto the brethren which dwelt in Judæa:
> v.30 Which also they did, and sent it to the elders by the hands of Barnabas and Saul."

19-22 V.19 represents a major turning-point in the book as a whole. It does not merely see a wider circumference for the spread of the gospel, it also sees the emergence of a new centre, Antioch. This new centre emerged as the direct result of that scattering which came about from the death of Stephen and the following persecution. 8:4 had said, "they that were scattered abroad went every where preaching the word". Thus Philip went to a city of Samaria; others had gone as far as Phenice (on the coastline of modern Syria), Cyprus (the island in the eastern Mediterranean), and Antioch (in Syria). In all three places the preaching was originally confined to Jewish audiences, and no doubt this continued until news reached them that God had granted repentance, forgiveness and the Holy Spirit to the Gentiles. But others who came to Antioch had a wider vision.

Some of these scattered christian preachers from Cyprus and Cyrene (presumably in Africa) had a wider evangelistic horizon, and extended their preaching to Grecians or Hellenes. The substance of their preaching was "the Lord Jesus". Gospel preaching with a minimum of the Lord Jesus tucked away in a corner is no gospel preaching at all. One small address in the Acts with no mention of the Lord is 14:15-17, but this was no gospel address, rather an attempt to avoid idolatry. Paul's address in Athens (17:22-31), where only the last verse mentions the Lord in judgment, is another example, but under unusual circumstances; it was not a gospel address.

The result was that "a great number believed", turning to the Lord; this must have changed the composition of the church at Antioch. Just as when the news of blessing from Samaria reached Jerusalem, the apostolic leaders Peter and John were sent to Samaria to see the work that God was doing, similarly, when the news about Gentile blessing at Antioch was received in Jerusalem (that is, by "the ears of the church") they sent one man to see what God had wrought. The man whom they trusted, Barnabas, was sent. Note that he did not choose by himself to go, as a result of an exercise before the Lord. Rather, the Jerusalem church decided that he should go, and he willingly agreed.

23-24 Barnabas has appeared in the Acts before; he was the large-hearted Cypriot who sold his family possessions and gave all the proceeds to the church (4:36-37). He had been the one whom the Jerusalem church could trust when he gave testimony

An Analysis of Peter's Addresses

	Acts 2	Acts 3	Acts 4	Acts 5	Acts 10
Life of Christ	"a man approved of God.... among you by miracles and wonders and signs, which God did by him" (2:22)				"God anointed Jesus of Nazareth... who went about doing good, and healing all that were oppressed of the devil" (10:38)
Death of Christ	"him, being delivered by the determinate counsel and foreknowledge of God, ye have taken, and by wicked hands have crucified and slain" (2:23)	"ye denied the Holy One and the Just, and desired a murderer to be granted unto you: and killed the Prince of life" (3:14-15)	"whom ye crucified" (4:10)	"whom ye slew and hanged on a tree" (5:30)	"whom they slew and hanged on a tree" (10:39)
Resurrection of Christ	"whom God hath raised up, having loosed the pains of death: because it was not possible that he should be holden of it" (2:24); "This Jesus hath God raised up" (2:32)	"whom God hath raised from the dead; whereof we are witnesses" (3:15)	"whom God raised from the dead" (4:10)	"The God of our fathers raised up Jesus" (5:30)	"him God raised up the third day, and showed him openly..." (10:40-41)

Ascension of Christ	"Therefore being by the right hand of God exalted ... God hath made that same Jesus, whom ye have crucified, both Lord and Christ" (2:33-36)	"whom the heaven must receive (3:21)		"Him hath God exalted with his right hand to be a Prince and a Saviour" (5:31)
Message for Audience	"Repent...for the remission of sins" (2:28)	"Repent...and be converted, that your sins may be blotted out" (3:19)	"Neither is there salvation in any other" (4:12)	"to give repentance ... and forgiveness of sins" (5:31)	"through his name whosoever believeth in him shall receive remission of sins" (10:43)
Holy Spirit	"he hath shed forth this, which ye now see and hear"; "ye shall receive the gift of the Holy Ghost", (2:33, 38)			"the Holy Ghost, whom God hath given to them that obey him" (v.32)	"these ... have received the Holy Ghost as well as we" (10:47)
The Coming of Christ		"whom the heaven must receive until the times of restitution of all things" (3:21)			"it is he which was ordained of God to be the Judge of quick and dead" (10:42)

to the conversion of Saul (9:27). Luke describes him in language that he uses of nobody else, "a good man, and full of the Holy Ghost and of faith". He uses this full description in spite of the fact that by the time he wrote the book, Barnabas was no longer the companion of Paul.

Luke's description of what Barnabas found at Antioch is interesting, "when he ... had seen the grace of God". The evidence of it lay in the fact that Gentiles were welcomed into the church. Barnabas' exhortation is one which must be valid in all circumstances, "with purpose of heart they would cleave unto the Lord". It is not only how we start that matters, but how we continue to the finish.

If the hand of the Lord had been with the preachers before Barnabas arrived, resulting in a great number believing, there was further blessing after he came, obviously because he was a man of spiritual gift. "Much people was added unto the Lord". There seems to be progression in the statements made:

1. "A great number believed, and turned unto the Lord" (v.21). This implies conversion.
2. "They would cleave unto the Lord" (v.23), implying a deep personal relationship with the Lord.
3. "Much people was added unto the Lord" (v.24), suggesting that there was now an adherence to church principles.

25 Seeing the magnitude of the task before him, Barnabas thought of Saul as a helper, and so departed from Tarsus to find him. It is instructive to note that he did not think that anyone else in Jerusalem could offer the same help as Saul could offer.

26 Barnabas' spiritual gift was that of "exhortation", but he knew that the exercise of other gifts also was necessary for the building up of a local church. Barnabas knew his limitations (we all have them when we restrict ourselves to the gift or gifts granted by the Holy Spirit), but he had already appreciated the truth of Rom 12:7-8, "he that teacheth, (let him wait) on teaching; or he that exhorteth, (let him wait) on exhortation". A young church such as at Antioch would not as yet have developed teachers, yet they needed teaching; Barnabas' exhortations were not enough. Saul was the man to fill the gap for as long as necessary – "a whole year".

How long Saul had been at Tarsus we can scarcely guess, and how he spent his time there is unknown to us. But Conybeare and Howson suggest the following: "Whatever length of time had elapsed since Saul came from Jerusalem to Tarsus, and however that time had been employed – whether he had already founded any of those churches in his native Cilicia, which we read about soon after (Acts 15:41), whether as is highly probable, he had there undergone any of those manifold labours and sufferings recorded by himself in 2 Cor 11, but omitted by Luke, or whether he had been waiting in silence for the call of God, praying for guidance, reflecting on the condition of the Gentiles, and gazing more and more closely on the plan of the world's redemption, it all ended with the arrival of his good friend, Barnabas, with the call to join him in the Syrian metropolis, Antioch". We must bear in mind, of course, the fact that he already knew that he would ultimately be called to testify to the Gentiles (9:15; 22:21; 26:17). The question in Saul's mind was, When?

"They assembled themselves with (or, in) the church" for a whole year, and much people were taught. Note that they did not have any particular status over and above the other believers in the church; one was an exhorter and one was a teacher, using gifts that the risen Lord had given them. At that stage, Saul had not even been designated as an apostle; this name of authority would not be used until the first missionary journey, when his name was changed from Saul to Paul. Neither were he and Barnabas "resident pastors" in the church at Antioch, as if their use of gifts gave them control and administrative rights over the church. We are not told how Saul lived financially, but it seems unlikely that he relied upon the other believers to support him. Elsewhere, he said that his own hands ministered to his necessities (20:34), and on his missionary journeys we never read that the church at Antioch sent him funds, for only the church at Philippi did that (Phil 4:15). Paul later wrote, "If we have sown unto you spiritual things, is it a great thing if we shall reap your carnal things? (1 Cor 9:11); "The labourer is worthy of his reward" (1 Tim 5:18).

Such an impact was made on the city by the believers that they earned for themselves (probably as a nickname) the designation "Christians", presumably meaning followers of Christ, the first time that it had been given to His followers anywhere. The name is used only three times in the NT (26:28; 1 Pet 4:16). Today, the name has a very wide application, firstly to the small number of true believers in the Lord Jesus, and secondly to the unbelieving masses of Christendom. This is unfortunate, for it now conveys a wrong impression to the world when a true believer uses the designation of himself. The same may also be said about the word "church".

27-28 V.27 introduces us to men with a new gift in the early church; they are given the same designation as a similar set of men in the OT, namely, prophets. Their function at both periods of history was to bring messages direct from God for their generation, whether of a moral, judgmental or foretelling nature. In the NT they certainly brought ministry direct from the Lord in days when the NT had not yet been given. Prophets are first mentioned in the Jerusalem church, and perhaps it is understandable that they should first have arisen there in direct collaboration with the apostles. They are then found in the church at Antioch 13:1). Later, prophets were working in the Corinthian church (1 Cor 14), while Eph 2:20 implies that the apostles laid the foundation of the NT church. But 1 Cor 13:8 shows that prophecies would cease when their particular function was no longer required. One can rightly be suspicious when individuals through church history – and today as well – claimed to be prophets. Generally their claims have conflicted with the Scriptures, while some of their wilder claims have had no fulfilment whatsoever. We have no need of prophets when we have the complete canon of Scripture.

A group of prophets from Jerusalem arrived at Antioch with a burden on their hearts. In particular, Agabus (who will reappear in 21:10) prophesied a world-wide famine and clearly the church believed his prediction. Agabus and the others were not deceivers like the "false prophets" (2 Pet 2:1); there would indeed be a famine. It is possible for churches to be deceived by false prophets – or just false men – about financial matters, and for churches unwittingly to deal out money in a spirit of love when the money is merely being collected by men engaged in trickery. The Lord commended the woman who gave two mites, but we are sure that the money was not spent by the temple authorities for God's service.

29 Luke then introduces the great relief problem which faced the early church. The famine would be the main cause of the problem, rather than the fact that the believers in Jerusalemm had given all that they possessed to the church funds. But the ultimate poverty of the Jerusalem church caused Paul later to refer to this church as "the poor saints which are Jerusalem" (Rom 15:26). This was a continuing practical problem which was to occupy the attention of the apostle Paul when he wrote several of his pre-imprisonment epistles. The subject is mentioned in Rom 15:16, 25-28; 1 Cor 16:1-4; 2 Cor 8, 9, when Paul was gathering together a large sum of money on his third missionary journey, to be taken especially to Jerusalem.

It was commendable that the first Christians should have taken care of their widows in ch.6, but it is an extra tribute to the grace of God that the new Gentile believers in Antioch should have responded to the needs of the Jews who until then (as a nation) had regarded them as dogs and outcasts. Long before Paul encouraged Gentile believers to respond to the fact that they were included in divine blessings, reserved in the old economy for Jews only, by sharing their material possessions with Jewish believers when they were in need, these Christians in Antioch had already done this, and Saul had witnessed it.

When distance intrudes, the community of goods which was practised when the church was almost entirely in Jerusalem is no longer possible. Paul later laid down the principle: "I mean not that other men be eased, and ye burdened: but by an equality, that ... your abundance may be a supply for their want, that their abundance also may be a supply for your want: that there may be equality" (2 Cor 8:13-14). Paul is not writing about equality in possessions and finance among all believers in all local assemblies; otherwise he would have soon ensured that some of the Corinthian wealth should be sent to Philippi; rather, he appears to be writing about an equality in the opportunity of providing for need when it arose. Sometimes, believers may long for guidance about how much to give, especially since tithing was well known in the OT before and after the giving of the law, but this was essentially for the priests and Levites. But no such guidance is given in the NT. Luke simply informs us that the Christians in Antioch gave "every man according to his ability". When Paul later urged believers in Corinth to join in relief work, he used the words "as God hath prospered" (1 Cor 16:2).

30 For the first time, though not the last, Paul, or Saul as he was still called, was one of the two chosen to carry the bounty of the saints to Jerusalem. (Other occasions are mentioned in Rom 15:25, 26, 28; 1 Cor 15:4; 2 Cor 8:19). He obviously did not consider this kind of service beneath his dignity as a teacher, evangelist and apostle. No "group of seven" was appointed to perform such tasks, as in Acts 6. But always at least two men were sent, chosen by the church or churches concerned, so that honesty should be seen as openly practised. That is what went wrong when Judas had the bag; he was a one-man treasurer and he was a thief. Only the Lord knew what he was doing when no one else was looking! Thus Saul was as willing to meet the material needs of the Lord's people as he was anxious later to meet their spiritual needs.

It is interesting to note that the relief was sent to the elders at Jerusalem. In ch.15 when the question of sharing the gospel with the Gentiles is in view, the apostles are prominent with the elders, but here in 11:30 it was the elders alone; the apostles had relinquished financial responsibilities in 6:2. and had not taken them back since. This highlights the fact that there were now apostles, prophets and elders in the church of God at Jerusalem. Saul's first visit to this city after his conversion (9:26) was presumably because at some previous stage he had made his home there, when he had sat at the feet of Gamaliel for instruction. Now his second visit was to convey material relief to hungry believers, and his third would be to resolve a difficult problem that was perplexing the early church. Although he had been called by Barnabas to help establish new converts in Antioch in the faith, yet after one year he and Barnabas could be spared to convey the love-gift of the Antiochan Christians to Jerusalem. Later they returned to Antioch (12:25), but Luke first inserts the story of the martyrdom of the first apostle at the hands of Herod, and the subsequent events occupy most of ch.12.

Notes

Names Given to the Believers

It need not be surprising that the Acts continues to call the believers "disciples". The word indicates one who follows with a view to learning. It is a very prominent word in all the Gospels; thus the Lord Jesus had His disciples; John the Baptist had his, and the Pharisees had theirs. It is used to describe believers in the Lord Jesus twenty-nine times in the Acts, far fewer than any of the Gospels, and the word is never used again in the NT, although new names for them are introduced. The last time the word is used is in 21:16, where we read of "one Mnason of Cyprus, an old disciple". We tend not to use the word today, no doubt because of Heb 8:13, "that which ... waxeth old is ready to vanish away."

The word "witness" is used by the Lord Himself to describe these disciples in Luke 24:48. Thereafter Luke uses it eleven times in the Acts. It ought not to require any great skill to be a witness. He is simply expected to tell what he knows and to say what he has seen. The strength of any movement, whether spiritual or secular, depends on such witnesses. To be a witness, there are no qualifications required in age, sex or in education.

The first new name given to the believers is that of "saints". It is first used by Ananias to God in 9:13. After this, it occurs only three other times in the Acts. It means "holy or separated ones", not because of any degree of practical holiness which they may have practised, but because of the Saviour's work for them. It was used in the OT to describe angels and priests among others, but in the NT is is used to describe all ordinary Christians. Christendom uses the word to describe those who are dead, but the Bible uses it to describe living ones. The apostle Paul loved the word, and used it to refer to his fellow-believers in every letter that he wrote.

The other new name given to them was "Christians". This word is used only three times in the NT, although now it has become the most common description of followers of the Lord Jesus, both nominal and genuine. The first occurrence is in 11:26. As we have remarked before, it is obviously a nickname adopted by the people of Antioch to describe those who had become followers of Christ. In a city considerably removed from Jerusalem, and where these people were unknown before, it is not hard to know why they were given a new distinguishing name.

In 5:14, these new disciples are called "believers". Since the word is a present participle, it may be translated "believing ones".

"Brother" and "brethren" soon came to be used among them to describe their new relationship in Christ to each other. Admittedly the apostles never seem to have ceased calling their fellow-Jews "brethren", but gradually they began to call their fellow-Christians "brethren". The former was a racial relationship, but the latter was based on the fact that those who had come to know God as Father must be brothers one of another. The first use of the word in this new connection appears in 6:3, "Wherefore, brethren, look ye out among you seven men". The sweetest use of it is when Ananias called Saul of Tarsus "brother" (9:17). After this it was commonly used, thirty-three times in the Acts, and frequently in Paul's epistles. John too loved to use it, but Peter used it only three times, and Jude not at all.

World Rulers

Luke pays more attention to historical detail than any other NT writer. He was anxious in his Gospel to show Theophilus the certainty of those things that Christians believe. In his second book he was concerned with the many infallible proofs of Christ's ascension, and Acts is full of the results of the Lord Jesus being alive in heaven.

He is the only NT writer who pays much attention to the names of rulers, both local and imperial, none of them very favourable to the gospel message. Thus he refers to no fewer than four Roman Emperors:

(i) In Luke 2:1 he tells of the world census demanded by Augustus Caesar to replenish his coffers, which made Joseph and Mary travel to the place of their origin, Bethlehem, for the birth of the Saviour, thereby fulfilling the prophecy of Micah 5:2.

(ii) Luke 3:1 mentions among other things that Tiberias Caesar was the Emperor when John Baptist commenced preaching.

(iii) In the Acts, Luke names Claudius Caesar, the subsequent Emperor, twice: first as being Emperor when the famine forecast by the prophet Agabus took place

(11:28), and as being the Emperor who ordered the expulsion of all Jews resident in Rome with the result that Aquila and Priscilla lived in Corinth when Paul came there to preach the gospel.

(iv) In Acts 25:21, Paul's appeal to be heard by Caesar is described by Festus as an appeal to Augustus. It must be borne in mind that "Augustus" is really a title passed on by the original Augustus, Julius Caesar's adopted son and heir. The Augustus Caesar for hearing Paul's appeal is really Nero, the Emperor of such ill-repute. A longer list of the Roman Emperors is given in ch.18.

The NT identifies four Herods:

(i) The king of Judaea who was troubled in Matt 2:1 by the news of the birth of another "King of the Jews", and took steps to exterminate Him, unsuccessfully.

(ii) The second was that tetrarch responsible for the beheading of John Baptist, mentioned in the three Synoptic Gospels and in Acts 4:27; 13:1.

(iii) The third Herod named is the king who was responsible for the death of the first apostolic martyr, James, John's brother, and also for the further imprisonment of Peter.

(iv) That Agrippa, who appears with his wife Bernice as the king who was anxious to hear Paul's "defence" in chs.25, 26, was really Herod Agrippa. He, of all the Herods, was probably the least opposed to the Saviour and His gospel.

We shall return to this subject at the end of ch.25.

2. A *Parenthesis: Herod and the First Apostolic Martyr* 12:1-25

v.1 "Now about that time Herod the king stretched forth *his* hands to vex certain of the church.

v.2 And he killed James the brother of John with the sword.

v.3 And because he saw it pleased the Jews, he proceeded further to take Peter also. (Then were the days of unleavened bread.)

v.4 And when he had apprehended him, he put *him* in prison, and delivered *him* to four quaternions of soldiers to keep him; intending after Easter to bring him forth to the people.

v.5 Peter therefore was kept in prison: but prayer was made without ceasing of the church unto God for him.

v.6 And when Herod would have brought him forth, the same night Peter was sleeping between two soldiers, bound with two chains: and the keepers before the door kept the prison.

v.7 And, behold, the angel of the Lord came upon *him,* and a light shined in the prison: and he smote Peter on the side, and raised him up, saying, Arise up quickly. And his chains fell off from *his* hands.

v.8 And the angel said unto him, Gird thyself, and bind on thy sandals. And so he did. And he saith unto him, Cast thy garment about thee, and follow me.

v.9 And he went out, and followed him; and wist not that it was true which was done by the angel; but thought he saw a vision.

v.10 When they were past the first and the second ward, they came unto the iron gate that leadeth unto the city; which opened to them of his own accord: and they went out, and passed on through one street; and forthwith the angel departed from him.

v.11 And when Peter was come to himself, he said, Now I know of a surety, that the Lord hath sent his angel, and hath delivered me out of the hand of Herod, and *from* all the expectation of the people of the Jews.

v.12 And when he had considered *the thing,* he came to the house of Mary the mother of John, whose surname was Mark; where many were gathered together praying.

v.13 And as Peter knocked at the door of the gate, a damsel came to hearken, named Rhoda.

v.14 And when she knew Peter's voice, she opened not the gate for gladness, but ran in, and told how Peter stood before the gate.

v.15 And they said unto her, Thou art mad. But she constantly affirmed that it was even so. Then said they, It is his angel.

v.16 But Peter continued knocking: and when they had opened *the door,* and saw him, they were astonished.

v.17 But he, beckoning unto them with the hand to hold their peace, declared unto them how the Lord had brought him out of the prison. And he said, Go shew these things unto James, and to the brethren. And he departed, and went into another place.

v.18 Now as soon as it was day, there was no small stir among the soldiers, what was become of Peter.

v.19 And when Herod had sought for him, and found him not, he examined the keepers, and commanded that *they* should be put to death. And he went down from Judæa to Cæsarea, and *there* abode.

v.20 And Herod was highly displeased with them of Tyre and Sidon: but they came with one accord to him, and, having made Blastus the king's chamberlain their friend, desired peace; because their country was nourished by the king's *country.*

v.21 And upon a set day Herod, arrayed in royal apparel, sat upon his throne, and made an oration unto them.

v.22 And the people gave a shout, *saying, It is* the voice of a god, and not of a man.

v.23 And immediately the angel of the Lord smote him, because he gave not God the glory: and he was eaten of worms, and gave up the ghost.

v.24 But the word of God grew and multiplied.

v.25 And Barnabas and Saul returned from Jerusalem, when they had fulfilled *their* ministry, and took with them John, whose surname was Mark."

Most of ch.12 is an insertion into the record of Barnabas and Saul carrying the love-gifts of the saints from Antioch to the famine-stricken believers in Judaea (11:30; 12:25). It is difficult to suggest why Luke should indulge in such a digression unless he wants to demonstrate that the gospel chariot runs on regardless of the opposition, and that the church is still very much active even when political leaders engage in murder and attempted murder. If Judaism has been less active in its suppression of the infant church since the conversion of Saul, then someone else has taken over, at least temporarily, namely, king Herod.

1 Herod is the third king with this name to appear in the NT narrative. Like his grandfather, he is called a king, though his father had been no more than a tetrarch (a ruler of a fourth part of a province; see Luke 3:1 for some of the provinces). However, all three of these Herods had this in common, that they opposed God and His Christ. The first, mentioned in Matt 2, was anxious to destroy the young child Jesus because the wise men had called Him "King of the Jews", and he wanted to preserve his position and authority against any possible opposition; he killed all the young boys around Bethlehem. The second in Matt 14 was responsible for the execution of John Baptist. The third in Acts 12 slew the apostle James, and proposed to take the life of Peter. So all three were murderers. It is easy to regard the Herods as representatives of the devil; other OT characters come to mind as serving the same purpose, and throughout secular history there have always been leaders ready to commit similar crimes for political and religious reasons.

2-4 Acts 12 raises one of the great enigmas of church history, namely, the will of God. This is not mentioned in these verses, nevertheless the question still remains: Why should God allow John's brother, James, to be cut off so early in life, while permitting John himself to serve for another fifty years approximately? Again, why should the God who is able to open prison doors for Peter not also open them for James, thus allowing him to be slain? The immediate answer is that of the hymn-writer:

> "Not now, but in the coming years,
>   It may be in the better land,
> We'll read the meaning of our tears,
>   Somehow, somewhere we'll understand."

It was a sad day for the church. It was Easter, the anniversary of their Lord's death. (This is the only time that the word for Passover, *pascha*, is thus translated in the AV.) James had just been slain with Herod's sword and, noting the Jewish pleasure at his action, the king had just imprisoned Peter for the third time. Herod did not intend to make the mistake that Jewish leaders had apparently made previously, that of having insufficient guards. Four squads of soldiers were commanded to guard him.

5-6 The church has only ever had one true weapon, prayer. Paul wrote that weapons are not carnal (2 Cor 10:4), prayer being the last piece of armour mentioned in Eph 6:18. But throughout most of history Christendom has made much use of the weapons of national armies, as during the Crusades of old.

The church had been born in the atmosphere of prayer (1:14; 2:42), and it continued in that attitude. The AV describes the prayers of the church on Peter's behalf as unceasing, but other translations describe them as being constant, or earnest. There is little doubt that in emergencies our prayers are even more earnest, real and sincere than usual. The prayer meeting continued during the night as well, such was their concern; those who stand by night in the house of the Lord, lifting up hands in the sanctuary, are blessed (Ps 134). Their prayers and their witnessing were according to need, rather than in accordance with any pre-arrangement.

As in earlier similar stories in the Acts, one wonders who were the more perturbed, the persecuted saints or the persecutors. Under the shadow of an approaching trial with the memory of a recently-executed colleague, Peter slept the sleep of the just. Perhaps he had recalled the Lord's words that he would die by crucifixion, and hence not by the sword. Certainly he had slept in failure on the Mount of Transfiguration and in the Garden of Gethsemane, but this time his sleep was in peace with the Lord, "I will both lay me down in peace, and sleep: for thou, Lord, only makest me dwell in safety" (Ps 4:8). Last time he was in prison the guards were outside the cell, but this time he had one on either side of him.

7-12 The ministry of angels is a regular feature in the Acts. The angel of the Lord may sometimes have been the Lord Himself in the OT, but we feel that he can hardly be the Lord in the NT. He appears on five different occasions in the Acts, where he intervened to help God's servants. (See the note on angels in ch.1; they are "ministering spirits".)

In ch.12 he wakened the sleeping Peter, without waking his guards. The angel showed the greatest consideration for him – a light was provided, the chains were removed, sandals were put on, and he had to dress completely, after which the angel led the way. The situation was so extraordinary that Peter did not believe it was happening; he thought it was all a vision in a dream. He still had the same feeling as he was escorted through successive prison wards with no alarm raised anywhere, and finally the massive iron gates leading to the city opened apparently automatically. Only then did the angel leave him on his own, and he knew that there was only one place to go in the circumstances, the house where prayer was in progress. The angel only did miraculously what Peter could not do for himself. Divine intervention generally works like that; God will not do for us what we can do for ourselves.

Only when he was alone in the city (v.11) did Peter realise that it was not a vision, but a reality – the Lord had delivered him. That is what Paul asked the Romans to pray for, "that I may be delivered from them that do not believe in Judaea" (Rom 15:31). In his last Epistle, Paul claimed that "out of them all the Lord delivered me" (2 Tim 3:11), and "I was delivered out of the mouth of the lion" (2 Tim 4:17). Contrast this with the Lord's words to the Father, "what shall I say? Father, save me from this hour: but for this cause came I unto this hour" (John 12:27).

13-17 Rhoda answered Peter's knocking. We have no idea how old she was, but evidently she was acting as a doorkeeper, with the church meeting inside. This reminds us of the verse: "I had rather be a doorkeeper in the house of my God" (Ps 84:10). In her excitement on recognising that it was Peter knocking, she rushed in to the others without as much as opening the door to him. Evidently this is another example of an interrupted meeting (10:44; 20:9). Sometimes the simple faith of the young accepts what older ones through experience do not accept. In the present story, they did not believe Rhoda's assertion – one may ask, How strong was their faith in prayer? What did they expect God to do? In fact, although they knew that Peter had previously been released from prison by divine intervention, those at this prayer meeting sought for other explanations of Rhoda's insistence that it was indeed Peter who was at the unopened door. To suggest, "Thou art mad" was unkindness indeed. Two explanations of "It is his angel" appear possible.

1. Those at the prayer meeting considered that the apparition implied that Peter was dead, and that further prayer was no longer necessary.

2. The Lord Himself had spoken of children having angels in heaven (Matt 18:10), so the Christians may have thought that each believer had a personal guardian angel, particularly since angels are stated to be "ministering spirits, sent forth to minister for them who shall be heirs of salvation" (Heb 1:14). Though it is not clear why they thought that a visible guardian angel should resemble the person in question, thus looking like Peter in the present case. But where faith is absent, irrationality can creep in.

18-23 Peter does not continue preaching as he had done on previous similar occasions. In 5:20, the angel had instructed all the apostles to "stand and speak in the temple to the people all the words of this life", but here no such command was given for what Peter was to do the following morning. Rather, he merely departs for another place, and we read no more of Peter's preaching in the Acts.

Herod is, of course, annoyed, and takes vengeance on the guards. What explanation could they give under examination? but the king commanded that they should be put to death. It was a similar fear that overtook the Philippian jailor when he thought that the prisoners had fled (16:27-30). Just as Peter departed, so Herod departed to his seat of authority, Caesarea. His estranged vassal state of Tyre and Sidon took steps to please him, and so to be restored to his favour. In their desperate desire to please him, they ascribed divine honours to him. "It is the voice of a god, and not of a man". Herod willingly accepted the description that he was a god, in the same way as there will be false Christs (Matt 24:5), and as throughout history there have arisen men who have claimed to be Christ. The man of sin will sit "in the temple of God, showing himself that he is God" (2 Thess 2:4). Herod was but a preview of worse things to come. The same angel of the Lord that delivered Peter now smote Herod for accepting divine status, although the idolaters themselves who worshipped him suffered no harm. Herod "gave up the ghost", whereas the man of sin and false prophet will be "cast alive into a lake of fire burning with brimstone" (Rev 19:20). Breaking the first commandment in any way has solemn consequences.

24-25 This whole episode is parenthetical, for it is immediately followed by the mention of the return of Barnabas and Saul from Jerusalem, the visit having commenced in 11:30. However, in 12:24 the return is preceded by another of Luke's summaries of the progress of the gospel. Let monarchs rise and fall, the word of God will grow and multiply regardless. So Luke injects into his story the relentless progress of the gospel, and accordingly illustrates the fact that the gates of hades will never prevail against the church.

When Barnabas and Saul returned to Antioch, they were accompanied by the first of two younger helpers whom Luke introduces to the reader during the course of his book. He is Mark, Barnabas' young relative, in whose mother's home in Jerusalem most of the major incidents recorded of the early church had taken place. The second younger helper will be Timothy (16:1-3).

So ends the first great section of the Acts, where all the action has been centred in and from Jerusalem.

3. Paul's First Missionary Journey
13:1-14:28

a. Antioch to Cyprus (13:1-13)

v.1 "Now there were in the church that was at Antioch certain prophets and teachers; as Barnabas, and Simeon that was called Niger, and Lucius of Cyrene, and Manaen, which had been brought up with Herod the tetrarch, and Saul.
v.2 As they ministered to the Lord, and fasted, the Holy Ghost said, Separate me Barnabas and Saul for the work whereunto I have called them.
v.3 And when they had fasted and prayed, and laid *their* hands on them, they sent *them* away.
v.4 So they, being sent forth by the Holy Ghost, departed unto Seleucia; and from thence they sailed to Cyprus.
v.5 And when they were at Salamis, they preached the word of God in the synagogues of the Jews: and they had also John to *their* minister.
v.6 And when they had gone through the isle unto Paphos, they found a certain sorcerer, a false prophet, a Jew, whose name *was* Bar-jesus:
v.7 Which was with the deputy of the country, Sergius Paulus, a prudent man; who called for Barnabas and Saul, and desired to hear the word of God.
v.8 But Elymas the sorcerer (for so is his name by interpretation) withstood them, seeking to turn away the deputy from the faith.
v.9 Then Saul, (who also *is called* Paul,) filled with the Holy Ghost, set his eyes on him,
v.10 And said, O full of all subtilty and all mischief, *thou* child of the devil, *thou* enemy of all righteousness, wilt thou not cease to pervert the right ways of the Lord?
v.11 And now, behold, the hand of the Lord *is* upon thee, and thou shalt be blind, not seeing the sun for a sason. And immediately there fell on him a mist and a darkness; and he went about seeking some to lead him by the hand.

v.12 Then the deputy, when he saw what was done, believed, being astonished at the doctrine of the Lord.

v.13 Now when Paul and his company loosed from Paphos, they came to Perga in Pamphylia: and John departing from them returned to Jerusalem."

The focus of attention now switches to Antioch, and brings an important development in the history of the church as a whole. Until now, Jerusalem has been the centre. But no place on earth can be the centre of something heavenly like the church. If the gates of hades are not to prevail against it, it can have neither earthly headquarters nor a human head. Jerusalem's destruction was only less than three decades away, and God would ensure that His church should not be involved in that destruction. Nor was Antioch's prominence to be of unlimited duration. The church that was to survive both the destruction of Jerusalem and the ultimate fall of Rome was not to have Antioch as its seeming headquarters for any length of time. The church is dependent neither on men nor on places.

Moreover, the time had come for the Lord's plans previously stated to be put into effect. He had said to Ananias, "He is a chosen vessel unto me, to bear my name before the Gentiles" (9:15), and He had said to Saul, "I will send thee far hence unto the Gentiles" (22:21; 26:17). The "far hence" was quite distinct from Caesarea where Peter first preached to the Gentiles, for it involved long visits even to Macedonia and Achaia as well as to Asia. At the end of his life, Paul recalled that he had been "appointed a preacher, and an apostle, and a teacher of the Gentiles" (2 Tim 1:11). But he awaited God's time for this great venture to commence; he was content to abide in Caesarea, Tarsus and Antioch before learning of the divine will for his mission to commence.

1-3 As a result of the spiritual nature of the church at Antioch described in 11:19-26, and the teaching of Saul and Barnabas, the church was flourishing. In v.1, the names of certain prophets and teachers are given. Barnabas (named first) and Saul (named last) are familiar names, but now for the first time two sons of Africa are mentioned as possessing particular spiritual gifts in the church. Moreover, turning from racial distinctions to the social, we find that another spiritually-able man in the church at Antioch was the foster-brother of Herod the tetrarch of Galilee.

The prophets were men who received doctrine directly from the Holy Spirit; the teachers were those who passed on and explained such doctrine already revealed. Today, as possessing the NT Scriptures, local churches do not need prophets, but teachers are still needed to expound and explain truth from the Scriptures to the saints.

In Antioch, prophets and teachers had been gifted by the risen Lord, and their ministry had been established through the work of Saul and Barnabas. These particular men met together for fasting and prayer, to learn the mind of the Lord regarding their own work and also that of Saul and Barnabas. This is the last mention of fasting in the NT; (the word does not exist in certain Greek texts in 1 Cor 7:5, and hence does not appear in the translation by JND). During this meeting, the Holy Spirit spoke, no doubt through one or more of the prophets present, and this intervention by the Spirit proved to be one of the great turning-points in the inspired history of the early church. The Spirit's words were few, but to the point, "Separate me Barnabas and Saul for the work whereunto I have called them", though no indication was given as to the nature of the work nor where it was to take place. It was going to be one step at a time as these two men went forth. Paul's subsequent guidance was not always as direct as this (see 15:36; 17:15; 18:21-23, and its contrast in 16:6-9). Individual exercise also plays an important part, though in the background this must be "if God will". There are principles here for all God's servants today. Service that is hastily and rashly conceived may lack the divine will, but a quiet waiting on the Lord, and with counsel taken with others whom one can trust as spiritually-minded, leads to the better pathway of service.

It cannot be overstressed that two parties were involved in this exercise in Antioch. No matter how much the servants to be commended are conscious of the divine intention for them, others in the assembly must also have the same certainty about the will of the Lord, else commendation will be cold and formal.

The record of the Acts presents the following picture:

1. The Jerusalem church sent Peter and John to Samaria (8:14)
2. The Jerusalem church sent Barnabas to Antioch (11:22)
3. The church at Antioch sent Barnabas and Saul to Jerusalem (11:30)
4. When a specific administrative ministry was needed, the church at Jerusalem chose people full of the Spirit to meet that need (6:3).
5. To the prophets and teachers in the church at Antioch, one of the most spiritually-ambitious of all NT churches, the Holy Spirit said, "Separate me Barnabas and Saul for the work whereunto I have called them". It was these men who also sent them away (13:2-3).
6. It was the church at Antioch which determined to send Paul, Barnabas and others to Jerusalem (15:2).

This does not, of course, cover every case in the Acts. But it can be seen clearly that missionary and other enterprise was a natural ongoing part of the life of christian churches. "It is therefore biblical to state that God calls individuals and confirms that call through the local fellowship of believers. The pattern of the NT is most certainly not one of rugged individualism" (*Rethinking Assembly Missionary Strategy*, by Kevin White, Papua, New Guinea).

To return to v.3, this revelation, received by the prophets and teachers from the Spirit of God, resulted in them carrying out the biblical practice of the laying on of hands. This was done neither by the elders nor by the church as a whole. It had little other significance than it had within the context of the OT sacrifices. There the offerer completely identified himself with the offering, either to have its perfection imputed to him as in the case of the burnt offering, or to have his sins imputed to it as in the case of the sin offering. In Antioch, the commending brethren identified themselves completely with the two servants being commended. This subject is further discussed in the Notes following v.13. In 14:26, Saul and Barnabas "had been recommended to the grace of God for the work which they fulfilled". This was not to any particular location nor to any other church, for these were unknown features at the beginning of this first missionary journey; it was "to the grace of God".

Note that "they sent them away". A better rendering of the one Greek word is "they let them go"; that is, they placed no hindrance whatsoever in their leaving Antioch, though both men would be greatly missed.

4-5 The first port of call on what has come to be called Paul's first missionary journey was the home country of his companion Barnabas. It may have been Barnabas' decision to visit his home island first (though, according to 11:19, others had visited Cyprus previously, a country missed out in 2:9-11), and Mark may have been on familiar ground also. In most places they visited, they first of all sought out the Jewish synagogues (v.5), for there might be found pious Jews waiting for the consolation of Israel, not knowing that He had already arrived. There might also be Gentile proselytes present who would understand the OT Scriptures, for Paul knew that his call was to the Gentiles. This was the first of eight places visited by the two newly-commended missionaries from the church at Antioch. What Paul did in Salamis in Cyprus set the pattern for the rest of his journeys. Ready-made audiences were to be found in Jewish synagogues, and as far as Saul was concerned (he is first referred to as Paul in v.9), the commission was to the Jew first and then to the Gentile (Rom 1:16). What duties John Mark did for the two preachers we are not told, but the word "minister" in v.5 used to describe Mark is not "deacon" but h$up\bar{e}ret\bar{e}s$, (strictly an "under-rower"), so formally an attendant or officer. We recall that there were faithful women who accompanied the Lord ministering unto Him (Luke 8:2-3).

It may be that Mark was an apprentice learning the spiritual art of soul winning and church planting from his more experienced brethren, though he had had plenty of opportunity to observe this in and from his mother's home in Jerusalem. The same may be said of Timothy, since in 19:22 he is said to "minister" (the verb now used is $diakone\bar{o}$ unto Paul. Many believers today have every reason to thank God for those with whom they have worked in their younger years, those who not only taught them the word of God but who also showed them the work of God.

6-12 The only place in Cyprus about which Luke gives much detail of the work done is Paphos, on the south-west corner of the island. It was the administrative capital of the island, and had a strong Roman garrison. Luke draws the reader's attention to the Roman proconsul, Sergius Paulus, who is described as a "prudent man". Evidently he was curious about the message brought by the preachers, since he desired to hear the word of God. The other man named in the story was Elymas (meaning "sorcerer"), his court magician. His Jewish name sounds most unpleasant, Bar-jesus, namely "son of Jesus". Everyone in the royal line from David onwards had a son, leading to the Lord Jesus (Matt 1:6-16) who was the final One in this royal line. It stopped at Him, the King of kings and Lords of lords. He had no natural sons, and spiritually believers are sons of the living God. Hence we may see in the name "Bar-jesus" something almost Satanic. Unlike Simon Magus in Samaria (ch.8), he did not join the movement, but he opposed it as an antichrist. Not for the last time (see 16:19) were there those who saw that the hope of their gains would disappear if the gospel made too much progress. So he sought to turn his master, the proconsul, from listening to the gospel. Many in Christendom today would adopt the same tactics, usually introducing practices of the flesh and the doctrines of demons, trying to make these more attractive than blessings through the gospel of Christ.

This was an occasion that called for a special enabling by the Holy Spirit – note that Paul deals with the situation rather than Barnabas. Apart from 9:17 just after his conversion, this is the first mention of Paul being filled with the Spirit, and this gave him the authority necessary for dealing with the Elymas. His condemnation is as severe as that administered by Peter to Simon Magnus. Paul went to the root of the man's heart by using very strong language, "O full of all subtilty and all mischief, thou child of the devil, thou enemy of all righteousness". It is doubtful whether any evangelist would use such words today, but it appears that Paul possessed that spiritual gift that he calls "discerning of spirits" (1 Cor 12:10), for this description goes further than merely trying to turn the proconsul from the faith. The Lord Jesus could discern all hearts; He knew "what was in man" (John 2:25), and therefore He said of the Pharisees, "Ye are of your father the devil" (John 8:44), again a name that evangelists today would not care to use of any unbeliever.

We have previously seen the hand of the Lord in the Acts as imparting blessing (11:21), but now we see the hand of the Lord moving in judgment, for Elymas was blinded for a season. The blindness and the leading by the hand remind us of events that accompanied Paul's conversion, but upon regaining his sight Paul (as Saul) was baptised and was a child of God, but Elymas is not recorded as being anything other than a child of the devil afterwards. In just the same way as "the hand of the Lord" is used in these two distinct connections, so too is the word "visit" in other contexts; God visited His people to give them bread on the one hand, but on the other hand He also visited the iniquity of the fathers on the children.

Luke does not give us any details of Paul's preaching in Cyprus, except that it was "the word of God", but it is interesting to note the impact that it had on Sergius Paulus, who did not have the same background knowledge as Cornelius. What he heard as doctrine, and what he saw as miraculous judgment, caused him to believe and to be "astonished at the doctrine of the Lord" (v.12). Whether Paul was able to use the OT as a background, or whether he preached only the facts of the historical Jesus, we are not told. But can we really envisage the wonder of a totally ignorant but civilised person, when he first heard the story of God manifest in flesh? Can we appreciate the impact of being told that this divine Person died for sins? And NT preaching was never complete without reference to the resurrection. All this must have been involved in "the doctrine of the Lord". This teaching was all climaxed by what the official saw. Miracles of judgment must be impressive, as were miracles of healing, but to these we can add the miracles of conversion. These were the factors that brought the proconsul to the point of believing. The Pharisees thought that they would believe if they saw a sign (Matt 16:1), while those at the cross claimed that they would believe if the Lord came down miraculously from the cross (Mark 15:32); such belief would not be faith at all and stands in contrast with that of the proconsul.

Every evidence of God working ought to be impressive, and the result was that the missionaries left a converted Roman official behind them in Cyprus. Luke does not inform us whether a church was established in Cyprus through other converts being gained as well, but Barnabas later returned to Cyprus (15:39) as if there was more work to be done there.

13 The second sea journey was now embarked upon. It took Paul and Barnabas north to Asia Minor, modern Turkey, first to Perga and then to the second Antioch in the NT, Antioch in Pisidia. What happened in Perga we do not know, but Mark decided to return home to his mother in Jerusalem. It seems that he took this decision as soon as he was on unfamiliar territory, because it would have been easier to go there from Cyprus, rather than waiting until they had visited Perga. Neither did he return to Antioch in Syria to give a report. The later dispute between Paul and Barnabas about John Mark rejoining them shows that Paul was disappointed in him (15:38). Many years later, Paul from prison in Rome could write approvingly about Mark (Col 4:10), so clearly in the period between he had become a changed man in the Lord's service, willing to visit the saints in Colosse in Asia.

Notes

The Laying on of Hands
Four separate uses for the laying on of hands can be identified in the Bible.

1. The first is in connection with the OT sacrifices. The instructions for the consecration of Israel's priests in Exod 29:10, 15, 19 show the priest being consecrated and credited with the unblemished nature of the bullock or ram which is being sacrificed, and he is therefore going to be fit to approach God. These instructions of Exod 29 are seen as being practised in Lev 8:14, 18, 22. And so it was always with Israel's priests. Of course their moral and physical qualifications both prior to and after their consecration had to be consistent with this ritual.

Offerers among the Israelites had to behave similarly when they were offering sacrifices.
(i) It applied to burnt offerings, according to Lev 1:4, presumably again with the symbolic meaning that the perfection of the offering was attributed to the offerer.
(ii) It applied to the peace offering, according to 3:2, 8, 13.
(iii) It applied to the sin offering according to 4:4, 15, 24, 29, 33, with the reverse meaning that the guilt of the offerer is transferred to the unblemished. It occurred again when the living goat was being let loose on the day of atonement carrying the people's

sins away into the uninhabited wilderness. As with the priests when they were being consecrated to serve God, so with the Levites in Num 8:12. Another example is 2 Chron 29:23.

2. If the first use of the laying on of hands in the Bible is peculiar to the OT, then the second is to be found in both Testaments.

(i) Moses laid his hands on Joshua (Deut 34:9) in accordance with the instructions given in Num 27:18, 23, so that Joshua would take over the leadership of Israel as his successor. This laying on of hands was a public act whereby the succession could be seen as having Moses' approval and endorsement.

(ii) Paul did something similar to Timothy according to 2 Tim 1:6. This was more of an act of identification than one of succession, for Paul as an apostle had no successor. This is the second time that such laying on of hands had been practised on the young man. The eldership of his assembly had obviously done this too, identifying themselves with the work to which his gift was leading him (1 Tim 4:14).

(iii) We have already seen that this was practised by the apostles in Acts 6:6 on the so-called six deacons.

(iv) A caution is given about this in 1 Tim 5:22 where Paul is virtually saying that Timothy was not to be in a hurry to identify with people whom he did not know well as being suitable for eldership.

3. The third use of the laying on of hands is found only in the Acts, and that only twice. On both occasions it was done with the intention of people receiving the Holy Spirit.

(i) The first was in 8:17 by Peter and John on the converts in Samaria, resulting in their receiving the Spirit, and in the impostor Simon Magus becoming desirous of using the same power.

(ii) The second case was when Paul laid his hands on the twelve in Ephesus who had not yet heard about the coming of the Holy Spirit.

Only three apostles used this ability, and each on one occasion only. The case in Acts 10 brought the Gentiles into the good of Pentecost without the laying on of hands. With no apostles today, all believers receive the Holy Spirit upon their conversion without any intermediary. Only God has the power to give His Holy Spirit to those who believe.

4. As long as it was God's purpose that miracles of healing should be performed, these were sometimes achieved by the laying on of hands, as the Lord promised (Mark 16:18). We may quote the example of Ananias laying his hands on Saul so that he could receive his sight (9:12), and Paul laying his hands on the father of Publius in 28:8.

The only one of these that could exist today is case 2: commendation of the Lord's servants, and even in the Acts this did not take place on every occasion when special men were sent forth into service. Certainly the spiritual equivalent ought to be practised, namely the personal identification of brethren with, and the prayerful and practical support of, the new missionary or worker when there is mutual exercise about the call.

The Filling of the Spirit

The only NT writer who mentions this subject in detail is Luke. He does so four times in his Gospel and ten times in the Acts. The four people in his Gospel whom he describes as having been filled with the Spirit are John the Baptist (1:15), his mother Elizabeth (1:41), his father Zacharias (1:67), and the Lord Jesus (4:1). John is said to have been filled with the Spirit from the womb, which means that he had nothing to do with the matter. His parents were filled with the Spirit for specific matters that they were going to say. The Lord had thus been anointed for service, and we can be certain that this filling was permanent.

Luke enlarges on the theme in his second book.

1. "They were all filled with the Holy Ghost", describing what happened involuntarily to all in the upper room on the day of Pentecost after they had been baptised into the one Spirit (2:4).
2. "Peter, filled with the Holy Ghost" (4:8).
3. "They were all filled with the Holy Ghost" (4:31).
4. "Seven men ... full of the Holy Ghost" for an administrative purpose (6:3).
5. "Stephen, a man full of faith and of the Holy Ghost" (6:5).
6. Stephen "being full of the Holy Ghost" (7:55).
7. "Saul ... filled with the Holy Ghost" (9:17).
8. Barnabas "full of the Holy Ghost and of faith" (11:24).
9. "Saul ... filled with the Holy Ghost" (13:9).
10. "The disciples were filled with joy, and with the Holy Ghost" (13:52).

The reader should note that in the AV the two words "Ghost" and "Spirit" are translations of one Greek word *pneuma*, and that these two words are used almost indiscriminately throughout the translation. No doubt it is better to use the word "Spirit" always. Certainly it is remarkable that the word "Ghost" is used in all the ten quotations given above, for which there appears to be no explanation. (Not all languages, such as French and German, have two distinct words for "Spirit".)

This word "Ghost" or "Spirit" is used far more times in Acts than in any other NT book, such as the Gospels. But there are no further mentions of being filled with the Spirit in the second part of the book. As a phenomenon, it could not have ceased. It was the case that it was a perfectly normal experience for Christians, and did not need to be mentioned any more when special service was engaged in. It was the regular experience of all Christians who were indwelt by the Spirit. The experience did not make life easier for them, or we would not have had the sad story of Stephen. It was a repeated experience in various aspects of service (and in dangerous circumstances as well), the first three mentions of it involving Peter. It was accompanied by faith and wisdom, enabling them to do and to say things according to the present will of God.

The only other NT reference is Eph 5:18 where it is a command. And that command occurs among a whole collection of others which would ask believers to behave like believers instead of being worldly in all kinds of behaviour and speech. It was intended to be the normal experience of every Christian in life and service.

b. *Antioch in Pisidia (13:14-52)*

v.14 "But when they departed from Perga, they came to Antioch in Pisidia, and went into the synagogue on the sabbath day, and sat down.
v.15 And after the reading of the law and the prophets the rulers of the synagogue sent unto them, saying, *Ye* men *and* brethren, if ye have any word of exhortation for the people, say on.
v.16 Then Paul stood up, and beckoning with *his* hand said, Men of Israel, and ye that fear God, give audience.
v.17 The God of this people of Israel chose our fathers, and exalted the people when they dwelt as strangers in the land of Egypt, and with an high arm brought he them out of it.
v.18 And about the time of forty years suffered he their manners in the wilderness.
v.19 And when he had destroyed seven nations in the land of Chanaan, he divided their land to them by lot.
v.20 And after that he gave *unto them* judges about the space of four hundred and fifty years, until Samuel the prophet.
v.21 And afterward they desired a king: and God gave unto them Saul the son of Cis, a man of the tribe of Benjamin, by the space of forty years.
v.22 And when he had removed him, he raised up unto them David to be their king; to whom also he gave testimony, and said, I have found David the *son* of Jesse, a man after mine own heart, which shall fulfil all my will.
v.23 Of this man's seed hath God according to *his* promise raised unto Israel a Saviour, Jesus:
v.24 When John had first preached before his coming the baptism of repentance to all the people of Israel.
v.25 And as John fulfilled his course, he said, Whom think ye that I am? I am not *he*. But, behold, there cometh one after me, whose shoes of *his* feet I am not worthy to loose.
v.26 Men *and* brethren, children of the stock of Abraham, and whosoever among you feareth God, to you is the word of this salvation sent.
v.27 For they that dwell at Jerusalem, and their rulers, because they knew him not, nor yet the voices of the prophets which are read every sabbath day, they have fulfilled *them* in condemning *him*.
v.28 And though they found no cause of death *in him*, yet desired they Pilate that he should be slain.
v.29 And when they had fulfilled all that was written of him, they took *him* down from the tree, and laid *him* in a sepulchre.
v.30 But God raised him from the dead:
v.31 And he was seen many days of them which came up with him from Galilee to Jerusalem, who are his witnesses unto the people.
v.32 And we declare unto you glad tidings, how that the promise which was made unto the fathers,
v.33 God hath fulfilled the same unto us their children, in that he hath raised up Jesus again; as it is also written in the second psalm, Thou art my Son, this day have I begotten thee.
v.34 And as concerning that he raised him up from the dead, *now* no more to return to corruption, he said on this wise, I will give you the sure mercies of David.

- v.35 Wherefore he saith also in another *psalm,* Thou shalt not suffer thine Holy One to see corruption.
- v.36 For David, after he had served his own generation by the will of God, fell on sleep, and was laid unto his fathers, and saw corruption:
- v.37 But he, whom God raised again, saw no corruption.
- v.38 Be it known unto you therefore, men *and* brethren, that through this man is preached unto you the forgiveness of sins:
- v.39 And by him all that believe are justified from all things, from which ye could not be justified by the law of Moses.
- v.40 Beware therefore, lest that come upon you, which is spoken of in the prophets;
- v.41 Behold, ye despisers, and wonder, and perish: for I work a work in your days, a work which ye shall in no wise believe, though a man declare it unto you.
- v.42 And when the Jews were gone out of the synagogue, the Gentiles besought that these words might be preached to them the next sabbath.
- v.43 Now when the congregation was broken up, many of the Jews and religious proselytes followed Paul and Barnabas: who, speaking to them, persuaded them to continue in the grace of God.
- v.44 And the next sabbath day came almost the whole city together to hear the word of God.
- v.45 But when the Jews saw the multitudes, they were filled with envy, and spake against those things which were spoken by Paul, contradicting and blaspheming.
- v.46 Then Paul and Barnabas waxed bold, and said, It was necessary that the word of God should first have been spoken to you: but seeing ye put it from you, and judge yourselves unworthy of everlasting life, lo, we turn to the Gentiles.
- v.47 For so hath the Lord commanded us, *saying,* I have set thee to be a light of the Gentiles, that thou shouldest be for salvation unto the ends of the earth.
- v.48 And when the Gentiles heard this, they were glad, and glorified the word of the Lord: and as many as were ordained to eternal life believed.
- v.49 And the word of the Lord was published throughout all the region.
- v.50 But the Jews stirred up the devout and honourable women, and the chief men of the city, and raised persecution against Paul and Barnabas, and expelled them out of their coasts.
- v.51 But they shook off the dust of their feet against them, and came unto Iconium.
- v.52 And the disciples were filled with joy, and with the Holy Ghost."

14-16 Antioch in Pisidia was the administrative centre of the entire district. There the customary visit was made to the synagogue, with the not unusual invitation to address the congregation. We recall that the Lord Himself "taught in their synagogues, being glorified of all", and in particular that He read from the OT in the synagogue at Nazareth, and He preached that Isa 61:1-2 was then being fulfilled concerning His own ministry (Luke 4:15-21).

Paul was doubtless delighted to have the opportunity of addressing the assembled congregation in any synagogue in any city that he visited in his zeal to spread the gospel message. He had, of course, given up the Jews' religion, since it was incompatible with faith in the Son of God (Gal 2:18-21). He did not go into the synagogue to take part in its formal proceedings, but to anticipate the opportunity of preaching a message that he knew would receive the opposition of the Jews. Certainly the Jews' religion (though not in its synagogue form) had been given by God, although men had changed it over the centuries, yet it attracted a fair number of proselytes from the Gentile world (2:10). After all, the alternatives were paganism and spiritism, and any honest person would be able to see how much superior the Jewish system was when contrasted with these.

In v.16, Paul draws a clear distinction between the "Men of Israel" and the "God-fearers" who were Gentiles; the same distinction is made in v.26. This idea is not entirely new; such men are referred to in the Psalms, namely 22:23 and 115:9-13, where such are distinguished from the house of Israel and the house of Aaron. This is not to say that God-fearers were always proselytes in the OT, but may well embrace all who fear God as in Mal 4:2.

17-18 The length of Paul's address is almost the same as Peter's address in ch.2. It may be clearly subdivided into sections, showing a logical train of thought throughout. These are:

1. Vv.16-22. The history of the nation from Egypt to king David. In particular, Saul was removed, and the true king, David, was raised up unto them. Saul came first, but David came second.
2. Vv.23-25. John the Baptist came first (shown by the words "first" and "fulfilled his course"), but then God raised "unto Israel a Saviour, Jesus", referring to the commencement of His service.
3. Vv.26-31. The historical facts concerning the death and resurrection of the Lord Jesus.
4. Vv.32-37. Several OT quotations concerning the Lord being raised unto service and being raised from the dead, showing that paragraphs 2 and 3 above were fulfilments of OT prophecy.
5. Vv.38-41. Paul's application of the sermon to the Jews and to the Gentile proselytes.

The different meanings of the word "raised" in the message must be clearly distinguished, referring to the beginning of the Lord's service and to His resurrection respectively.

Paul's address emphasises the later period of Israel's history (in particular, the establishment of the monarchy), rather than the earlier period on which Stephen had concentrated. As in all the great evangelical addresses in the Acts, the emphasis is on what God had done: God chose His people; He exalted them; He brought them out. It is impossible to establish with certainty whether v.18 ("suffered he their manners in the wilderness") refers to God's tolerance or God's provision. The AV says that for forty years He suffered their manners in the wilderness, with the marginal alternative, "He fed them as a nurse beareth or feedeth her child". Other translations adopt this rendering rather than the former. The reason for the difference is that in the rather long Greek word involved, some Greek texts have just *one* letter altered, and this changes completely the meaning of the word. Several versions cite Deut 1:31 as a parallel passage, "the Lord thy God bare thee, as a man doth bear his son".

19-22 Paul mentions various periods of time: forty years in the wilderness (v.18); about four hundred and fifty years for the time of the judges (v.20) (though this figure causes difficulties, depending on whom one takes as the first judge and the last one; see 1 Kings 6:1); forty years for Saul's reign (v.21). The story of what God did for Israel continues, and the reader can easily find these events as recorded in the OT. God destroyed seven nations in Canaan (Deut 7:1); He divided the land by lot among His people (Josh 14:1-2); He gave them judges (Jud 2:16); He gave them Saul to be king because of the false desire of the people to be like the nations around (1 Sam 10:1), finally removing him (1 Sam 13:14; 15:23). And then David was raised up to replace Saul (1 Sam 16:12-13). The OT quotation given by Paul appears to be a double one, taken from two places and joined together to appear as a single quotation. "I have found David" is taken from Ps 89:20, while "a man after mine own heart" is taken from 1 Sam 13:14. How possible it is to stray from the will of God, for on many occasions David certainly did not do the will of God.

23-25 So this has been a story of continuous action, and no doubt his audience was completely familiar with it. Paul passes over completely the period between David and "a Saviour, Jesus", so as to emphasise the royal connection between David and the Lord Jesus. The full genealogy was known (Matt 1:6-16), but the OT had to be known properly for anyone to realise that the Saviour came by "promise". In writing his letter to the Ephesians later, Paul stresses that the gospel brings Gentile sinners into the blessings of "the covenants of promise" (Eph 2:12-18) usually taken to mean those made with Abraham, Isaac and Jacob before the giving of the law (see Heb 6:13-19). But here in Antioch the apostle stresses what God promised David, indicating that such promises are realised by Gentile sinners upon conversion.

Having established that Jesus Christ came from the seed of David according to the flesh, Paul now deals briefly with the ministry of John the Baptist who is mentioned several times in the Acts. In just the same way as the character of David far outweighed that of Saul before him, so too with the Saviour Jesus when contrasted with John the Baptist. John was sent to prepare the people for the Lord's coming and ministry, by preaching the baptism of repentance. And the difference between the two was complete, for some had thought that John was Christ, but he made the positive disclaimer, "Whom think ye that I am? I am not he". Rather One was coming after him fulfilling a divine ministry, and John was willing to be absolutely humble before the Son of God; he was unworthy to loose the shoes from off His feet. By this argument, Paul has developed his subject to the pre-eminence of Christ, whether the Jews would accept it or not.

26-31   It is at this point in v.26 that Paul shows that he has a message for the people, namely that of "this salvation" ("to you is the word of this salvation sent"), the message being sent through the apostolic preaching for he also had been sent. He does not develop this application until v.38, but in the meantime he dwells upon the crucifixion and resurrection of the Lord Jesus, first without reference to the OT and then by ample quotations from it. To expound plain historical facts is one thing, but to prove them from the Scriptures is another, and this is certainly necessary.

Thus in vv.27-31, he follows Peter in his sermon structure. Paul recalls very recent history, afterwards showing three times that what had happened to the Lord Jesus had been prophesied in the OT Scriptures.

In v.27, Paul places the responsibility for the Lord's death on (i) the dwellers at Jerusalem, and (ii) the rulers, such as the priests, Pharisees and Sanhedrin as a whole. He does not include the vast numbers of pilgrims who were at Jerusalem for the the Passover. The ignorance of these people was complete; "they knew him not" in spite of the testimony of His works and teaching. Their ignorance was in spite of the OT prophets to whom they listened every Sabbath day. Had they known the truth of their Messiah revealed in the OT, they would not have crucified the Lord of glory. But ignorance of the OT caused them to condemn Him, "Let him be crucified". Only false witnesses concocted any reason why the Lord should be crucified, and the envy of the leaders that here was a Leader who should properly supersede them. They desired Pilate that He should be slain because He was a new King of the Jews, and they would rather have Caesar as king so as to retain their own authority.

In v.29 the implied subjects of the verbs are of course different. In "when they had fulfilled", the subject "they" refers to the betrayers and murderers (7:52), but those who took the Lord down from the tree and laid Him in a sepulchre were Nicodemus and Joseph of Arimathaea (John 19:38-42). The power of God in the resurrection of Christ is almost the keynote of the Acts. Peter revelled it in 2:24, 32; 3:15; 4:10; 5:30; 10:40. God undid what men did; He reversed their action. The apostle makes reference to it in his Epistles (Eph 1:20; Phil 2:9).

There was no doubt about His resurrection, for there were many witnesses, as Paul noted in 1 Cor 15:4-8, over a period lasting for "many days". In v.31, Paul announces a new fact. In the Gospel records, the witnesses in Jerusalem were mainly the apostles and a few women, but here Paul adds those "which came up with him from Galilee to Jerusalem", though the five hundred mentioned in 1 Cor 15:6 may well refer to witnesses in Galilee when the Lord went there after His resurrection. Just two witnesses would have been sufficient to establish the truth, but God would select large numbers for so important an event upon which the whole of Christianity would rest.

32-33   Paul refers again to "the promise" made in the OT, taking the subject back to v.23, where "according to his promise (he) raised unto Israel a Saviour, Jesus". The OT references are given in order, matching the history of the Lord from the beginning of His ministry to His resurrection. It must be clearly seen that "raised" in v.23 goes with "raised" in v.33, and "raised" in v.30 goes with "raised" in v.34, and that both the history and and the OT reference refer to different events. Confusion arises if this is not understood, and Paul could be accused of losing himself in his argument. The AV reader may well be confused by the word "again" in v.33, which is a translator's insertion, with no authority from the Greek manuscripts, suggesting resurrection, whereas in the order of Paul's thoughts resurrection is not in view in v.33.

Admittedly expositors have suggested both the Lord's birth and His resurrection as being satisfactory as an interpretation of "Thou art my Son, this day have I begotten thee". An inspection of Ps 2:7 will show that this is a millennial Psalm, and there the interpretation must be that the figurative expression refers to the manifestation of the Son as King of kings. Similarly in v.33. The context from v.23 shows that the quotation is given to establish the fact that after the Father's commendation at His baptism, "This is my beloved Son" (Matt 3:17), He was then manifested for service.

34-37 In v.34 Paul turns to resurrection, the other reference to "raised" in v.30. The change of subject is shown by the words "as concerning that he raised him up from the dead". "The sure mercies of David" from Isa 55:3 may appear to our minds to be a strange reference to embrace resurrection, but clearly not to Paul's mind. But God was promising to restore something that His people had lost. What else could He do? After all, He cannot revoke an everlasting covenant. So here the apostle Paul revives the idea of "the sure mercies of David"; they could not derive from a dead Christ but from a living One.

It appears that "the sure mercies of David" are what the prophet Nathan told David about both in 2 Sam 7 and 1 Chron 17. The promise consisted of three main items;

1. "I will set up thy seed after thee ... I will be his father, and he shall be my son" (2 Sam 7:12,14). The "seed" refers to the Lord as promised, not a succession of offspring. For concerning the word "seed", we can say, as Paul wrote in Gal 3:16, "He saith not, And to seeds, as of many; but as of one, And to thy seed, which is Christ". (The word "seed" is singular in number in Gen 3:15; 12:7; 2 Sam 7:12.)

2. God promised David through Nathan, "He shall build an house for my name" (2 Sam 7:13). In Acts 15:16-17, James quoted Amos 9:11-12 about the rebuilding of the tabernacle of David which had fallen down. When Solomon undertook the task of building that house, he expressed its inadequacy, "Behold, heaven and the heaven of heavens cannot contain thee; how much less this house which I have built!" (2 Chron 6:18). Stephen in Acts 7:47 said, "But Solomon built him an house", and this is almost a reference to Nathan's statement. But in Acts 7:47-49

Stephen contrasted Solomon's temple with God's new dwelling-place, the house not made with hands. This is the aspect of "the sure mercies of David" which Paul had in mind when he addressed the congregation in the synagogue in Antioch.

3. "I will stablish the throne of his kingdom for ever" (2 Sam 7:13). "For ever" occurs eight times in 2 Sam 7, showing how sure are these mercies (or holy or just things). The resurrection of Christ was necessary in order that "for ever" should be applicable.

Time after time in the Acts we are shown fulfilments of the OT Scriptures in connection with the christian age, although another fulfilment has yet to take place. It is very important to note that the Lord is coming again. What men did to Him at Calvary does not prevent Him having a glorious future both with His church in heaven, and with His people Israel on earth.

In v.35, once again Ps 16:10 is quoted in the Acts. Here Paul is claiming its fulfilment, just as Peter did in Acts 2:27. God's Holy One did not see corruption, and it certainly was not himself of whom David was speaking, since he "fell on sleep" (1 Kings 2:10) after a reign of forty years. (This is the first time that Paul uses the word "sleep" to describe the death of an OT character. It has already been used by Luke himself to describe the homecall of Stephen in 7:60. In his Epistles, Paul uses it several times to describe the death of God's saints; see 1 Cor 11:30; 15:51; 1 Thess 4:14.) Whereas David's body saw corruption, this was impossible in the case of the Lord's body. His body in resurrection ascended to the Father's throne; "death hath no more dominion over him" (Rom 6:9); He is made "after the power of an endless life" (Heb 7:16).

38 Having put things in historical and scriptural perspective, explaining the connection between the Old and the New, just as Peter had done in Acts 2 in particular, Paul was now ready to apply the message to the audience in the synagogue. On the basis of that death and resurrection, the message of the gospel was being preached. In the OT forgiveness of sins was possible through offering a sin offering to God, though strictly "it is not possible that the blood of bulls and of goats should take away sins" (Heb 10:4). Throughout the Acts, forgiveness is offered as the result of the finished work of Christ on the cross. Peter presented forgiveness to his audience in Jerusalem in 2:38, and to a smaller audience outside the temple in the same city in 3:19. This message was repeated to the Jewish Sanhedrin in 5:31, and to those gathered in Cornelius' house in 10:43. Stephen did not mention the possibility of forgiveness to those who "gnashed on him with their teeth" (7:54); some men put themselves outside the bounds of the preaching of forgiveness. We have now reached the point where Paul preached the same subject in the synagogue in Antioch of Pisidia, and later he confesses that the offer was contained in his vision of the risen Christ on his conversion day, "that they may receive forgiveness of sins" (26:18).

39 Having spoken about this great offer, made several times in the Gospels by the Lord Himself, Paul then turned over the coin and introduced the positive side of the truth forever associated with his teaching, namely, the truth of justification by faith. The twin truths are the basis of all blessing. The first delivers the believer from his sins and their penalty; the second places him forever in a position of no condemnation, as though he had never sinned at all. There is no equivalent position for the guilty in the legal systems of the world. Paul elaborates on the subject in his two Epistles, Romans and Galatians. The law of Moses made some provision for the guilty in the passing over of their sins in view of the forthcoming sacrifice of Christ, but it could make no provision for the justification of the ungodly.

40-41 Once again, Peter's example is followed by the giving of a word of warning (see 3:23). Of all the warnings appearing in the OT prophets, Paul used a quotation from Hab 1:5. The context foreshadows God's use of the Gentiles to punish His earthly people. It is used here by Paul to introduce the subject of the setting aside of God's earthly people with subsequent Gentile blessing. This is the meaning of the work that God was going to do. (Isa 28:11-12 is similarly quoted in 1 Cor 14:21 within the context of Gentile blessing.) Note that Jewish unbelief was expected. Thus similarly in John 12:37-40; the apostle quotes Isa 53:1; 6:10 as showing beforehand that "they believed not on him" and "Therefore they could not believe". Thus the OT was used to show Jewish unbelief both when the Lord Jesus was here on earth, and afterwards when the gospel was preached.

42-43 We are not told what the reaction of the Jews in the synagogue was to this address, but the closing words of warning may have indicated that Paul feared for them. It was the Gentiles who were affected spiritually; they asked for a further opportunity of hearing the word of God "the next sabbath". It may appear strange that any gospel preacher would be happy to postpone preaching an urgent message for a whole week; certainly v.44 indicates that "the next sabbath day" was used for preaching. But v.43 shows what really happened. During the week, "many of the Jews and religious proselytes" followed Paul and Barnabas, and he spoke to them and persuaded them to continue in the grace of God. This word "continue" suggests that there were converts on the first Sabbath day, or at least during the days of the following week.

To "follow" preachers does not give them a position of importance and elevation. Rather, they were following them for further instruction immediately after their conversion. The follow-up teaching was simple in nature, "continue in the grace of God". This was the new message that was being given to the world. It was "the grace of God" that Barnabas saw when he first arrived in Antioch in Syria (11:23). This was a message so different from that always preached in the synagogue; it was a message of free grace, not of compulsory law. Grace is the overflowing of God's bounty to Gentile sinners in particular, and to all those who believed, and now these new believers are being exhorted to continue in it. (Barnabas is now included, as being a man endowed with the gift of exhortation.) So "the grace of God" can be added to the list of 2:42, as something in which believers should continue. Of course they would never abandon God's moral law as a way of life, though they would now no longer regard it as the way of obtaining eternal life; they would pay less attention to the ceremonial law, though false teachers and special circumstances would often arise to draw Jewish believers back to ceremony, as is the case today in Christendom. And pressure would sometimes be put on the Gentiles to adopt old Jewish practices.

44-46 A bigger crowd than before gathered to hear the message the next Sabbath day. "Almost the whole city" recalls what happened in Nineveh (Jon 3:5-10) where "the people of Nineveh believed God ... from the greatest of them even to the least of them", and also what happened in Lydda when "all that dwelt in Lydda ... turned to the Lord" (Acts 9:35). In Antioch, for the unregenerate Jews the preachers were being too successful; the priests and Pharisees thought the same about the Lord Jesus, that "all men will believe on him", thus taking away their own place and nation (John 11:47-48). So the Jews obdurately insisted on Judaism as the means of blessing, contradicting what the missionaries were saying. If ch.11 marked a turning-point in the story of God's dealings with men, then ch.13 sees a crisis point being reached. The two types of people in the audience are described in very different ways.

1. The Jews are described as being "unworthy of everlasting life" (v.46). This was the attitude taken by the Jews themselves.

2. Some Gentiles "were ordained to eternal life" (v.48). This was the attitude taken by God. (Note that in both these passages in the Greek text the same word "eternal" is used.)

No wonder when this point was reached, the apostle said, "lo, we turn to the Gentiles". Many years later in Rome, he said effectively the same thing (28:28). This occasion in Antioch may well be the first time that election is stated as being the portion of Gentiles, although it is not the last. What was specified for God's earthly people in the OT, and what is stated for them in the future ("for the elect's sake", Matt 24:22) is here declared to be the portion of converted Gentile sinners. How marvellous is that grace of God which was now being preached! In Rom 9-11 Paul later expounded the matter at greater length.

47 Paul quoted Isa 49:6 to show them that, like so much else in his preaching, even Gentile blessing was envisaged in the Jewish Scriptures, "It is a light thing that thou shouldest be my servant to raise up the tribes of Jacob, and to restore the preserved of Israel: I will also give thee for a light to the Gentiles, that thou mayest be my salvation unto the end of the earth". (In Rom 15:9-12, Paul quotes another four OT passages indicating the divine intention to bless the Gentile world, and these do not necessarily exhaust the number.)

48-49 It is a very appropriate place for another of Luke's summaries or progress reports: "as many as were ordained (appointed) to eternal life believed. And the word of the Lord was published throughout all the region". This "region" must embrace the country around Antioch only, not extending to the cities evangelised in ch.14 lying further to the east. We are not told who did the evangelising, but these must have included Paul and Barnabas, together with converts from Antioch. The last three verses of the chapter suggest that they made excursions out from their central base, Antioch. There was liberty to start with, unlike the expansion of the testimony from Jerusalem, where most of the believers had to leave because of persecution (8:4); they too "went every where preaching the word". There was no such thing as preaching a political or social gospel; it was always "the word".

50-52 Ultimately, persecution broke out. Unbelieving Jews enlisted the support of the most unexpected of people – "devout and honourable women" together with the city authorities. In 16:22, it was the multitude and magistrates of Philippi; in 17:5 it was the Jews and "certain lewd fellows of the baser sort" in Thessalonica; in Corinth it was the Jews though not the deputy of Achaia (18:12); in Ephesus it was the silversmiths who were losing their idolatrous trade (19:24-25). Opposition to Christ brings out the worst in strange allies.

The list of experiences that Paul later compiled in 2 Cor 11:23-33 is being built up, in keeping with the Lord's words, "I will show him how great things he must suffer for my name's sake" (9:16). The apostle knew that he was made "as the filth of the world" and "the offscouring of all things" (1 Cor 4:13). He escaped from Damascus through being let down over the city walls in a basket; his life was in danger in Jerusalem, so he was taken down to Caesarea and then despatched to Tarsus; and now he is expelled from the borders of Antioch in Pisidia. The preachers, therefore, did what the Lord had told their predecessors to do, "Whosoever will not receive you, when ye go out of that city, shake off the very dust from your feet" (Luke 9:5), and they proceeded to Iconium. However, they left behind them another of those groups of believers who are described as being full of joy and of the Holy Spirit.

Readers will be familiar with the idiom "shake off the dust of their feet". The Lord Jesus instructed His disciples to do this with unresponsive audiences in the Gospels. See Matt 10:14; Luke 9:5; 10:11. It seems to imply that no further responsibility can be accepted for the future of their never-dying souls. It may be that the OT equivalent could be the quitting of the right of redemption as illustrated in the ceremony described in Ruth 4:4-8. The near kinsman who ought to have been kinsman-redeemer renounced his right by taking off his shoe and handing it to Boaz, the person who was going to accept the responsibility. God denied such a right over Edom in Pss 60:8;108:9. Whether *we* have the right to renounce responsibility for the souls of persons or places is another matter. It may be wise at times to decide not to speak any more to an individual about his soul, but the passing of time means that we cannot do this for places in successive generations. At least, Paul did visit Antioch again in spite of this original method of leaving the city (14:21; 15:36).

c. *Iconium, Lystra and Derbe (14:1-20)*

v.1 "And it came to pass in Iconium, that they went both together into the synagogue of the Jews, and so spake, that a great multitude both of the Jews and also of the Greeks believed.
v.2 But the unbelieving Jews stirred up the Gentiles, and made their minds evil affected against the brethren.
v.3 Long time therefore abode they speaking boldly in the Lord, which gave testimony unto the word of his grace, and granted signs and wonders to be done by their hands.
v.4 But the multitude of the city was divided: and part held with the Jews, and part with the apostles.
v.5 And when there was an assault made both of the Gentiles, and also of the Jews with their rulers, to use *them* despitefully, and to stone them,
v.6 They were ware of *it,* and fled unto Lystra and Derbe, cities of Lycaonia, and unto the region that lieth round about;
v.7 And there they preached the gospel.
v.8 And there sat a certain man at Lystra, impotent in his feet, being a cripple from his mother's womb, who never had walked:
v.9 The same heard Paul speak: who stedfastly beholding him, and perceiving that he had faith to be healed,
v.10 Said with a loud voice, Stand upright on thy feet. And he leaped and walked.
v.11 And when the people saw what Paul had done, they lifted up their voices, saying in the speech of Lycaonia, The gods are come down to us in the likeness of men.
v.12 And they called Barnabas, Jupiter; and Paul, Mercurius, because he was the chief speaker.
v.13 Then the priest of Jupiter, which was before their city, brought oxen and garlands unto the gates, and would have done sacrifice with the people.
v.14 *Which* when the apostles, Barnabas and Paul, heard *of,* they rent their clothes, and ran in among the people, crying out,
v.15 And saying, Sirs, why do ye these things? We also are men of like passions with you, and preach unto you that ye should turn from these vanities unto the living God, which made heaven, and earth, and the sea, and all things that are therein:
v.16 Who in times past suffered all nations to walk in their own ways.
v.17 Nevertheless he left not himself without witness, in that he did good, and gave us rain from heaven, and fruitful seasons, filling our hearts with food and gladness.
v.18 And with these sayings scarce restrained they the people, that they had not done sacrifice unto them.
v.19 And there came thither *certain* Jews from Antioch and Iconium, who persuaded the people, and, having stoned Paul, drew *him* out of the city, supposing he had been dead.
v.20 Howbeit, as the disciples stood round about him, he rose up, and came into the city: and the next day he departed with Barnabas to Derbe."

1-2 Iconium was the fourth place visited on Paul's first missionary journey where it is recorded that he preached the gospel. This city was situated about one hundred miles to the east of Antioch. Their first preaching point was again the synagogue, where there was once again a mixed audience of Jews and Gentile proselytes. The response was exceptional, "a great multitude both of the Jews and also of the Greeks believed". This kind of evangelistic success always presented a danger that a riot would be produced. At Antioch it had been devout and honourable women together with the chief men of the city who were used against the preachers, but in Iconium it was the Gentiles (v.4 suggests that these Gentiles were outside the synagogue, and hence they were not all proselytes). Jews were only too willing to use people with whom they had little in common to make trouble for the preachers of the gospel. This is what the Jews did when they allied themselves with Pilate at the trial of the Lord Jesus. They hated the Roman occupiers of the land, but willingly took sides with Caesar as their king when it was to their advantage.

3-7 In spite of the opposition, it was not a brief visit that the missionaries paid to Iconium, but a lengthy one, during which time the preaching was confirmed with "signs and wonders" following, the fifth time that such miraculous phenomena accompanied the preaching in the Acts. It was the Lord Himself who gave this special testimony to the preaching of "the word of his grace". Like Peter in 3:12, they would have denied that the power was their own. As always, there were two responses to the preaching: some people supported the Jewish opponents of the gospel, while others took sides with the apostles and their teaching. V.4 is the first time in which Barnabas is referred to as an apostle (and also in v.14). This is the first time that Paul also is referred to as an apostle. The final resort of the hatred of the opponents of the gospel (Gentiles, Jews and their rulers) was a plan to stone the apostles. Just as the Lord Jesus did not invite trouble before His hour was come, escaping out of the hands of the Jews who intended to stone Him (John 8:59; 10:39), so too in the case of Paul and Barnabas. They avoided trouble by fleeing to Lystra, and Derbe, where we are told that "they preached the gospel". The word does not mean formal preaching so much as spreading the good news. Note that they did not continue eastwards to the safer parts of Tarsus, but later returned to the cities of their persecution.

8-14 Lystra, the first city of Lycaonia, seems to have been a more heathen city than the others, and no synagogue is mentioned. But Paul and Barnabas preached the gospel there before a specific miracle was performed by Paul, that of the healing of a cripple. This man first heard Paul speak, and evidently faith was formed, and the apostle perceived his faith and appreciated that circumstances were right for the miracle. The man's faith lay at the basis of the miracle, unlike the case in 3:5 where the lame man had no thought except that of receiving money. Paul's miracle was not done privately, so he commanded with "a loud voice" that the man should stand up. Every NT miracle is instantaneous, complete and lasting, so the man "leaped and walked". In the Gospels, unbelieving Jews wanted to attribute miracles to anybody but God, even to Beelzebub (Matt 12:24), but these heathen people wanted to attribute this miracle to their gods, for there were "gods many, and lords many"

(1 Cor 8:5). Note how the heathen religions copy the truth. The Lord Jesus was God manifest in flesh; He came down and took upon Himself flesh and blood; these heathen claimed, "The gods are come down to us in the likeness of men". In other words, they considered that they were having a visit from the Greek gods Jupiter (or Zeus) and Mercury (or Hermes). (Consider a similar idolatrous statement by the people of Ephesus in 19:35.) The priest of Jupiter was anxious to make a festive occasion of the incident, and was doubtless astonished when the preachers refused divine honours. Angels refused to be treated like God in the book of Revelation (19:10; 22:8-9), while Paul and Barnabas certainly declined such an honour here. The Lord's people ought always to remember that they are only servants, possessing nothing that they did not receive. Everything that detracts from God must be repudiated. He is too great to share His glory with any other. The sole Creator of heaven, earth and sea can have no rivals. Herod may accept worship (12:22), but the two evangelists could but rend their clothes in indignant protest.

15 Paul's address in the synagogue in Antioch included many references to Jewish history in the OT, such as any Jew would understand even if they had no capacity to interpret the Scriptures in terms of Christ. But this approach was of no value when resisting idolatry from heathen men. In other words, NT preachers addressed their audiences in language which they could understand, even if the OT and Christ Himself were absent. The evangelists' approach here was through the creation, which they could not help but know about, though not through scriptural history, of which they were totally ignorant.

The preachers insisted that they were human, "men of like passions with you", and indeed would condemn their idolatrous practices. The gospel required them to turn from their idolatry. Five times in the Acts people are asked to repent, or are described as having repented. Repentance implies a *change of mind*. But in v.15, we have the idea of to "turn". Eight times people in the Acts are asked to turn, or are said to have turned. Turning is a *change of action*. Generally the second concept would be the evidence that the first had taken place. Twice in the AV the word *epistrephō* is translated "be converted".

When God is called "the living God" in the NT it is usually in contrast to the lifeless idols of the heathen world (1 Thess 1:9). However, it may appear to be strange that in the most Jewish Epistle of all He is called the living God four times (Heb 3:12; 9:14; 10:31; 12:22).

God is called the God of creation numerous times in the Bible. Each time the reader should pay attention to the reason for His being so called. Usually it is to emphasise His greatness and our dependence on Him. He is too great to be represented by lifeless idols. He created the three great spheres in which life exists (heaven, earth and sea) with all the biological specimens in each: see, for example, Neh 9:6; Jer 32:17; Acts 4:24.

16-18 From the realm of creation, Paul passed to the ream of human government.

God allowed all nations to walk in their own ways. It was specially sad when all in His own nation "turned every one to his own way" (Isa 53:6), when "every man did that which was right in his own eyes" (Jud 21:25). That did not mean that He paid no attention to nations, for "he left not himself without witness". Creation did not suffer irreparable drought when men turned to their own ways. The Lord Jesus had said that He "sendeth rain on the just and on the unjust" (Matt 5:45). The effect of rain, particularly in Bible lands, is "fruitful seasons", and the effect of fruitful seasons is gladness. The people still wanted to offer sacrifices to the preachers, and these words only just restrained them. But hostile Jews from the last two places visited arrived to stir up trouble.

19-20 People who were with difficulty restrained from offering sacrifice to the preachers were very quickly persuaded to stone them. How quickly can a mob be turned from idolising to persecuting. A form of public execution which unregerate Jews had attempted twice against the Lord in John's Gospel (8:59; 10:31), and in which Paul in his unregenerate days had played a part against Stephen, was now experienced by himself for the only time in this life as a missionary (see the word "once" in 2 Cor 11:25).

Paul was left for dead. Bible teachers generally agree that this is the occasion to which the apostle refers in 2 Cor 12:1-4 some fourteen years afterwards. It is amazing how God compensates His servants for bitter experiences. Paul does not claim that he was actually dead when this happened, but he does claim that he was caught up to the third heaven, to paradise, and heard indescribable words which he was not allowed to pass on. The compensations of the Lord are exceedingly great. In addition, the apostle was better equipped through personal experience to tell others that it is through much tribulation that we enter the kingdom of God.

Paul did not continue eastwards to regions of safety, but returned to Lystra where the persecution began, only on the next day departing for Derbe many miles to the south. We are not told what happened at Derbe, except that the gospel was preached and that many were taught. Presumably this was the time when Timothy trusted the Saviour (16:1); he owed a great deal to his mother and grandmother (2 Tim 1:5; 3:15), though he must have been saved through Paul's testimony since he refers to him as "my own son in the faith" (1 Tim 1:2).

Persecution did not stop these first preachers from accomplishing their work for the Lord; it merely caused them to change their venue so that the gospel might spread the faster. Thus Derbe was the fourth city over the sea from Cyprus which had the opportunity of hearing the gospel on Paul's first missionary journey.

d. *Confirming the Churches (14:21-28)*

> v.21 "And when they had preached the gospel to that city, and had taught many, they returned again to Lystra, and *to* Iconium, and Antioch,

v.22 Confirming the souls of the disciples, *and* exhorting them to continue in the faith, and that we must through much tribulation enter into the kingdom of God.
v.23 And when they had ordained them elders in every church, and had prayed with fasting, they commended them to the Lord, on whom they believed.
v.24 And after they had passed throughout Pisidia, they came to Pamphylia.
v.25 And when they had preached the word in Perga, they went down into Attalia:
v.26 And thence sailed to Antioch, from whence they had been recommended to the grace of God for the work which they fulfilled.
v.27 And when they were come, and had gathered the church together, they rehearsed all that God had done with them, and how he had opened the door of faith unto the Gentiles.
v.28 And there they abode long time with the disciples."

21-24 In spite of the obvious dangers attendant upon a return journey through three places full of hostility to the preachers, Paul and Barnabas retraced their steps. Groups of believers had been left behind in each city, and they needed encouragement and spiritual organisation. Harold St. John called the nature of the Lord's work on the outward trip from Antioch *the mission stage of the church*, preceding the next stage when elders took their place by apostolic recognition and appointment (v.23). Elders already existed in the Jerusalem church (11:30), and Paul and Barnabas knew how rule should be maintained in a local church particularly in the absence of apostolic leadership. These elders had obviously emerged during the time since the original formation of the churches, and this is the pattern for all churches. Since the apostolic period, we do not need them to be present to appoint elders, for even Paul himself told the Ephesian elders later that it was the Holy Spirit who had made them overseers (20:28). These were not blind appointments, but a confirmation of what was already taking place. Believers will not follow hirelings, but will "know them which ... are over you in the Lord, and admonish you" (1 Thess 5:12). Within the relatively short time that these new churches existed, men were emerging to take the lead, not lording it over the Lord's people, but being examples to the flock (1 Pet 5:3). These were the men whom Paul and Barnabas apppointed elders. Being engaged in such work should always precede the recognition of, or appointment to, eldership. The word "ordained" in the AV was a concession to the established ecclesiastical system of the seventeenth century. The word simply means "appointed". NT teaching on elders occurs again in 20:28-31, as well as in several of the Epistles. Note that these churches existed before there were recognised elders, and that while it is desirable for churches to have elders, yet they do not cease to be churches because they do not, at the moment, have any.

25-28 For the fourth time in this chapter, the subject of preaching is mentioned, this time in Perga. This was their business, and they continued in it regardless of the opposition. The first missionary journey began and ended with a sea voyage. It also began and ended in the same place, Antioch in Syria. From there they had been commended, and there they reported. Commended to the grace of God, they returned and now reported on the grace of God. Bible teachers may claim that Peter used the keys of the kingdom to admit the Gentile world through Cornelius and his company, but it is really at the end of the first missionary journey that we are told that "the door of faith" had been opened to the Gentiles, but see 15:7. No doubt this has special reference to Gentile conversion outside the homeland of the Jews. But it was this work of Paul that created the problem that needed to be solved in ch.15.

So half way through the Acts the gospel has spread from Palestine where the story all began, to one of the islands of the sea and into parts of Asia Minor. Little did even Paul know that the next step was to be over the sea into Europe.

A Comparison of Acts 13 and 14

Acts 13	Acts 14
A Miracle of Judgment (vv. 6-10)	A Miracle of Healing (vv. 8-10)
Result of Miracle: Proconsul Believed	Result of Miracle: People Wanted to Worship the Preachers
An Address to Jews	An Address to Idolaters
The God of this People, Israel	He Left not Himself without Witness
The Jews were Filled with Envy	The Jews Came and Persuaded Multitudes
The Jews Stirred up the Women	
	Note: Stoning Contemplated (v. 5)
	Stoning Practised (v. 19)
A Light to the Gentiles (v.47)	Door of Faith Opened to Gentiles (v.27)

4. The Apostolic Council
15:1-35

v.1 "And certain men which came down from Judæa taught the brethren, *and said,* Except ye be circumcised after the manner of Moses, ye cannot be saved.

v.2 When therefore Paul and Barnabas had no small dissension and disputation with them, they determined that Paul and Barnabas, and certain other of them, should go up to Jerusalem unto the apostles and elders about this question.

v.3 And being brought on their way by the church, they passed through Phenice and Samaria, declaring the conversion of the Gentiles: and they caused great joy unto all the brethren.

v.4 And when they were come to Jerusalem, they were received of the church, and *of* the apostles and elders, and they declared all things that God had done with them.

v.5 But there rose up certain of the sect of the Pharisees which believed, saying, That it was needful to circumcise them, and to command *them* to keep the law of Moses.

- v.6 And the apostles and elders came together for to consider of this matter.
- v.7 And when there had been much disputing, Peter rose up, and said unto them, Men *and* brethren, ye know how that a good while ago God made choice among us, that the Gentiles by my mouth should hear the word of the gospel, and believe.
- v.8 And God, which knoweth the hearts, bare them witness, giving them the Holy Ghost, even as *he did* unto us;
- v.9 And put no difference between us and them, purifying their hearts by faith.
- v.10 Now therefore why tempt ye God, to put a yoke upon the neck of the disciples, which neither our fathers nor we were able to bear?
- v.11 But we believe that through the grace of the Lord Jesus Christ we shall be saved, even as they.
- v.12 Then all the multitude kept silence, and gave audience to Barnabas and Paul, declaring what miracles and wonders God had wrought among the Gentiles by them.
- v.13 And after they had held their peace, James answered, saying, Men *and* brethren, hearken unto me:
- v.14 Simeon hath declared how God at the first did visit the Gentiles, to take out of them a people for his name.
- v.15 And to this agree the words of the prophets; as it is written,
- v.16 After this I will return, and will build again the tabernacle of David, which is fallen down, and I will build again the ruins thereof, and I will set it up:
- v.17 That the residue of men might seek after the Lord, and all the Gentiles, upon whom my name is called, saith the Lord, who doeth all these things.
- v.18 Known unto God are all his works from the beginning of the world.
- v.19 Wherefore my sentence is, that we trouble not them, which from among the Gentiles are turned to God:
- v.20 But that we write unto them, that they abstain from pollutions of idols, and *from* fornication, and *from* things strangled, and *from* blood.
- v.21 For Moses of old time hath in every city them that preach him, being read in the synagogues every sabbath day.
- v.22 Then pleased it the apostles and elders, with the whole church, to send chosen men of their own company to Antioch with Paul and Barnabas; *namely,* Judas surnamed Barsabas, and Silas, chief men among the brethren:
- v.23 And they wrote *letters* by them after this manner; The apostles and elders and brethren *send* greeting unto the brethren which are of the Gentiles in Antioch and Syria and Cilicia:
- v.24 Forasmuch as we have heard, that certain which went out from us have troubled you with words, subverting your souls, saying, *Ye must* be circumcised, and keep the law: to whom we gave no *such* commandment:
- v.25 It seemed good unto us, being assembled with one accord, to send chosen men unto you with our beloved Barnabas and Paul,
- v.26 Men that have hazarded their lives for the name of our Lord Jesus Christ.
- v.27 We have sent therefore Judas and Silas, who shall also tell *you* the same things by mouth.

WHAT THE BIBLE TEACHES / ACTS 15   157

> v.28 For it seemed good to the Holy Ghost, and to us, to lay upon you no greater burden than these necessary things;
> v.29 That ye abstain from meats offered to idols, and from blood, and from things strangled, and from fornication: from which if ye keep yourselves, ye shall do well. Fare ye well.
> v.30 So when they were dismissed, they came to Antioch: and when they had gathered the multitude together, they delivered the epistle:
> v.31 *Which* when they had read, they rejoiced for the consolation.
> v.32 And Judas and Silas, being prophets also themselves, exhorted the brethren with many words, and confirmed *them*.
> v.33 And after they had tarried *there* a space, they were let go in peace from the brethren unto the apostles.
> v.34 Notwithstanding it pleased Silas to abide there still.
> v.35 Paul also and Barnabas continued in Antioch, teaching and preaching the word of the Lord, with many others also."

1-2 Paul and Barnabas' stay at Antioch was lengthy (14:28). It appears that they resumed the work of teaching and preaching in which they had engaged prior to their commendation to the grace of God for the first missionary journey. While in Antioch, they had unwelcome visitors from Jerusalem, men who were trying to prevent the separation of Christianity from Judaism. Such men seem to have plagued Paul for the entire duration of his missionary service. Had these men succeeded, Christianity would have become but a sect of Judaism, but God ensured that the result of ch.15 was the salvation of Christianity itself. Unfortunately, most of the branches of Christendom have not learned the lesson even to the present day.

How serious this development was considered to be by Paul can be seen both from the action taken in this chapter, and from his letter to the Galatians. (See the companion volume in this series which includes *Galatians* by J. Hunter.) Any other gospel which adds to the simple gospel of God's free grace must be resisted. Paul called such false preachers "accursed" and "false brethren" (Gal 1:8-9; 2:4). Any addition, whether it be child-baptism or circumcision, rites and ceremonies, sacrifices or offerings, and even good works, makes void the one true gospel which requires that Christ does everything for the salvation of those who believe. Such additions mean that here is a gospel which implies "ye cannot be saved", and this is no good news at all.

Acts 15 is a most unhappy chapter. It begins and ends with a dispute. The first was the more serious, and although the matter was resolved by the Holy Spirit, yet its effects have survived to the present. The second was personal and temporary. "Dissension and disputation" can never provoke a happy atmosphere in a local church, and it is wise to settle such debate as soon as possible.

This Council of Jerusalem is the only NT example of a high level conference convened to settle an outstanding issue in the story of the church. All others belong to church history outside the NT era. They belong to a time when unauthorised bishops had come to the fore and their pronouncements are merely of academic interest, though sometimes they dealt with important issues of doctrine. It is quite another matter today on the mission field when elders and missionaries from various churches come together in conference and fellowship, both for teaching and for discussion of prospects and difficulties. This can be very profitable and spiritually reinvigorating.

3 A deputation was formed from the church in Antioch to go to Jerusalem about the matter; it consisted of Paul, Barnabas and "certain other of them". After all, Jerusalem was the source of this "other gospel", as Paul called it in Gal 1:6. All evils, whether moral, practical or doctrinal, should be checked at their sources. For the first time, an important NT custom is brought to the attention of readers, "being brought on their way by the church"; this will appear on several other occasions in Acts. Firstly this implies that a party of Christians escorted those journeying for part of their way, to identify themselves with them in their business, and to encourage them in the doing of it. In 28:15 it consisted of going out to meet them. Secondly it suggests that the various local churches en route offered hospitality to the travellers, for v.3 shows that other churches were involved in listening to reports by Paul and Barnabas. We should, in fact, never expect that Paul would fail to use the journey for spiritual purposes. Calls were made on churches in both Phenice and in Samaria. If there was great joy in Samaria when they themselves were converted in 8:8, then there was again great joy when they heard of Gentiles being converted as well. There was not the same prejudice among those converts as there was among Jewish ones (see 11:1-3).

4-5 Another "report meeting" appears to have been held in Jerusalem, the church being involved as well as the apostles and elders. This drew the ire of the converted Pharisees, and brought the whole controversy into the open. Note carefully the two sides of the argument.

1. "Certain of the sect of the Pharisees which believed". How strong their faith was we are not told, nor what spiritual gifts they possessed, nor whether they knew what it meant to be filled with the Holy Spirit. They insisted on the law of Moses, and the rite of circumcision for Gentile converts.

2. Paul and Barnabas "declared all things that God had done with them", making quite clear that their work had really been "the Lord working with them" (Mark 16:20). They had confessed the same thing in Antioch (14:27); see also Rom 15:18. Paul had declared in Pisidian Antioch that this gospel "justified from all things, from which ye could not be justified by the law of Moses" (13:39). This was in direct opposition to these men who were demanding that new converts be compelled to conform to the law of Moses.

6-11 Now we have not a meeting of the whole church, but of its leaders, the apostles and elders, though ultimately their decision, taken though the Holy Spirit "pleased ... the whole church" (v.22). On this occasion, unlike that mentioned in

Gal 2:11, Peter lent his weight against these converted Pharisees. After many had taken part in the dispute, we finally have addresses by Peter, Barnabas and Paul, with a conclusion by James. In v.7 Peter referred to his own experience in Cornelius' house (ch.10), and he claimed divine approval for what had happened through the giving of the Holy Spirit. There was therefore no difference between Jews and Gentiles in the matter of salvation. Their hearts had been purified by faith, so Peter was quite clear that salvation was through faith and not by rites in any added form. The two sides of salvation were firstly the gospel of grace on the part of God, and secondly faith on the part of the hearer. "The grace of the Lord Jesus Christ" (v.11) is unusual in this connection, for by itself it is usually the final greeting in the NT letters. Here in v.11 it is synonymous with "the grace of God". Its equivalent in the NT is Paul's use of the expression in 2 Cor 8:9, "ye know the grace of our Lord Jesus Christ, that, though he was rich, yet for our sakes he became poor, that ye through his poverty might be rich".

Peter emphasised the common ground occupied by Jew and Gentile in the new situation that had come to exist. His words "no difference" are parallel to those of Paul in Rom 10:12, "For there is no difference between the Jew and the Greek: for the same Lord over all is rich unto all that call upon him". Thus Peter concluded, "giving them the Holy Ghost, even as he did unto us; and put no difference between us and them ... we believe that ... we shall be saved, even as they". Note that he did not say, "they shall be saved, even as we", for that might have played into the hands of the Pharisees, placing the Gentiles upon Jewish ground. These men were tempting God by seeking to replace liberty by "a yoke on the neck of the disciples", which pressed men downwards into fear and despair instead of raising them up to hope and blessings in Christ.

12 Peter was the first apostle to express his mind on the matter. With this introduction by a leader, the multitude (i.e., the apostles and elders in v.6) was ready to hear what Barnabas, one of themselves originally, and Paul had seen among the Gentiles. (It should be remembered that only two of the miracles performed by the Lord Jesus Himself had been performed on non-Jews. V.12 proves that it had now been happening on a considerable scale among Gentiles.) These miracles and wonders that God had wrought proved the validity of the message that they preached, namely, justification by faith. What a contrast to the unprofitableness of circumcision (Rom 2:25).

13-18 The next and last recorded speaker was James, understood to be the Lord's brother according to the flesh, and author of the Epistle of James (1 Cor 15:7). He quoted a further witness to the truth of Gentile blessing, namely from the OT prophet Amos (9:11-12). There are two points:

1. that God intended the revival of His dwelling-place on earth;

2. that God intended Gentile blessing. (See the comments on 13:44-47.)

The Greek word for "agree" is interesting. Our word for "sympathy" is derived from it. The NT fulfilment is in harmony with the OT prophecy. James made reference to the tabernacle. David's tabernacle was not Moses' tabernacle, which had been forsaken by God in Samuel's time (Ps 78:60). David's tabernacle was a tent specially erected on mount Zion to receive the ark (2 Sam 6:17), but it ceased to be functional when the ark was brought into Solomon's temple, together with Moses' tabernacle (1 Kings 8:4). What had ceased to be functional ceremonially would be built again spiritually.

James identified a people upon whom God's name is called (v.17). A Christian is a person who initially called on the name of the Lord and was saved (Acts 2:21). Thereafter such people are called by His name. It is interesting to note that the very Greek word in v.17 is translated "surnamed" several times in Acts, so that a Christian is a person who could easily be surnamed "the Lord's". Interesting parallels are found in the OT for God's earthly people which could easily be transferred to us (2 Chron 7:15; Isa 43:1). His people are surely those on whom His name is called.

James here insisted that everything was happening in accordance with a divine plan, not only forecast in the OT, but actually foreknown from the foundation of the world, "Known unto God are all his works from the beginning of the world" (v.18). So the believers ought not to be taken by surprise since such a thing as Gentile blessing had always been in the purpose of God, just as the crucifixion and resurrection of Christ had been. (Acts 2, 4 stress the same two points.) These developments ought not to take any by surprise, since what happened to Christ, and now what was (and still is) happening in the gospel and in the church, are both in the counsels of God and in the Scriptures of truth. Before circumcision was commanded and before the law was given, there stood the promise to Abraham, "In thee shall all families of the earth be blessed" (Gen 12:3).

19-21 With the evidence of Peter, Barnabas and Paul, and that of the Scriptures, James finally gave his judgment that ceremonial issues like circumcision should never be insisted on for Gentiles believers (the words "that we trouble them not" imply this) but that moral issues should be, for example, prohibitions against idolatry and fornication. The moral standards of the Mosaic law are expected from all Christians since they are a reflection of the standards of a holy God. Since Gentile believers have already been brought out of idolatry (1 Thess 1:9), it is best to understand "idolatry" in the sense that Paul discussed the matter in Rom 14 and 1 Cor 8; 10:23-33, namely to avoid partaking of flesh that had been offered in idolatrous practices and then sold on the open market, thereby avoiding offence to Jew, Gentile or the church of God. Fornication is understood in its primary meaning, since it was regarded as normal in heathen circles, and hence several times Paul warns against it in the church. Although some modern translations suggest that abstention from things strangled is not fully authenticated in all Greek manuscripts, we must admit that the law of Moses, preached in every synagogue every Sabbath day, did forbid the eating of things strangled and of blood, and pious Jews are still meticulous in their observance of such prohibitions. There are still Christians who have reservations about not taking heed to these last two prohibitions, while others take 1 Tim 4:4-6 as being final, "every creature of God is good, and nothing to be refused, if it be received with thanksgiving: for it is sanctified by the word of God and prayer". On the one hand there are certain features of conduct in which Christians should never be engaged, while there are other features that should be avoided if they cause offence to others.

22-29 This judgment obtained the approval of the whole church in Jerusalem, so it was proposed that not only Barnabas, Paul and their companions should carry the decision back to Antioch, but that they should be accompanied by a group of "chief men among the brethren" or "chosen men" from Jerusalem who would verify the report. Barnabas and Paul are called "men that have hazarded their lives for the name of our Lord Jesus Christ". Various copies of the letter were taken, not only for the church at Antioch but for the churches planted during the first missionary journey (16:4). Additionally, the letter stated that it was the mind of the Holy Spirit, as well as of the brethren with one accord. The letter consists of the following ideas:

1. Greetings from all in the Jerusalem church to the Gentiles (v.23).

2. The fact that the false doctrine had not been commanded by the Jerusalem church (v.24); circumcision is mentioned particularly.

3. Those who would be sent with the letter, including chosen men from Jerusalem, would testify verbally of the truth (vv.25-27).

4. The Holy Spirit approves the contents of the letter (v.28).

5. The substance of the decision (v.29).

This was the authoritative answer to those unauthorised persons who had upset the Gentile believers with their preposterous demands that new believers should become little better than Jewish proselytes. There are several references to unauthorised teachers in the epistles, such as grievous wolves and false elders in Ephesus (20:29-30); those who do not teach the words of the Lord Jesus (1 Tim 6:3-5); those whose words eat as a canker (2 Tim 2:17); false teachers who will be followed (2 Pet 2:1-2); those who deny that Jesus Christ is come in the flesh (1 John 4:1-3). Such men dominate Christendom today.

This letter constituted the last-mentioned communication between the parent Jerusalem church and the daughter church in Antioch. The Council of Jerusalem resolved the difficulty, but such councils must not be regarded as a precedent for NT churches, since the presence of apostles was necessary. Believers today have the whole NT as their guide, rather than depending solely on the advice and counsel of others. When we look for guidance in the Acts, we have not only the progress of revealed doctrine to take into consideration, but also the completion of the canon of Scripture. We should imitate the zeal of the first Christians, aware that their Lord had so recently risen from the dead, note their practices, and watch the development of the church which owed more to the revelations received directly from God than it does to Judaism. Sir Robert Anderson fought so much against the re-introduction of ritualism into the church, which he regarded as simply a reversion to Judaistic practices which had served their purpose (as a "schoolmaster" or "child instructor" bringing us up to the time of Christ, Gal 2:14-16), but which were completely superseded by the christian revelation.

30-35 The word "confirmed" in the AV is interesting (v.32). It is used on a number of occasions, in the sense of encouraging or strengthening those first disciples and churches; it is never used, as in Christendom, to describe a ceremony performed on an individual. The exhortations of Judas and Silas had this effect on the saints in Antioch (v.32), and the further visit of Paul and Silas had the same effect on the new churches in Syria and Cilicia (v.41).

With their mission accomplished, it was time for the visitors from Jerusalem to return home "to the apostles", but Silas chose to stay at Antioch, just as Barnabas had done previously. V.35, like previous verses as 11:26; 13:1, 27-28, indicates what a privileged place Antioch was, with so many preachers and teachers, "Paul and Barnabas continued in Antioch, teaching and preaching the word of the Lord, with many others also" (v.35).

5. Paul's Second Missionary Journey
15:36-18:22

a. Derbe and Lystra (15:36-16:5)

v.36 "And some days after Paul said unto Barnabas. Let us go again and visit our brethren in every city where we have preached the word of the Lord, *and see* how they do.

v.37 And Barnabas determined to take with them John, whose surname was Mark.

v.38 But Paul thought not good to take him with them, who departed from them from Pamphylia, and went not with them to the work.

v.39 And the contention was so sharp between them, that they departed asunder one from the other: and so Barnabas took Mark, and sailed unto Cyprus;

v.40 And Paul chose Silas, and departed, being recommended by the brethren unto the grace of God.

v.41 And he went through Syria and Cilicia, confirming the churches."

16 v.1 "Then came he to Derbe and Lystra: and, behold, a certain disciple was there, named Timotheus, the son of a certain woman, which was a Jewess, and believed; but his father was a Greek:
v.2 Which was well reported of by the brethren that were at Lystra and Iconium.
v.3 Him would Paul have to go forth with him; and took and circumcised him because of the Jews which were in those quarters: for they knew all that his father was a Greek.
v.4 And as they went through the cities, they delivered them the decrees for to keep, that were ordained of the apostles and elders which were at Jerusalem.
v.5 And so were the churches established in the faith, and increased in number daily."

36-36 Now that the standing of Gentile believers had been established, Paul felt that it was necessary to make a return visit to their previous converts of his first missionary journey. A considerable time had elapsed, and no doubt he had heard that it would be beneficial to deliver the letter from Jerusalem to them also. Note in v.36 that the exercise was Paul's; the Holy Spirit is not mentioned in this connection, although obviously he was guided by the Spirit as 16:6-9 makes clear. However, when he spoke to Barnabas about the subject, he found that his partner had a proposal which did not meet with his approval. Paul was not prepared to give the young relative of Barnabas a second chance immediately, since he had caused a difficulty on the previous occasion (13:13), almost as soon as they had reached the mainland from Cyprus. Luke would not belittle anybody by providing the reason for Mark's return home. Suggestions have been made by expositors, but Scripture is silent. At least Mark was profitable again in the hands of the Lord (Col 4:10; 2 Tim 4:11), and when he wrote his Gospel.

39-41 There is no attempt to disguise the fact that there was a major contention between Paul and Barnabas concerning Mark. The result was that two pairs of christian workers set out on the Lord's service instead of one. Barnabas and Mark went to where the first missionary journey had commenced, whereas Paul and Silas began where it had concluded, namely Derbe and Lystra. This time they travelled overland through Syria and Cilicia where churches had been formed (though how and when we are not told). What is specifically stated is that Paul received a second recommendation to the grace of God for this work. Note that the word "recommended" is singular, applying to Paul, but we need not doubt that Silas and also Barnabas were also recommended.

Note that Paul "chose" Silas. This does not displace the prerogative of the Holy Spirit to chose the Lord's servants, for several times Paul is seen as choosing servants to accomplish various aspects of the Lord's work. But clearly when a servant is chosen by another, there must be a direct contact with the Lord's will, with the qualifications of the one chosen being taken into account carefully before the Lord. This remark applies particularly when speakers are chosen for the "platform", whether for ministry or for gospel preaching.

And so one of the few men (Luke 23:50) in the NT to be called "a good man" disappears from the record in the Acts. He does not drop out of the Lord's work, but only out of that aspect of it described in the book. He is mentioned again in Gal 3:13 and 1 Cor 9:6.

16:1-5 Paul and Silas arrived in Derbe and Lystra, the furthest points reached in the first missionary journey. There they met a young man Timothy, who, to begin with at least, was going to occupy the role previously occupied by John Mark. He was destined to have Paul's mantle fall upon him (though not apostleship), and to be the helper who had most in common with Paul, "I have no man likeminded, who will naturally care for your state" (Phil 2:20), in spite of the fact that there was an age gap, a racial gap and a personality gap.

Since the last visit, Timothy had obviously made spiritual strides; he was "well reported of by the brethren that were at Lystra and Iconium". He had become well-known among the believers in the places covered in the previous missionary journey, and this good report must have formed the basis of Paul's decision to take him with him on the second journey. In spite of the fact that Paul was carrying the decision of the Jerusalem Council relative to circumcision, Paul felt it necessary to have Timothy circumcised before he became his companion in missionary work. The only explanation that we can suggest is that if Timothy's uncircumcised condition (his father was a Greek) would reduce his effectiveness in service, then Paul would be happy to have that impediment removed. It is an illustration of the principle stated in 1 Cor 9:20, "unto the Jews I became as a Jew, that I might gain the Jews; to them that are under the law, as under the law, that I might gain them that are under the law". But contrast he positively refused to have Titus circumcised, since that would have been a concession to the bondage of Judaism with its distortion of the gospel (Gal 2:3-4). The section ends with another of Luke's summaries, "And so were the churches established in the faith, and increased in number daily".

b. *The Gospel Comes to Europe: Philippi (16:6-40)*

> v.6 "Now when they had gone throughout Phrygia and the region of Galatia, and were forbidden of the Holy Ghost to preach the word in Asia,
> v.7 After they were come to Mysia, they assayed to go into Bithynia: but the Spirit suffered them not.
> v.8 And they passing by Mysia came down to Troas.
> v.9 And a vision appeared to Paul in the night; There stood a man of Macedonia, and prayed him, saying, Come over into Macedonia, and help us.
> v.10 And after he had seen the vision, immediately we endeavoured to go into Macedonia, assuredly gathering that the Lord had called us for to preach the gospel unto them.

- v.11 Therefore loosing from Troas, we came with a straight course to Samothracia, and the next *day* to Neapolis;
- v.12 And from thence to Philippi, which is the chief city of that part of Macedonia, *and* a colony: and we were in that city abiding certain days.
- v.13 And on the sabbath we went out of the city by a river side, where prayer was wont to be made; and we sat down, and spake unto the women which resorted *thither*.
- v.14 And a certain woman named Lydia, a seller of purple, of the city of Thyatira, which worshipped God, heard *us*: whose heart the Lord opened, that she attended unto the things which were spoken of Paul.
- v.15 And when she was baptized, and her household, she besought *us*, saying, If ye have judged me to be faithful to the Lord, come into my house, and abide *there*. And she constrained us.
- v.16 And it came to pass, as we went to prayer, a certain damsel possessed with a spirit of divination met us, which brought her masters much gain by soothsaying:
- v.17 The same followed Paul and us, and cried, saying, These men are the servants of the most high God, which shew unto us the way of salvation.
- v.18 And this did she many days. But Paul, being grieved, turned and said to the spirit, I command thee in the name of Jesus Christ to come out of her. And he came out the same hour.
- v.19 And when her masters saw that the hope of their gains was gone, they caught Paul and Silas, and drew *them* into the market-place unto the rulers,
- v.20 And brought them to the magistrates, saying, These men, being Jews, do exceedingly trouble our city.
- v.21 And teach customs, which are not lawful for us to receive, neither to observe, being Romans.
- v.22 And the multitude rose up together against them: and the magistrates rent off their clothes, and commanded to beat *them*.
- v.23 And when they had laid many stripes upon them, they cast *them* into prison, charging the jailor to keep them safely:
- v.24 Who, having received such a charge, thrust them into the inner prison, and made their feet fast in the stocks.
- v.25 And at midnight Paul and Silas prayed, and sang praises unto God: and the prisoners heard them.
- v.26 And suddenly there was a great earthquake, so that the foundations of the prison were shaken: and immediately all the doors were opened, and every one's bands were loosed.
- v.27 And the keeper of the prison awaking out of his sleep, and seeing the prison doors open, he drew out his sword, and would have killed himself, supposing that the prisoners had been fled.
- v.28 But Paul cried with a loud voice, saying, Do thyself no harm: for we are all here.
- v.29 Then he called for a light, and sprang in, and came trembling, and fell down before Paul and Silas,
- v.30 And brought them out, and said, Sirs, what must I do to be saved?
- v.31 And they said, Believe on the Lord Jesus Christ, and thou shalt be saved, and thy house."

v.32 And they spake unto him the word of the Lord, and to all that were in his house.
v.33 And he took them the same hour of the night, and washed *their* stripes; and was baptized, he and all his, straightway.
v.34 And when he had brought them into his house, he set meat before them, and rejoiced, believing in God with all his house.
v.35 And when it was day, the magistrates sent the serjeants, saying, Let those men go.
v.36 And the keeper of the prison told this saying to Paul. The magistrates have sent to let you go: now therefore depart, and go in peace.
v.37 But Paul said unto them, They have beaten us openly uncondemned, being Romans, and have cast *us* into prison; and now do they thrust us out privily? nay verily; but let them come themselves and fetch us out.
v.38 And the serjeants told these words unto the magistrates: and they feared, when they heard that they were Romans.
v.39 And they came and besought them, and brought *them* out, and desired *them* to depart out of the city.
v.40 And they went out of the prison, and entered into *the house of* Lydia: and when they had seen the brethren, they comforted them, and departed."

The new territory opened up for the gospel, principally in Europe, focusses mainly on five cities, implying that this second journey could well be called A *Tale of Five Cities*. There is only one speech recorded compared with two during the first missionary journey. This speech (hardly a sermon, 17:22-31) was delivered in Athens, and could well be compared with that to the people of Lystra in 14:15-17. But the amount of other detail given by Luke, now an eye-witness for part of the time, is greater than that given for the various places visited on the first journey. This detail embraces the kind of officials responsible for local government in all the places except Athens, and in every case Luke informs us about the condemnatory accusations made against the preachers, in addition to the usual stories of converts and reactions to the preachers. Features of these five cities and of the missionaries' work in them are as follows:

1. Philippi

Description of city: "The chief city of that part of Macedonia, and a (Roman) colony" (16:2).

Nature of city: Commercial, attracting business people such as Lydia from Thyatira and sharp businessmen who capitalised on the fortune-telling abilities of the demon-possessed girl (v.16).

Local officials: Roman *praetores* or magistrates (vv.20, 22, 38), together with "serjeants" who carried out their orders.

Preaching place: Presumably there were not enough Jews to justify having a synagogue, but any that dwelt there, together with possible proselytes, met each Sabbath day by the river side for prayer (v.13).

Converts: The household of Lydia (v.15); the jailer's household (v.33); "the brethren" (v.40). At some stage, Euodias and Syntyche were converted (Phil 4:2).

Baptisms: The households of Lydia and of the jailer (vv.15,33).

Miracles: The casting out of the demon from the soothsayer (v.18); the earthquake, with all doors opened and bands loosed (v.26).

Accusation: "These men, being Jews, do exceedingly trouble our city, and teach customs, which are not lawful for us to receive, neither to observe, being Romans" (vv.20-21). Compare this with the words of the demon-possessed girl, "These men are the servants of the most high God, which show unto us the way of salvation" (v.17).

Persecution: Beaten or flogged, "many stripes" (v.22-23); compare this with "in stripes above measure" (2 Cor 11:23).

Preachers: Paul, Silas, Luke, Timothy.

Lodgings: Unknown address for "certain days" (v.12), thereafter in Lydia's house (vv.15,40).

Follow up: Luke was left behind; visit to Macedonia (19:22); collection from Macedonia for the Jerusalem church (2 Cor 8:1); Paul's letter to Philippi; Paul's later visit to Macedonia (1 Tim 1:3). (Note the emphasis on "gain" or "win" in Phil 1:21; 3:2-8.)

2. Thessalonica

Description of city: Accessible from Macedonia and Achaia (1 Thess 1:8), these being provinces of ancient Greece.

Nature of city: Idolatrous (1 Thess 1:9).

Local officials: The rulers or politarchs (Acts 17:6, 8).

Preaching places: The synagogue for three Sabbath days (v.2).

Converts: "Some believed ... of the devout Greeks a great multitude, and of the chief women not a few" (v.4); Jason (vv.6-9); Aristarchus and Secundus (20:4).

Accusation: "These that have turned the world upside down are come hither also ... these all do contrary to the decrees of Caesar, saying that there is another king, one Jesus" (vv.6-7).

Persecution: "The Jews ... took ... certain lewd fellows of the baser sort ... and set all the city on an uproar" (v.5).

Preachers: Paul, Silas and Timothy.

Lodgings: Jason's house (v.7).

Follow up: Two letters, 1 & 2 Thessalonians. Paul sent Timothy to establish and comfort them (1 Thess 3:1-13). Note emphasis on the second advent, "there is another king, one Jesus".

3. Athens

Description of city: The intellectual capital of the ancient world with philosophers of the Epicureans and of the Stoicks (v.18); "all the Athenians and strangers ... spent their time in nothing else, but either to tell, or to hear some new thing" (v.21). The city was full of images, or "wholly given to idolatry" (v.16), with one

altar named "To the unknown god" in case one had been missed out (not of course the true God) (v.23).
Local officials: Traditionally, Athens was a democracy, excluding the great slave population. Intellectuals tended to argue rather than to persecute.
Preaching places: The synagogue (v.17); in the market (*agora*) daily with those chancing to be there; a once-for-all meeting in the Areopagus (v.19).
Converts: Dionysius the Areopagite, a woman Damaris and others (v.34). There is no mention of a church being formed.
Accusation: Paul was a "babbler" or an ignorant plagiarist; "a setter forth of strange gods" (v.18); "thou bringest certain strange things to our ears" (v.20).
Preacher: Paul alone, since Silas and Timothy had remained in Berea (v.14); they caught up with him in Corinth (18:5).
Preaching: "Jesus, and the resurrection" (vv.18,31).

4. Corinth

Description of city: Leading seaport of the Eastern Mediterranean. Highly immoral as one would expect from a seaport (1 Cor 6:9-10); idolatrous (1 Cor 8:1-13; 10:24-29); "the Greeks seek after wisdom" (1 Cor 1:19-31). 1 Corinthians does not only refer in ch.1 to the Greeks' love of knowledge, but also reveals that there were those who, like the Athenians, did not believe in resurrection, even amongst believers (15:12).
Local officials: Gallio, deputy or proconsul of Achaia (Acts 18:12).
Preaching place: Synagogue every Sabbath day (v.4), until he left for the house next door (v.7).
Converts: Justus (v.7); Sosthenes (v.17; 1 Cor 1:1); Crispus, the chief ruler of the synagogue (v.8); "much people" (v.10); "house of Chloe" (1 Cor 1:11); Gaius (v.14); "household of Stephanas" (1:16; 16:15); Fortunatus and Achaicus (16:17).
Baptisms: "Many of the Corinthians hearing believed, and were baptized" (v.8).
Accusation: "This fellow persuadeth men to worship God contrary to the law" (v.13).
Persecutions: They opposed or resisted, and blasphemed (v.6); the Jews made insurrection and brought Paul to the judgment seat before Gallio (v.12).
Preachers: Paul alone at first; joined later by Silas and Timothy (v.5).
Lodgings: With Aquila and Priscilla, recently driven from Rome on account of persecution of Jews (vv.2-3).
Follow-up: Visits by Apollos (18:27-28), and by Timothy and Titus (1 Cor 4:17; 16:10; 2 Cor 7:4-16; 8:6,16,23). Paul's two epistles to the Corinthians. His later visit in Acts 20:2-3 in keeping with 1 Cor 4:19 and 2 Cor 12:20.

5. Ephesus

Description of city: Located in Asia (Asia Minor for a period, but now modern Turkey); centre of worship of Artemis or Diana whom "all Asia" worshipped (19:27). From this city "all ... Asia heard the word of the Lord" (v.10).
Local officials: The townclerk (v.35), a more important official than former United

Kingdom townclerks; deputies or proconsuls (v.38).
Preaching places: The synagogue for three months (v.8); the school of Tyrannus daily for two years (v.9).
Converts: "Many that believed came, and confessed, and showed their deeds" (v.18); "Many ... which used curious arts brought their books together, and burned them" (v.19).
Baptisms: About twelve were initially baptised (vv.5,7), previously having been baptised unto John's baptism.
Miracles: Speaking with languages (v.6); special miracles, or powerful deeds out of the ordinary, by the hands of Paul, with diseases cured and evil spirits departing (vv.11-12); pseudo-miracles attempted by the sons of Sceva (v.26).
Accusation: Many spoke "evil of that way" (v.9); "this Paul hath persuaded and turned away much people, saying that there be no gods, which are made with hands" (v.26).
Persecution: "Full of wrath ... the whole city ... caught Gaius and Aristarchus" (v.28); a two-hour riot when the mob chanted, "Great is Diana of the Ephesians" (v.34); uproar or insurrection (v.40).
Preachers: Paul, with Timothy and Erastus for a time, until Paul sent them to Macedonia (v.22); Gaius and Aristarchus unto the end (v.29).
Follow-up: The Ephesian elders were summoned to meet Paul at Troas (20:17-38); the letter to the Ephesians is considered to have been a circular letter rather than a specific one to that church alone. Later Timothy was left at Ephesus after Paul's first imprisonment (1 Tim 1:3).

We have omitted Berea (17:10-14) owing to the lack of much information. Note that in Philippi, Thessalonica and Corinth the accusers played on the idea that the new Christians were undermining the loyalty of citizens to Rome (16:20-21; 17:6-7; 18:13). In Athens and Ephesus Paul condemned men worshipping things made with hands.
We now return to Paul's work in Philippi (16:6-40).

6-7 Leaving the territory covered on the first missionary journey, Paul and Silas ran into apparent difficulties. They may not have been sufficiently motivated to head directly for Europe themselves, but found their way blocked to anywhere else. They had passed through Phrygia and Galatia, and intended first to preach the gospel in the province of Asia (then only a part of what we now call Turkey). When that door was closed to them, they planned to visit Bithynia (bordering the Black Sea to the north). But both roads were blocked by the Spirit of God, "they ... were forbidden of the Holy Ghost" (v.6); "the Spirit suffered them not" (v.7).
The interesting feature of the two closed doors is that the first one is accredited to the Holy Spirit (v.6), whereas almost all Greek MSS state that it was the "Spirit of Jesus" that closed the door into Bithynia. We cannot offer an explanation of the difference. This is the only mention of this precise title in the NT. We read of "the

Spirit of Christ" (Rom 8:9; 1 Pet 1:11); "the Spirit of his Son" (Gal 4:6); "the Spirit of Jesus Christ" (Phil 1:19).

In neither case can there have been a direct revelation. There was no question of the preachers saying, "The Spirit speaketh expressly", for the missionary group had still to await the vision of the man from Macedonia calling for their help. But Paul always relied on the will of God (18:21). It is, therefore, more likely to have been circumstantial guidance, the nature of which we are not told, but the one situation is attributed to the Holy Spirit, and the other to the Spirit of Christ.

8-9 So the only route lay westwards between Asia and Bithynia through Mysia. It was that vision, the sixth in the historical record of the Acts (9:10; 9:12; 10:3; 10:10; 22:17), which directed the preachers from Troas at the western end of this route. Troas was in the district of ancient Troy, and the vision would direct the evangelists to brand new territory, the continent of Europe. It forms a major turning-point in God's dealings with men. Nor should we be concerned about the places which were not visited by Paul and Silas, for the Lord who was directing them elsewhere for their service made sure that Asia and Bithynia heard the gospel from other lips, as indicated by the provinces listed in 1 Pet 1:1. The elect are reached by whomsoever God chooses to be His servants, wherever they live.

From now on, the great Gentile world beyond Asia is going to be the apostle's sphere of service, but he was guided to it regardless of any natural instinct. He had never objected to including Gentiles among the subjects of his preaching, and had contended for their being included in God's sphere of blessing, but he may not have considered how far the Lord would have him to advance into the Gentile continent beyond. The vision of the man from Macedonia gave him direction and the certainty of God's will. It is impossible to identify this man; no doubt he was a representative of Europe, an idolater with a veneer of civilisation, a man who needed Christ through the gospel.

10-11 Although only Paul had the vision, yet all in the missionary group assuredly understood that the Lord had called them all, and they reacted "immediately" to this call. Here we discover that Luke was among the preaching party. He makes his presence known by changing the pronoun "they" (v.8) to "we" and "us" (from v.10). We therefore begin to have actual eyewitness accounts of what was happening on the following missionary journeys. During the following chapters, the author's presence is indicated by the pronouns "we" and "us", and his absences by a return to "they" and "them". The result is that we have a writer who never intrudes into his writings (except briefly in Luke 1:3), but expresses the spirit of Christ by remaining in the background. "We" continues throughout ch.16 in vv.11, 12, 13, 15, 16, 17 while Paul and his company remained in Philippi. The change to "they" and "them" continues from 17:1. Paul and his company returned to Macedonia from Ephesus in Acts 20 and then to Greece proper. The use of "we" and "us" recommences in v.5, and continues in vv.6, 13 ,15, etc. In other words, Luke rejoined the apostle as he followed the others to Troas, and the eyewitness account is then continued through to the last chapter. The "we" in 27:1 shows that Luke was present on the isle of Melita, and on the ship that took Paul to Puteoli on the Italian mainland. According to vv.16-17, he was also on the walk to Rome. Finally, he was with Paul during his last imprisonment in Rome, "Only Luke is with me" (2 Tim 4:11).

12-13 The first scene of gospel activity in Europe was the city of Philippi slightly inland, a Roman colony with all the status that went with it, but there was too small a Jewish population to justify a synagogue.

14 Three parties appear in the story of this first missionary visit to Philippi. First, on the Sabbath day because there was no synagogue in the city, the evangelists sought out the group of praying women who were found meeting for prayer each Sabbath day by the riverside. This was unusual, but the Lord often used to pray outside, and so did Paul (21:5; 28:15). To such an audience the story of the Lord Jesus was told; the outstanding conversion was that of Lydia, a proselyte from Thyatira, whose presence in the city was explained by her business activity. There was nothing spectacular in her story, except the statement "whose heart the Lord opened", which strictly must describe every conversion. In Lydia's case, this means that the bud of Judaism, which she readily accepted because there was nothing else to accept as a proselyte, blossomed out, as she received the preachers' claim about the Lord Jesus, namely, "the things which were spoken by Paul". Christ was found by her to be the end of the law for righteousness.

15 The natural corollary was to be baptised, implying that Paul had also taught this subject (as Philip had to the Ethiopian eunuch in the chariot). This happened almost immediately with every new convert in the Acts. The happy feature of this first baptism in Philippi and in Europe was that it was of a household. We must surmise that the members of her household believed just like herself. NT baptism was only for believers and disciples, though mistakes might sometimes be made as in 8:13.

Not only was Lydia's household (no doubt her staff of servants if she did not have a family or her own) the first christian household in Europe, but it was also the first to show the christian grace of hospitality. Wherever the evangelists had been staying previously in Philippi, she insisted that they come and lodge with her. An open heart was followed by an open door. (In the case of the jailer later, an open door was followed by an open heart.) Paul was counted faithful by the Lord (1 Tim 1:12), and now he was able to discern that Lydia was faithful. The NIV "If you consider me a believer in the Lord" is a poor paraphrase, since one can be a believer and yet not be faithful, and the AV definitely follows the Greek text (the word is an adjective not a noun).

The first preachers owed a lot to such open doors (as did Andrew and Peter in John 1:39-42). It is suggested that the church commenced in John Mark's mother's house in Jerusalem, and made use of these premises for meetings as late as 12:12. Peter was lodging in such a hospitable house in Joppa (9:43). This is the first lodging, but by no means the last, into which Paul and his company were welcomed, according to Luke's record. What an important part such homes have played in the spread of the gospel and of the church over the centuries! How blessed are those who have provided accommodation for the Lord's servants!

16-23 The second person contacted and blessed was the demon-possessed girl. In a commercial city like Philippi, shrewd men had capitalised on her condition, and used her fortune-telling for their gain and not hers. Just as the Lord was recognised by demons in the Gospels (Mark 1:23-28; 3:11-12; 5:1-20; etc.), so was Paul in the Acts. See also 19:13-17.

The girl fortune-teller's description of the preachers whom she followed day after day is interesting and complex. She called them "servants (slaves) of the most high God". In normal circumstances we would not expect one demon-possessed to admit that God was most High. And yet elsewhere in Acts (19:15) as well as in Mark 1:24 we have examples of the indwelling demons acknowledging the presence of deity. James tells us that the demons believe that there is only one God, and that they tremble (2:19).

Luke mentions this title of God, most High, or Highest, many more times than any other NT writer. In the OT its meaning is "possessor of heaven and earth" (Gen 14:19). Luke quotes Stephen using it in his speech before he was stoned to death (7:48), and it also occurs five times in his Gospel (1:32, 35, 76; 6:35; 8:28). It would appear to be almost automatic that one who was demon-possessed should acknowledge the most High God, since the demon within her knew this fact. But many translations state that she was saying that what was being preached was "a way" of salvation rather than "the way" of salvation. (The RV margin has "a", and JND brackets the word "the"). The reason is that the Greek text does *not* have the definite article "the".

At the beginning in 3:6, the power of the name of Jesus Christ is used by Peter. What that power did for the paralysed man at the temple gate, it also did for the demon-possessed girl through Paul's instrumentality. We would believe that this girl was now converted, and followed Paul and the others in quite a different sense from previously, namely in a spiritual way.

The casting out of the spirit of Python from this fortune-telling girl is one of the six specific miracles performed by Paul in the Acts. It was this miracle that caused her masters to bring Paul and Silas before the magistrates, which produced the uproar in Philippi, leading to their imprisonment. Here too were inflicted one session of those stripes about which Paul wrote in 2 Cor 11:23. ("Divination" or "Python" (v.16) was the name of the Pythian serpent or dragon killed by Apollo in Greek mythology. The word came to be used of Apollo himself, and then it was applied to diviners or soothsayers (W.E. Vine).)

24-34 From a human point of view, to Paul and Silas it must have seemed strange divine guidance that led to a dungeon-prison in Philippi. But the prisoners behaved magnificently. What they did could only come from believing that they were in the current of the will of God. What a wonderful illustration they were of that peace, which Paul later described when he wrote to those inhabitants of Philippi who became Christians, "the peace of God, which passeth all understanding, shall keep your hearts and minds through Christ Jesus" (Phil 4:7). With backs bleeding and sore, with their feet cramped in stocks and in the blackness of the inner dungeon at midnight, they sang praises to God. At the critical moment, there was a divine intervention from heaven; an earthquake burst open the prison doors, but not to let the prisoners scatter for freedom. We do not know what prompted the asking of that famous question, "What must I do to be saved?" (v.30). Was it the collapse of the jailer's world about him? Was it the behaviour of the prisoners who could so easily have escaped? Was it to be saved from the Roman authorities who would put him to death if prisoners were lost? Or was it a call for genuine salvation? Certainly he could not have heard the songs of praise of Paul and Silas since v.27 states that he was asleep, unlike the other prisoners who heard their prayer and praise. We do not know, but the outcome was the creation of a second christian household in Philippi, and that of a very different kind from the first. A second baptism took place, and the jailer proved that he had been changed when his attitude towards the preachers changed. His callousness gave place to gentleness, and his pitilessness to kindness, providing simple medical care and food.

The third mentioned, but nameless, beneficiary from the preaching of the gospel in Philippi was this jailer. It needed a vastly different set of circumstances to gain his conversion from those required in Lydia's case, but this is how God works. Lydia was met at a religious prayer meeting; the jailer at his place of employment. The former was converted at a place where "prayer was wont to be made"; the latter where praise was raised, perhaps for the only time in history. Lydia had a background of Jewish religion and the OT Scriptures; the jailer was no doubt an ignorant heathen. Relative to his imprisonment, Paul might well have used the words that he later wrote to the Philippians, "the things which happened unto me have fallen out rather unto the furtherance of the gospel" (Phil 1:12).

The church at Philippi was the first individual church formed for which we have a letter preserved in the NT from the apostle's pen. (Though it must be realised that the epistles to the Thessalonians, Corinthians and Romans were written previously to churches that had been formed after that at Philippi, and that the epistle to the Galatians was written to a group of churches.) We would expect links between Acts 16 and the epistle to the Philippians. We have already referred to two such (Phil 1:12; 4:7). It is also interesting to note the mentions of the word "gain" in the epistle (1:21; 3:7-8) to believers in a city where gain was considered to be so important. Paul's manner of life while he was among them was also to be an example, "Those things, which ye have ... seen in me, do" (Phil 4:9).

Once again God opened prison doors in the Acts. The first time in 4:3,7 was normal; the following two occasions with the apostles and Peter it was the angel of the Lord who opened the doors (5:19; 12:7-10); the fourth time in 16:26 it was through an earthquake by divine intervention. "Omnipotence has servants everywhere", in humans, in angels and in nature; on earth, in heaven, and in the forces of the universe.

35-38 On the morning after that memorable night, the magistrates ordered the release of the prisoners, who promptly claimed the privileges of Roman citizenship which had not been respected in their case. Not for the only time in the Acts did the apostle claim such rights and embarrass those who had denied them to him (22:25; 24:11). Certain rights Paul would renounced for the gospel's sake, as in 1 Cor 9:5, 15; 2 Cor 11:9. But others he would claim when he felt it right to do so. It is not necessarily a wise unworldliness that causes a Christian to deny that he has rights. "Use it rather" might well be Paul's outlook in a situation like this, which is well illustrated by him in the various circumstances mentioned in 1 Cor 7:21.

39-40 Having roused the magistrates' apprehensions about exceeding their own powers, the imprisoned evangelists received a visit from them, so that they should be released by those who had commanded their imprisonment in the first place. At the same time they were requested to depart from the city, which they did in their own time. First they returned to their lodgings in Lydia's house, who must have spent a night in prayer for her two lodgers. Then they had a session with the brethren for their encouragement (showing that others unmentioned had been converted in the city), and only then did they move on. There was no point in staying if further trouble would ensue.

The word "church" is never used to describe this group of believers in Philippi, but there can be no significance in this. They are all simply referred to as "the brethren" (v.40), but when Paul writes to them in his epistle, he identifies those groups that constitute any local church: saints, bishops and deacons (Phil 1:1). But in 2 Cor 8:1 he does include them amongst "the churches of Macedonia".

Although the evanglists moved on, it appears that the church at Philippi was not left without outside help. This is indicated by the fact that in 17:1 the pronoun reverts to "they" instead of "we", which means that Luke must have remained in Philippi. Do we give him credit for the healthy state of that assembly (2 Cor 9:1-5), where they "first gave their own selves to the Lord"? Luke did not rejoin the preachers until they returned to Macedonia in 20:1-6. We learn from verses such as Phil 1:29-30 that the church suffered for their faith and testimony afterwards, "unto you it is given in the behalf of Christ, not only to believe on him, but also to suffer for his sake; having the same conflict which ye saw in me".

c. *Thessalonica and Berea (17:1-14)*
    v.1   "Now when they had passed through Amphipolis and Apollonia, they came to Thessalonica, where was a synagogue of the Jews:
    v.2   And Paul, as his manner was, went in unto them, and three sabbath days reasoned with them out of the scriptures.

v.3 Opening and alleging, that Christ must needs have suffered, and risen again from the dead; and that this Jesus, whom I preach unto you, is Christ.
v.4 And some of them believed, and consorted with Paul and Silas; and of the devout Greeks a great multitude, and of the chief women not a few.
v.5 But the Jews which believed not, moved with envy, took unto them certain lewd fellows of the baser sort, and gathered a company, and set all the city on an uproar, and assaulted the house of Jason, and sought to bring them out to the people.
v.6 And when they found them not, they drew Jason and certain brethren unto the rulers of the city, crying. These that have turned the world upside down are come hither also;
v.7 Whom Jason hath received: and these all do contrary to the decrees of Caesar, saying that there is another king, *one* Jesus.
v.8 And they troubled the people and the rulers of the city, when they hard these things.
v.9 And when they had taken security of Jason, and of the other, they let them go.
v.10 And the brethren immediately sent away Paul and Silas by night unto Berea: who coming *thither* went into the synagogue of the Jews.
v.11 These were more noble than those in Thessalonica, in that they received the word with all readiness of mind, and searched the scriptures daily, whether those things were so.
v.12 Therefore many of them believed; also of honourable women which were Greeks, and of men, not a few.
v.13 But when the Jews of Thessalonica had knowledge that the word of God was preached of Paul at Berea, they came thither also, and stirred up the people.
v.14 And then immediately the brethren sent away Paul to go as it were to the sea: but Silas and Timotheus abode there still."

1-4   The main highway westwards led to Thessalonica. We are not informed of any evangelistic activities in the towns of Amphipolis and Apollonia on the Aegean coastline before the missionaries arrived in Thessalonica, modern Salonica. Although there were sufficient Jews here to justify a synagogue, and this was, as usual, Paul's first preaching place, the church that was formed on his visit seemed to have been largely a Gentile one. For there is not a single OT quotation in the epistles written to them shortly afterwards by Paul.

Not only was the Jewish synagogue Paul's first preaching point in Thessalonica, but his message was typical of his approach to Jews and proselytes; he reasoned with them from the OT Scriptures. He proved that Jesus was the suffering Saviour and the risen Lord of the OT, and consequently He must be Israel's Messiah. V.4 relates to those who believed, while v.5 provides information about those who did not. The Lord came into the world to create division, and Paul found this always to be so: "some believed the things which were spoken, and some believed not" (28:24). Those who did believe are described as a great multitude of devout Greeks, and not a few of the chief women. Based on the Greek word for "chief" (*protos*), it has been suggested that these women were the wives of the leading men of the city. From the beginning there were the makings of a christian church in this city, indicated by the new believers consorting together, or gathering around Paul. They became followers of Paul, and of the Lord (1 Thess 1:6). Those converted in the synagogue could not have been idolaters, so there must also have been converts from outside the synagogue, since Paul wrote that they "turned to God from idols" (v.9). Paul also preached truth not contained in the OT, namely that they had to "wait for his Son from heaven" (v.10). The news of their faith spread abroad rapidly, through Macedonia and Achaia, and "in every place" (vv.7-8).

The true character of a missionary is seen in Paul's behaviour amongst the Thessalonians. He was bold (1 Thess 2:2); there was no deceit, uncleanness or guile in his exhortation (v.3); he sought to please God as having been put in trust with the gospel (v.4); he would not use flattering words (v.5); he sought glory from none (v.6); he was gentle as a nursing mother would cherish her own children (v.7); he desired to impart to them his own soul, that is, his own appreciation of the Lord and the truth of the Scriptures (v.8); he would work night and day to avoid being a burden to them (v.9); he behaved "holily and justly and unblameably" amongst them (v.10); he acted as a father when he exhorted, comforted and charged them (v.11). And when he left them, it was not in heart but desiring greatly to see them again (v.17). In no other place does Paul open out his heart like this; his manner of life had to match his doctrine. Here was no authoritative dictator, but one in whom the person of Christ was dwelling. In Rom 15:15-33 Paul opens out his life of service, and in 2 Cor 11:23-33 he opens out his life of suffering, but nowhere else than in 1 Thess 2 do we find his manner of life in service so sweetly, spiritually and personally described. It is an example for all the Lord's servants.

5-6 Doubtless Paul's success in gaining converts produced this reaction among the unbelieving Jews, for Paul preached only for three Sabbath days in the synagogue, and then those who believed gathered with him outside the synagogue. Envy in the unbelieving Jews caused them to arrange the assault. In contrast to the chief women who believed, we find that their opponents enlisted the rabble of the city to serve their purpose in creating a riot. In Ephesus later it was the words of a heathen Gentile which caused a riot (19:28). In Jerusalem Jews from Asia gave false testimony that caused a riot (21:27, 30). In other words, in city after city, there was no depth to which unregenerate Jews and Gentiles would not stoop to enlist violence to oppose the spread of the gospel. The opposition in Thessalonica was as fierce as it was anywhere.

It appears that the missionaries' lodging place was Jason's house. Even the preachers' hosts were likely to find themselves in trouble for sheltering them. Mention of those who gave shelter to God's servants is frequently given by Luke (16:15; 18:3; 21:16), and its importance cannot be over-emphasised; did not Mary and Martha do the same for the Lord Jesus? Those who offered such hospitality shared in the successes of the gospel, and often shared equally in the sufferings connected with it. When "that day" dawns, God will not overlook the helping hand given by those who took the Lord's servants into their homes. The Lord used this idea in His parable in Matt 25:35, 38, 43, 44. Peter commended it (1 Pet 4:9) and so did John (3 John 5-8); certainly Peter had experienced it in Joppa in 9:43, and in Cornelius' house in 10:48.

The preachers were accused of having "turned the world upside down". Readers may well feel, with the old Puritan, that the situation was rather that they found the world upside down, and attempted through the gospel to turn it right side up, at least in those who were converted, with the majority still remaining facing downwards. Certainly the devil loved the world as it was, and made it exceedingly difficult for those who by their preaching attempted to change some men and women in it.

7-8 The various charges laid against the preachers are worth summarising. Taken together they illustrate how much the gospel cuts across what is generally accepted in the world.

This time they are not accused of moving contrary to Jewish tradition, but of undermining Caesar's rule. The Jews adopted this false concept when they accused the Lord Jesus before Pilate (Luke 23:2). Paul had already been similarly accused in Philippi (16:21). Whether the preachers talked about the Lord Jesus as king or not, we do not know, but it is evident that that was how people in Thessalonica interpreted it. After all, they did announce another kingdom, the kingdom of God, which, however, was moral in its application (Rom 14:17); Paul wrote to them that they had been called "unto his kingdom and glory" (1 Thess 2:12). The Lord Jesus does require undivided loyalty from His followers. And we know from the epistles to the Thessalonians that Paul taught them much about prophecy, when the Lord as King will be fully manifested. These Jews in Thessalonica might have misunderstood Paul's teaching about the future from his teaching about the present. 2 Thess 2:1-2 shows that even the believers were confused about certain prophetic matters owing to false teachers being active amongst them.

9-12 Jason had to pay bail for the good behaviour of his guests. Once again, the brethren considered that in the interests of his own safety Paul should be escorted away from danger. Their next port of call was Berea, about fifty miles west of Thessalonica. Here the Jews in the synagogue seemed to be much more fair-minded than in most Jewish communities, and they compared what the preachers had to say with the OT Scriptures. For them to do this, it shows the necessity for all preachers of the gospel to use thoroughly Bible-based messages. The example of the Berean's is a very worthy one, both for every child of God and also for those exercised about finding the truth, "they ... searched the scriptures daily, whether those things were so". Timothy, who was with Paul, might well have recalled his upbringing, "from a child thou hast known the holy scriptures" (2 Tim 3:15). Believers today may tend to be far too prone to accept that things are right, without searching the Scriptures for confirmation that their conduct, service and doctrine are consistent with the Scriptures or not. Some preachers can be very persuasive, with the subtle intention of drawing away disciples after them (20:30). So after having heard Paul preach, the

Bereans were not prepared to rest on Jewish tradition; they realised that there was doctrine and prophecy in the OT Scriptures that they had not perceived before. They examined the evangelists' preaching to check whether it was in harmony with the word of God or not. Again, both women and men believed. Both in his Gospel and in the Acts, Luke pays special attention and gives special tribute to women-folk. Paul also did likewise; see Rom 16:1-6 (and other feminine names in the chapter); Phil 4:2-3.

13-14 It is surprising to discover that, in spite of the distance between Thessalonica and Berea in days when transport was not easy, news travelled quickly; the persecutors from the former city arrived in Berea to stir up the people. They had great determination that the new message should not take root. Again the local brethren considered that discretion was the better part of valour, and so Paul was brought to Athens by those who "conducted" him (God's destination for him ultimately was Corinth). His travelling companions, Silas and Timothy remained in Berea meanwhile. We do not know why this separation took place, but we do know that Paul in Athens felt the need of their help. Neither in Athens nor in Rome (2 Tim 4:10-11) did Paul like to be alone.

Notes

Timothy

Paul's first letter to the Thessalonians supplements the story in Acts 17 more than any other NT letters do for the apostle's corresponding visit to particular cities. Paul's deep concern for the infant church in Thessalonica caused him to send Timothy to see how they were faring under persecution. Paul had arrived in Athens only with an escort. That escort was instructed, when they returned to Berea, to request Silas and Timothy to join him "with all speed" in Athens where he was alone.

What happened to Silas after that we do not know. Timothy was quickly despatched back to Thessalonica because of Paul's concern for the new persecuted church (1 Thess 3:1-10). Paul called him "our brother, and minister of God, and our fellowlabourer in the gospel of Christ". The name of Silas, as "Silvanus", appears at the head of both epistles to the Thessalonians, and he reappears for the last time in Acts, together with Timothy in 18:5, when they both arrived back from Macedonia, but this time to Corinth. It therefore appears that the arrival in 18:5 refers, not to their arrival in Athens (17:15-16) but in Corinth (18:5), as if Silas left Athens either with Timothy (1 Thess 3:2) or at some later time. One of the features of the Acts is that there was plenty of movement by the evangelists between cities, and yet there was always onward progress. It may appear that a lot of "human" decisions were being taken, but we can rest assured that the will of God was motivating all decisions.

It should be noted that this is the first time that Timothy is mentioned as having been given a special task by the apostle Paul. It was certainly not the last. Paul was learning, as he watched Timothy day by day, that he had "no man likeminded, who will naturally care for your state" (Phil 2:19-24); Paul recalled "ye know the proof of him, that, as a son with the father, he hath served with me in the gospel". Several times afterwards, when Paul needed to be in two places at once, he sent Timothy to be his spokesman (Acts 19:22; 1 Cor 4:17; 16:10-11; 1 Tim 1:3-4). Such "proof" is necessary before a church can commend a servant of the Lord to service elsewhere, otherwise commendation is reduced to a formality, and spiritual disaster may result. In Timothy's case, Paul was certain what he would do and teach "in every church" (1 Cor 4:17). This is a true commendation.

d. Athens (17:15-34)

v.15 "And they that conducted Paul brought him unto Athens: and receiving a commandment unto Silas and Timotheus for to come to him with all speed, they departed.
v.16 Now while Paul waited for them at Athens, his spirit was stirred in him, when he saw the city wholly given to idolatry.
v.17 Therefore disputed he in the synagogue with the Jews, and with the devout persons, and in the market daily with them that met with him.
v.18 Then certain philosophers of the Epicureans, and of the Stoicks, encountered him. And some said, What will this babbler say? Other some, He seemeth to be a setter forth of strange gods: because he preached unto them Jesus, and the resurrection.
v.19 And they took him, and brought him unto Areopagus, saying, May we know what this new doctrine, whereof thou speakest *is*?
v.20 For thou bringest certain strange things to our ears: we would know therefore what these things mean.
v.21 (For all the Athenians and strangers wich were there spent their time in nothing else, but either to tell, or to hear some new thing.)
v.22 Then Paul stood in the midst of Mars' hill, and said, Ye men of Athens, I perceive that in all things ye are too superstitious.
v.23 For as I passed by, and beheld your devotions, I found an altar with this inscription, TO THE UNKNOWN GOD. Whom therefore ye ignorantly worship, him declare I unto you.
v.24 God that made the world and all things therein, seeing that he is Lord of heaven and earth, dwelleth not in temples made with hands;
v.25 Neither is worshipped with men's hands, as though he needed any thing, seeing he giveth to all life, and breath, and all things;
v.26 And hath made of one blood all nations of men for to dwell on all the face of the earth, and hath determined the times before appointed, and the bounds of their habitation;
v.27 That they should seek the Lord, if haply they might feel after him, and find him, though he be not far from every one of us:
v.28 For in him we live, and move, and have our being; as certain also of your own poets have said, For we are also his offspring.
v.29 Forasmuch then as we are the offspring of God, we ought not to think that the Godhead is like unto gold, or silver, or stone, graven by art and man's device.
v.30 And the times of this ignorance God winked at; but now commandeth all men every where to repent:

v.31   Because he hath appointed a day, in the which he will judge the world in righteousness by *that* man whom he hath ordained; *whereof* he hath given assurance unto all *men,* in that he hath raised him from the dead.
v.32   And when they heard of the resurrection of the dead, some mocked: and others said, We will hear thee again of this *matter.*
v.33   So Paul departed from among them.
v.34   Howbeit certain men clave unto him, and believed: among the which *was* Dionysius the Areopagite, and a woman named Damaris, and others with them."

15-17 Athens was different from any other city that Paul had already visited. It was the cultural capital of the world, and it had produced more outstanding men of many different disciplines than any other city. Paul's approach, therefore, had to be different. The Athenians' hostility was of a very distinct kind from that which occurred in religious Jerusalem or idolatrous Ephesus. The opposition of the cultured can be less violent physically but more hurtful intellectually.

Present day evangelistic preachers, those with the gift of, and calling to evangelism (Eph 4:11), should pay careful attention to where Paul preached: in the synagogue to the Jews, presumably weekly; in the market-place with whoever happened to be there, definitely daily; and on Mars' Hill or the Areopagus, the great open-air Academy, on a once-for-all occasion. There was no fixed practice, and no unbending rules, but just a willingness to seek out people on their own ground wherever that might be.

18-21 The apostle's approach is also worthy of note. In the synagogue, he no doubt preached in his familiar style using the OT Scriptures, but Paul's lengthy address recorded here is different from all previous and later ones. At least they already knew that he preached "Jesus, and the resurrection", but the understanding of the philosophers was abysmal, because they thought that these two words were two "strange gods". There is not the slightest suggestion that he was adopting a wrong approach. As always, he met people on their own ground, and his address concluded with Jesus and the resurrection (v.31) when he was mockingly interrupted. The meeting-place was virtually of their own choosing, and so was the nature of the address when they asked him about "this new doctrine". A religious address would be given in the synagogue, to people who had the Jewish knowledge of God, but to Gentile idolaters who had no such knowledge the address had to be based on the God of creation.

The tragedy of Athens was that the city was as idolatrous as any, in spite of the fact that the Greeks sought after wisdom, which could never lead to the true God (1 Cor 1:19, 21). Their's was a more sophisticated idolatry than that of Ephesus, Thessalonica or any other. The Ephesians might have Diana, but the Athenian idolatry was pantheistic, the idolatry of Homer and of the Greek myths. What a contrast with the "Word" (*logos*), the eternal description given by John to the Lord Jesus (John 1:1).

Even though Paul was alone, "his spirit was stirred in him" when he saw the religious state of the city. This was a "pre-preaching" state of heart towards the unbelievers and idolaters, in contrast to that described in 1 Thess 2 where we read of a "post-preaching" state of heart towards the believers. And yet what Paul found in Athens had occurred before even in Jerusalem and Judah, "according to the number of thy cities are thy gods, O Judah" (Jer 2:28); "For according to the number of thy cities were thy gods, O Judah; and according to the number of the streets of Jerusalem have ye set up altars to that shameful thing, even altars to burn incense unto Baal" (11:13). Hence Paul not only preached, but he "disputed" or "reasoned" with men of all persuasions.

Paul's spiritual sensitivity was horrified by what he saw in Athens. Yet seemingly his greatest opportunity for testimony took him to the Areopagus, or Mars' Hill, also connected with Apollo, the patron saint of the city. Here his audience consisted of the Stoics and Epicureans. The reader who desires further information about these kinds of philosophers must consult fuller references, such as Conybeare and Howson, or any comprehensive Bible Encyclopaedia. Basically, the Stoics believed that the soul was corporeal and would be burned at death. Their ideal was self-denial, austere apathy untouched by human feeling or change in circumstances. They were rationalists and pantheists. The Epicureans were equally opposed to the God of the Jew or Christian. They did not believe in the Creator (as is the case with so many today), and therefore owned no accountability to One higher than themselves. Body and soul were to be dissolved together, and that was the end of existence. The policy behind 1 Cor 15:32 was also their's, "Let us eat and drink; for tomorrow we die".

These "philosophers" referred to Paul as a "babbler" or an "ignorant plagiarist". They claimed that he was an announcer of foreign demons (as the word "gods" in v.18 should be translated literally). They had never heard of Jesus in their learned work, and had only heard of Him and the resurrection through Paul's testimony, so the concept of resurrection was foreign to their philosophy and to human experience, and was too ridiculous to consider. Still, his message was both new and startling, and both they and the foreigners who had been attracted to their teaching and way of life spent their time teaching and listening to new things.

And so in three different venues in the world's intellectual capital, Paul presented Christ and Him crucified. Only one address is recorded, presented to the intellectuals whose response was negative contrasted with most other places and different kinds of audiences. After all, "not many wise men after the flesh ... are called" (1 Cor 1:26).

22-30 Paul's starting point in his sermon was the multitude of idols that he saw in their city. They were not satisfied with the battery of them named in Homer, etc., but in case they had left out one they inscribed one, "To the unknown god". His finishing point was to be "Jesus, and the resurrection" (vv.18-31).

Firstly, the God of creation is introduced (vv.24-25), the Owner of all things, and hence as the Giver He needed nothing Himself. Greek mythology attributed creation in all its elements to a series of gods; Paul attributed all creation to the one God.

Greek mythology caused temples and shrines to be erected to each of their gods, plus the extra one and its altar. Paul insisted that the God of creation was too great to be contained in any temple made with hands. Elsewhere Paul has shown that the heathen should know God through His creation, but "when they knew God, they glorified him not as God, neither were thankful" (Rom 1:19-21).

But He is not only the God of creation, He is also the God of history. The men of Athens were also told that God "hath determined the times before appointed, and the bounds of their habitation" (v.26). Their responsibility was to "seek the Lord". But men did not, and those historical times are described as "the times of this ignorance". They did not know that men could seek the Lord; that He was not very far from men; that their life derived from Him. It was no use quoting the OT Scriptures to demonstrate these facts; Paul had to resort to one of their own poets who declared, "For we are also his offspring". This quotation is by Aratus a Cilician poet, and almost the same words are used by Cleanthes, both of whom were Stoics. Paul used another profane quotation in Titus 1:12, not that we are to assume that Paul had a good knowledge of Greek literature; as a Pharisee and then as a Christian he had other things to occupy his attention.

As far as the Jews were concerned, those times of ignorance saw God overlooking their sins in view of the coming sacrifice of Christ (Rom 3:25), but as far as Gentiles were concerned, those days of ignorance were succeeded by days when they had (and have) the opportunity to repent.

31-32 The last period identified by Paul is future; v.31 is the gospel given both as a warning and as an assurance. Paul knew that either none or perhaps only a few of these men would repent, so the warning is that God has already appointed a day "in the which he will judge the world (or, inhabited earth) in righteousness" (v.31). Many Psalms had mentioned such a day (Pss 7:8; 50:4; 67:4; 72:2; 76:8; 96:10; 98:9; 135:14), but Paul could not refer to any such OT quotations. Rather he claimed that that day was guaranteed by the resurrection of "that man", though he did not mention that name of Jesus. So Paul ended his declaration of truth where it began, with his previous preaching of "Jesus, and the resurrection". This produced a mixed reaction – mocking, procrastination, and a little faith. This reaction was prompted by the very idea that dead persons could rise from the dead. The word "dead" at the end of v.31 is plural, implying that those who had not repented in the past remained dead, not having eternal life. Human intelligence laughed at the whole idea of resurrection, and today people generally give no thought to the matter or willingly accept false teaching about the subject as in 2 Tim 2:18. On the other hand, the resurrection of Christ also gives "assurance unto all men" provided that they repent and believe, since as He has risen, so will they also rise in that coming day. He is "the firstfruits of them that slept" (1 Cor 15:20).

33-34 The hope that they would hear Paul again would not be possible, as far as the record is concerned. God is not mocked if men mock Him and His Christ. Just as the Lord departed from the temple courts and never returned (Matt 24:1), so too Paul departed. It would be more tolerable for the land of Sodom and Gomorrha in the day of judgment that for the city which would not hear the apostolic words (Matt 10:14-15).

1 Cor 1:26 explains why there were so few converts in Athens, "not many wise men after the flesh". But two are named and "others with them". There is no reference to a local church being formed in Athens, composed of those few who believed. Paul had no time to explain what a local church was, nor what was expected of it in worship, service and testimony. But this truth may have been acquired by news filtering back from Corinth, some eighty miles away.

e. Corinth (18:1-17)

v.1 "After these things Paul departed from Athens, and came to Corinth;
v.2 And found a certain Jew named Aquila, born in Pontus, lately come from Italy, with his wife Priscilla; (because that Claudius had commanded all Jews to depart from Rome:) and came unto them.
v.3 And because he was of the same craft, he abode with them, and wrought: for by their occupation they were tentmakers.
v.4 And he reasoned in the synagogue every sabbath, and persuaded the Jews and the Greeks.
v.5 And when Silas and Timotheus were come from Macedonia, Paul was pressed in the spirit, and testified to the Jews *that* Jesus *was* Christ.
v.6 And when they opposed themselves, and blasphemed, he shook *his* raiment, and said unto them, Your blood *be* upon your own heads; I *am* clean: from henceforth I will go unto the Gentiles.
v.7 And he departed thence, and entered into a certain *man's* house, named Justus, *one* that worshipped God, whose house joined hard to the synagogue.
v.8 And Crispus, the chief ruler of the synagogue, believed on the Lord with all his house; and many of the Corinthians hearing believed, and were baptized.
v.9 Then spake the Lord to Paul in the night by a vision, Be not afraid, but speak, and hold not thy peace:
v.10 For I am with thee, and no man shall set on thee to hurt thee: for I have much people in this city.
v.11 And he continued *there* a year and six months, teaching the word of God among them.
v.12 And when Gallio was the deputy of Achaia, the Jews made insurrection with one accord against Paul, and brought him to the judgment seat.
v.13 Saying, This *fellow* persuadeth men to worship God contrary to the law.
v.14 And when Paul was now about to open *his* mouth, Gallio said unto the Jews, If it were a matter of wrong or wicked lewdness, O *ye* Jews, reason would that I should bear with you:
v.15 But if it be a question of words and names, and *of* your law, look ye *to it*; for I will be no judge of such *matters*.

> v.16   And he drave them from the judgment seat.
> v.17   Then all the Greeks took Sosthenes, the chief ruler of the synagogue, and beat *him* before the judgment seat. And Gallio cared for none of those things."

1-2   In most other parts of the ancient world, Paul's visits were not accompanied by the outright opposition to the truth that he received in Athens. Again, in other places he had to sustain more physical opposition that he had to in Athens. Apart from mockery, there is an easy-going tolerance to the gospel that is worse for the gospel's progress than outright opposition in whatever form. Paul arrived in Corinth, apparently alone. He awaited the arrival of Timothy and Silas from Thessalonica, and they arrived in v.5, having been redirected from Athens which they had originally left. Paul arrived in Corinth before them, evidently because his departure from Athens had been somewhat precipitate. Yet his journey to Corinth took him to a city where God had "much people" (v.10).

In Corinth, he was glad to find a godly couple, Aquila and Priscilla, and he was able to lodge with them. The first mention of this couple calls for an assessment of their contribution to the whole story of the furtherance of the gospel of the Lord Jesus. They belonged to that part of the ancient world where Paul was not allowed by God to preach the gospel, Pontus on the southern shores of the Black Sea. But before Paul found lodgings with them in Corinth, they had been resident in Rome. There has been no more persecuted race or nation in world history than the Jewish nation, and Emperor Claudius Caesar had his own contribution to make towards anti-Semitism. This second mention of such a Caesar greatly helps towards attaching a date to this part of the story; this would be about AD 51-52. (See the notes at the end of v.17.) That persecution (whether of Jewish believers or unbelievers) drove Aquila and Priscilla to Corinth, where they met the apostle Paul, and a lifelong partnership was formed. (The NT gives three different places where they lived, Rome, Corinth and Ephesus, and in all of them they had an open door for the Lord's people, including NT churches that met in their home, Rom 16:3-5; 1 Cor 16:19.) There was an additional reason for staying with them: like Paul, they were tentmakers. The reason for this is that every Jewish boy had to learn a craft, and this was evidently the one chosen by both Paul and Aquila. Staying with them enabled Paul to earn his living while preaching the gospel and establishing a new church.

Paul had every right to "live of the gospel" (1 Cor 9:14), but he was glad to renounce his rights for the gospel's sake. He certainly received no financial gifts from the Corinthians, and only the Philippians sent him anything when he departed from Macedonia (Phil 4:15-16). So much so, that the Corinthians refused to recognise that he was an apostle! In addressing the Ephesian elders, Paul stated that he worked there with his own hands to meet his own necessities and those of others (Acts 20:34-35). In many cases there would be an advantage in the Lord's servants earning their own living, although this is increasingly difficult in advanced societies. Unless this is impossible to practise, and we recognise that this is often the case, it may well be accepted as a good guide as to how the work of God could be done.

Returning to Aquila and Priscilla, we read that Paul sent them his greetings when writing to the church at Rome (Rom 16:3-4), and this suggests that by that time they had returned to Rome from Ephesus (Acts 18:18-27); this epistle was written towards the end of the third missionary journey. Some years later, he expressed his final greetings to them in 2 Tim 4:19 prior to his martyrdom.

4 In Corinth, as in most other places that he visited with the gospel, Paul first visited the synagogue where there were Jews and Gentile proselytes. There he always had a ready audience, even if it was usually an unsympathetic one. There was now no hurry for the apostle to move on as from some previous places that he had visited, for he was to stay for eighteen months in Corinth, and for double that time, three years, in Ephesus during his third missionary journey.

Corinth, with its two ports, constituted the commercial capital of the eastern Mediterranean. It was the capital of the Greek state of Achaia, and a powerful rival of Athens; they were only forty-five miles apart by sea, though much farther by land. Sailing was a better means of transport for Paul than any other means, hence his perils in the sea, and his many shipwrecks, of which we have no record (2 Cor 11:25). Operating between two continents and many islands, it could not have been otherwise for the apostle.

Cicero has written, "Maritime cities suffer corruption and degeneration of morals, for they receive a mixture of strange languages and customs, and import foreign ways as well as foreign merchandise", and he cited Corinth as an outstanding example. Liddell & Scott's *Greek Lexicon* gives the meaning of the Greek word *korinthiazesthai*, "to practise whoredom", while the word was known in Regency England (the beginning of the 19th century) for a polished rake. It could not have been the most attractive of cities for a gospel preacher to visit, but it was certainly one of the most needy. The immoral state of some of the Corinthian believers before their conversion is recalled by Paul in 1 Cor 6:9-11, together with the grace of God that had washed, sanctified and justified them in the name of the Lord Jesus. Blaiklock renders this background in 1 Cor 6:9-11 as, "No fornicator or idolater, none who are guilty of either adultery or sexual perversion, no thieves, or drunkards, or slanderers or swindlers can enter the kingdom, and such were some of you". We do well to remember that Calvary can remove all such guilt, but repentance is necessary and a turning away from such sins. After men had repented at the preaching of the gospel, they were in the church and the kingdom of God. More details about Corinth are given in volume 4 of this series *What the Bible Teaches*, *First Corinthians* by J. Hunter and *Second Corinthians* by A. McShane.

5-6 The AV translation "Paul was pressed in the spirit" is distinct from modern translations, such as "pressed by the word", "Paul began to devote himself entirely to preaching", "Paul was deeply engaged with the message". The reason for the difference is that different Greek manuscripts are used. The word "spirit" (sometimes taken by expositors to be the Holy Spirit) occurred in the MSS used by the AV translators, whereas "word" occurs in the MSS used by modern translators. JND has "word" in his translation and "spirit" in his footnote. Certainly there is truth in both possibilities. The idea seems to be that as long as Paul was alone he was content to lodge with Priscilla and Aquila and work at their occupation of tentmaking, preaching in the synagogue on the Sabbath days. But after Silas and Timothy arrived from Thessalonica, he gave up tentmaking as a fulltime occupation (though still working to meet his daily necessities of life) and concentrated on the word, testifying that Jesus was Christ.

Whether it was the greater intensity of Paul's exercise imparted to his spirit by the Holy Spirit, or whether it was the greater intensity of his preaching, we do not know. One or the other caused the Jewish reaction of opposition and blasphemy, and this led Paul to take the symbolic step of shaking his raiment in their presence, in effect washing his hands of responsibility for their rejection of the gospel, laying the burden of responsibility on their own shoulders, "Your blood be upon your own heads". Ezekiel is the OT prophet who repeatedly used this figure to audiences that rejected his message (3:18; 18:13; 33:4, 5, 6, 8). The shaking of the garments would be similar to that of the dust, but Paul was not quitting Corinth as he had Antioch, but giving others – the Gentiles – the opportunity to hear.

How many weeks it was before Silas and Timothy arrived we do not know. Until they came, Paul kept pressing the claims of the Lord Jesus on his weekly congregation of Jews and Greeks. Their arrival seems to have coincided with the final rejection of the message by those attending the synagogue, but instead of a riot resulting in the apostle fleeing from the city, there was a positive decision about a change of tactics. Until now Paul, although already noted as the apostle to the Gentiles (Gal 2:8), had given preference in every city to the Jews and Gentile proselytes, but now there is a notable departure from this policy; he would devote himself particularly to the Gentiles: "from henceforth I will go unto the Gentiles" (v.6).

7-11 When v.7 states that Paul "departed thence, and entered into a certain man's house, named Justus, one that worshipped God, whose house joined hard to the synagogue", it is not clear whether this means that he actually changed his lodgings from the house of Aquila and Priscilla to the house of Justus, or whether the house of Justus was used only as a preaching point next to the synagogue. He might have known that there were sympathetic people still in the synagogue whom he wanted to influence with the gospel. In the house of Justus next to the synagogue, he had the joy of seeing the household of Crispus, the synagogue ruler, trusting the Saviour. Was his home the first household of new converts in in Corinth? But here in v.8 we have the last but one mention of baptism following conversion in the Acts; the last mention is the special case in Ephesus (19:5). From now on we can take for granted the baptism of new converts. Paul was very careful that he should appear not to be baptising in his own name. It is worth while quoting 1 Cor 1:14-16 in this connection, "I thank God that I baptized none of you, but Crispus and Gaius; lest any should say that I had baptized in my own name. And I baptized also the household of Stephanus:

besides, I know not whether I baptized any other". It is interesting that he thanked God for this fact, and that the Spirit of inspiration allowed for the forgetfulness of Paul regarding the full facts of events several years earlier. It would almost appear that Paul was acting so as to avoid potential trouble, namely the rising of a "Paul party". Clearly others did the baptising, for "many of the Corinthians hearing believed, and were baptised".

In v.9 we have another of Paul's many visions, for "Where there is no vision, the people perish" (Prov 29:18). In other words, without this vision of the will of the Lord, Paul might have moved on to fresh fields. Rather he was told to stay in Corinth because of the many people that God had in prospect there. For this service, God promised him both the divine presence and protection. Thus he continued for one and a half years, teaching the word of God, both the gospel to the unconverted and the Scriptures for the edification of the believers.

Hence a church was established in Corinth. Facts about it may be found in Corinthians. It was addressed by Paul as "the church of God which is at Corinth" (1:2), the members of which were called "saints". The Epistle, though corrective of many faults in Corinth, was nevertheless addressed to "all that in every place call upon the name of Jesus Christ our Lord" (v.2). Paul recalled what he had taught when amongst them: the gospel and the resurrection of Christ (15:1,3), and the Lord's Supper (11:23). He also recalled what he did, that he was their spiritual father having begotten them in Christ Jesus through the gospel (4:15), as well as planting the word of God (3:6) and laying the one foundation (3:10). He also described the nature of his preaching, that he was "determined not to know anything among you, save Jesus Christ, and him crucified" (2:2). This church was "enriched by him, in all utterance, and in all knowledge" (1:5), and although these gifts were being misused, nevertheless in chs.12-14 he expounded in detail what God expects in a local church. The subject of prophecy is essential in a church, for they were "waiting for the coming of our Lord Jesus Christ" (1:5), and the Lord's Supper was to take place "till he come" (11:26). Features such as these enable a believer today to recognise what group of Christians constitutes a local church according to the will of God. Others features, such as elders and the nature of service, are found in other Epistles.

12-17 Presumably it was the progress made by the gospel that caused the next Jewish uprising. Luke informs us who the proconsul was at the time. As in other cities, citizens seem to have had the right to arrest a man and bring him to the judgment seat, the local magistrate's court. Once again the accusation concerned the upsetting of the established way of things, whether Jewish or civil. This time it was the religious aspect that was pursued (v.13), and this proved to be a failure for the Jews. There was no sympathy from the Roman proconsul, who like many another, was tired of the things, petty and religious to them (v.15), that so aroused the Jewish citizens. Frustrated by the proconsul, they decided to vent their anger on the ruler of the synagogue, Sosthenes, presumably Crispus' successor, who seems also to have become a Christian.

Notes

Commission Given by the Lord

There is an interesting comparison between the great commission given by the Lord Jesus in Matt 28:18-20 and Paul's ministry in Corinth.

The Lord's Commission	Paul's Ministry
"Go ye therefore" (Matt 28:19)	Paul came to Corinth (Acts 18:1)
"teach all nations" or "make disciples" (v.19)	Many heard and believed (v.8)
"baptising them" (v.19)	"and were baptised" (v.8)
"teaching them" (v.20)	"a year and six months, teaching the word of God" (v.11)
"lo, I am with you" (v.20)	"for I am with thee" (v.10)

Emperors of Rome
BC 30-AD 180

1. Augustus .... (Christ born) .... BC 30-AD 14
2. Tiberius .... (Christ crucified) .... AD 14-37
3. Caligula .... AD 37-41
4. Claudius .... (Acts 18) .... AD 41-54
5. Nero .... (Paul's third journey onwards) ... AD 54-68
6. Galba .... AD 68-69
7. Otho .... AD 69 (3 months)
8. Vitellius .... AD 69 (1 month)
9. Vespasian .... (Destruction of Jerusalem) .... AD 69-79
10. Titus .... AD 79-81
11. Domitian .... (Writings of John) .... AD 81-96
12. Nerva .... AD 96-98
13. Trajan .... AD 98-117
14. Hadrian .... AD 117-138
15. Antoninus Pius .... AD 138-161
16. Marcus Aurelius .... AD 161-180

f. *Ephesus (18:18-22)*

   v.18 "And Paul *after this* tarried *there* yet a good while, and then took his leave of the brethren, and sailed thence into Syria, and with him Priscilla and Aquila; having shorn *his* head in Cenchrea: for he had a vow.

   v.19 And he came to Ephesus, and left them there: but he himself entered into the synagogue, and reasoned with the Jews.

v.20 When they desired *him* to tarry longer time with them, he consented not;
v.21 But bade them farewell, saying, I must by all means keep this feast that cometh in Jerusalem: but I will return again unto you, if God will. And he sailed from Ephesus.
v.22 And when he had landed at Cæsarea, and gone up, and saluted the church, he went down to Antioch."

18-21   Still Paul was in no hurry to leave Corinth, presumably choosing his own time to go. He was no longer a Jew in the sense that he gave them the first opportunity of hearing the gospel in any place, but he still was in the sense that he had taken a vow. Luke does not explain what this means. However, when he sailed from Corinth with Syria as his destination, he is accompanied by Priscilla and Aquila. Expositors have long noted the reversal of the order of their names, pointing out that after their first appearance (18:2), Priscilla is mentioned before Aquila, suggesting that she was the more prominent member of the partnership. It should be pointed out that this is not impossible in Christian life in the family circle, in spite of the prohibition in letters both to Corinth and to Ephesus (via Timothy) that the woman was to be silent in the church itself (1 Cor 14:34-35; 1 Tim 2:8-13).

A note on the "vow" that Paul had may help readers. The great vow that Israelites could take was that of the Nazarite (Num 6:1-21). The indication that Paul might have taken this vow is suggested by the fact that he let his hair grow. The indication that his vow was ended was the shaving of his head. Vows were for ordinary people, and there was no necessity to take them then, just as there is no necessity today. However, a person was to take any vow seriously (Eccl 5:1-7). By the time Paul reached Jerusalem (not as in 18:22 "gone up", but in 21:17-32 at the end of the third journey), he was asked by James to join four others who had taken vows to complete the matter in the temple, thus to prove that the rumoured accusations against him were untrue.

Vows and fasting are similar in that neither is obligatory for the Christian but neither are they wrong. Still, neither should be taken lightly once it has been embarked upon.

Paul's stay in Ephesus was short. The main feature of this first visit was to leave Aquila and Priscilla in the idolatrous city while he moved on, but not before he had addressed a synagogue congregation. Opposition did not arise immediately, and the Jews desired that he should remain "longer time" with them. However, Paul wanted to return to Antioch. The explanation that he gave to the Jews related to the responsibility of all Jewish males to visit Jerusalem three times a year on special feast days, but his spiritual intentions were to visit the churches at Jerusalem and Antioch (the "up" in v.22 refers as usual to Jerusalem). This responsibility of Jewish males to visit Jerusalem at the feast days (as in 2:9-11) lasted until AD 70 when the city was finally destroyed by Titus, the future Emperor of Rome.

But Paul promised to return to Ephesus "if God will". This is the first definite example of how the planning of life and service should be conducted. The earliest of the NT Epistles states that believers should say or do this on all occasions, "Go to now, ye that say, to day or to morrow we will go into such a city, and continue there a year, and buy and sell, and get gain. Whereas ye know not what shall be on the morrow ... ye ought to say, If the Lord will" (James 4:13-15).

22 Landing at the Roman seaport city of Caesarea, Paul visited the church at Jerusalem, before making a return visit to Antioch, his commending assembly (13:3; 14:26; 15:40).Previously it was "some days after" that he left Antioch (15:36); here it is "some time". Previously the Council of Jerusalem had taken place during the visit, but here nothing of note took place. But Paul perceived the poverty amongst the believers in Jerusalem, and this caused much exercise on his part during the third missionary journey.

Paul then took the opportunity of revisiting the disciples throughout Galatia and Phrygia, the territory reached on his first missionary journey and that he visited at the beginning of his second journey (15:36 16:1-6). This visit is referred to in 1 Cor 16:1, "concerning the collection for the saints (in Jerusalem), as I have given order to the churches of Galatia, even so do ye". "Strengthening all the disiples" was, and is, a necessary task for evangelists, even many years after a work for the Lord has been started.

6. Paul's Third Missionary Journey 18:23-20:2

a. *Apollos at Ephesus and Corinth (18:23-28)*

> v.23 "And after he had spent some time *there*, he departed, and went over *all* the country of Galatia and Phrygia in order, strengthening all the disciples.
> v.24 And a certain Jew named Apollos, born at Alexandria, an eloquent man, *and* mighty in the scriptures, came to Ephesus.
> v.25 This man was instructed in the way of the Lord; and being fervent in the spirit, he spake and taught diligently the things of the Lord, knowing only the baptism of John.
> v.26 And he began to speak boldly in the synagogue: whom when Aquila and Priscilla had heard, they took him unto *them*, and expounded unto him the way of God more perfectly.
> v.27 And when he was disposed to pass into Achaia, the brethren wrote, exhorting the disciples to receive him: who, when he was come, helped them much which had believed through grace:
> v.28 For he mightily convinced the Jews, *and that* publickly, shewing by the scriptures that Jesus was Christ."

23-28 Meanwhile, a restricted work continued at Ephesus. But we may infer that the spiritual gift possessed by Aquila and Priscilla was one of personal teaching in the home, rather than that of being able to engage in any public evangelism. That kind of work had to remain until Paul returned.

Another visitor arrived, an Alexandrian Jew named Apollos, who knew only part of the truth. He was "mighty" in the OT Scriptures, and able to expound these boldly in the synagogue with great fervency of spirit. What he did teach in addition to the OT Scriptures were "the things of the Lord, knowing only the baptism of John". Other Greek MSS and hence translations based on them, such as JND, have instead "concerning Jesus". The fact that his knowledge was imperfect, thereby making him acceptable in the synagogue, depended on the obvious fact that he had never had the opportunity of hearing any advance on truth that he knew concerning John's baptism. It appears safe to conclude that he knew only the beginning of the ministry of the Lord, "concerning Jesus", that took place at the same time as John was baptising. The facts of the crucifixion, resurrection and ascension of the Lord he knew nothing about, together with the subsequent giving of the Holy Spirit to all believers, and the gathering of believers after christian baptism into local churches. But he was zealous about that part of the truth that he knew, he proved to be very willing to accept the rest of the truth that he did not know, once Aquila and Priscilla "expounded unto him the way of God more perfectly" (v.26). Thus we see that once again Priscilla and Aquila took a preacher into their home, this time as his instructors rather than to be taught themselves (by Paul).

Apollos' next wish was to visit Achaia (v.27). It was then that the small company of Christians (there must have been more at the time than only Aquila and Pricilla, seen by the word "brethren" in v.27) at Ephesus decided to help him on his way by writing the first letter of commendation in the NT. Other previous commendations had been given by word of mouth, as when Barnabas spoke for Saul at Jerusalem (9:27), and when Timothy was "well reported of" by his local church and nearby brethren to accompany Paul and Silas in the work of the Lord (16:1-2). In both these cases, the commendation was to the grace of God rather than to any particular church, since Paul did not know where he was going apart from special divine guidance. Our days are in no way different from their's, and this kind of worthy practice cannot be dispensed with. A letter, particularly from brethren that are known to the recipients (though this is often not possible) avoids suspicion and possible difficulties such as being a herald of false doctrine, breaks down barriers and helps to gain approval for the Lord's servant, instead of requiring him to start afresh to prove himself in the Lord's work in every new place to which he goes. Although the name "Achaia" is used, the particular place to which Apollos was commended was obviously Corinth.

The description of Apollos' contribution to the spiritual life of the new Corinthian Church, "he ... helped them much which had believed through grace" is given by Paul in 1 Cor 3:6, "Apollos watered". Moreover, under Apollos' preaching in Corinth, the city's Jews were granted to have pressed upon their attention once again the claims of Jesus as the true Messiah, the OT Scriptures being used to this end. His eloquence (v.24) resulted in his audience being "mightily convinced" (v.28). So the object of his preaching was both private to the church and public on the outside. Other translations imply that Apollos vigorously refuted the Jews in the synagogue rather than convincing them, as if he engaged in debate that could not be resisted.

It is tragic to realise that an "Apollos party" arose in the Corinthian church, not necessarily based on doctrine but on his method of presentation (1 Cor 1:12). To answer this growth of parties, Paul declared that both he and Apollos were but "ministers by whom ye believed, even as the Lord gave to every man" (3:5). Several years later, the apostle wanted Apollos with others to go to Corinth, but he had no desire to go until a later time, no doubt until after these parties had seen the error of their ways and had repented (16:12).

b. *Ephesus (19:1-20:2)*

- v.1 "And it came to pass, that, while Apollos was at Corinth, Paul having passed through the upper coasts came to Ephesus: and finding certain disciples,
- v.2 He said unto them, Have ye received the Holy Ghost since ye believed? And they said unto him, We have not so much as heard whether there be any Holy Ghost.
- v.3 And he said unto them, Unto what then were ye baptized? And they said, Unto John's baptism.
- v.4 Then said Paul, John verily baptized with the baptism of repentance, saying unto the people, that they should believe on him which should come after him, that is, on Christ Jesus.
- v.5 When they heard *this*, they were baptized in the name of the Lord Jesus.
- v.6 And when Paul had laid *his* hands upon them, the Holy Ghost came on them; and they spake with tongues, and prophesied.
- v.7 And all the men were about twelve.
- v.8 And he went into the synagogue, and spake boldly for the space of three months, disputing and persuading the things concerning the kingdom of God.
- v.9 But when divers were hardened, and believed not, but spake evil of that way before the multitude, he departed from them, and separated the disciples, disputing daily in the school of one Tyrannus.
- v.10 And this continued by the space of two years; so that all they which dwelt in Asia heard the word of the Lord Jesus, both Jews and Greeks.
- v.11 And God wrought special miracles by the hands of Paul:
- v.12 So that from his body were brought unto the sick handkerchiefs or aprons, and the diseases departed from them, and the evil spirits went out of them.
- v.13 Then certain of the vagabond Jews, exorcists, took upon them to call over them which had evil spirits the name of the Lord Jesus, saying, We adjure you by Jesus whom Paul preacheth.
- v.14 And there were seven sons of *one* Sceva, a Jew, *and* chief of the priests, which did so.
- v.15 And the evil spirit answered and said, Jesus I know, and Paul I know; but who are ye?

- v.16 And the man in whom the evil spirit was leaped on them, and overcame them, and prevailed against them, so that they fled out of that house naked and wounded.
- v.17 And this was known to all the Jews and Greeks also dwelling at Ephesus; and fear fell on them all, and the name of the Lord Jesus was magnified.
- v.18 And many that believed came and confessed, and shewed their deeds.
- v.19 Many of them also which used curious arts brought their books together, and burned them before all *men:* and they counted the price of them, and found *it* fifty thousand *pieces* of silver.
- v.20 So mightily grew the word of God and prevailed.
- v.21 After these things were ended, Paul purposed in the spirit, when he had passed through Macedonia and Achaia, to go to Jerusalem, saying, After I have been there, I must also see Rome.
- v.22 So he sent into Macedonia two of them that ministered unto him. Timotheus and Erastus; but he himself stayed in Asia for a season.
- v.23 And the same time there arose no small stir about that way.
- v.24 For a certain *man* named Demetrius, a silversmith, which made silver shrines for Diana, brought no small gain unto the craftsmen;
- v.25 Whom he called together with the workmen of like occupation, and said, Sirs, ye know that by this craft we have our wealth.
- v.26 Moreover ye see and hear, that not alone at Ephesus, but almost throughout all Asia, this Paul hath persuaded and turned away much people, saying that they be no gods, which are made with hands:
- v.27 So that not only this our craft is in danger to be set at nought; but also that the temple of the great goddess Diana should be despised, and her magnificence should be destroyed, whom all Asia and the world worshippeth.
- v.28 And when they heard *these sayings,* they were full of wrath, and cried out, saying, Great is Diana of the Ephesians.
- v.29 And the whole city was filled with confusion: and having caught Gaius and Aristarchus, men of Macedonia, Paul's companions in travel, they rushed with one accord into the theatre.
- v.30 And when Paul would have entered in unto the people, the disciples suffered him not.
- v.31 And certain of the chief of Asia, which were his friends, sent unto him, desiring *him* that he would not adventure himself into the theatre.
- v.32 Some therefore cried one thing, and some another: for the assembly was confused: and the more part knew not wherefore they were come together.
- v.33 And they drew Alexander out of the multitude, the Jews putting him forward. And Alexander beckoned with the hand, and would have made his defence unto the people.
- v.34 But when they knew that he was a Jew, all with one voice about the space of two hours cried out, Great *is* Diana of the Ephesians.
- v.35 And when the townclerk had appeased the people, he said, *Ye* men of Ephesus, what man is there that knoweth not how that the city of the Ephesians is a worshipper of the great goddess Diana, and of the *image* which fell down from Jupiter?
- v.36 Seeing then that these things cannot be spoken against, ye ought to be quiet, and do nothing rashly.

> v.37 For ye have brought hither these men, which are neither robbers of churches, not yet blasphemers of your goddess.
> v.38 Wherefore if Demetrius, and the crafstmen which are with him, have a matter against any man, the law is open, and there are deputies: let them implead one another.
> v.39 But if ye inquire any thing concerning other matters, it shall be determined in a lawful assembly.
> v.40 For we are in danger to be called in question for this day's uproar, there being no cause whereby we may give an account of this concourse.
> v.41 And when he had thus spoken, he dismissed the assembly.
> 20 v.1 And after the uproar was ceased, Paul called unto *him* the disciples, and embraced *them,* and departed for to go into Macedonia.
> v.2 And when he had gone over those parts, and had given them much exhortation, he came into Greece."

1-7 While Apollos was at Corinth, Paul returned to Ephesus by land via "the upper coasts", probably Galatia and Phrygia. Having learned of the "poor saints" at Jerusalem (Rom 15:26), he was determined to help them financially, and gave command to the Gentile churches of his first missionary journey to make a financial collection that he would take to Jerusalem at the end of the third journey (v 25; 2 Cor 8:4). This collection was also raised by the churches of his second missionary journey, and was finally delivered to the Jerusalem church in Acts 21:17-18. The remarkable thing is that its receipt is not mentioned!

Upon Paul's arrival in Ephesus, he found a group of about twelve men whose spiritual standing was identical to that of Apollos when he had arrived in Ephesus; they are called "disciples" in the sense that they believe in something beyond OT teaching. The suggestion is made that they were disciples of Apollos' teaching prior to his learning ways of God more perfectly. Paul discerned that this group of twelve men could not possibly be regarded as a local church, since there was no manifestation of spiritual gifts amongst them. In the AV, he asked the question, "Have ye received the Holy Ghost since ye believed?" Strictly speaking, the insertion of the word "since" gives a wrong meaning to Paul's question. In the Greek text, the second verb *pisteusantes* is is an aorist participle, and no exact grammatical construction exists in English for the sentence. It must be translated, for example following JND, as "Did ye receive the Holy Spirit when ye believed?". In other words, the moment of faith is the same moment as the reception of the Holy Spirit. These men then confessed ignorance of the Holy Spirit; they had only reached the stage of John's baptism. They had never heard of the important event of Pentecost in Acts 2.

Paul's assessment of the position in v. 5 makes it quite clear that these men were not christian believers. John's baptism implied, not a faith in Christ, but repentance together with a forthcoming faith in the One who would follow Him, namely Jesus Christ. It is also clear that Paul must have engaged in some substantial teaching at this point, so that they knew what it meant to be baptised in the name of the Lord Jesus, and that faith in Him would imply the reception of the Holy Spirit. Like

Corinthians, therefore, these men "hearing, believed, and were baptized". Note that a second baptism was required, not because the *mode* of the first was wrong, but because the *meaning* of it was deficient. Today the *process* and *meaning* of infant baptism are wrong, and a believer is therefore baptised "in the name of the Father, and of the Son, and of the Holy Ghost" (Matt 28:19).

There was only one Pentecost. V.6 "the Holy Ghost came on them; and they spake with tongues, and prophesied" is not a repetition of Pentecost. Even in the Acts, spiritual gifts did not usually arise immediately, but were developed in God's time in a believer. But Paul, under the present circumstances, had the miraculous power, by the laying on of hands, to hasten the granting of certain spiritual gifts, so that they could be used by the twelve men as they were added usefully in service to the church at Ephesus. The speaking in languages was for testimony outside, as in Acts 2 (see 1 Cor 14:21-22) for the proclamation of the gospel, while prophecy was a gift to be exercised in church meetings. It was God speaking directly through individuals, and certainly this was needed at the beginning since these men were so ignorant of basic truth. A difference must be made between receiving the Spirit at conversion, bringing blessings that the Lord promised in John 14-16 and that are found elsewhere in the epistles, on the one hand, and the activity of the Spirit in believers through spiritual gifts on the other hand. There are no apostles today who can confer the latter immediately on new converts.

By this means, the gospel was validated in Ephesus, and to this must be added the special miracles that God wrought by the hands of Paul (v. 11). Since those early days, all these particular spiritual gifts (some listed in Cor 12:7-11) are no longer operative in the will of God, though there may be pseudo-operators ready to deceive the Lord's people (Matt 7:22). There are plenty of gifts that remain now that the canon of Scripture is complete, and these should all be used for spiritual edification.

8-10 We do not know if Paul's synagogue preaching in Ephesus lasted longer than it did in Corinth, since only the duration of the former is stated, namely, three months. It is remarkable that they allowed the apostle such a long time to dispute and persuade "the things concerning the kingdom of God". Only when the Jewish reaction was hardened in unbelief did Paul change his venue for preaching to "the school of one Tyrannus". When we read in v. 9, "he ... separated the disciples", we conclude that other believers were supporting him in the synagogue, and that every one departed with Paul. This gospel testimony was additonal to the development of the church in Ephesus, and indeed brought converts into it from a Jewish and Gentile proselyte background, while later converts from the idol worship of Diana were brought in as well. Three months in the synagogue and two years in the school of Tyrannus formed the major part of Paul's stay in Ephesus, which lasted three years altogether (20-31). This was his longest stay in any city as far as we know, and throughout he was surrounded by the idolatrous practices associated with one of the Seven Wonders of the Ancient World, the temple of Diana. But the ripples of his preaching were widespread, "all they which dwelt in Asia heard the word of the Lord

Jesus, both Jews and Greeks". Thus the church at Colosse and the six other Asian churches named in Rev 2-3 must have been established at this time. For example, it seems that Paul heard of the faith of the Colossians through Epaphras, and he knew that "the gospel ... is come unto you, as it is in all the world" (Col 1:5-9).

11-16 Not only were miracles of healing of a special kind wrought by God at Ephesus, but also exorcism, "evil spirits went out of them". Attempts were made to imitate this kind of miracle, but even the spirits rebelled by saying, "Jesus I know, and Paul I know; but who are ye?" Just as they knew Paul's Saviour when He was here, so they knew His servant who was instrumental in doing the same things as the Lord.

These seven sons are examples of those whom the Lord referred to in the Sermon on the Mount (Matt 7:22). Their father was a high priest, not just a priest. It may appear strange that such a man should be found in Ephesus rather than in Jerusalem, but he might have been an apostate Jew, a high priest of the goddess Diana. The reaction of the spirit who refused to come out of the victim was to overwhelm those would-be exorcists, producing the same fear in Ephesus as was evidenced when miracles were wrought in 2:43 and 5:11, whether in Jew or Greek, in believer or unbeliever. Certainly God's presence was acknowledged, and believers magnified the name of the Lord Jesus.

17-20 The last part of v. 17 together with v. 20 resemble one of Luke's normal summaries or progress reports, "the name of the Lord Jesus was magnified" and "So mightily grew the word of God and prevailed". Faith was followed by confession and deeds. Those who had been followers of Diana displayed a new behaviour; the destruction of their books has been called "the burning of the vanities", and certainly sets an example of the transformation produced in those who turn to the Saviour in idolatrous lands. Even in non-idolatrous countries, there are plenty of pre-conversion activities that should be given up when a person is genuinely converted. In Ephesus, the cost was considerable – 50,000 pieces of silver. The earlier journals of George Müller gave examples of this kind of thing happening in Victorian England; believers today should ask themselves whether they had a spring-cleaning upon conversion.

21 It was Paul's intention after two or three years in Ephesus to revisit Europe, namely, Macedonia and Achaia, in which provinces Philippi, Thessalonica and Corinth were situated. News had reached him "by them which are of the house of Chloe" (1 Cor 1:11) that there was trouble in Corinth, regarding divisions, immorality, the misuse of spiritual gifts, and doctrine. Hence he wrote the First Epistle to the Corinthians from Ephesus to correct them. He wrote this later in "trouble ... pressed out of measure, above strength, insomuch that we despaired even of life" (2 Cor 1:8). Such was the state of his soul as he contemplated this trouble in Corinth. He intended to go to the Corinth "if the Lord will" (1 Cor 4:19), with a rod or in love. But he would not go until he heard of the effects of the First Epistle upon the Corinthians. He awaited the return of Titus with news. He moved on to Troas, but still Titus had not arrived, and he had no rest in his spirit as if he could not preach there although the door was opened by the Lord (2 Cor 2:12-13). So he passed over into Macedonia, where at last he met Titus, who brought good news of the Corinthians' repentance (7:6, 7, 13). He therefore wrote Second Corinthians to precede him down to Corinth, the first nine chapters referring to the majority who had repented, but the last four chapters referring to the minority who would not repent. In chs. 8-9 he took the opportunity to remind the Corinthians about the collection being gathered for the poor believers in Jerusalem. Exactly what happened when he finally reached Corinth we are not told; 20:2-3 refer to this visit lasting three months.

Paul's plans are similarly found in Rom 15:23-28, an epistle written from Corinth. He wrote that he would go first to Jerusalem (v. 25), and then he would "come by you into Spain" (v. 28). His visit to Jerusalem would be to take the gifts from the Galatian churches, from the Macedonian churches and from Corinth. Then he would proceed to Spain via Rome – a journey that would have taken months by sea. He planned "by the will of God" (v. 32), but the divine will was quite different for His servant. Instead he would be taken prisoner in Jerusalem, kept in Caesarea for several years, and then he would arrive in Rome still as a prisoner. Prayers are not always answered according to one's asking, for Paul asked the Romans to pray that he might "be delivered from them that do not believe in Judaea" (v. 31), but this was not to be so in the will of God.

22 The advance party consisted of Timothy and Erastus (presumably a Corinthian as Rom 16:23 suggests), while Paul stayed in Asia. We do not know where this man named Erastus first heard the gospel and responded to its claims, but he did become a believer, and returned to his own city of Colosse to proclaim it and to establish a NT church. No doubt he is just one example of how all Asia heard the word of the Lord.

23-28 But opposition was mounting in Ephesus. It appears that this city was another of those places where they called the first believers "people of the way" (v.9). Their numbers were increasing too much for the comfort of craftsmen whose businesses would suffer as a result of Christians refusing to purchase silver shrines. With the gospel spreading through the whole province the threat was great. Hence the riot, during which for two hours the devotees of Diana chanted, "Great is Diana of the Ephesians". They knew that "all Asia" had yielded converts who refused gods made with hands (v.26), but their idolatrous expectations were that "all Asia" should worship Diana (v.27). The repetition of "all Asia" is a remarkable contrast.

Not only did Paul have a longer stay in Ephesus than anywhere else, but he also had a greater battle. While the conflict was not so much with the Jews as with the priests of Artemis (translated "Diana" in the AV), it was still the conflict between the living God and what was man-made. If Stephen had aroused trouble for himself by insisting that the most High did not dwell in temples made with hands, thereby condemning the Jews' temple built by Herod, Paul aroused trouble for himself, both in Athens and in Ephesus, by contrasting his God and His dwelling-place with their man-made idols and their residences (17:24; 19:26). This belittling contrast struck at the very foundations of Ephesus' popularity. The chief building was four times larger than Athens' most famous building, the Parthenon. As with most shrines, both then and now, it was not only worshippers who were cared for, but also souvenir-collectors, presumably believing that these souvenirs had magical qualities.

29-41 The whole scene was confused, as one would expect in a riot; the next uproar that Paul experienced would be in Jerusalem (21:31). Two of Paul's companions were taken hostage, and Paul was restrained by his friends from going into the theatre to address the crowd. The riot is probably what Paul described shortly afterwards in 1 Cor 15:32, "I have fought with beasts at Ephesus". A riot on a smaller scale had previously taken place at Philippi for a very similar reason; compare "her masters saw that the hope of their gains was gone" (16:19) with "by this craft we have our wealth" and "this our craft is in danger" (19:25, 27).

As elsewhere, the authorities were brought in. In Philippi they locked up the Lord's two servants overnight and then released them hastily when they discovered that they had done this to Roman citizens without a trial. A similar occurrence happened in Corinth where the deputy did not want to know of their complaint because it was a question of words and names relative to Jewish law. Here in Ephesus the city's leading official (not a "townclerk" in our sense of the word) claimed that the preachers had done nothing that could be condemned and if they had then it could be resolved in a lawful assembly rather than by a riot.

20:1-2 Paul's stay in Ephesus was longer than those in other places, but the outcome was very much the same: a delayed uprising caused him to leave the city. This means that the price paid for the establishment of a church of God was a visit lasting three years to evangelise the city, culminating in a riot. Paul left the disciples not knowing whether he would see them again. Here he "embraced them", though when he left the elders of the church in Ephesus they fell on his neck weeping, and "kissed him" (20:37).

He then passed over into Macedonia, as described in our comments on vv. 21, 22. This was another of those trips that would encourage the new churches; he gave them "much exhortation". The following visit to Greece (including Corinth) lasted three months, but his life was still in danger, this time again from the Jews. This danger caused a change of plans, and instead of travelling by sea from Greece, he returned through Macedonia, intending to take the shorter sea route to Syria.

7. *Paul's Journey to Jerusalem*
   20:3-21:16

a. *Via Miletus (20:3-38)*

- v.3 "And *there* abode three months. And when the Jews laid wait for him, as he was about to sail into Syria, he purposed to return through Macedonia.
- v.4 And there accompanied him into Asia Sopater of Berea; and of the Thessalonians, Aristarchus and Secundus; and Gaius of Derbe, and Timotheus; and of Asia, Tychicus and Trophimus.
- v.5 These going before tarried for us at Troas.
- v.6 And we sailed away from Philippi after the days of unleavened bread, and came unto them to Troas in five days; where we abode seven days.
- v.7 And upon the first *day* of the week, when the disciples came together to break bread, Paul preached unto them, ready to depart on the morrow; and continued his speech until midnight.
- v.8 And there were many lights in the upper chamber, where they were gathered together.
- v.9 And there sat in a window a certain young man named Eutychus, being fallen into a deep sleep: and as Paul was long preaching, he sunk down with sleep, and fell down from the third loft, and was taken up dead.
- v.10 And Paul went down, and fell on him, and embracing *him* said, Trouble not yourselves; for his life is in him.
- v.11 When he therefore was come up again, and had broken bread, and eaten, and talked a long while, even till break of day, so he departed.
- v.12 And they brought the young man alive, and were not a little comforted.
- v.13 And we went before to ship, and sailed unto Assos, there intending to take in Paul; for so had he appointed, minding himself to go afoot.
- v.14 And when he met with us at Assos, we took him in, and came to Mitylene.
- v.15 And we sailed thence, and came the next *day* over against Chios; and the next *day* we arrived at Samos, and tarried at Trogyllium; and the next *day* we came to Miletus.
- v.16 For Paul had determined to sail by Ephesus, because he would not spend the time in Asia: for he hasted, if it were possible for him, to be at Jerusalem the day of Pentecost.
- v.17 And from Miletus he sent to Ephesus, and called the elders of the church.
- v.18 And when they were come to him, he said unto them, Ye know, from the first day that I came into Asia, after what manner I have been with you at all seasons,
- v.19 Serving the Lord with all humility of mind, and with many tears, and temptations, which befell me by the lying in wait of the Jews:
- v.20 *And* how I kept back nothing that was profitable *unto you*, but have shewed you, and have taught you publickly, and from house to house,
- v.21 Testifying both to the Jews, and also to the Greeks, repentance toward God, and faith toward our Lord Jesus Christ.

v.22 And now, behold, I go bound in the spirit unto Jerusalem, not knowing the things that shall befall me there:
v.23 Save that the Holy Ghost witnesseth in every city, saying that bonds and afflictions abide me.
v.24 But none of these things move me, neither count I my life dear unto myself, so that I might finish my course with joy, and the ministry, which I have received of the Lord Jesus, to testify the gospel of the grace of God.
v.25 And now, behold, I know that ye all, among whom I have gone preaching the kingdom of God, shall see my face no more.
v.26 Wherefore I take you to record this day, that I *am* pure from the blood of all *men*.
v.27 For I have not shunned to declare unto you all the counsel of God.
v.28 Take heed therefore unto yourselves, and to all the flock, over the which the Holy Ghost hath made you overseers, to feed the church of God, which he hath purchased with his own blood.
v.29 For I know this, that after my departing shall grievous wolves enter in among you, not sparing the flock.
v.30 Also of your own selves shall men arise, speaking perverse things to draw away disciples after them.
v.31 Therefore watch, and remember, that by the space of three years I ceased not to warn every one night and day with tears.
v.32 And now, brethren, I commend you to God, and to the word of his grace, which is able to build you up, and to give you an inheritance among all them which are sanctified.
v.33 I have coveted no man's silver or gold, or apparel.
v.34 Yea, ye yourselves know, that these hands have ministered unto my necessities, and to them that were with me.
v.35 I have shewed you all things, how that so labouring ye ought to support the weak, and to remember the words of the Lord Jesus, how he said, It is more blessed to give than to receive.
v.36 And when he had thus spoken, he kneeled down, and prayed with them all.
v.37 And they all wept sore, and fell on Paul's neck, and kissed him.
v.38 Sorrowing most of all for the words which he spake, that they should see his face no more. And they accompanied him unto the ship."

3-4 Paul returned to Macedonia overland. V.4 gives a list of Paul's companions, all of them interesting characters. Some were from Europe and some from Asia, evidently from churches established during the apostle's first, second and third missionary journeys. Some accompanied him for shorter periods, and some for longer. They make a proper study in themselves; see Appendix 2. They certainly "accompanied him into Asia", but they went "before" and waited at Troas (v.5). Whether they sailed directly from Greece, leaving Paul himself to return over land to Macedonia, we are not told, though the former appears to be the more probable. But these companions certainly went ahead, and waited for him at Troas, the wait being of a somewhat long duration. Troas was, of course, the site of the ancient city of Troy.

5 It is now that Luke re-enters the story. We last noted his presence when Paul and his company left Philippi during his second journey (16:40); they did not join up again when Paul went into Macedonia in 20:1. The pronouns used by the author now revert to "us" and "we", indicating that Paul called at Philippi, and that Luke rejoined him to return into Asia. We can attribute the healthy spiritual and practical state of the Philippian church to the efforts of this man of God, Luke.

6-7 The reference to "the days of unleavened bread" merely shows the time of the year when the sailing took place, just as the Passover is mentioned in 12: 3-4. It does not mean that the Jewish feasts had any religious significance to Paul and Luke. Paul was more interested in "Christ our passover is sacrificed for us: therefore let us keep the feast: with the unleavened bread of sincerity and truth" (1 Cor 5:7-8).

The meeting-place for Paul and Luke with the rest of Paul's travelling companions was Troas, where previously Paul had been unable to preach although there was an open door (2 Cor 2:12-13). Here they had the happy privilege of breaking bread with the disciples. V. 7 indicates that the church had been guided to accept the practice of remembering the Lord Jesus on the first day of the week. It was the day on which the Lord Jesus had risen from the dead, and a complete break with Judaism and the Sabbath was necessary in order to appreciate it. The christian revelation constituted a new beginning. This is the second, and the last, mention of breaking bread in the Acts (the previous one is in 2:42, although Paul had earlier written on the subject in 1 Cor 11: 20-32, where it is called "the Lord's supper"). But this change from the last day to the first day created practical problems. The first day of the week was an ordinary working day. It seems clear that the Jewish way of reckoning the length of the day was adopted. Their day did not extend from midnight to midnight, but from sunset to sunset; and we find the same order for a day in Gen 1, "the evening and the morning were the first day" (vv. 5, 8, 13, 19, 23, 31). We can therefore safely deduce that the breaking of bread was held on what we would call Saturday evening just after six o'clock.

The NT indicates that meetings of the church were what we may call composite; perhaps the church met only once per week as a matter of necessary convenience rather than as a formal regulation. Today, we have more freedom, and meetings on the Lord's Day and also during the week are arranged according to the needs of the Lord's people based on this freedom, and the Lord's Day is also wholly available for a variety of meetings. Thus in Acts 20, they broke bread, and this was followed by a lengthy address by Paul lasting until midnight. 1 Cor 11-14 may suggest another such lengthy gathering, and this was so extended that a meal was called for at some point. Circumstances of the saints must always be considered when such arrangements are made, though the Lord's Supper should always be celebrated on the first day of the week.

It is, of course, necessary to distinguish between the two mentions of breaking bread in the chapter. That in v. 7 was the spiritual activity of the disciples comprising the church at Troas, while that in v. 11 was the act of taking food. The context must decide. The same kind of distinction is also found in ch. 2; v.42 was the communal act of remembrance of the Lord by the church, while that in v.46 was the domestic act of partaking of a meal.

8-12 Lengthy sermons can create problems, and the result in this case was that one young man fell asleep in a window of the upper room, and fell out of the window to the ground below. We cannot blame the young man; we do not know how busy he had been at his work during the day. Neither can we blame people today if they fall asleep; we do not know their circumstances, and the sermon may be boring, uninspired, badly presented and monotonously spoken. Perhaps such a speaker should not be on the platform in the first place. There are various cases of disciples falling asleep in the NT:

1. Peter, James and John on the mount of transfiguration (Luke 9:32). This was inexcusable, in the presence of divine glory.

2. Peter, James and John in the Garden of Gethsemane (Luke 22:45). This also was inexcusable, since the Lord had instructed them to watch and pray. This occurred three times.

3. Peter in prison (Acts 12:6), rightly and peacefully, anticipating martyrdom the next day.

4. This young man in Troas; no blame was attached to him.

5. Morally and spiritually, "let us not sleetp" (1 Thess 5:6). See also Rom 13:11; Eph 5:14.

The present case gave the occasion for another of Paul's specific miracles, and the greatest: that of a person being raised from the dead. How disconcerting that kind of accident can be in a work recently established. How gracious of God to confirm His work in the early church in such a remarkable way!

There was no sleep for the apostle that night. They ate and talked until daybreak, before Paul"s departure from Troas. Some expositors spiritualise this story, without of course denying its historicity, but the present author believes that NT truth is not reinforced by imaginative interpretations or imagined allegories, although it is admitted that there are found some rather strange allegories, used even in the NT (Gal 4:22-31; Heb 4:1-11; 7:9-10).

13-16 Once again, Paul travelled alone on foot. The others went by ship, the arrangement being that they would collect him at Assos. We can only conclude that, in the middle of a busy life, he required a quiet period of time for meditation and reflection; even Luke was not with him. On one occasion the Lord had invited His disciples to come apart and rest awhile, and He often used the Garden of Gethsemane for such a purpose when in Jerusalem.

The sea-route can best be studied from a map, but it involved the by-passing of Ephesus because Paul wanted to be in Jerusalem by the day of Pentecost, if possible. It can scarcely be imagined that there was any intention of celebrating a feast which had been fulfilled by the giving of the Holy Spirit. It is more likely that the names of the feasts continued to be used like dates in the calendar by Christians, although unregenerate Jews would continue to celebrate them, as they had been required to do by the law during the previous centuries since Moses' time.

17-21 Although Paul did not want to call at Ephesus itself, yet he desired to communicate with the church through its elders. The result was that he sent to the elders to meet him at Ephesus. We have read about elders in the Acts previously in 11:30; 14:23; 15:6,22. There were several elders in one local church; in v.28 they are called "overseers" otherwise translated "bishops". The word "elder" implies spiritual maturity, while the word "overseer" denotes their work. There is no such NT concept as a single bishop ruling over many churches, thereby forming a hierarchy of ecclesiastical officials.(Some have put forward a false interpretation of v.17, that there were many churches involved, and that one elder or bishop came from each church, seeking thereby partly to justify traditional established practice.)

There followed Paul's moving address in which he recalled his previous visit of three years to Ephesus. He spoke of his conduct, service, dangers and testimony. His testimony commenced "from the first day" that he arrived in Ephesus; there is another "first day" in Phil 1:5. No sight-seeing for Paul to commence with; the work of God came first. His ministry was complete; "I kept back nothing that was profitable unto you", declaring "all the counsel of God" (v.27), enabling him to write at the end, "I have finished my course, I have kept the faith" (2 Tim 4:7). Paul's recollection of his service in v.19 reminds us of his longer explanation in 1 Thess 2. Paul's manner of service in Ephesus had been the same as that of the first disciples in Jerusalem. They had preached in the public place (the temple courts) and in private places (people's homes) (5:42). Similarly with Paul in Ephesus: publicly in the synagogue and in the school of Tyrannus, and privately "from house to house". Paul's gospel preaching consisted of the subjects "repentance toward God, and faith toward our Lord Jesus Christ". There were no learned discourses with the gospel message given a brief mention at the end; "woe is unto me, if I preach not the gospel!" (1 Cor 10:16). Some preachers today have never learned this lesson.

22-25 The apostle now looks towards the future concerning himself in these verses. We are not informed why he was so anxious to go to Jerusalem, apart from the fact that he was helping to carry the love-gift from the churches to the saints there (Rom 15: 25-28). His anticipation of his arrival at his destination was full of foreboding, yet he persevered with his intentions. Later we have a few examples of the Holy Spirit testifying about the bonds and afflictions that awaited him (21:11). He had already experienced afflictions in almost every city that he had visited, in keeping with the Lord's words, "I will show him how great things he must suffer for my name's sake" (9:16).

Yet Paul was indomitable in spirit; his life was of no importance provided that the service of the Lord was accomplished. Just as he claimed at the end of his life that he had finished his course (2 Tim 4:7), so here at this critical point of his service he claimed that he wanted to finish his course with joy. He wanted to complete the race and to reach the winning post. The finishing of the course consisted of completing his service of testifying to "the gospel of the grace of God", the first time that Paul had called his message by such an impressive name. The sad part of this was that Paul acknowledged that they would see his face no more. Not that Paul knew what his future movements would be, since 1 Tim 1:3 suggests that he visited Ephesus again after his first imprisonment, though he did not remain there.

26-27 These words are reminiscent of Moses' farewell address in Deut 32; Moses declared all, as he had done throughout the book of Deuteronomy. Paul, like Moses, was "pure from the blood of all men". Both had proclaimed all that God had given them, and the responsibility was no longer their problem. Israel had the option given them to choose life or death; the Ephesians too had the option of remaining faithful to the Lord, or reverting to Judaism.

28 Thus Paul gave a charge to the elders. V.28 teaches a great deal about the work of elders. They were fit to exercise overseership only if they first took heed unto themselves. Vv.29-31 refer to this, since even the elders can go astray. Their responsibility had to be exercised towards "the flock", the first time that a NT church is referred to by such a term. The Lord had used it when speaking of his disciples (Luke 12:32), while Peter also used it of a local church, again in the context of elders (1 Pet 5:3). These men are called "overseers", and this is the only time in the NT when the Greek word *episkopos* is so translated. On the other four occasions (Phil 1:1; 1 Tim 3:2; Titus 1:7; 1 Pet 2:25) the word is translated "bishops", possessing false ecclesiastical connotations. The Anglo-Saxon "overseer", or the classical "supervisor", would be equally appropriate on all occasions. A church leader or elder had the duty to oversee or supervise the well-being, especially the spiritual well-being, of the flock. In Acts 11:30, they also had to deal with financial matters.

There is no contradiction between these verses and others dealing with the appointment of such elders (or presbyters, as the Greek word may be translated), as they are called in v. 17. Paul stated that it was the Holy Spirit that had made them overseers; it was not an appointment or election decided by men. But it is the responsibility of every local church to recognise these man as having divine appointment. Nobody should be an elder (or evangelist, or Bible teacher) officially before he has been one actually. Practice precedes the office.

The Thessaslonian church was young when Paul wrote to them, but the existence of elders is assumed, the believers being exhorted to "know them" (1 Thess 5:12), and to esteem them highly (5:13). They should have a desire for the work entrusted to them, and their qualifications or characteristics are particularly detailed (1 Tim 3:1-7; Titus 15-10). There is no human "ordination" involved; only the apostolic church-planters had the ability to recognise such men and to point them out to the church. Once they exist, it is the duty of the local saints comprising a church to behave as in Heb 13:7, 8, 17, 24.

The same men are elders (v. 17), overseers (v.28) and shepherds or pastors, as indicated by the further mention of their work: to "feed" (AV) or "shepherd" the church of God. Peter was commanded to engage in this work (John 21:16).

We are perfectly familiar with the truth that the body of Christ was loved so much by Him that he gave Himself for it (Eph 5:25). But here in v. 28 Paul stated that a local church, the church of God, was purchased by the blood of His own (presumably, "by the blood of His own Son", though the word "Son" does not occur in the Greek text).

29-31 Paul's anxiety to see the Ephesian elders was obviously prompted by the dangers that he foresaw. He stated, "I know", just as Moses said "I know that after my death ye will utterly corrupt yourselves" (Deut 31:29). Paul could see two dangers, both regarding the elders:

1. These elders would be exposed to special dangers from outside the church; these would be dividers whom Paul described as "grievous wolves" – the figure of the flock is being continued, with the enemy depicted as wolves. These would be false men who would seek church membership, and rapidly seek to become elders and thereby to destroy the flock. But their end is sure; "If any man defile the temple of God, him shall God destroy" (1 Cor 3:17). These men may be the men whom the Lord describes as "apostles, and are not" in Rev 2:2. Here are false elders, just as there would be false gospels, false teachers, false brethren and even a false Jesus (2 Cor 11:4). Every believer must take heed, noting who is a "hireling" and who is the "good shepherd" (John 10:11-14).

2. Paul also foresaw internal enemies who would divide the flock with false teaching – men from among the elders, "of your own selves", seeking to make a separate grouping under their leadership.

By such means, false denominations and cults have developed over the centuries. They were the cause of every weakness witnessed by the Lord in the seven churches in Rev 2-3.

32 The Lord's servants cannot remain in the same place all the time for the sake of averting trouble if it arises. Paul, therefore, commended the Ephesians to God and the word of His grace. Also in this verse we find his first mention of the believer's inheritance; in his letters he often wrote about the subject (Gal 3:18; Eph 1:14, 18; Col 3:24).

	Audience	Where Preached	Subject	Instruction	Parallel Scripture	References in Sermons
Acts 13	Unregenerate Jews	Synagogue of Antioch in Pisidia (v.14)	God of revelation (vv.17-38)	Believe and be justified (v.39)	Rom 2:17-3:31	OT - from Genesis NT - John Baptist and Christ
Acts 14	Idolaters	City gates of Lystra (v.13)	God of creation (v.15)	Turn from these vanities (v.15)	Rom 1:18-32	Creation (v.17)
Acts 17	Philosophers, Intelligentsia	Mar's Hill in Athens or in the court of the Areopagites (v.22)	God of creation and human government (vv.24-29)	Seek the Lord and find Him (v.27)	Rom 2:1-16	A Greek poet - Aratus from three centuries before (v.28)
Acts 20	Elders of Ephesian church	Miletus (v.17)	Paul's burden for any church (vv. 20-21, 27-31)	Take heed to yourselves, and to all the flock, and feed the church of God (v.28)	1 Tim 2:1-3:16 Titus 1:4-16	His visit to Ephesus recalled from ch.19, and the words of the Lord Jesus not mentioned in the Gospels (v.35)

Any NT mention of an inheritance for the people of God must stand in contrast to that of the people of Israel. This contrast exists more strongly in 1 Pet 1:4-5 than anywhere else. The Christian's inheritance is heavenly and therefore cannot be lost like an earthly one. W.E. Vine defines it as "the prospective condition and possessions of the believer in the new order of things to be ushered in at the return of Christ".

Believers have already been referred to as saints in the Acts, but v.32 is the first time the word "sanctified" is used to describe them. The heavenly inheritance is not for unconverted Jews, but for "set-apart" people out of every nation.

While believers wait for that inheritance, Paul commends then to God (some Greek MSS have "the Lord") and to the word of His grace. This last would build them up or edify them, for Paul's objective was, "Let all things be done unto edifying" (1 Cor 14:26; 2 Cor 12:19). This word "grace" plays a large part in Paul's writings. All this inheritance given to the Ephesians and to every believer (unlike Israel because of their physical birth) comes rather because of God's exceeding grace.

33-35 Paul repeatedly recalled his visit to Ephesus and the example that he set for the saints as well as the ministry that he gave them. As in Corinth and obviously in Ephesus, Paul sought to be self-supporting while evangelising and church-planting.

He behaved in the same fashion in Thessalonica according to 1 Thess 2:9. There are situations where many of the Lord's full-time servants could not possibly be self-supporting, but this was Paul's policy before the Lord. He would never have funds diverted from other directions (like supporting needy saints) in his favour. If he had coveted other men's possessions, he could not possibly have written a verse such as 1 Tim 3:3, "not covetous". There is never any shortage of good causes for a church to support in preference to supporting a preacher who is well able to support himself. But note that this same Paul had already stated in 1 Cor 9:14 that it was the right of the evangelist to "live of the gospel"; it would be wrong, however, for a preacher to make any such claims for funds, since that would not be an exercise of faith.

In v.35 we are given the only example in the NT of a statement attributed to the Lord Jesus, but not found any of the four Gospels: "It is more blessed to give than to receive". The word "remember" suggests that the elders knew these words already. How unlike the hypocrites who gave alms openly and receive glory from men (Matt 6:1-2). The widow gave two mites, but received commendation from the Lord (Mark 12:42-44).

36-38 Paul obviously feared for his personal future. He later accepted the prophecies about the dangers that awaited him in Jerusalem (21:13). He did not expect to see the Ephesians again. Only when he wrote to the Philippians more than four years later while in prison in Rome, did he become sure that he could survive this captivity (Phil 1:19-26).

It was a tearful parting when the Ephesian elders escorted Paul to the ship that was to take him further on his journey to Jerusalem. Further NT references show that Paul was the weeping apostle. Paul's burden was emphasised by his kneeling down to pray (v.36). The act of kneeling would normally indicate how great is the person before whom one kneels (see Matt 27:29; Mark 15:19, where it was done in mockery). In Phil 2:10 it is the acknowledgement that Jesus is Lord. The pressure of the occasions made Stephen kneel in Acts 7:60: Peter in 9:40 and Paul again in 21:5. Paul also bowed his knees in prayer in Eph 3:14, whether physically or metaphorically is hardly of relevance. But the Christian who prays *only* on his knees does not pray enough! Paul prayed constantly night and day (1 Thess 3:10; 2 Tim 1:3), and could not always have been on his knees. Thus David sat before the Lord in prayer (2 Sam 7:18), while Nehemiah was obviously standing as butler before the king when he "prayed to the God of heaven" (Neh 2:4).

b. *Tyre to Caesarea (21:1-16)*

v.1 "And it came to pass, that after we were gotten from them, and had launched, we came with a straight course unto Coos, and the *day* following unto Rhodes, and from thence unto Patara:
v.2 And finding a ship sailing over unto Phenicia, we went abroad, and set forth.

v.3 Now when we had discovered Cyprus, we left it on the left hand, and sailed into Syria, and landed at Tyre: for there the ship was to unlade her burden.

v.4 And finding disciples, we tarried there seven days: who said to Paul through the Spirit, that he should not go up to Jerusalem.

v.5 And when we had accomplished those days, we departed and went our way; and they all brought us on our way, with wives and children, till *we were* out of the city: and we kneeled down on the shore, and prayed.

v.6 And when we had taken our leave one of another, we took ship; and they returned home again.

v.7 And when we had finished *our* course from Tyre, we came to Ptolemais, and saluted the brethren, and abode with them one day.

v.8 And the next *day* we that were of Paul's company departed, and came unto Cæsarea: and we entered into the house of Philip the evangelist, which was *one* of the seven; and abode with him.

v.9 And the same man had four daughters, virgins, which did prophesy.

v.10 And as we tarried *there* many days, there came down from Judæa a certain prophet, named Agabus.

v.11 And when he was come unto us, he took Paul's girdle, and bound his own hands and feet, and said, Thus saith the Holy Ghost, So shall the Jews at Jerusalem bind the man that owneth this girdle, and shall deliver *him* into the hands of the Gentiles.

v.12 And when we heard these things, both we, and they of that place, besought him not to go up to Jerusalem.

v.13 Then Paul answered, What mean ye to weep and to break mine heart? for I am ready not to be bound only, but also to die at Jerusalem for the name of the Lord Jesus.

v.14 And when he would not be persuaded, we ceased, saying, The will of the Lord be done.

v.15 And after those days we took up our carriages, and went up to Jerusalem.

v.16 There went with us also *certain* of the disciples of Cæsarea, and brought with them one Mnason of Cyprus, an old disciple, with whom we should lodge."

1-4 Apart from shorter and longer addresses by Paul in chs. 21-28, the material is mainly historical, and our comments of necessity be more brief.

Luke had now become Paul's permanent companion, and he gives us an eyewitness account of all subsequent events. To start with, there is the slow voyage to Caesarea, calling at several ports and involving more than one ship. The text in v.1 suggests a reluctance on the part of the Ephesian elders to let Paul depart, believing that it was for the last time. The route taken can be traced on a map. Certainly they changed ships, and were therefore brought to Tyre, a renowned city of OT times, and capital of Syria. They had to spend seven days in this city, presumably while the ship was unloading.

Needless to say, Paul and his fellow travellers searched for and found a group of disciples in Tyre, and endeared themselves to them in fellowship during the week that they spent there. Seven days must have involved a "first day of the week", when the local church would have gathered for the breaking of bread. Here there were prophets who could speak "through the Spirit", giving advance warning of what awaited Paul at Jerusalem. They pleaded with Paul not to go, but he was determined to go, since he had work to do whatever the consequences. He was not fatalistic in his outlook, but he knew that he was in the will of God.

5-6 In 20:38, they accompanied "him" to the ship, but this time the whole party was escorted out of the city to the shore and as far as the ship. All the church including women and children were determined to see them off. It is touching to see how people who had probably never met each other before were so attached just because they belonged to Christ in a hostile world. View the beauty and wonder of the two groups of Christians kneeling in prayer on a beach committing each other to God for the unknown future.

7 While the folk from Tyre returned home, Paul and those accompanying him continued on their way. Their next port of call was Ptolemias where again a company of brethren was found. Some of these churches are not mentioned elsewhere in Scripture, but their very existence must have been a thrill to Paul, for within a space of a few years new churches had been planted in so many different places. Their individual stories could not possibly all be recounted, but God was at work, and in place after place, mentioned and unmentioned, there were NT churches following the pattern of the apostolic teaching.

The visit to Ptolemais lasted only one day, presumably that could be given because that was the duration fo the ship's stay there, but doubtless the opportunity was taken to encourage the brethren, before moving on to the final port of call, Caesarea, one of the nearest ports to Jerusalem (Joppa was nearer).

8-9 Lodgings in Caesarea were found in the home of Philip the evangelist. He first appeared many years previously as one of the men of honest report appointed in 6:5 to arrange the fair distribution of church funds among the widows in the church at Jerusalem. He went on to earn the title which is accorded here, "Philip the evangelist", being very successful with the gospel in Samaria, culminating in the conversion of the Ethiopian (ch. 8). Now he is found resident in Caesarea where he had brought up four daughters who had become prophetesses, and where he became host for many days to Paul and his company. In the light of Paul's teaching elsewhere, they would not have exercised their gift of prophecy in gatherings of the church, but amongst women. This led to a teaching ministry amongst women by women. (Titus 2: 3-5).

10-14 It was necessary for a visiting prophet from Jerusalem to convey the prophecy about Paul's forthcoming arrest in that city, rather than one of Philip's daughters. This prophet has appeared before, since he was the man who had prophesied the great famine mentioned in 11:28. (The prophetic gift seems to have continued until the NT was complete.) Paul's response to this prophecy was to persevere with his intention, in spite of the entreaties of his companions and of the Caesarean Christians. In the light of subsequent knowledge, we can see that God furthered His pupose in Paul's imprisonment, but Luke does not explain why the warnings were given, if Paul was expected to insist upon going up to Jerusalem. Perhaps it was a test of his faithfulness. He was afraid neither of imprisonment nor death in the Lord's service, so that the apostle's company submitted with a kind of resignation which the NT would enjoin upon us all, "The will of the Lord be done". James tells us that we should all say this, and say it always(4:13-15).

15-16 The final stage of the journey to Jerusalem was overland. There is no question in the Greek text of "carriages" being provided; "carriages" refer to objects being carried in old English. There may have been no carriages in the modern sense of the word, but there was a christian escort, including an old disciple who lived in Jerusalem but who previously had been visiting Caesarea. (This is the last time that the word "disciple" occurs in the NT). One cannot help but notice the number of homes in which christian hospitality was offered, and to appreciate the enormous contribution that such homes must have made to the progress of the gospel and of the church. "Use hospitality one to another without grudging", wrote Peter (1 Pet 4:9).

Notes

> **15**   The RV translates this verse as "we took up our baggage" with a marginal reading "made ready". Obviously its modern equivalent is "we packed our bags". Recall that Paul and others were still carrying the financial gift to the Jerusalem church.
>
> Campbell Morgan cites Henry Ward Beecher's observation that Paul travelled through these Asiatic cities packed with things of beauty and artistry, "and never by a line referred to one of them". But Packer's comment is, "There was no scenery to Paul; there was no geography; there was nothing but lost humanity, and the redeeming cross of Christ".

8. Paul's Arrest and Witness
21:17-26:32

a. Jerusalem (21:17-40)

> v.17   "And when we were come to Jerusalem, the brethren received us gladly.
> v.18   And the *day* following Paul went in with us unto James; and all the elders were present.
> v.19   And when he had saluted them, he declared particularly what things God had wrought among the Gentiles by his ministry.
> v.20   And when they heard *it*, they glorified the Lord, and said unto him, Thou seest, brother, how many thousands of Jews there are which believe; and they are all zealous of the law:

- v.21 And they are informed of thee, that thou teachest all the Jews which are among the Gentiles to forsake Moses, saying that they ought not to circumcise *their* children, neither to walk after the customs.
- v.22 What is it therefore? the multitude must needs come together: for they will hear that thou art come.
- v.23 Do therefore this that we say to thee: We have four men which have a vow on them;
- v.24 Them take, and purify thyself with them, and be at charges with them, that they may shave *their* heads: and all may know that those things, whereof they were informed concerning thee, are nothing; but *that* thou thyself also walkest orderly, and keepest the law.
- v.25 As touching the Gentiles which believe, we have written *and* concluded that they observe no such thing, save only that they keep themselves from *things* offered to idols, and from blood, and from strangled, and from fornication.
- v.26 Then Paul took the men, and the next day purifying himself with them entered into the temple, to signify the accomplishment of the days of purification, until that an offering should be offered for every one of them.
- v.27 And when the seven days were almost ended, the Jews which were of Asia, when they saw him in the temple, stirred up all the people, and laid hands on him,
- v.28 Crying out, Men of Israel, help: This is the man, that teacheth all *men* every where against the people, and the law, and this place: and further brought Greeks also into the temple, and hath polluted this holy place.
- v.29 (For they had seen before with him in the city Trophimus an Ephesian, whom they supposed that Paul had brought into the temple.)
- v.30 And all the city was moved, and the people ran together: and they took Paul, and drew him out of the temple: and forthwith the doors were shut.
- v.31 And as they went about to kill him, tidings came unto the chief captain of the band, that all Jerusalem was in an uproar.
- v.32 Who immediately took soldiers and centurions, and ran down unto them: and when they saw the chief captain and the soldiers, they left beating of Paul.
- v.33 Then the chief captain came near, and took him, and commanded *him* to be bound with two chains; and demanded who he was, and what he had done.
- v.34 And some cried one thing, some another, among the multitude: and when he could not know the certainty for the tumult, he commanded him to be carried into the castle.
- v.35 And when he came upon the stairs, so it was, that he was borne of the soldiers for the violence of the people.
- v.36 For the multitude of the people followed after, crying, Away with him.
- v.37 And as Paul was to be led into the castle, he said unto the chief captain, May I speak unto thee? Who said, Canst thou speak Greek?
- v.38 Art not thou that Egyptian, which before these days madest an uproar, and leddest out into the wilderness four thousand men that were murderers?

v.39 But Paul said, I am a man *which am* a Jew of Tarsus, *a city* in Cilicia, a citizen of no mean city: and, I beseech thee, suffer me to speak unto the people.

v.40 And when he had given him licence, Paul stood on the stairs, and beckoned with the hand unto the people. And when there was made a great silence, he spake unto *them* in the Hebrew tongue, saying,"

17-20 This final visit of Paul to Jerusalem was his fifth as recorded in the Acts (9:26; 11:30; 15:4; 19:21-22; 21:17). His reception by the church was very different from that on the first occasion in ch. 9. Then he was suspect until Barnabas declared how he had been converted, but now he is a respected missionary-evangelist who had done more than any other to propagate the faith that he had once sought to destroy. He had laboured more than the other apostles. He recounted to James and the elders in detail what God had been doing among the nations. Paul took no credit to himself for anything that had been done; his work was "all that God had done" (14:27). They "glorified God" in Paul (Gal 1:24). Even unbelieving Jews "glorified God" for the miracle which was done (Acts 4:21), though without accepting the message concerning Christ. However, in Acts 21 the church in Jerusalem still seems to think that it was right for Jewish believers to be "zealous of the law". They needed to read the Epistle to the Hebrews to correct themselves on that point.

Note: originally the responsible brethren were the apostles (6:2). Then those responsible were "the apostles and elders" (15:6). Finally, it was "the elders" (v.18). This marks the change from apostolic times to what is normal in any local church.

21-25 There was in Jerusalem still much suspicion about the inclusion of Gentiles in local churches. The Lord's brother, James, and the elders were delighted with the progress of the gospel among Gentiles, but were concerned about the attitude of the thousands of Jews who had also believed, but who were still very much devoted to Moses' law. These attitudes were two opposites, as different as the first covenant was from the new and second covenant. Could the gap between the two be bridged? Could Paul display that he was still devoted to the law, although he had proved that he was the apostle to the Gentiles (and this had been agreed in Gal 2:9)? After all, he had written that, to the Jews he became as a Jew if that would further the work of the gospel amongst Jews (1 Cor 9:20), with which Epistle they were probably unfamiliar. So the elders encouraged Paul to join four men who had taken a vow, in shaving his head as a concession to the Jews who could then see clearly that Paul was identifying himself with their traditions, at least in a point that did not damage the true and fundamentally distinct doctrines of Christianity. (A clear example of an OT vow is found in 2 Sam 15:8, though the present case may be another Nazarite vow.) Thus they hoped that the Jews would see that Paul kept the law; of course he did morally, in fact better than did the Jews, for they said but did not do (Rom 2:18-23). At the same time, the elders restated the decisions of the Council of Jerusalem, something he knew already, since he had been involved in delivering the letter to many churches. The decisions were that not such requirements regarding the law should be imposed on believing Gentiles.

26 Paul did as he was asked, and joined the four men entering the temple, for the completion of their purification, with an offering. Luke merely provided the facts, but without an explanantion. Just as we shall never find the answer to the problem as to why Paul persisted in going to Jerusalem in the first instance, equally we shall never find the answer to the question why he went so far in attempting to please the Jews. Expositors may speculate, but these are mere guesses. Paul obviously went the second mile, even to the point of being willing for an offering to be offered for all five men, which we would expect to serve absolutely no purpose in view of the one great and final offering of Christ.

27-29 But the plans of James and the elders went completely astray; was this God's answer to their strange behaviour? They had thought that, by what appears to be compromise, peace with the Jews could be maintained; instead, a riot occured which altered all Paul's plans for his future service.

It was when the seven days of purification were almost ended that the uproar broke out, this time at the hands of unregenerate Jews stirred up by men from Asia. The charges laid against him were almost identical to those laid against his great christian predecessor Stephen, at whose martyrdom he had almost presided. They claimed that Stephen had asserted that Jesus of Nazareth would destroy their holy place, the temple, and would change the customs or rules delivered to them by Moses. Now they claimed that Paul taught everywhere against their people, the law and the holy place, and that he had proved this by bringing Greeks into the temple, thereby polluting it. They had spotted there one of his companion, the Ephesian Trophimus, and presumed that it had been Paul who had brought him in. As far as they were concerned, the middle wall of partition (Eph 2:14) had not been broken down, and Trophimus had presumably ignored the notice on that literal partition warning Gentiles of the consequence of passing that point. Certainly Paul had never taken anybody, Gentile or fellow-Nazarite, into the temple building itself *(naos)* which was for the priests only and it is not clear that he personally had brought anyone into the external temple courts either *(hieron)*.

30-36 Once again, as on so many occasions in his missionary service, Paul was in real danger of being killed, this time in Jerusalem where his Lord had been slain, and where he had participated in the death of the first christian martyr Stephen. His was one of the most adventurous lives in history, but for the greatest of all causes – that of spreading the gospel of the Lord Jesus, which he had once upon a time tried to destroy.

Dragged out of the temple courts by the mob, whereupon the doors were shut, Paul was rescued from being killed only by the arrival of the chief Roman captain. Although Paul was taken into custody for his own safety, he was nevertheless bound with two chains. He was once again in the midst of a riot not of his own making. How often did this happen in his lifetime of christian service! So great was the commotion that the chief captain could not make out the cause of all the trouble, and so many were the threats that Paul had to be carried by the soldiers into the barracks for his safety. "The castle" adjoined the temple courts. The cry of the Jews, "Away with him" (v.36), recalls a similar cry in Jerusalem made against the Lord Jesus (Luke 23:18). Thus Paul knew "the fellowship of his sufferings" (Phil 3:10).

37-40 Speaking to the chief captain, Paul surprised him by speaking in Greek, for Jerusalem was a multilinguistic city in those days, as shown by the superscription on the cross. Instead, the captain expected him to be an Egyptian who had recently created a riot and then led out four thousand murderers; Jerusalem seems to have been a dangerous city to live in at that time. Paul was anxious to address the mob which had threatened him. He then gave his pedigree in Greek, and proceeded to give an account of his conversion in Hebrew. This was diplomacy itself, for the use of their own tongue guaranteed a ready audience.

b. *Paul's Defence before the Jewish Mob (22:1-30)*

> v.1 "Men, brethren, and fathers, hear ye my defence *which I make* now unto you.
>
> v.2 (And when they heard that he spake in the Hebrew togue to them, they kept the more silence; and he saith,)
>
> v.3 I am verily a man *which am* a Jew, born in Tarsus, *a city* in Cilicia, yet brought up in this city at the feet of Gamaliel, *and* taught according to the perfect manner of the law of the fathers, and was zealous towards God, as ye all are this day.
>
> v.4 And I persecuted this way unto the death, binding and delivering into prisons both men and women.
>
> v.5 As also the high priest doth bear me witness, and all the estate of the elders: from whom also I received letters unto the brethren, and went to Damascus, to bring them which were there bound unto Jerusalem, for to be punished.
>
> v.6 And it came to pass, that, as I made my journey, and was come nigh unto Damascus about noon, suddenly there shone from heaven a great light round about me.
>
> v.7 And I fell unto the ground, and heard a voice saying unto me, Saul, Saul, why persecutest thou me?
>
> v.8 And I answered, Who art thou, Lord? And he said unto me, I am Jesus of Nazareth, whom thou persecutest.
>
> v.9 And they that were with me saw indeed the light, and were afraid; but they heard not the voice of him that spake to me.
>
> v.10 And I said, What shall I do, Lord? And the Lord said unto me, Arise, and go into Damascus; and there it shall be told thee of all things which are appointed for thee to do.
>
> v.11 And when I could not see for the glory of that light, being led by the hand of them that were with me, I came into Damascus.

v.12	And one Ananias, a devout man according to the law, having a good report of all the Jews which dwelt *there,*
v.13	Came unto me, and stood, and said unto me, Brother Saul, receive thy sight, And the same hour I looked up upon him.
v.14	And he said, The God of our fathers hath chosen thee, that thou shouldest know his will, and see that Just One, and shouldest hear the voice of his mouth.
v.15	For thou shalt be his witness unto all men of what thou hast seen and heard.
v.16	And now why tarriest thou? arise, and be baptized, and wash away thy sins, calling on the name of the Lord.
v.17	And it came to pass, that, when I was come again to Jerusalem, even while I prayed in the temple, I was in a trance;
v.18	And saw him saying unto me, Make haste, and get thee quickly out of Jerusalem: for they will not receive thy testimony concerning me.
v.19	And I said, Lord, they know that I imprisoned and beat in every synagogue them that believed on thee:
v.20	And when the blood of thy martyr Stephen was shed, I also was standing by, and consenting unto his death, and kept the raiment of them that slew him.
v.21	And he said unto me, Depart: for I will send thee far hence unto the Gentiles.
v.22	And they gave him audience unto this word, and *then* lifted up their voices, and said, Away with such a *fellow* from the earth: for it is not fit that he should live.
v.23	And as they cried out, and cast off *their* clothes, and threw dust into the air,
v.24	The chief captain commanded him to be brought into the castle and bade that he should be examined by scourging; that he might know wherefore they cried so against him.
v.25	And as they bound him with thongs, Paul said unto the centurion that stood by, Is it lawful for you to scourge a man that is a Roman, and uncondemned?
v.26	When the centurion heard *that,* he went and told the chief captain, saying, Take heed what thou doest: for this man is a Roman.
v.27	Then the chief captain came, and said unto him, Tell me, art thou a Roman? He said, Yea.
v.28	And the chief captain answered, With a great sum obtained I this freedom. And Paul said, But I was *free* born.
v.29	Then straightway they departed from him which should have examined him: and the chief captain also was afraid, after he knew that he was a Roman, and because he had bound him.
v.30	On the morrow, because he would have known the certainty wherefore he was accused of the Jews, he loosed him from *his* bands, and commanded the chief priests and all their council to appear, and brought Paul down, and set him before them."

1-3 In Acts 9 we have already had Luke's direct description of Paul's conversion. Here (22:1-21) we have the first of two accounts of this conversion from the apostle's own lips, the second being related before Agrippa (26:2-29). The reader should compare and constrast these three passages, to see what information is and is not included in each. The account of his birthplace and his education at Gamaliel's feet are repeated, though such a gain in the flesh now meant nothing to Paul as it contrasted with "the excellency of the knowledge of Christ Jesus my Lord" (Phil 3:3-8). We have already learned in 5:34 that Gamaliel, a doctor of the law, was a member of the Sanhedrin. All this recollection was no doubt designed to quieten the crowd and to give him an attentive audience to which he could present the gospel as based on his personal testimony. Paul claimed that he used to be as much of a zealot of God as they still were (cf. Rom 10:1-3).

4-16 Once again he designated Christians as being "this way", and recognised his persecutors' zeal for their law, which was so much like his had been. It has frequently been pointed out that, whereas the light which struck Saul to the ground in the story of his conversion in 9:3 was called "a light from heaven", here he calls it "a great light". It did not become dim in his memory with the passing years. (Similarly Peter's memory of the light on the mountain top did not become dim in 2 Pet 1:16-18.) Rather did it brighten, since the wonder of what happened to him on the Damascus road never diminished.

The only mentions of this particular man Ananias in the NT are the two connected with Paul's conversion story. God used an otherwise-unknown disciple to lead Saul into the way. This is not unusual in God's dealings with His servants. What Ananias said to Paul is not identical in the two accounts either. His choice by God is mentioned in both, but here Ananias is recalled as having said that he was to know God's will, to see the Just One (the only other two occasions when the Lord Jesus is called this are in 3:14 and 7:52, all in contrast to the evil of men and of Saul), and to hear His voice. This was all in view of his becoming a witness to all men, which embraces "the Gentiles, and kings, and the children of Israel" (9:15). (In 26:16-18 the Lord Himself spoke to Saul about this on the Damascus road.) Paul's sins were obviously forgiven at that moment on the Damascus road. His baptism in water took place three days later. The baptism was no doubt public, though the forgiveness was private. The public act is evidence that his guilty past is washed away.

17-24 Paul continued in his address to explain that, when he visited Jerusalem for the first itme after his conversion, he was warned by the Lord to flee because of the dangers with which he was threatened. He suggested that he was reluctant to do so since he wanted to make amends for the damage that he had apparently inflicted on the christian cause. 9:28-29 shows that he did actually testify openly in Jerusalem. The Lord's answer even at that early stage was that Paul's major service would be among the Gentiles; in fact, He had already informed him of this even on the Damascus road (26:27). It was this mention of the Gentiles that provoked the vast Jewish audience into a further riot. Even though the christian message would be different, the Jews were greedy of their privileges. Once again the chief captain had to intervene. Paul was cross-examined, scourging being the method by which the truth was obtained. Once more Paul learnt "the fellowship of his sufferings" (Phil 3:10).

25-30 Again Paul's rights as a Roman citizen were violated as at Philippi (16:37). He did not hesitate to claim these rights (see 25:11). He would certainly renounce those that he had as an evangelist (1 Cor 9:15), but not those that he had as a Roman. Either way would further the gospel of Christ. Taking his stand on the grounds that he was a Roman citizen, Paul may well have escaped being lynched, but the chief captain then tried to have the cross-examination carried out by Jewish Sanhedrin.

The greatest prize for non-Romans living in the Roman Empire was the obtaining of Roman citizenship. The centurion had obviously valued it so much that he purchased it for himself, but Paul replied equally proudly that he was born a citizen of that same Empire.

c. Paul's Defence before the Jewish Sanhedrin (23:1-9)

v.1   "And Paul, earnestly beholding the council, said Men *and* brethren, I have lived in all good conscience before God until this day.
v.2   And the high priest Ananias commanded them that stood by him to smite him on the mouth.
v.3   Then, said Paul unto him, God shall smite thee, *thou* whited wall: for sittest thou to judge me after the law, and commandest me to be smitten contrary to the law?
v.4   And they that stood by said, Revilest thou God's high priest?
v.5   Then said Paul, I wist not, brethren, that he was the high priest: for it is written, Thou shalt not speak evil of the ruler of thy people.
v.6   But when Paul perceived that the one part were Sadducees, and the other Pharisees, he cried out in the council, Men *and* brethren, I am a Pharisee, the son of a Pharisee: of the hope and resurrection of the dead I am called in question.
v.7   And when he had so said, there arose a dissension between the Pharisees and the Sadducees: and the multitude was divided.
v.8   For the Sadducees say that there is no resurrection, neither angel, nor spirit: but the Pharisees confess both.
v.9   And there arose a great cry: and the scribes *that were* of the Pharisees' part arose, and strove, saying, We find no evil in this man: but if a spirit or an angel hath spoken to him, let us not fight against God."

1-5 All of this scene with the whole subsequent story – trial, address, imprisonment, voyage to Rome, shipwreck, arrival in Rome – are given in detail, as one might expect from Luke.

The first dignitary of the Sanhedrin to intervene was the high priest Ananias. This name was obviously a common one among the Jews, for this is the third time that we find a man bearing it in the Acts (5:1; 9:10). This one was hostile to Paul from the very beginning, and gave orders for him to be struck on the mouth immediately he commenced to speak. This is another example of "the fellowship of his sufferings" (Matt 26:67). Paul responded by calling him a whited wall, reminiscent of the Lord's reference to scribes and Pharisees in Matt 23:27, "Woe unto you, scribes and Pharisees, hypocrites! for ye are like unto whited sepulchres, which indeed appear beautiful outward, but are within full of dead men's bones, and of all uncleanness". As far as Paul was concerned, these men were acting contrary to God's decree through Moses (Deut 25: 1-2). Paul certainly knew the law and quoted it when necessary; the Sanhedrin also knew the law, but disregarded it when it suited their purpose.

Paul was rebuked for his answer to the high priest, and it may appear that Paul apologised, claiming that he did not know that the man was the high priest, and reacalling that the Scriptures taught that people must not speak evil about rulers (Exod 22:28). But it may certainly be that Paul acknowledged the high priest as a civil ruler, but not as God's high priest. At least when he replied to the accusation he did not mention God and also did not use the definite article "the" concerning him. He said, "I wist not that he was high priest", unlike the men who said in v.4, "Revilest thou the high priest of God?", using both words "the" and "God's". After all, these high priests were chosen by the Romans, and remind us of Eli who took the title high priest, but not according to God's choice that the high priests should proceed from the line of Eleazar.

6-9 Paul detected that the Sanhedrin was divided between Pharisees and Sadducees, and decided to exploit their differences by referring to "the hope and resurrection of the dead". He recalled that he had been a Pharisee, and the son of a Pharisee (some Greek MSS have "Pharisees"), just as he was a Hebrew of the Hebrews. By saying "resurrection of the dead", he used the Pharisees' concept, not the christian concept which would be "resurrection out from among the dead".

Paul's appeal to the Pharisees simply resulted in a deep cleavage between the two sections of the Sanhedrin; evidently resurrection was a subject that could not be mentioned in any discussion of doctrine! The Pharisees sided with him even to the extent of suggesting that a spirit or angel might have spoken to him, in which the Sadducees did not believe. Once again Gamaliel's old fear in 5:39 was raised, "Let us not fight against God". They little knew that they had been fighting against God on every occasion that persecution was raised against His servants. But "He that sitteth in the heavens shall laugh: the Lord shall have them in derision" (Ps 2:1-5).

d. *Paul's Rescue from Jerusalem (23:10-35)*

> v.10 "And when there arose a great dissension, the chief captain, fearing lest Paul should have been pulled in pieces of them, commanded the soldiers to go down, and to take him by force from among them, and to bring *him* into the castle.

v.11 And the night following the Lord stood by him, and said, Be of good cheer, Paul: for as thou hast testified of me in Jerusalem, so must thou bear witness also at Rome.
v.12 And when it was day, certain of the Jews banded together, and bound themselves under a curse, saying that they would neither eat nor drink till they had killed Paul.
v.13 And they were more than forty which had made this conspiracy.
v.14 And they came to the chief priests and elders, and said, We have bound ourselves under a great curse, that we will eat nothing until we have slain Paul.
v.15 Now therefore ye with the council signify to the chief captain that he bring him down unto you to morrow, as though ye would inquire something more perfectly concerning him: and we, or ever he come near, are ready to kill him.
v.16 And when Paul's sister's son heard of their lying in wait, he went and entered into the castle, and told Paul.
v.17 Then Paul called one of the centurions unto *him*, and said, Bring this young man unto the chief captain: for he hath a certain thing to tell him.
v.18 So he took him, and brought *him* to the chief captain, and said, Paul the prisoner called me unto *him*, and prayed me to bring this young man unto thee, who hath something to say unto thee.
v.19 Then the chief captain took him by the hand, and went *with him* aside privately, and asked *him*, What is that thou hast to tell me?
v.20 And he said, The Jews have agreed to desire thee that thou wouldest bring down Paul to morrow into the council, as though they would inquire somewhat of him more perfectly.
v.21 But do not thou yield unto them: for there lie in wait for him of them more than forty men, which have bound themselves with an oath, that they will neither eat nor drink till they have killed him: and now are they ready, looking for a promise from thee.
v.22 So the chief captain *then* let the young man depart, and charged *him*, See thou tell no man that thou hast shewed these things to me.
v.23 And he called unto *him* two centurions saying, Make ready two hundred soldiers to go to Cæsarea, and horsemen threescore and ten, and spearmen two hundred, at the third hour of the night;
v.24 And provide *them* beasts, that they may set Paul on, and bring *him* safe unto Felix the governor.
v.25 And he wrote a letter after this manner:
v.26 Claudius Lysias unto the most excellent governor Felix *sendeth* greeting.
v.27 This man was taken of the Jews, and should have been killed of them: then came I with an army, and rescued him, having understood that he was a Roman.
v.28 And when I would have known the cause wherefore they accused him, I brought him forth into their council:
v.29 Whom I perceived to be accused of questions of their law, but to have nothing laid to his charge worthy of death or of bonds.
v.30 And when it was told me how that the Jews laid wait for the man, I sent straightway to thee, and gave commandment to his accusers also to say before thee what *they had* against him. Farewell.

v.31 Then the soldiers, as it was commanded them, took Paul, and brought *him* by night to Antipatris.
v.32 On the morrow they left the horsemen to go with him, and returned to the castle:
v.33 Who, when they came to Cæsarea, and delivered the epistle to the governor, presented Paul also before him.
v.34 And when the governor had read *the letter,* he asked of what province he was. And when he understood that *he was* of Cilicia;
v.35 I will hear thee, said he, when thine accusers are also come. And he commanded him to be kept in Herod's judgment hall."

10-11 This historical passage needs but little comment. For the third time in this single incident Paul had to be rescued by the chief captain. That night, as on several occasions in his career (18:9; 22:18; 27:23; 2 Tim 4:17), the Lord stood by him and said, "Be of good cheer, Paul: for as thou hast testified of me in Jerusalem, so must thou bear witness also at Rome" (v.11). This testimony in Jerusalem (22:1-21) was as prisoner of the Romans, and the Lord seemed to imply that it would be as a prisoner that he would testify at Rome; whether Paul appreciated this we cannot discern, but see 20:23. In spite of all our questions about his going to Jerusalem in the first place, God was in control. Paul's desire to visit Rome (19:21; Rom 1:10; 15:24, 32) would be fulfilled, though not with the liberty that he had anticipated. God's servant had not run away from His presence, nor ever could do so.

12-35 The Jews were still determined to kill him. They drew up a plot and bound themselves by an oath to do so. They were not going to eat or drink until they had fulfilled their objective, and the number in the conspiracy was more than forty. They took the Sanhedrin into their confidence, and asked them to bring the apostle before them the next day, as though they wished to question him further. They were going to lie in wait and seize him before he arrived at the meeting-place. Paul's nephew, a "young man" (v.22), heard of the plot and visited his uncle in prison to tell him about it. This is the only time that we hear of one of Paul's near relatives; it was remarkable, naturally speaking, that he was near at hand! Paul used a great deal of common sense as well as divine guidance. The Lord had told him only the night before that he would see Rome, and what Paul did was only to further the divine will. He asked a centurion to take his nephew to tell the chief captain about his information. The chief captain responded by arranging for a military escort of about five hundred men to escort Paul, under cover of darkness, to Caesarea, where the Romans were stronger. It was probably Paul's most comfortable journey ever on that route, for he was given a beast of burden on which to ride. (The strength of the oath taken by those forty men is seen in the word used, *anathematizō*, a verb in Greek (vv.12, 14, 21). These men were prepared to be accursed if they did not succeed in murdering Paul, but we are not informed what happened to them ultimately.)

The letter written by Claudius Lysias to the governor Felix was factual, except that it commenced with an untruth (v.27). He wrote that he came and rescued him (the first time), having understood that he was a Roman. But he only learned this important fact afterwards (22:27). How unlike the truthful letter written on behalf of Apollos (18:27), and the seven letters in Rev 2-3 containing the truthful discernment of the churches by the Lord.

e. *Paul's Trial before Felix (24:1-27)*

- v.1 "And after five days Ananias the high priest descended with the elders, and *with* a certain orator *named* Tertullus, who informed the governor against Paul.
- v.2 And when he was called forth, Tertullus began to accuse *him,* saying, Seeing that by thee we enjoy great quietness, and that very worthy deeds are done unto this nation by thy providence,
- v.3 We accept *it* always, and in all places, most noble Felix, with all thankfulness.
- v.4 Notwithstanding, that I be not further tedious unto thee, I pray thee that thou wouldest hear us of thy clemency a few words.
- v.5 For we have found this man *a* pestilent *fellow,* and a mover of sedition among all the Jews throughout the world, and a ringleader of the sect of the Nazarenes:
- v.6 Who also hath gone about to profane the temple: whom we took, and would have judged according to our law.
- v.7 But the chief captain Lysias came *upon us,* and with great violence took *him* away out of our hands,
- v.8 Commanding his accusers to come unto thee: by examining of whom thyself mayest take knowledge of all these things, whereof we accuse him.
- v.9 And the Jews also assented, saying that these things were so.
- v.10 Then Paul, after that the governor had beckoned unto him to speak, answered, Forasmuch as I know that thou has been of many years a judge unto his nation, I do the more cheerfully answer for myself:
- v.11 Because that thou mayest understand, that there are yet but twelve days since I went up to Jerusalem for to worship.
- v.12 And they neither found me in the temple disputing with any man, neither raising up the people, neither in the synagogues, nor in the city:
- v.13 Neither can they prove the things whereof they now accuse me.
- v.14 But this I confess unto thee, that after the way which they call heresy, so worship I the God of my fathers, believing all things which are written in the law and in the prophets:
- v.15 And have hope toward God, which they themselves also allow, that there shall be a resurrection of the dead, both of the just and unjust.
- v.16 And herein do I exercise myself, to have always a conscience void of offence toward God, and *toward* men.
- v.17 Now after many years I came to bring alms to my nation, and offerings.
- v.18 Whereupon certain Jews from Asia found me purified in the temple, neither with multitude, nor with tumult.
- v.19 Who ought to have been here before thee, and object, if they had aught against me.

v.20 Or else let these same *here* say, if they have found any evil doing in me, while I stood before the council,

v.21 Except it be for this one voice, that I cried standing among them, Touching the resurrection of the dead I am called in question by you this day.

v.22 And when Felix heard these things, having more perfect knowledge of *that* way, he deferred them, and said, When Lysias the chief captain shall come down, I will know the uttermost of your matter.

v.23 And he commanded a centurion to keep Paul, and to let *him* have liberty, and that he should forbid none of his acquaintance to minister or come unto him.

v.24 And after certain days, when Felix came with his wife Drusilla, which was a Jewess, he sent for Paul, and heard him concerning the faith in Christ.

v.25 And as he reasoned of righteousness, temperance, and judgment to come, Felix trembled, and answered, Go thy way for this time; when I have a convenient season, I will call for thee.

v.26 He hoped also that money should have been given him of Paul, that he might loose him: wherefore he sent for him the oftener, and communed with him.

v.27 But after two years Porcius Festus came into Felix' room: and Felix, willing to shew the Jews a pleasure, left Paul bound."

Thus Paul's case passed from the hands of the Jewish Sanhedrin into those of the Roman governor Felix. Five days later his accusers arrived, namely the Jewish Sanhedrin led by Ananias the high priest and the orator (not a professional lawyer, but a professional speaker) to present their case. It was almost a replica of the Lord's situation when He appeared before Pilate: once again Paul shared "the fellowship of his sufferings". He was being bandied about between Jews and Romans, and between different officials in the Roman establishment.

1-21 The orator spoke first. He flattered Felix (something that Paul would never do in his evangelistic work (1 Thess 2:4-5)), and went on to accuse Paul in vehement terms. He was "a pestilent fellow", a "mover of sedition" throughout world Jewry, a ringleader of the sect of the Nazarenes, a profaner of the temple. Some Greek MSS omit v.7 in which Lysias is condemned for his part in rescuing Paul. Tertullus claimed that what he had accused Paul of would be confirmed by an examination of the prisoner (the AV may read as if the examination would be of the high priest and elders, but strictly the examination is of Paul).

The apostle commenced in v.10 by saying a pleasing thing about Felix, but what he said was not flattery – it was true. He declared that some of the charges were impossible, since it was only twelve days since his arrival in Jerusalem. He had not engaged in dispute in the temple, synagogues nor in the city. He confessed that he did follow after "the way which they call heresy", but stressed the common features between Judaism and Christianity: the worship of the God of their fathers, the things which were written in the prophets, the hope of Israel, and the resurrection of both kinds of dead people. In order to calm the situation, he did not expound the doctrines that were peculiar to Christianity. His attitude was to offend nobody, neither God nor men, but his presence in the city was to do what he had done on a previous occasion, namely to take alms and offerings to his nation (strictly, to the church in Jerusalem). This corresponds to his stated intention for such a visit to Jerusalem in Rom 15:25; 1 Cor 16:3-4; 2 Cor 8:4. He claimed that in the temple he was purified, and that there was no disturbance whatsoever. He stated that those Asiatic Jews who found him in the temple ought to have been present to answer his objections, or alternatively that the members of the Sanhedrin who were present ought to be pressed about any evil that they found in him. He insisted that the crux of the matter was the subject of the resurrection of the dead, the dividing point between Pharisees and Sadducees. How unlike this unrighteous judgment of men from God's judgment, for He will judge the world in righteousness (17:31).

22-26 Felix was obviously not ignorant of the christian way, and decided that the only other evidence that he needed was that of Lysias. He entrusted Paul to the care of a centurion, permitting a fair degree of liberty including that of open visiting. A few days later, Felix summoned Paul again in the presence of his wife who was a Jewess, and gave him the opportunity of speaking to them. All that we are told is that Paul spoke to them of righteousness, self-control and coming judgment. We are left to imagine the details, but we are told of the effect on Felix: he became afraid. But once again he postponed the decision about his prisoner, telling him that when it was convenient he would send for him again. So vivid is the AV rendering that it might suggest that he was almost persuaded, like Agrippa, to believe. That does not seem really likely, since we are told quite plainly in v.26 that Felix was looking for a bribe. In fact, to increase the opportunities for bribing him, he sent for him often, indicating all the time that his motives were very mixed, and that no convenient season ever arrived. (Some have suggested the Paul, poor in 2 Cor 6:10, had inherited some money, and that Felix was seeking some of it.)

Felix had still made no decision about Paul before his successor, Festus, arrived. Like his Lord's judge, Pilate before him, he was more concerned with men-pleasing and with himself, than with righteous judgment. Thus the Caesarean part of Paul's captivity extended to two years. With another two years lying ahead in Rome after a long voyage, this period constituted a significant interval in the life of such an energetic and busy man.

f. Paul's Trial before Festus (25:1-27)

v.1 "Now when Festus was come into the province, after three days he ascended from Cæsarea to Jerusalem.
v.2 Then the high priest and the chief of the Jews informed him against Paul, and besought him,

v.3   And desired favour against him, that he would send for him to Jerusalem, laying wait in the way to kill him.
v.4   But Festus answered, that Paul should be kept at Cæsarea, and that he himself would depart shortly *thither*.
v.5   Let them therefore, said he, which among you are able, go down with *me*, and accuse this man, if there be any wickedness in him.
v.6   And when he had tarried among them more than ten days, he went down unto Cæsarea; and the next day sitting on the judgment seat commanded Paul to be brought.
v.7   And when he was come, the Jews which came down from Jerusalem stood round about, and laid many and grievous complaints against Paul, which they could not prove.
v.8   While he answered for himself, Neither against the law of the Jews, neither against the temple, nor yet against Cæsar, have I offended any thing at all.
v.9   But Festus, willing to do the Jews a pleasure, answered Paul, and said, Wilt thou go up to Jerusalem, and there be judged of these things before me?
v.10 Then said Paul, I stand at Cæsar's judgment seat, where I ought to be judged: to the Jews have I done no wrong, as thou very well knowest.
v.11 For if I be an offender, or have committed any thing worthy of death, I refuse not to die; but if there be none of these things whereof these accuse me, no man may deliver me unto them. I appeal unto Cæsar.
v.12 Then Festus, when he had conferred with the council, answered, Hast thou appealed unto Cæsar? unto Cæsar shalt thou go.
v.13 And after certain days king Agrippa and Bernice came unto Cæsarea to salute Festus.
v.14 And when they had been there many days, Festus declared Paul's cause unto the king, saying, There is a certain man left in bonds by Felix:
v.15 About whom, when I was at Jerusalem, the chief priests and the elders of the Jews informed *me*, desiring *to have* judgment against him.
v.16 To whom I answered, It is not the manner of the Romans to deliver any man to die, before that he which is accused have the accusers face to face, and have licence to answer for himself concerning the crime laid against him.
v.17 Therefore, when they were come hither, without any delay on the morrow I sat on the judgment seat, and commanded the man to be brought forth.
v.18 Against whom when the accusers stood up, they brought none accusation of such things as I supposed:
v.19 But had certain questions against him of their own superstition, and of one Jesus, which was dead, whom Paul affirmed to be alive.
v.20 And because I doubted of such manner of questions, I asked *him* whether he would go to Jerusalem, and there be judged of these matters.
v.21 But when Paul had appealed to be reserved unto the hearing of Augustus, I commanded him to be kept till I might send him to Cæsar.
v.22 Then Agrippa said unto Festus, I would also hear the man myself. To morrow, said he, thou shalt hear him.

v.23 And on the morrow, when Agrippa was come, and Bernice, with great pomp, and was entered into the place of hearing, with the chief captains, and principal men of the city, at Festus' commandment Paul was brought forth.

v.24 And Festus said, King Agrippa, and all men which are here present with us, ye see this man, about whom all the multitude of the Jews have dealt with me, both at Jerusalem, and *also* here, crying that he ought not to live any longer.

v.25 But when I found that he had committed nothing worthy of death, and that he himself hath appealed to Augustus, I have determined to send him.

v.26 Of whom I have no certain thing to write unto my lord. Wherefore I have brought him forth before you, and specially before thee, O king Agrippa, that, after examination had, I might have somewhat to write.

v.27 For it seemeth to me unreasonable to send a prisoner, and not withal to signify the crimes *laid* against him."

1-5 Three days after his arrival to take up his new post, Festus visited Jerusalem, and the leaders of the Sanhedrin took the opportunity to raise the subject of Paul with him; after two years they had never forgotten their enemy in Caesarea. They tried to repeat the plot whereby Paul was to be disposed of by themselves. Would he bring him up to Jerusalem and have his case tried there? Festus disagreed, but declared that he was returning shortly to Caesarea and would deal with the case then, if they would send down his accusers.

6 Festus spent ten days in Jerusalem and sent for Paul the day after his return. We are not given any details about the "many and grievous complaints" that they pressed against him, but, as with his Lord those years before, we are told that they could not prove them. Paul did protest his innocence (v.8); there had been no escape for the Lord at His trial (indeed, Pilate had power given to him from above, John19:11), else atonement would not have been made, but there needed to be an escape route for His servant Paul, so that the divine will for his services be fulfilled. He said, "Neither against the law of the Jews, neither against the temple, nor yet against Caesar, have I offended any thing at all". This is obviously what he meant when he spoke about "void of offence toward God, and toward men" (24:16). Festus was prepared to vacillate as much as Felix had done. He was prepared to play right into their hands and to send the prisoner back to Jerusalem with all its dangers, so Paul appealed to Caesar.

The Jews surprisingly seem to have agreed (v.12). Did they reckon that Nero would slay him? They certainly did not communicate with the Jewish leaders in Rome to continue with the case (28:21). So Paul's ordeal continued.

The words "judgment seat" *(bema)* three times appear in this chapter (vv.6, 10, 17), meaning the tribunal of a magistrate or ruler (usually a Roman). There are four occasions in the NT where it has this sense:

1. When the Lord Jesus appeared before Pilate in Jerusalem (Matt 27:19; John 19:13).

2. When Herod sat on his "throne" in Caesarea (Acts 12:21) and accepted the people's claim of deity.

3. In Corinth, when Paul appeared before Gallio (18:12, 16, 17).

4. In Caesarea, when Paul appeared before Festus (25:6, 10, 17). In v.10, Paul said, "I stand at Caesar's judgment seat", referring to the delegated authority from Caesar in Rome to the governor Festus in Caesarea.

In Rom 14:10 and 2 Cor 5:10 the "judgment seat" is that of Christ, before which believers will appear after the rapture. Before the four judgment seats quoted above, unrighteous decisions were taken or strange things occurred, but at the judgment seat of Christ pure righteous divine discernment will be exercised so that rewards may be granted to the Lord's people.

13-27 In spite of the decision to remit the prisoner to the court of Nero in Rome, Paul was not yet finished with the Roman and Jewish authorities in Caesarea. King Agrippa (one of the Herods – see the family tree at the end of this section) and Bernice came to pay a call on Festus and eventually, either having nothing further with which to occupy his guests, or seeking more definite information about Paul to transmit to Caesar, Festus gave them the opportunity to listen to this interesting prisoner. Time and again in the Acts, mobs, both Jewish and heathen, put magistrates into difficult situations with their knowledge of the law, and the impossibility of condemning the gospel preachers on the grounds of it. Thus Pilate wanted to release the Lord Jesus, but the Jews made it impossible for him to do so. The first missionaries were very careful to behave properly in spite of all the rough handling that they suffered. They made very sure that they did not practice wrong-doing, so that their accusers could have no legal substance for their complaints. Any sufferings that they experienced were purely because they were Christians. They practised Peter's precept before he wrote about it in 5:29, "We ought to obey God rather than men". See 1 Pet 2:11-15; 4:15-16, "let none of you suffer as a murderer, or as a thief, or as an evildoer ... Yet if any man suffer as a Christian, let him not be ashamed, but let him glorify God on this behalf".

Festus related Paul's story to Agrippa. He found the accusations against him to be in connection with their own religion, of which Roman rulers tended to be ignorant, and its connection with a man called Jesus. He explained that he had no accusations to present before Caesar. (Note that "Augustus" in v.21 was a general title; Nero was the Roman Emperor at that time.) The subsequent public appearance of Paul in ch. 26 before an august assembly might not have contributed anything to what Festus had to communicate to Caesar, but it did give Paul another opportunity to witness for his Lord, and it also gives us another narration of his famous testimony.

Notes

The Herodian Family

Eleven members of the Herodian family are mentioned in the NT, in the Gospels and Acts, and it is important that their relation the one to the other be understood, and that the several Herods be distinguished.

The following names are not inclusive, some have been omitted because they are not relevant to our exposition.

(a) Diagram

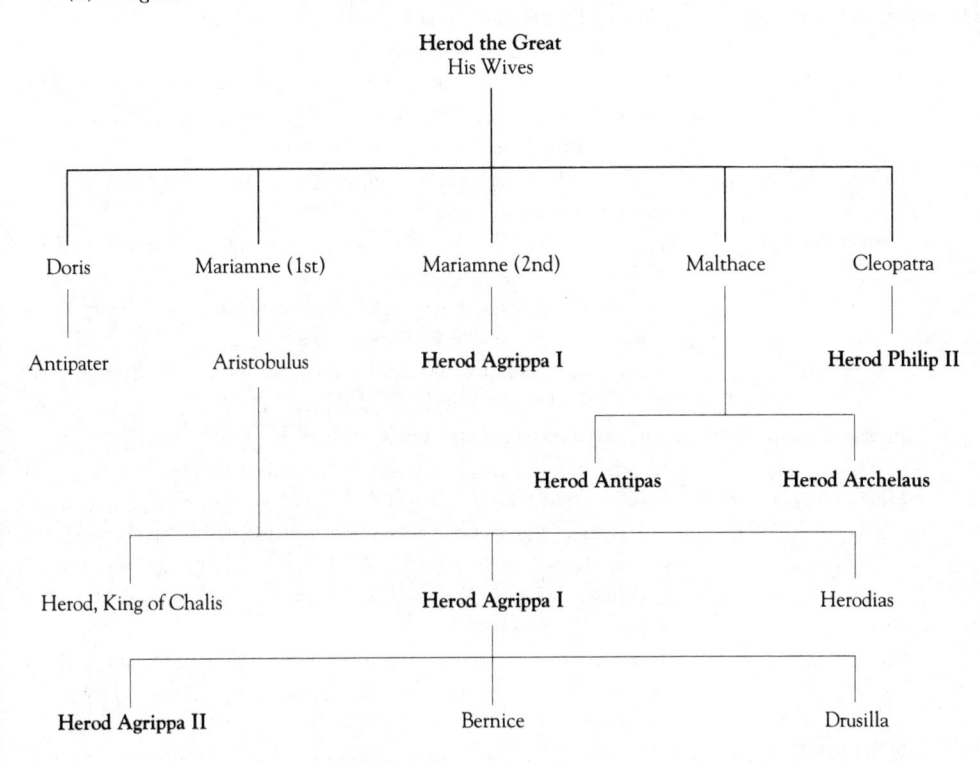

```
                        Herod the Great
                           His Wives
    ┌───────┬──────────────┬──────────────┬──────────────┬──────────────┐
  Doris   Mariamne (1st)  Mariamne (2nd)    Malthace       Cleopatra
    │         │                │                │                │
Antipater  Aristobulus    Herod Agrippa I                   Herod Philip II
              │
              │                        ┌──────────────┬──────────────┐
                                   Herod Antipas           Herod Archelaus

      ┌──────────────┬──────────────┬──────────────┐
Herod, King of Chalis    Herod Agrippa I        Herodias
                              │
              ┌──────────────┬──────────────┐
      Herod Agrippa II     Bernice        Drusilla
```

(The names in bold type are of importance for the Gospels and Acts)

(b) References

Herod the Great	Matt 2:1-3, 7, 9, 12-19; Luke 1:5
Herod Philip I	Matt 14:3; Mark 6:17; Luke 3:19
Herod Antipas	Matt 16:1, 3, 6, 9; Mark 6:14, 16-22, 25-27; Luke 3:1, 19; 8:3; 9:7, 9; 23:7-12, 15; Acts 4:27; 13:1

Herod Archelaus	Matt 2:22; (Luke 19: 12-27)
Herod Philip II	Luke 3:1
Salome	Matt 14:6-11; Mark 6:22-28 (not named)
Herod Agrippa I	Acts 12:1-6; 19-23
Herodias	Matt 14:3, 6-11; Mark 6:17, 19, 22-28
Herod Agrippa II	Acts 25:13-27; 26:1-32
Bernice	Acts 25:13, 23; 26:30
Drusilla	Acts 24:24

(c) Notes

Herod the Great	Made king by the Romans, BC 40. Sole king of Judaea BC 27. Died BC 4. Christ was born in his reign.
Aristobulus	Married Bernice, tha daughter of Salome, and sister of Herod the Great. He was the son of the first Miriamne, and was put to death by his father in BC 6.
Herod Philip I	The son of the second Miriamne. He married Herodias, and Salome was his daughter.
Herod Antipas	The tetrarch of Galilee. He married the daughter of Aretas king of Arabia, and later Herodias the wife of Herod Philip I. He was the son of Malthace. He beheaded John the Baptist. Jesus appeared before him in the Passion week. He was banished in AD 40.
Archelaus	Son of Malthace. Ethnarch of Judaea, Idumaea and Samaria, BC 4. He was desposed and banished in AD 6.
Herod Philip II	Son of Cleopatra. Tetrarch of Ituraea and Trachonitis. He married Salome, the daughter of Philip I and Herodias. He died in AD 34.
Herod Agrippa I	Son of Aristobulus, and grandson of Herod the Great by the first Miriamne. He succeeded to the Tetrarchy of Philip II in AD 37, and of Herod Antipas in AD 40. Judaea and Samaria were added in AD 41. He killed James, the brother of John and was eaten of worms in AD 44.
Herodias	The daughter of Aristobulus and the first Miriamne. She married Philip I, whom she left for Herod Antipas. Salome was her daughter.
Herod Agrippa II	Son of Agrippa I, AD 48-53. Succeeded to Tetrarchy of Philip II, AD 53-70. Was the last Herodian Prince. He heard Paul's defence. After the fall of Jerusalem in AD 70, he retired to Rome, and died in AD 100.
Bernice	Daughter of Herod Agrippa I, and sister of Agrippa II. She married Herod king of Chalcis, the son of Aristobulus and the first Miriamne.
Drusilla	Daughter of Herod Agrippa I; sister of Agrippa II and of Bernice. She married Felix, governor of Judaea, before whom Paul made his defence.

WHAT THE BIBLE TEACHES / ACTS 26

g. *Paul's Trial before Agrippa (26:1-32)*

v.1 "Then Agrippa said unto Paul, Thou art permitted to speak for thyself. Then Paul stretched forth the hand, and answered for himself:

v.2 I think myself happy, king Agrippa, because I shall answer for myself this day before thee touching all the things whereof I am accused of the Jews:

v.3 Especially *because I know* thee to be expert in all customs and questions which are among the Jews: wherefore I beseech thee to hear me patiently.

v.4 My manner of life from my youth, which was at the first among mine own nation at Jerusalem, know all the Jews;

v.5 Which knew me from the beginning, if they would testify, that after the most straitest sect of our religion I lived a Pharisee.

v.6 And now I stand and am judged for the hope of the promise made of God unto our fathers:

v.7 Unto which *promise* our twelve tribes, instantly serving *God* day and night, hope to come. For which hope's sake, king Agrippa. I am accused of the Jews.

v.8 Why should it be thought a thing incredible with you, that God should raise the dead?

v.9 I verily thought with myself, that I ought to do many things contrary to the name of Jesus of Nazareth.

v.10 Which thing I also did in Jerusalem: and many of the saints did I shut up in prison, having received authority from the chief priests; and when they were put to death, I gave my voice against *them*.

v.11 And I punished them oft in every synagogue, and compelled *them* to blaspheme: and being exceedingly mad against them, I persecuted *them* even unto strange cities.

v.12 Whereupon as I went to Damascus with authority and commission from the chief priests,

v.,13 At midday, O king, I saw in the way a light from heaven, above the brightness of the sun, shining round about me and them which journeyed with me.

v.14 And when we were all fallen to the earth, I heard a voice speaking unto me, and saying in the Hebrew tongue, Saul, Saul, why persecutest thou me? *it is* hard for thee to kick against the pricks.

v.15 And I said, Who are thou, Lord? And he said, I am Jesus whom thou persecutest.

v.16 But rise, and stand upon thy feet: for I have appeared unto thee for this purpose, to make thee a minister and a witness both of these things which thou hast seen, and of those things in the which I will appear unto thee;

v.17 Delivering thee from the people, and *from* the Gentiles, unto whom now I send thee,

v.18 To open their eyes, *and* to turn *them* from darkness to light, and *from* the power of Satan unto God, that they may receive forgiveness of sins, and inheritance among them which are sanctified by faith that is in me.

v.19 Whereupon, O king Agrippa, I was not disobedient unto the heavenly vision:

v.20 But shewed first unto them of Damascus, and at Jerusalem, and throughout all the coasts of Judæa, and *then* to the Gentiles, that they should repent and turn to God, and do works meet for repentance.
v.21 For these causes the Jews caught me in the temple, and went about to kill *me*.
v.22 Having therefore obtained help of God, I continue unto this day, witnessing both to small and great, saying none other things than those which the prophets and Moses did say should come:
v.23 That Christ should suffer, *and* that he should be the first that should rise from the dead, and should shew light unto the people, and to the Gentiles.
v.24 And as he thus spake for himself, Festus said with a loud voice, Paul, thou art beside thyself; much learning doth make thee mad.
v.25 But he said, I am not mad, most noble Festus; but speak forth the words of truth and soberness.
v.26 For the king knoweth of these things, before whom also I speak freely: for I am persuaded that none of these things are hidden from him; for this thing was not done in a corner.
v.27 King Agrippa, believest thou the prophets? I know that thou believest.
v.28 Then Agrippa said unto Paul, Almost thou persuadest me to be a Christian.
v.29 And Paul said, I would to God, that not only thou, but also all that hear me this day, were both almost, and altogether such as I am, except these bonds.
v.30 And when he had thus spoken, the king rose up, and the governor, and Bernice, and they that sat with them:
v.31 And when they were gone aside, they talked between themselves, saying, This man doeth nothing worthy of death or of bonds.
v.32 Then said Agrippa unto Festus, This man might have been set at liberty, if he had not appealed unto Cæsar."

1-7 Paul's attitude was always one of the utmost respect. Even his remarks in 23:3 show no sign of disrespect, even if Ananias had no God-given authority whatsoever. He gave credit to Agrippa for his familiarity with Jewish ways; this was not flattery. (For Agrippa's connection with the Herodian family, see the Herodian family genealogy preceding this section.) Paul stressed his Jewish upbringing in Jerusalem to illustrate how devoted he had been to the faith of his fathers. He stressed that he was still standing for the hope of Israel. It must be emphasised that Christianity does not repudiate Judaism, but builds upon the fact that Christ came in keeping with "the things ... which were written in the law of Moses, and in the prophets, and in the psalms" concerning Himself (Luke 24:44). All the ceremonial law is fulfilled in Christ, whereas the moral law was magnified by Christ, and superceded by higher standards made possible by the indwelling Spirit. "The hope" of Israel, to which Paul referred in v.6, was obviously the coming of the Messiah with the establishment of His kingdom. Peter has beautifully called the christian hope "a living hope" (1 Pet 1:3).

8-13 But the critical point both for Jew and Gentile was the christian claim that God had raised Jesus from the dead (the word "dead" in vv.8, 23 is plural). Before his conversion, Paul as a Pharisee had believed in resurrection, but not that of the Lord Jesus. He had been so identified with Judaism that he here recalled how he opposed Jesus of Nazareth. He gave more details here than in his first account of his pre-conversion life in 22:4-5; those whom he persecuted he called "saints" (v.10). The recollection of this persecution gave him the opportunity to lead on to his Damascus road experience. In 22:6, Paul stated that he had been struck down by "a great light", whereas here in v.13 he used the description "a light from heaven, above the brightness of the sun". This recalls Matthew's description of the Lord on the mount of transfiguration, "his face did shine as the sun" (Matt 17:2), and John's description on the Isle of Patmos, "his countenance was as the sun shineth in his strength" (Rev 1:16). For a believer today, only the lustre of conversion's day will maintain a christian zeal.

15-18 Equally the direction of Paul's life is elaborated in more detail than formerly – in particular we are given further words spoken by the Lord to him as he had fallen to the earth (vv.16-18). In 22:25, Ananias by divine revelation told Paul that he was chosen to be a witness to "all men". In 26:17 the Lord had already told him that these would be "the Gentiles", and that they were to be turned from darkness to light, from the power of Satan unto God, receiving forgiveness of sins (surely a strange concept for Gentile sinners), and an inheritance among the sanctified (a word having the same root as "saints" in v.10). See 20:32 for comments on this inheritance.

Paul must have loved this description of conversion involving "from darkness to light". This is spiritual and moral, and is the reverse of what happened to him for three days, when the blinding light that he saw from heaven was replaced by natural blindness until his sight was restored. The darkness certainly means the darkness of paganism, but the unbelief of Judaism is also darkness. See Eph 5:8; Col 1:13; 1 Thess 5:5. Peter's uplifting description was certainly written to converted Jews, "that ye should show forth the praises of him who he hath called you out of the darkness into his marvellous light" (1 Pet 2:9).

19-21 Paul now stressed the divine part in his personal story. He therefore could not be disobedient, Obedience forms part of Paul's gospel, that takes men from being "children of disobedience" (Eph 2:2; Col 3:6) to "obedient children" (1 Pet 1:14). Again, the concept of obedience particularly marks the Epistle to the Romans, from "for obedience of the faith among all nations" (1:5) to "made known to all nations for the obedience of faith" (16:26).

We are familiar with Paul's activities at Damascus, and with his first visit to Jerusalem, but not with his preaching through all the country of Judaea. We are not given any details in the Acts of these last labours, except that in 9:31 churches are mentioned as being in existence in Judaea and Galilee, the very regions in which the Lord's own ministry was conducted during the days of His sojourn here below. The scenes of Saul's persecution became the early scenes of his evangelisation. Naturally he must also mention why he finally went to the nations of the world. After all, that was the crux of the Jewish objection to his activities.

Paul's preaching demanded repentance from those who responded to the gospel message. This may be one of the big omissions from much preaching at the present time; suggestions are made that this is the main reason why many professions of faith appear to lack reality. This is worth pondering, for to be a true follower of God, there must be a genuine repudiation of one's past; immersion by baptism is a testimony to this repudiation. Paul had told the Ephesian elders in 20:21 that the burden of his preaching had been "repentance toward God, and faith toward our Lord Jesus Christ". He seems to emphasise the first part of the truth even more here (v.20), for he claimed that he told the Gentiles to repent and turn and do works worthy of repentance, showing the enormous care that he took to ensure that the Gentile converts were genuine. They were indeed expected to turn from their idols, and from everything associated with them.

The actual wording, "works meet for repentance" is reminiscent of the preaching of John the Baptist (Matt 3:8). This simply means worthy of repentance, to prove that one had repented.

22-23 Before he was interrupted by Festus, following his brief account of his arrest in the temple, Paul returned to his great insistence in all his addresses to Jewish audiences, that he preached what the OT prophecies had forecast, "Christ should suffer, and that he should be the first that should rise from the dead, and should show light ... to the Gentiles". Paul was convinced that what he was doing was of God, in keeping with His revealed will in the OT, and therefore beyond disputation by anybody. He witnesses to "small and great", the commoners and kings. And certainly the "small and great" are responsible to God, for all unbelievers will stand before the great white throne (Rev 20:12).

24-29 Speakers were used to being interrupted in those days, particularly when they reached a critical (and oftentimes controversial) point of their discourse (see 4:1; 5:26; 7:54; 10:44; 17:32; 20:9; 22:22; 23:7). But Paul was able to handle his interrupter. Probably Festus had had enough; his remark "thou art beside thyself" reminds us of the words that the Lord's kinsmen said about Him, "He is beside himself" (Mark 3:21), another example of "the fellowship of his sufferings". But Paul was able to reply with a direct appeal to Agrippa, who seems to have had a personal acquaintance with the prophets, and a personal knowledge that what Paul had been telling him was factual. We cannot assess how genuine the king's response was, "Almost thou persuadest me to be a Christian", but Paul, obviously unafraid, took advantage of that remark as well, revealing that his deep wish for all the audience was that they could be like him, "except these bonds". He had the same desire towards the Thessalonian believers, that he could have imparted his own soul to them (1 Thess 2:8). (It should be pointed out that this is the second of only three mentions of the name "Christian " in the NT, Acts 11:26; 1 Pet 4:16. Its popularity increased after the NT was complete, and its major use in Christendom rather belittles its true meaning in the minds of the general public.)

Translators differ as to how to render Agrippa's words and Paul's reply. *En oligō* are words used by both. It can be rendered as, "with a little persuasion I could become, a Christian", Paul's reply "both almost, and altogether" (AV) has been rendered, "short time or long" or "whether with little or much". Whether as free or as a prisoner, he desired men to be like him, a believer. He was, of course, never happy being a prisoner, yet he was able to accomplish much by being one. His longing here is re-echoed in Rom 10:1, "My heart's desire and prayer to God for Israel is that they might be saved".

30-32 The consequent private discussion between the dignitaries about Paul confirmed his blamelessness even in the minds of two such different kinds of men, Agrippa and Festus. But it was too late to cancel his appeal to Caesar. This simply adds to the enigma. Why did Paul persist in going up to Jerusalem in spite of all the warnings about the danger awaiting him there? He appealed to Caesar in all good faith to avoid being slaughtered at the hands of the Jews, and now a Roman representative suggests that the appeal to Caesar was a mistake.

Paul wanted to go to Rome. Twice in his letter to them, he had written of this (Rom 1:9-15; 15:22-32). But doubtless when he wrote, he imagined himself calling at Rome as a free man on an intended journey to Spain. Instead he was to go as a prisoner, admittedly at Caesar's charge, but without the liberty to move around in the great metropolis as a missionary would like to do. The whole story is utterly bewildering for people who think that Paul's knowledge of the will of God was all foreseen and complete. On the other hand, the story is helpful to others who find the will of God a difficult thing to ascertain, particularly when they themselves must take decisions. Yet they, like Paul, can look back and admit that though they had definite objectives before them, in the end it all fell out to the furtherance of the gospel and the work of God. All should be able to exclaim, "I being in the way, the Lord led me" (Gen 24:27). This is in keeping with Rutherford's words:

> "I'll bless the hand that guided,
>   I'll bless the heart that planned,
> When throned where glory dwelt,
>   In Immanuel's land."

7. Paul's Mission to Rome
   27:1-28:31

a. *Shipwrecked (27:1-44)*

v.1 "And when it was determined that we should sail into Italy, they delivered Paul and certain other prisoners unto *one* named Julius, a centurion of Augustus' band.

v.2 And entering into a ship of Adramyttium, we launched, meaning to sail by the coasts of Asia; *one* Aristarchus, a Macedonian of Thessalonica, being with us.

v.3 And the next *day* we touched at Sidon. And Julius courteously entreated Paul, and gave *him* liberty to go unto his friends to refresh himself.

v.4 And when we had launched from thence, we sailed under Cyprus, because the winds were contrary.

v.5 And when we had sailed over the sea of Cilicia and Pamphylia, we came to Myra, a *city* of Lycia.

v.6 And there the centurion found a ship of Alexandria sailing into Italy; and he put us therein.

v.7 And when we had sailed slowly many days, and scarce were come over against Cnidus, the wind not suffering us, we sailed under Crete, over against Salmone;

v.8 And, hardly passing it, came unto a place which is called The fair havens; nigh whereunto was the city *of* Lasea.

v.9 Now when much time was spent, and when sailing was now dangerous, because the fast was now already past, Paul admonished *them,*

v.10 And said unto them, Sirs, I perceive that this voyage will be with hurt and much damage, not only of the lading and ship, but also of our lives.

v.11 Nevertheless the centurion believed the master and the owner of the ship, more than those things which were spoken by Paul.

v.12 And because the haven was not commodious to winter in, the more part advised to depart thence also, if by any means they might attain to Phenice, *and there* to winter; *which is* an haven of Crete, and lieth toward the south west and north west.

v.13 And when the south wind blew softly, supposing that they had obtained *their* purpose, loosing *thence,* they sailed close by Crete.

v.14 But not long after there arose against it a tempestuous wind, called Euroclydon.

v.15 And when the ship was caught, and could not bear up into the wind, we let *her* drive.

v.16 And running under a certain island which is called Clauda, we had much work to come by the boat:

v.17 Which when they had taken up, they used helps, undergirding the ship; and, fearing lest they should fall into the quicksands, strake sail, and so were driven.

v.18 And we being exceedingly tossed with a tempest, the next *day* they lightened the ship;

v.19 And the third *day* we cast out with our own hands the tackling of the ship.
v.20 And when neither sun nor stars in many days appeared, and no small tempest lay on *us,* all hope that we should be saved was then taken away.
v.21 But after long abstinence Paul stood forth in the midst of them, and said, Sirs, ye should have hearkened unto me, and not have loosed from Crete, and to have gained this harm and loss.
v.22 And now I exhort you to be of good cheer: for there shall be no loss of *any man's* life among you, but of the ship.
v.23 For there stood by me this night the angel of God, whose I am, and whom I serve,
v.24 Saying, Fear not, Paul; thou must be brought before Cæsar: and, lo, God hath given thee all them that sail with thee.
v.25 Wherefore, sirs, be of good cheer: for I believe God, that it shall be even as it was told me.
v.26 Howbeit we must be cast upon a certain island.
v.27 But when the fourteenth night was come, as we were driven up and down in Adria, about midnight the shipmen deemed that they drew near to some country;
v.28 And sounded, and found *it* twenty fathoms: and when they had gone a little further they sounded again, and found *it* fifteen fathoms.
v.29 Then fearing lest we should have fallen upon rocks, they cast four anchors out of the stern, and wished for the day.
v.30 And as the shipmen were about to flee out of the ship, when they had let down the boat into the sea, under colour as though they would have cast anchors out of the foreship,
v.31 Paul said to the centurion and to the soldiers, Except these abide in the ship, ye cannot be saved.
v.32 Then the soldiers cut off the ropes of the boat, and let her fall off.
v.33 And while the day was coming on, Paul besought *them* all to take meat, saying, This day is the fourteenth day that ye have tarried and continued fasting, having taken nothing.
v.34 Wherefore, I pray you to take *some* meat: for this is for your health: for there shall not an hair fall from the head of any of you.
v.35 And when he had thus spoken, he took bread, and gave thanks to God in presence of them all; and when he had broken *it,* he began to eat.
v.36 Then were they all of good cheer, and they also took *some* meat.
v.37 And we were in all in the ship two hundred threescore and sixteen souls.
v.38 And when they had eaten enough, they lightened the ship, and cast out the wheat into the sea.
v.39 And when it was day, they knew not the land: but they discovered a certain creek with a shore, into the which they were minded, if it were possible, to thrust in the ship,
v.40 And when they had taken up the anchors, they committed *themselves* unto the sea, and loosed the rudder bands, and hoised up the mainsail to the wind, and made toward shore.
v.41 And falling into a place where two seas met, they ran the ship aground; and the forepart stuck fast, and remained unmoveable, but the hinder part was broken with the violence of the waves.

v.42 And the soldiers' counsel was to kill the prisoners, lest any of them should swim out, and escape.
v.43 But the centurion willing to save Paul, kept them from *their* purpose; and commanded that they which could swim should cast *themselves* first *into the sea,* and get to land:
v.44 And the rest, some on boards, and some on *broken pieces* of the ship. And so it came to pass, that they escaped all safe to land."

1-2 Most of the Roman centurions who figure in the NT were sympathetic to the Jewish people or to the Christians. The centurion who was put in charge of the prisoners heading for Rome of whom Paul was one, became quite sympathetic to his unusual prisoner. Luke still accompanied Paul, together with one other attendant, Aristarchus, who, Luke informs us for the second time, was from Thessalonica (20:4).

3-6 The first port of call was the Sidon on the Syrian coast, and Paul was given the liberty to visit "his friends" there. Elsewhere they are called "brethren", as in 28:14. Every place of note had a group of them. No wonder Paul was later to write that the gospel had been "preached to every creature which is under heaven" (Col 1:23). The next calling place was Myra in Asia Minor where ships were changed; and there does not appear to have been any organised, regular boat sailing from Caesarea to Rome. An even stranger circumstance was that the transportation of these prisoners to Rome took place at a time of the year when there was little chance of arriving before winter.

7-10 The new ship obviously set sail at the time of the autumn gales, and made slow progress to Crete. The delay was such that Paul, presumably by divine revelation, advised against setting sail, but the majority believed that there was a better port in Crete in which to spend the winter. They never reached that port, for the gentle wind in which they set out gave place to a gale-force wind. All these events gave Luke a splendid opportunity to use his considerable literary powers to produce one of the most vivid descriptions in early literature of a tempestuous voyage. This is an example of how divine inspiration uses the particular style of an author.

11-14 While the centurion had been sympathetic enough to Paul, and had permitted him to go ashore to visit his friends at Sidon, yet here he had more respect for the ship-master's opinion of sailing conditions and of commodious harbours than he had for Paul's. He had yet to learn that Paul was in regular touch with the God of the winds and the waves. Paul had warned that they should stay in Crete, and when his advice was not heeded he remained silent until v.21 when he rebuked them for ignoring his original advice.

15-41 At the height of the gale, Paul prophesied that they would all be saved even if the ship were lost. He had received a message that very night direct from the angel of the Lord, a fellow-messenger from God, even if of a higher order than himself.

Appearing before Caesar in Rome, which the angel promised, was better than perishing in a shipwreck in a stormy sea. The promise was not only that Paul would reach Rome, but that the lives of all with him would be spared. It is not a question of numbers, but that the providential care of God may extend to the fellow-travellers of the people of God, even if these men are criminals or escorting soldiers. Paul stated his unbounded confidence in God that He would do what He had said: "I believe God". It now becomes clear that the whole voyage, including the shipwreck, was of God.

Readers with an interest in seafaring will note how they sounded to ascertain the depth of the sea, and the fact that the ship was large enough to carry 276 people, and had four anchors to hold it in rough seas. Mention is also made of the near-loss of the ship's boat, and of "helps" (frapping) for undergirding the ship. It is also vivid, a veritable eyewitness account of a great storm which lasted for at least a fortnight. In v.18 the cargo was thrown overboard to lighten the ship (and again in v.38 when the last of the food was disposed of), reminding us of the storm in Jonah's day, when idolaters "cast forth the wares that were in the ship into the sea, to lighten it of them" (Jonah 1:5). Again, in v.19 the tackling was dispensed with, while in v.30 the shipmen were preparing to abandon ship, pretending that they were just casting the anchors. Paul was not deceived and alerted the centurion, declaring that the soldiers would not be saved if the sailors abandoned ship. The soldiers, therefore, cut loose the only means of escape, the boat, and let it drop into the sea. Paul virtually took charge then, thanking God publicly for food, and eating it in front of them all while they were terrified. The man who had sung praises to God while in the inner prison in Philippi could now set an example of freedom from fear, even when experienced sailors were terrified in a tempest. Having jettisoned the remainder of the cargo after this meal, they attempted to beach the ship in a creek, but it broke up and the entire complement got ashore by swimming, or on boards and pieces of the ship.

42-44 If the shipmen had thoughts of abandoning their prisoners to their fate, it was now the soldiers' intention to slay the prisoners, since they could no longer maintain control over them. Only the intervention of the centurion, who could see Paul's faith and authority, prevented this. In 2 Cor 11:23-25, Paul had written previously that he had been "in deaths oft … thrice I suffered shipwreck", so he had been in this situation several times before. We cannot tell how many narrow escapes he had between his arrest in Jerusalem (21:30) until this shipwreck on Malta, but he knew the truth of Ps 107:23-31, "He bringeth them out of their distresses … he bringeth them unto their desired haven … Oh that men would praise the Lord for his goodness".

b. *Wintering on Malta (28:1-10)*

> v.1 "And when they were escaped, then they knew that the island was called Melita.
> v.2 And the barbarous people shewed us no little kindness: for they kindled a fire, and received us every one, because of the present rain, and because of the cold.
> v.3 And when Paul had gathered a bundle of sticks, and laid *them* on the fire, there came a viper out of the heat, and fastened on his hand.
> v.4 And when the barbarians saw the *venomous* beast hang on his hand, they said among themselves, No doubt this man is a murderer, whom, though he hath escaped the sea, yet vengeance suffereth not to live.
> v.5 And he shook off the beast into the fire, and felt no harm.
> v.6 Howbeit they looked when he should have swollen, or fallen down dead suddenly: but after they had looked a great while, and saw no harm come to him, they changed their minds and said that he was a god.
> v.7 In the same quarters were possessions of the chief man of the island, whose name was Publius; who received us, and lodged us three days courteously.
> v.8 And it came to pass, that the father of Publius lay sick of a fever and of a bloody flux: to whom Paul entered in, and prayed, and laid his hands on him, and healed him.
> v.9 So when this was done, others also, which had diseases in the island, came, and were healed:
> v.10 Who also honoured us with many honours; and when we departed, they laded *us* with such things as were necessary."

1-10 The Maltese people proved to be very kind, although they were "barbarous", that is, they were barbarians. If Paul had impressed his authority on the centurion during the voyage, he now impressed it on the Maltese people with the first miracle on the island. The main purpose of such miracles was to confirm that God was there: it was unusual for a miracle to be performed directly on the apostle. At first, the superstition of the Maltese suggested that the viper which emerged from the fire meant that fate was catching up with Paul; what the shipwreck did not do, the viper could do. But when Paul survived the experience, they considered him to be a god, as in Lystra (14:11). Perhaps it was this miracle that influenced the leading citizen of the island to lodge some of the castaways, certainly Luke and Paul, in his own house for three days. The whole situation was cumulative, for a second miracle was performed on Publius' father, and this was followed by a series of miracles, such as had taken place in the earlier chapters of Acts (2:43; 5:12; 6:8; 8:6-7; 9:34, 40; 19:11). As a consequence of this, the believers, centred on an apostolic prisoner of the Romans, were honoured in various ways and showered with supplies, presumably food and clothing, which would replace all that they had lost in the shipwreck. Such gifts were readily accepted (not, we are assured, as a "payment" for the miracles performed), and this acceptance stands in complete contrast with 14:13 when Paul and Barnabas refused "oxen and garlands" as sacrifices in Lystra.

c. *Paul's Ministry at Rome (28:11-31)*

v.11 "And after three months we departed in a ship of Alexandria, which had wintered in the isle, whose sign was Castor and Pollux.
v.12 And landing at Syracuse, we tarried *there* three days.
v.13 And from thence we fetched a compass, and came to Rhegium: and after one day the south wind blew, and we came the next day to Puteoli:
v.14 Where we found brethren, and were desired to tarry with them seven days: and so we went toward Rome.
v.15 And from thence, when the brethren heard of us, they came to meet us as far as Appii forum, and The three taverns: whom when Paul saw, he thanked God, and took courage.
v.16 And when we came to Rome, the centurion delivered the prisoners to the captain of the guard: but Paul was suffered to dwell by himself with a soldier that kept him.
v.17 And it came to pass, that after three days Paul called the chief of the Jews together: and when they were come together, he said unto them, Men *and* brethren, though I have committed nothing against the people, or customs of our fathers, yet was I delivered prisoner from Jerusalem into the hands of the Romans.
v.18 Who, when they had examined me, would have let *me* go, because there was no cause of death in me.
v.19 But when the Jews spake against *it*, I was constrained to appeal unto Cæsar; not that I had aught to accuse my nation of.
v.20 For this cause therefore have I called for you, to see *you,* and to speak with *you*: because that for the hope of Israel I am bound with this chain.
v.21 And they said unto him, We neither received letters out of Judæa concerning thee, neither any of the brethren that came shewed or spake any harm of thee.
v.22 But we desire to hear of thee what thou thinkest: for as concerning this sect, we know that every where it is spoken against.
v.23 And when they had appointed him a day, there came many to him into *his* lodging; to whom he expounded and testified the kingdom of God, persuading them concerning Jesus, both out of the law of Moses, and *out of* the prophets from morning till evening.
v.24 And some believed the things which were spoken, and some believed not.
v.25 And when they agreed not among themselves, they departed, after that Paul had spoken one word, Well spake the Holy Ghost by Esaias the prophet unto our fathers,
v.26 Saying, Go unto this people, and say, Hearing ye shall hear, and shall not understand; and seeing ye shall see, and not perceive:
v.27 For the heart of this people is waxed gross, and their ears are dull of hearing, and their eyes have they closed; lest they should see with *their* eyes, and hear with *their* ears, and understand with *their* heart, and should be converted, and I should heal them.
v.28 Be it known therefore unto you, that the salvation of God is sent unto the Gentiles, and *that* they will hear it.

v.29 And when he had said these words, the Jews departed, and had great reasoning among themselves.
v.30 And Paul dwelt two whole years in his own hired house, and received all that came in unto him,
v.31 Preaching the kingdom of God, and teaching those things which concern the Lord Jesus Christ, with all confidence, no man forbidding him."

11-14 There was a wait of three months before a ship was available, once the winter was past, to carry the lost ship's complement onwards to Rome. Paul's counsel had been to winter in Crete, but the captain's foolhardiness resulted in their spending the remainder of the winter on another island, Malta, much further to the west. (Contrast this with the reception of Paul's counsel in 16:10.) It was in a second ship from Alexandria that they completed the voyage. (Counterclaims that Malta was the name of an island off the coast of Yugoslavia can neither be confirmed nor rejected.)

The first port of call was Syracuse, on the island of Sicily. The ship's business occupied three days, but there is no mention of brethren, to use a term by which believers are described in the various places at which the missionary group called. They finally disembarked at Puteoli; why the centurion allowed a stay of seven days is not explained – perhaps further evidence of his indulgent treatment of his unusual prisoner.

15-16 In spite of the military escort, the apostle had various privileges; the presence of soldiers did not prevent a second escort formed of brethren from Rome accompanying Paul, Luke and Aristarchus on their way. No wonder Paul thanked God and took courage, since the seat of the Caesars contained Christians. The city in which he had arrived as a total stranger was not entirely hostile. His letters to Rome, written several years before in advance of his arrival, had identified four groups of Christians, presumably in different districts of the great city (see Rom 16:5, 10, 14, 15).

While the other prisoners brought from Caesarea to appear before Caesar in person were imprisoned in Rome, Paul was kept under house arrest. He was continually chained to a Roman soldier, but he could have as many visitors as he liked. Among the people whom Paul evangelised was a group that he never would have been able to contact had he visited the metropolis as a free man. In his letter to the Philippians, he wrote, "My bonds are manifest in all the Praetorian Guard and in all other places" (1:13). If it fell to each of the imperial guardsmen to guard Paul for four hours during his two year's imprisonment, then it can be appreciated why he claimed that the whole palace guard heard the gospel!

17-20 A second group of people who had heard the gospel from Paul while he was a prisoner in Rome was the leadership of the Jewish comminity there. Paul waited three days after his arrival before summoning them in order to present his case to them. At no time did Paul castigate his fellow Jews. He tried to find as much common ground as possible in discussion. He would insist that his present plight as a prisoner was for "the hope of Israel". He explained in detail why he had to appeal to Caesar, and hence why he was in Rome as a prisoner.

21-22 The Jewish leaders knew plenty about the christian "sect", none of it commendatory, but they had no communication from the Jewish leaders in Judaea about its chief protagonist. (What Festus had written to Nero we are not told.) They arranged another suitable date when they would come to Paul's lodgings in order to hear him speak for himself. This must have been the only occasion in his life of service when the apostle invited an audience to come to hear him (apart from 14:27). At other times he went to his audience. He loved to meet people in their meeting-places, and the explanation for this exception is obviously that he was not a free man.

23-24 His theme was a familiar one: the kingdom of God in its latest aspect, not in manifestation as the Jews expected, but in mystery. In a lengthy address stretching from morning to evening, he followed the example of the Lord in Luke 24:27, 44, presenting Christ from their OT Scriptures. We too follow a good example when we find Him there. Passage after passage in the law of Moses, in the Psalms of David, and in the prophets of Israel speak of Him. NT writers bring a large number of quotations to our attention. The effect of such teaching divided the Jews into believers and unbelievers (see John 3:18; Acts 13:43).

25-28 There seems to have been some acrimony between the two groups, and the meeting ended with Paul speaking rather forcibly with the backing of the OT Scriptures. From Isa 6:9-10 their lost condition was described (also quoted in John 12:40-41). The passage in Isaiah goes on to answer Isaiah's question as to how long he was to go and tell this people. Paul indicated clearly that his mission now lay with Gentiles, although he was a prisoner. He had written to believers in Rome that he would preach the gospel to the Jew first and also to the Gentile (Rom 1:16); that order would now take place in Rome itself.

(Just as early in Acts there are claims that the divine voice spoke through David (4.25), so now the book ends with the assertion that the Holy Spirit also spoke through Isaiah.)

29 This verse is not found in some Greek MSS, in which case Acts virtually ends with "the Gentiles ... will hear it".

> "Ye Gentile sinners ne'er forget
>   The wormwood and the gall.
> Go spread your trophies at His feet.
>   And crown Him Lord of all."

30-31 Paul still had two years to spend in custody before appearing before Caesar. We have mention of a third audience to which he presented the kingdom of God and the things concerning the Lord Jesus, "all that came in unto him", many of whom must have been believers in the church in Rome as well as visitors from elsewhere. Other verses in Paul's epistles mention some of these: Onesimus, who was converted as a result (Col 4:9; Philem 10); Epaphras (a "fellowprisoner") from Colosse, who was already a Christian (Col 1:7); Epaphroditus from Philippi (Phil 2:25); Aristarchus (a "fellowprisoner", Col 4:10), amongst others.

Human writers seldom end their books as Luke ended his second one – with the main character in prison. It is idle speculation to suggest that Luke intended to write a third book; we have only two from his pen. (It has been suggested that the length of many NT books was governed by the length of the parchments available.) But the unfinished nature of Acts is not a mark of imperfection, since the Holy Spirit was in control. This is not the end of Paul's missionary work, nor of God's. This kind of work is not finished even today; it will continue until the end of the age. Each believer is intended to add his or her contribution. Paul made tremendous use of his prison experience, yet he still wanted to be free (Phil 1:24-26; Philem 22). Readers should ask themselves how they make use of their freedom.

Notes

Summary of Places Mentioned on the Journey to Rome

	Having appealed from the tribunal of Festus to that of the Emperor at Rome (25:10-11), Paul set sail from
Caesarea	On a ship of Adramyttium, a seaport of Mysia in Roman Asia, with Julius in charge, a centurion of the Augustan Cohort (27:1-2). They first touched at
Sidon	probably for the purpose of trade, and the apostle received on shore the kind attention of his friends. Thence they sailed "under the lee" (27:4 RV), that is, along the north side of
Cyprus	and "across the sea which is off" Cilicia and Pamphylia, to
Myra	then a flourishing seaport of Lycia. Here the centurion found an Alexandrian corn-vessel bound for Italy, and transferred his prisoners into it, setting sail with a heavy cargo and with 276 people on board. Owing to unfavourable winds, it was only after many days (v.7) that they came over against
Cnidus	a promontary of Caria, at the extreme south-west of the peninsula of Asia Minor. Here the wind stopped their direct course (v.7), and the vessel was driven southwards to

Salmone	the eastern promontory of Crete. Rounding it, the ship worked its way with difficulty under the shelter of the southern coast to
Fair Havens	near which was the city of Lasea about five miles to the east. Here Paul advised them to winter, but the harbour not being commodious, they resolved to try to reach
Phoenix (RV)	the town of palms, with a harbour looking north-east and south east. Weighing anchor, they set sail, but were caught by a violent wind called Euroclydon ("Euraquilo", v.14 RV) beating down from the heights of Ida on Crete, and were driven under the lee of
Cauda (RV)	or Clauda an island south-west of Crete, and with much difficulty they succeeded in hoisting on board the boat, which was being towed behind (vv.16-17). They then proceeded to undergird the vessel, that is, to pass strong cables round its hull, and being afraid that they should drift onto the Syrtis, a dangerous sandbank north of Libya, they lowered the gear (v.17 RV), and were driven slowly before the wind. On the next day, they proceeded to lighten the ship by throwing the freight overboard (v.18), and on the third day they cast out the tackling, probably the mainyards of the ship. At midnight of the fourteenth day, as they were drifting to and fro in "the sea of Adria" (v.27 RV), the sailors suspected from the noise of the breakers that they were nearing land. After sounding they cast out four anchors from the stern, and on the next day ran the ship aground in a creek where two seas met. This was the island of
Melita (Malta)	at that time largely uncultivated, and inhabited by a people of Phoenician origin. Here by swimming or floating on portions of the wreck, they were able to reach the shore. The people received them hospitably, kindled a fire, and welcomed them to its genial warmth. A viper came out of the sticks that Paul was gathering, and fastened on his hand. At first the people thought that he was a murderer, but when he flung it off and was unharmed, they regarded him as a god. Paul miraculously healed the father of Publius, the chief Roman officer of the island, who was afflicted with fever and dysentery. After a stay of three months, they sailed in another Alexandrian corn-ship called "The Twin Brothers" (28:11 RV), and reached

Syracuse	the chief city of Sicily. Here they stayed three days, and from thence they sailed northwards towards the straits of Messina. But the wind being against them, they were constrained after "making a circuit" (v.13 RV) to put into
Rhegium	at the extreme south-west of Italy, where they remained for one day. On the following morning they reached
Puteoli	(modern Pozzuoli) in the Bay of Naples, at that time the regular harbour for the Alexandrian corn-ships. Here they rested seven days with certain of the brethren, and then proceeded by land to
Appii Forum	about forty miles from Rome, where a welcome company of brethren met them, and the apostle "thanked God, and took courage" (v.15). Ten miles further on, they reached
The Three Taverns	where a second company greeted them, and thus at length the apostle reached
Rome	the Imperial City, and was handed over by Julius to the "captain of the guard", namely the prefect of the praetorian guard.

Acts Postscript

And so the curtain falls on the scene of Paul's missionary exploits, during which time he had "laboured more abundantly" than all the other apostles (1 Cor 15:10). It is a most unusual ending; the main character of the second half of the book is in custody, and although he will be released, the writing of the story is never resumed. When Paul finally came to the end of his life, Luke was still with him (2 Tim 4:11), so he did not lack a historian or biographer. Nor was there any shortage of material for such a story as an examination of 2 Cor 11:22-33 and the Pastoral Epistles (written after his release) will reveal.

And yet the last chapter of the Acts is a landmark in the story of the furtherance of the gospel. When Paul wrote to the Romans, he indicated that his approach was still "to the Jew first, and also to the Greek" (1:16). When the apostle arrived in Rome, he sent for the Jewish leaders to inform them of his message and of the trouble that he had suffered through preaching it. We have noticed several occasions in the Acts when wider audiences heard the gospel: Samaritans in ch.8; a Roman centurion in ch.10; Grecians in ch.11: Gentiles in ch.13; but it was still Paul's practice to give precedence in every place to the Jews usually in their synagogues.

That was not now to be his future intention. He told these Jewish leaders in Rome

	Where	Audience	Subject	Related Scriptures	Results for Paul	Results for others
Acts 22:1-21	Jerusalem	Jewish mob	Paul's preconversion activity; his conversion; the Lord's purpose for him	Acts 8:1; 9:1-31; 26:1-29	To leave Jerusalem; to be sent to the Gentiles	Paul should die; brought into castle for examination
Acts 23:1-6	Jerusalem	Jewish Sanhedrin	The high priest; the resurrection	Matt 22:23-33	His life before; hope of the resurrection	Strife between Pharisees and Sadducees
Acts 24:10-21	Caesarea	Felix, high priest and elders	What Paul had done in Jerusalem	Acts 21: 26-40; 23:1-6	Remained a prisoner for two years	Felix sought to bribe him, though he trembled
Acts 25:8, 10-11	Caesarea	Festus, high priest and Jewish chiefs	No offence committed; appeal to Caesar	Acts 25:21; 26:32; 28:19; 2 Tim 4:16-18	Paul remained a prisoner; he appeared before Agrippa	Festus in a dilemma as to what to write to Nero
Acts 26:1-29	Caesarea	Festus, Agrippa, Bernice and others (25:23)	Original life; his conversion; divine command; his service	Acts 8:1; 9:1-31; 22:1-21	No liberty; had to go to Rome	"Almost persuaded"
Acts 27:10,21-26, 31-34	Ship	Master, centurion and soldiers	Warning; safety; partaking of food	2 Cor 11:25	Unheeded and heeded	All saved by following Pauls counsel
Acts 28:17-28	Rome	Jews	Reason for imprisonment; the kingdom of God; Gentiles will hear	Acts 25:11; Isa 6: 9-10; John 12:39-41	Continued preaching and teaching	Some believed; some believed not

that he was bound with that chain for the hope of Israel. As he wrote his prison letters during the next two years, he called himself "the prisoner of Jesus Christ for you Gentiles" (Eph 3:1), and "the prisoner of the Lord" (4:1). Just as the restrictions caused by the chains and soldiers were to be removed, so were the restrictions imposed by Judaism.

It was still too early to say that Rome was now the centre of christian activity, as Jerusalem had been at the beginning, and Antioch afterwards, but it was going to become the centre in the future. It is widely believed in Spain that Paul realised his desire expressed in Rom15:24, 28. He also had work to do in Crete, according to his letter to Titus, with which island he became familiar on his voyage to Rome.

It is likely that northern Europe, like Britain, was evangelised from Rome, which probably became the kind of centre that Antioch had been, before Rome ultimately became the headquarters of the false church. It is noticeable that the believers there are never called the "church at Rome" anywhere in the NT. The Epistle to the Romans is addressed "to all that be in Rome, beloved of God, called (to be) saints" (Rom 1:7), while when Peter referred to it he wrote, "She that is at Babylon, elected together with you, saluteth you" (1 Pet 5:13) (though some expositors assert that the actual physical Babylon is alluded to by Peter). Even the Catholic Douai Bible suggests that Rome is intended under the cloak of the name "Babylon", though this has important implications in prophecy.

So the Lord's work proceeds as it is intended to proceed until the end of the age. Luke added no more to his account of it, but we are intended to add our own chapters to complete the account of God's work, not as Paul's companions, but as his successors. Yet there are some parts of the world that have had to wait until the twentieth century before the message of salvation has been taken to them.

The Gospels and the Acts reveal conflicts. Neither local nor imperial rulers were favourable to the new movement of God, revealed first in Herod acting against the Babe of Bethlehem and then in the Jewish Sanhedrin acting against the early church in Jerusalem. But the story of the Lord Jesus did not end with His death; His resurrection, ascension and the giving of the Holy Spirit ensured that the church would commence and continue. It certainly did not end with the imprisonment and later martyrdom of its greatest servant. If this work had been of men, it would have come to nothing, as Gamaliel had suggested, but the work was of God, so it not only survived but flourished.

Purple has long been a symbol of royalty – in the present case of the Herods and the Caesars. And a scarlet thread runs through the Bible from beginning to end. The two colours come into conflict. In the natural course of things, the strong would triumph over the weak, the purple over the scarlet. But in the spiritual realm, God takes away the first that He might establish the second.

Within a few years of the apostle finishing his course, the temple in Jerusalem which meant so much to pious Jews was destroyed by the Romans, together with the city in which it had such a commanding position. And that city, the city of the great King, the capital of what is called "Immanuel's land", was completely incorporated into the Roman Empire. That situation was to exist, with successive conquerors taking over, for 1877 years. But by contrast, that new temple not made with hands was to continue growing. Being not natural but spiritual, being not of this building but the building of God, it was not going to fall at the hands of any human armies, "the gates of hell shall not prevail against it" (Matt 16:18).

As with the religious opposition, so with the political. Imperial Rome had longer to run than religious Jerusalem. But local Herods and imperial Caesars, who figure so strongly in Luke's writings, would have no more success in suppressing the new movement than Jewish leaders. 1500 years of Imperial Rome passed into oblivion, while the church remains. "They overcame him by the blood of the Lamb" (Rev 12:11). The scarlet survives, while the purple has long since passed away. "Hail Thou once despised Jesus", and His great church victorious. And in the future, when "These shall make war with the Lamb", then "the Lamb shall overcome them: for he is Lord of lords, and King of kings" (Rev 17:14).

Appendix 1

How the Gospel was Spread

A variety of words is used by Luke to describe the ways in which the first gospel preachers spread their message. They did not have literature, but they had their voices. Except in a few places, there were no restrictions placed on them by any authority, "they that were scattered abroad went everywhere preaching the word" (Acts 8:4). We discuss a list of Greek words that describe how the message was spoken.

1. Before the Lord Jesus left His apostles in ch.1, He had told them that they were to be witnesses (v.8). The verb for witness (*diamarturomai*) is first used in 2:40 where it is translated "testify". It is subsequently used another seven times of believers. All that is required of a witness is that he tells what he knows (8:25; 10:42; 18:5; 20:21, 24; 23:11; 28:23). Peter in 2:40; Peter and John in 8:25; and Paul in 18:5; 20:21, 24; 23:11; 28:23 all responded to the Lord's command (10:42). The noun occurs in 1:8, 22; 2:32; 3:15; 5:32; 10:39, 41; 13:31; 22:15, 20; 26:16 (translated "martyr" in 22:20).

2. The second word "to teach" (*didaskō*) is used fifteen times. This is a much more formal word, but is must be distinguished from the word "preach". Both words are used to describe what the first believers did. The apostles taught the people in the temple courts about Jesus and the resurrection (4:2). They were forbidden to do so in v.18. They were teaching again in the same place early one morning in 5:21, 25, 28. Nor did they cease even when ordered to do so by the Sanhedrin (5:42). Barnabas taught at Antioch for a year (11:26), while he and Paul continued there according to 15:35. The word is used of false teaching in 15:1. Paul spent eighteen months teaching at Corinth (18:11), while Apollos did the same at Ephesus (18:25) before he knew the truth more perfectly. Paul recalled to the elders from Ephesus that he had taught there publicly and from house to house (20:20). Church leaders were informed that Paul taught all the Jews among the Gentiles (21:21) and he was accused of doing that by Jews from Asia in v.28. The Acts ends with Paul teaching while a prisoner in Rome (28:31). The occasions on which such teaching took place tended to be more formal, in many cases Jews being taught in their synagogues to

accept the teaching that Jesus was the Christ. (It should be pointed out that the Acts opens with Luke recalling that the Lord taught, 1:1.)

3. At an early stage, the commonest of all these words is used for their witnessing, namely "to speak" (*laleō*). Only dumb people cannot do this; believers can do it anywhere and at almost any time. No doubt this is why we are often reminded that those first believers "gossiped" their message. Peter and John were doing this quite informally, when they were arrested in 4:1. They were forbidden to do this in v.17, but insisted in v.20 that they could not cease. In v.31 the whole assembled company is described as still speaking boldly. An angel told Peter to speak in 5:20, while Stephen was criticised for speaking in 6:13. Peter and John did this in Samaria, although the word is translated "preached". Saul spoke boldly in 9:29 as soon as he was converted, and Cornelius was told by an angel to send for Peter to speak to him in 10:6, 32. Peter spoke in Cornelius' house in v.44. The word is again translated "preaching" in 11:19 (but "spake" in v.20) to describe the activity of the scattered believers. In Pisidian Antioch, Gentiles asked that the word might be spoken to them in 13:42 (again translated "preached"). Paul and Barnabas spoke to a vast audience in 14:1, while the lame man heard Paul speak in Lystra (v.9). Both Paul and Barnabas spoke in Perga (v.25), where again the word is translated "preached". The Holy Spirit forbade Paul to speak the word in Asia (16:6), but he did at the riverside in Philippi and Lydia was saved (vv.13, 14). He and Silas spoke to the jailor (v.32). The Lord spoke to Paul in a vision in Corinth (18:9), with exceptional results, while Apollos did the same in Ephesus (v.25). The final mention is in Paul's request to the Roman chief captain to be allowed to speak to the people (21:39). Obviously this speaking was to a fair variety of groups and individuals, in places that were both formal and informal. The word is also used many other times in the Acts, but not in the sense of testimony being involved.

4. The commonest word used is *euangelizō*, from which the English word "evangelise" is obviously derived. It is often translated in the AV as "preach the gospel", but sometimes to show, declare or bring the glad tidings. Evangelism does not only depend on preaching; it is much wider in scope than that, and should involve all believers, whether they are gifted as evangelists or not. The noun "gospel" means "good news", and it occurs seventy-two times in the NT, fifty-four of them in Paul's letters. The noun is found only twice in the Acts (15:7; 20:24). The verb is used fifteen times in the Acts. The words represent the summation of the whole christian message.

The first occasion of its use in the Acts ought to be a guide and example to all believers, "daily in the temple, and in every house, they ceased not to teach and preach the gospel" (5:42). But when it is realised that the word "preach" is so restricted in many people's vocabularies, a suitable paraphrase would be that the believers never stopped teaching and proclaiming the good news. In 8:4, they went everywhere proclaiming the good news (strictly, "the word" is the object of the verb).

V.12 shows that this good news was about the kingdom of God and the name of the Lord Jesus. It was announced in many villages of the Samaritans as Peter and John returned to Jerusalem (v.25); they would not miss this opportunity as they passed through this region on their way home. Philip told the Ethiopian the good news about Jesus (v.35) (strictly "Jesus" is the object of the verb). Afterwards, he presented it in all the cities up the coast to Caesarea (v.40). When Peter spoke to Cornelius, he said that God sent the word, preaching peace by Jesus Christ (10:36). This good news reached Antioch through persecuted saints (11:20). Later in Antioch of Pisidia, we have the best translation, "we declare unto you glad tidings" (13:32); Paul is speaking here in the synagogue though the pronoun "we" is used. Barnabas and Paul did the same in Lystra and Derbe according to 14:7, illustrated in v.15 as "We ... preach unto you (announcing the glad tidings to you) that ye should turn from these vanities". The same word also occurs in v.21 when they were in Derbe.

After the Council of Jerusalem, Paul and Barnabas returned to Antioch in Syria with the report of victory, and also kept on announcing the glad tidings (15:35). In 16:10, Paul and his party prepare to cross over to Macedonia, concluding from the vision that the divine plan was that they should carry the glad tidings "to them". The final mention of the verb in Acts occurs in 17:18; the Athenian philosophers had heard the good news about Jesus and the resurrection; they almost mocked him for this subject, but desired to have a fuller account presented to many others in the Areopagus.

5. Several words cognate with the verb *euangelizō* are also used to describe how those first believers spread their message. For instance, we have the verb *katangellō* ten times in the Acts, most of them in the second half of the book. The word has several renderings in the AV: "preached" six times; "teach" once; "show" twice, and "declare" once. Note that these cognate words all contain the central root "angel", meaning messenger.

It is first found in 4:2, translated "preach", and this upset the Jewish leaders who had hoped that they had finished with the subject of Jesus. The verb is not used again until 13:5, where the AV "preached" describes what Paul and Barnabas did in the synagogues of Salamis in Cyprus. It is used again of Paul in Antioch of Pisidia. It carries a more official meaning, and can be translated "proclaimed". This is confirmed in 15:36, where Paul suggested that he and Barnabas should retrace their steps to all places where they had preached or proclaimed the word. The word appears twice in ch.16 where it is translated "show" in v.17 in the exclamation of the demon-possessed fortune-teller drawing attention to the message of the preachers, and "teach" in v.21 in the condemnatory language of her masters. It is again translated "preach" relating to Paul's message to the Thessalonians from the OT in 17:3, and also in v.13 relating to Berea. The word is translated "declare" in v.23 in Paul's address to the Athenian philosophers. Finally, it is used by the apostle, translated "show", in his address to king Agrippa in 26:23, where its unexpected object is "light". Paul was proclaiming light to both Jews and Gentiles.

6. The Greek word *anangellō* is used only four times in Acts: in 14:27 it is "rehearsed"; in 15:4 it is "declared"; and in 20:20, 27 the word is used twice to the Ephesian elders.

7. The Greek word *apangellō* occurs many times in the Gospels and the Acts in purely historical contexts, and is translated by several different words, such as "announced". For our present purpose, we may mention 15:27 where, in the letter from the Jerusalem Council, Judas and Silas would "tell" the church at Antioch about the decisions. And also 26:20, where Paul was describing the nature of his service to king Agrippa, that he "showed" first at Damascus, then at Jerusalem, Judaea and to the Gentiles that they should repent.

8. Another word *kērussō* is used many times in the Gospels, and eight times in the Acts, seven being of relevance to our purpose. It signifies to proclaim as a herald. Its use in the three Synoptic Gospels relates to the preaching of John the Baptist, the apostles and the Lord Jesus. In the Acts, this verb is used of Philip in Samaria (8:5), and of Saul in Damascus (9:20). In line with the descriptions of John the Baptist in the Gospels, Peter used the word when he described John's preaching in 10:37, and again in 10:42 to describe the work that the Lord had given His disciples (where it translated "preach"). It is used by the Jewish exorcists in 19:13 to describe Paul's message in Ephesus. Paul also used it to describe his own mission in his address to the Ephesian elders (20:25). Finally it is used again in 28:31 to describe how Paul presented his message in his hired house in Rome for the two years that he was waiting to appear before Caesar; it is translated "preaching". It appears to be the most high-powered word of all with which to describe the activity of the gospel preacher. He is indeed a herald of the cross, of God's great salvation. In Mark and Luke it is sometimes translated "publish".

9. The next word is one that implies disucssion, questioning and answering. It is *dialegomai*, translated "reasoned, disputed, preached". In the Acts, "reason" occurs four times: "dispute" four times: and "preach" twice. It is used only in the second half of the book, during and after the second journey. First it describes what Paul did in the synagogue in Thessalonica (17:2), and again in the synagogue in Athens (17:17). Similarly, the word is used for Paul's work in the synagogues in Corinth (18:4) and in Ephesus (v.19). This shows how he used the OT Scriptures to present the truth to those who were well-taught in the law. It is translated "disputing" in 19:8, 9 both in the synagogue and in the school of Tyrannus in Ephesus. It is translated "preached" in 20:7, 9 (perhaps rather unnecessarily) in relation to Paul's discourse to the believers in the church at Troas, where obviously he was doing more than expounding the Scriptures, but was reasoning with them about vital church matters. The word finally appears in 24:12, where Paul denies that he had been disputing with anybody in the temple at Jerusalem, and in v.25 where he reasoned with Felix about "righteousness, temperance, and judgment to come". This method of reasoning is sometimes the best way of presenting the truth in formal and informal situations,

provided the audience is such that they can appreciate a discourse based on reasoning. It is not suitable for simpler folk.

10. A word with a similar meaning to the previous one is *suzeteō*, occurring twice in the Acts, but only once of relevance to our subject (9:29). Here Paul "disputed against the Grecians" in Damascus concerning the gospel.

11. The word *parakaleō* occurs many times in the Gospels, Acts and Epistles, but only a few times in the Acts for our present purpose. We may quote the references: 2:40 where Peter exhorted the Jews in Jerusalem to save themselves by repentance and faith from that generation; 11:23 where Barnabas exhorted the church at Antioch to cleave unto the Lord; 14:22 where Paul and Barnabas exhorted the disciples to continue in the faith; 15:32 where Judas and Silas exhorted the brethren in Antioch with many words; 16:40 where Paul and Silas "comforted" the brethren in Philippi; and 20:2 where Paul gave much exhortation to the churches of Macedonia.

12. The Greek word *ektithēmi* is used three times in Acts in the sense of "expounded". First in 11:4 where Peter "expounded" to the "circumcision party" in Jerusalem all that had happened to him in ch.10; then in 18:26 where Aquila and Priscilla expounded to Apollos the way of God more perfectly; and finally in 28:23 where Paul addressed the Jews in his prison-lodgings in Rome,. where it is also coupled with another word "testified".

13. A further verb *parrēsiazomai* describes the freedom, openness and boldness which these first preachers approached their work. The corresponding noun also appears in the Acts, and even more times in John's writings translated "openly, plainly, confidence". In Acts 9:27, the verb describes Paul's bold preaching in Damascus. The same verb is used of his preaching when he came to Jerusalem, in spite of danger (v.29). It describes the approach of Paul and Barnabas when confronted with the opposition of the Jews in 13:46 in Pisidian Antioch. It also describes their preaching when the unbelieving Jews aroused opposition to them in Iconium (14:3). According to 18:26 Apollos spoke boldly in the synagogue in Ephesus before he knew the way of God more perfectly. Similarly Paul spoke boldly in the synagogue in Ephesus for three months, though with a different message from that of Apollos (19:8). Frequently more than one word is used to describe the approach of the preachers; thus in 19:8, three words are used, relating to speaking boldly, disputing and persuading.

14. Finally, the verb *peithō* is used in the sense of persuading a number of times in the Acts (it is also translated "obey" many times in the NT). Apart from 13:43 where the word is used of believers being persuaded in Pisidian Antioch, it is used in 18:4 (together with "reasoned", or "lectured") to describe what Paul did in Corinth. It is used again together with the same word to describe his similar activity in Ephesus

(19:8). In v.26, he is condemned for having succeeded in persuading the people. Paul almost succeeded in persuading king Agrippa in 26:28. Finally as a prisoner in Rome Paul was still trying to persuade his Jewish audience about the gospel (28:23), from Moses and the prophets, expounding and testifying from morning to evening.

So over one hundred times in the Acts believers are described by a variety of Greek verbs to have spread their message. Some words applied to all believers, but others to those who had specific gifts. Such zeal demands much heart-searching on the part of all believers today.

Appendix 2

Paul's Companions in Travel

As we have stated before, it appears that the apostle Paul did not like to be on his own in the Lord's service. No doubt he was familiar with the Saviour's practice of sending out His disciples two and two (Luke 10:1), for "the testimony of two men is true" (John 8:17). After all, the wise man had said, "Two are better than one; because they have a good reward for their labour" (Eccles 4:9-12). Humans are human, and hence it is often better for two to share any honour when things go well, rather than allow only one to be puffed up with unique pride! Equally, when things are difficult, one can help by sharing disappointment with the other.

We are not surprised, therefore, to discover the phrase, "Paul's companions in travel" in Acts 19:29 (this is one word in Greek, Paul's "fellowtravellers") and the other phrase, "we which were of Paul's company" in 21:8 (more simply in Greek, "those with Paul", which is omitted in some Greek MSS). Many of these companions in service joined Paul on his missionary journeys when he called at the places where they lived.

Barnabas

We have already read about Paul's first companion, Barnabas (13:28). The only missionary journey that they shared was the first. Their partnership was broken when Barnabas wanted to reinstate John Mark, his relative, to the missionary group in spite of the fact that he had let them down on the first missionary journey. The result was that they split up, and two missionary groups set out instead of one. Paul was joined by Silas, while Barnabas took Mark with him, leaving for Cyprus where John Mark apparently was happier. They went to the scene of his faithfulness rather than to the scene of his defection. It is better that believers work where others will not remember their failures. We should not read too much into the fact that Barnabas is not mentioned again in the Acts. After all, nine of the apostles are not mentioned again after the prayer meeting in ch.1, and five of the "deacons" are not mentioned again after ch.6. The preaching of the gospel in all the world (Col 1:6) was the work of many, rather than of the few, so many names could not be mentioned again.

It should be pointed out that Barnabas is mentioned again in 1 Cor 9:6, which was written a few years later than the time when Paul and Barnabas split up. As late as AD 60 Paul was claiming that Barnabas, like himself, had the right to live of the gospel. There is also a mention of Barnabas in Gal 2:1, 9, 13.

Mark disappeared from the scene in Acts 15:39, but he reappears, obviously recovered and profitable, in Col 4:10 when Paul was a prisoner in Rome. He is still commendable when Paul wrote his last Epistle (2 Tim 4:11). If there is one thing better than beginning well, it is ending well (Heb 6:10-11).

Silas

Silas is first mentioned as accompanying Saul and Barnabas to Antioch on their return from the Council of Jerusalem (15:27). In this respect he followed in the footsteps of Barnabas (although he was with Barnabas on this return). He came to strengthen the recommendations of the Council to the church in Antioch relative to the attempts to make the new Gentile Christians accept the Jewish law and rites. He stayed at Antioch, and took Barnabas' place on Paul's second missionary journey. He therefore earned the distinction of being one of the first preachers of the gospel in Europe, and, of course, shared Paul's imprisonment at Philippi.

(Some Greek manuscripts omit 15:34, which would mean that Silas did return to Jerusalem with Judas; this would make the pronoun "they" in v.33 more comprehensible. However, it creates the problem of how Silas, instead of Barnabas, was available to join Paul on his second missionary journey.)

Silas was present when the gospel was first preached in Thessalonica and Berea, and also in Corinth (18:5), after which we read nothing further about him. It is taken for granted that Silas is a shorter form of the name Silvanus, of whom we read in 2 Cor 1:19; 1 Thess 1:1 and 2 Thess 1:1. The letters sent by Paul to the Thessalonians during the second missionary journey contain the names of the three preachers in the missionary group. It is not likely that the Silvanus in 1 Pet 5:12 (Peter's scribe) is the same person.

Mark

We have already commented on Mark under "Barnabas", and no further notes are necessary.

Timothy

Apart from Barnabas, Timothy (or Timotheus) is the most frequently mentioned of all Paul's companions. He must have been quite young when he joined the two missionaries on the second missionary journey (see 16:1-3), but he was already "well reported of" by the brethren at Lystra and Iconium. What better apprenticeship could a young man have served! Thereafter he is linked with Paul as long as he lived, as Paul's last Epistle witnesses (2 Tim 4:9, 13, 21).

From one point of view, it was an unusual partnership. Paul was older and Timothy younger; Paul was a pure Jew (Phil 3:5), while Timothy was a half-caste (Acts 16:1);

Paul could well be likened to a lion, Timothy to a lamb. In the two letters that Paul wrote to him, he seems to have been of a much more timid disposition that his older friend, yet he had a very important mission given to him in Ephesus (1 Tim 1:3). Men who are very distinct one from the other have often been linked together in the work of the Lord. Service for Christ can overcome every kind of difference, if devotion to the Lord prevents any disharmony.

About the young man, Paul could write later, "I have no man likeminded, who will naturally care for your state" (Phil 2:20). On several occasions, when Paul could not be in two places at the one times, because he trusted Timothy, he could send him to various places. Thus he sent him to Macedonia from Ephesus (Acts 19:22); to Corinth from Ephesus (1 Cor 4:17); to Philippi from Rome (Phil 2:19); to Thessalonica from Athens (1 Thess 3:2). He did not share Paul's short imprisonment in Philippi, but Phil 1:1 suggests that he was a prisoner in Rome at some stage. He is mentioned in Heb 13:23 as being in prison, and he was asked to join Paul quickly in the apostle's final imprisonment in Rome (2 Tim 4:9), though it is not known whether he reached Paul before his martyrdom. It was effectively on Timothy that Paul's mantle was to fall (not, of course, as an apostle), in spite of the many distinctions between them. He was to be the second link in the chain of 2 Tim 2:2 for the continuation of the Lord's work after Paul's departure from the scene of his labours.

He shares with Titus (who is never mentioned in the Acts) and Onesimus the intimate title "my son" (1 Cor 4:17; Phil 2:22; 1 Tim 1:2, 18; 2 Tim 1:2; 2:1; Titus 1:4; Philem 10), implying that Paul was the Lord's instrument in their conversion.

Luke

Luke is one of the most self-effacing characters in the NT. He wrote two Bible books without ever mentioning his own name. We would not even know his occupation had Paul not called him "the beloved physician" in Col 4:14, though this might be deduced from the events described and words used in his writings.

His Gospel was the result of research (Luke 1:1-4), but from Acts 16:10 he was more often an eye-witness. This means that he joined the missionary group at Troas and, from then on, he and Paul were separated only when he was left behind at Philippi, an excellent example to the Philippians of one who had in him that mind which was also in Christ Jesus.

His service consisted of writing two books, caring for the Philippian church in its infancy, and caring for Paul until the end of his life. In 2 Tim 4:11, Paul wrote, "Only Luke is with me", but it cannot be deduced from this that Luke shared the apostle's imprisonment. The influence of his medical vocabulary is strong in the three pastoral Epistles, which makes it hard to understand why such vocabulary is not found in Paul's first prison Epistles.

In Acts 19:29 we find the phrase "Paul's companions in travel", though Luke never once mentions his own name as being among them; the Greek word really means "fellow-travellers".

Erastus

His name is found only three times in the NT. He first appears at Ephesus in Acts 19:21. He and Timothy had left the city before the riot broke out, since Paul had sent them into Macedonia to prepare for a return visit. He may have belonged to Corinth and held high office in the city, since a believer with such a name sent greetings via Paul's letter to the Christians in Rome (Rom 16:23); in 2 Tim 4:20 he is mentioned again as having stayed in Corinth. This means that on two occasions Erastus was Timothy's companion, although his service was not as long as Timothy's. Paul's second and final Roman imprisonment was a much lonelier one than his first. Only Luke was with him, and he wanted Timothy and Mark to join him. Is there a hint of regret that Erastus had not done so, to minister unto him?

Gaius

This name is common in the NT, so references cannot all be associated with the same person. The Gaius who was one of Paul's companions appears first in Acts 19:29. He and Aristarchus, in the absence of Timothy and Erastus, were caught up in the Ephesian riot, when they were seized by the mob. The two are mentioned again in 20:4, but we learn that this Gaius belonged to Derbe, a city of Asia Minor, where Paul had preached Christ towards the end of his first missionary journey.

Aristarchus

Mentioned in Acts 19:29 along with Gaius from the same part of the world, he is again listed in 20:4 as a member of the company that crossed from Europe back into Asia, and headed for Caesarea and Jerusalem. He is found in Caesarea in 27:2 about to set out on the voyage to Rome, and is mentioned in two of the prison Epistles (Col 4:10; Philem 24). He is called a "fellowprisoner" in the former, and a "fellowlabourer" in the latter.

Sopater

This man is referred to only in Acts 20:4, where he is stated to have come from Berea. (Note that in this verse there were companions in travel with Paul from all three of his missionary journeys.) In Berea, Paul had a much more reasonable response than in many other places, for they (no doubt including Sopater) searched the OT Scriptures to see if they endorsed Paul's claims regarding Jesus of Nazareth. He may have been the same man Sosipater mentioned in Rom 16:21. Whether Sopater travelled with Paul to Caesarea and Jerusalem, we are not told, and we do not read of him again.

Secundus

Like Aristarchus, Secundus (Acts 20:4), meaning "second", came from Thessalonica and journeyed into Asia with the others named. His fellow-countryman continued with Paul to Rome (27:2), but we do not read of Secundus again. It has been pointed out that if the NT presents us with an early believer called "second", it also presents us with one named Tertius (meaning "third", Rom 16:22), and Quartus (meaning "fourth", Rom 16:23). Only the Leader can be called First and Last (Rev 1:17).

Tychicus

This man was another of the group who travelled from Europe into Asia with Paul's company (Acts 20:4). Although not mentioned again in the Acts, his name is found in two of the prison Epistles as being with Paul in Rome (Eph 6:21; Col 4:7). Paul described him as "a beloved brother and faithful minister in the Lord" and a fellowservant, able to declare Paul's state truthfully to the churches of Asia; he carried with him the Epistles to the Ephesians and Colossians, and we presume the Epistle to Philemon. He was sent by Paul on important missions to Crete and Ephesus (Titus 3:12; 2 Tim 4:12), showing how much Paul could trust him.

Trophimus

Like Tychicus, Trophimus came from Asia (Acts 20:4), and is called "Trophimus an Ephesian" (21:29), showing that he came from Ephesus. Like Tychicus he was a member of that considerable party who crossed the Bosphorus into Asia, continuing all the way with Paul to Jerusalem, for we learn in 21:29 that when he was seen in Jerusalem with Paul (on the assumption that Paul had ignored the Jewish conscience by taking him into the forbidden parts of the temple courts), the Jews staged a riot that resulted in Paul being arrested.

He does not appear to have gone to Rome with Paul, but he and his fellow-Asian Tychicus were faithful to the end. When Paul wrote his final letter, he indicated that Trophimus might well have been with him in Rome, but he had to leave him behind sick at Miletus (which was not his home city) before the apostle reached Rome for his second and last imprisonment (2 Tim 4:20).

Others who are not mentioned in the Acts became Paul's companions while he was in prison in Rome, notably Epaphras and Onesimus, both from Colosse. To these we can add Epaphroditus from Philippi, who became ill nearly unto death while taking a gift from the Philippian saints to the apostle as a prisoner in Rome (Phil 2:25), described as "my brother, and companion in labour, and fellowsoldier".

All these believers must have been a mixed collection, drawn from two races and two continents, including at least one slave and quite a number of freemen, but all belonging to Christ, all prepared to suffer for Him and to find themselves bound together in the closest fellowship which time will never dissolve.

Appendix 3

The Apostle Paul on his Missionary Journeys
(approximate distances travelled in miles)

First Journey

Place Names	By Land	By Sea
Antioch to Seleucia	20	–
Seleucia to Salamis	–	150
Salamis to Paphos	90	–
Paphos to Perga	–	175
Perga to Antioch	110	–
Antioch to Iconium	80	–
Iconium to Lystra	45	–
Lystra to Derbe	30	–
Derbe to Antioch	160	–
Antioch to Perga	110	–
Perga to Attalia	10	–
Attalia to Antioch	–	300
Total distance	555	625

Second Journey

Place Names	By Land	By Sea
Antioch to Syria	75	–
Syria to Cilicia	–	85
Cilicia to Derbe-Lystra	120	–
Lystra to Phyrgia	230	–
Phyrgia to Galatia	180	–
Galatia to Mysia	240	–
Mysia to Troas	140	–
Troas to Philippi	–	160
Philippi to Thessalonica	80	–
Thessalonica to Berea	35	–
Berea to Athens	185	–
Athens to Corinth	80	–
Corinth to Cenchrea	75	–
Cenchrea to Ephesus	–	230
Ephesus to Caesarea	–	570
Caesarea to Antioch	–	275
Total distance	1440	1320

PAUL'S JOURNEY No. 1

PAUL'S JOURNEY No. 2

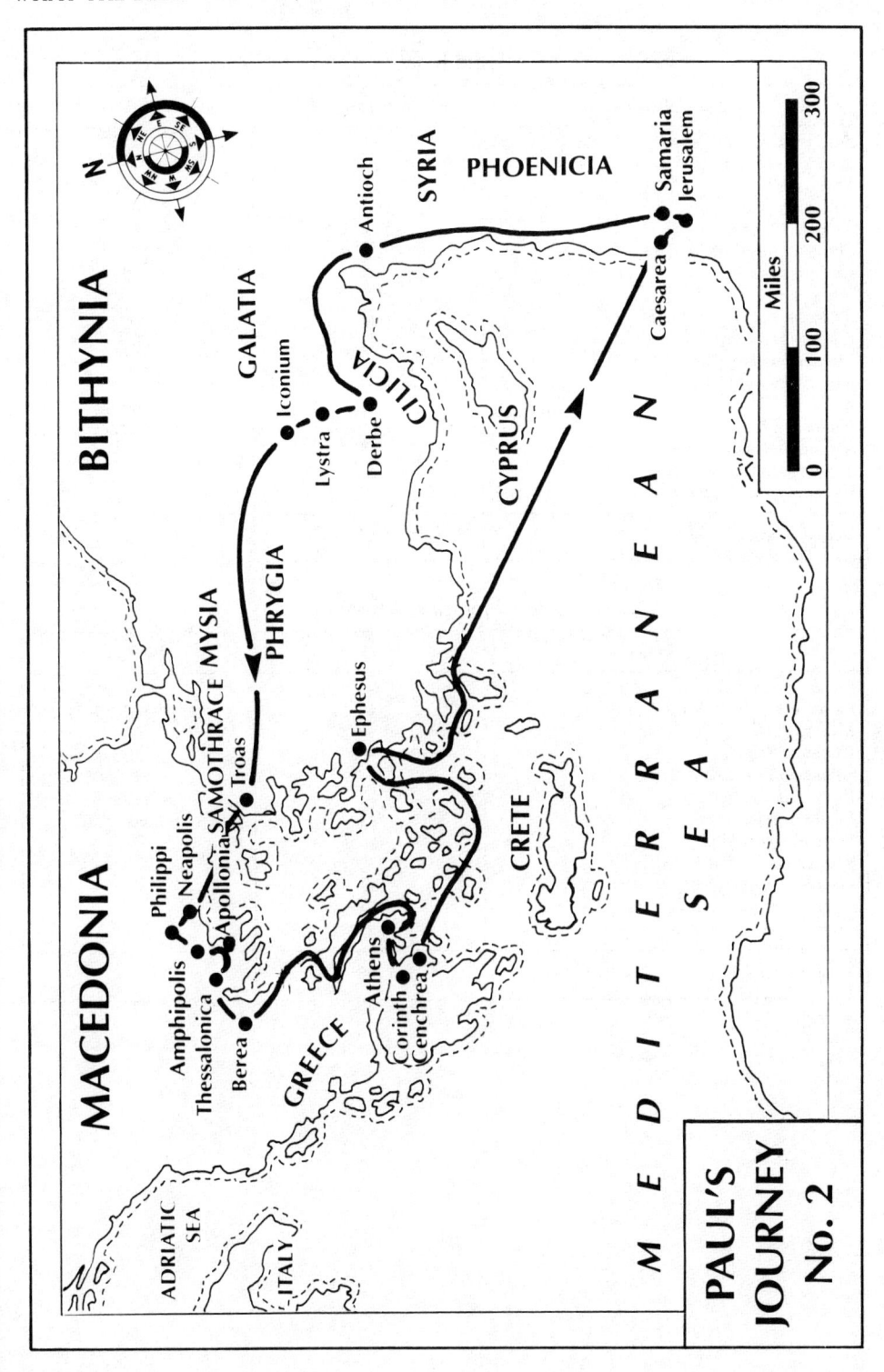

Third Journey

Place Names	By Land	By Sea
Antioch to Galatia	340	–
Galatia to Phyrgia	190	–
Phyrgia to Ephesus	150	–
Ephesus to Troas	–	160
Troas to Philippi	–	160
Philippi to Corinth	–	250
Corinth to Philippi	–	250
Philippi to Troas	–	160
Troas to Assos	20	–
Assos to Mitylene	–	30
Mitylene to Trogyllium	–	120
Trogyllium to Miletus	–	30
Miletus to Patara	–	160
Patara to Tyre	–	400
Tyre to Ptolemais	25	–
Ptolemais to Caesarea	30	–
Caesarea to Jerusalem	50	–
Total distance	805	1720

Fourth Journey to Rome

Place Names	By Land	By Sea
Caesarea to Sidon	–	75
Sidon to Myra via Cyprus	–	360
Myra to Cnidus	–	160
Cnidus to Salmone	–	140
Salmone to Fairhavens	–	80
Fairhavens to Melita	–	530
Melita to Syracuse	–	90
Syracuse to Rhegium	–	75
Rhegium to Puteoli	–	220
Puteoli to Appii forum	80	–
Appii forum to Three Taverns	20	–
Three Taverns to Rome	30	–
Total distance	130	1820

PAUL'S JOURNEY No.3

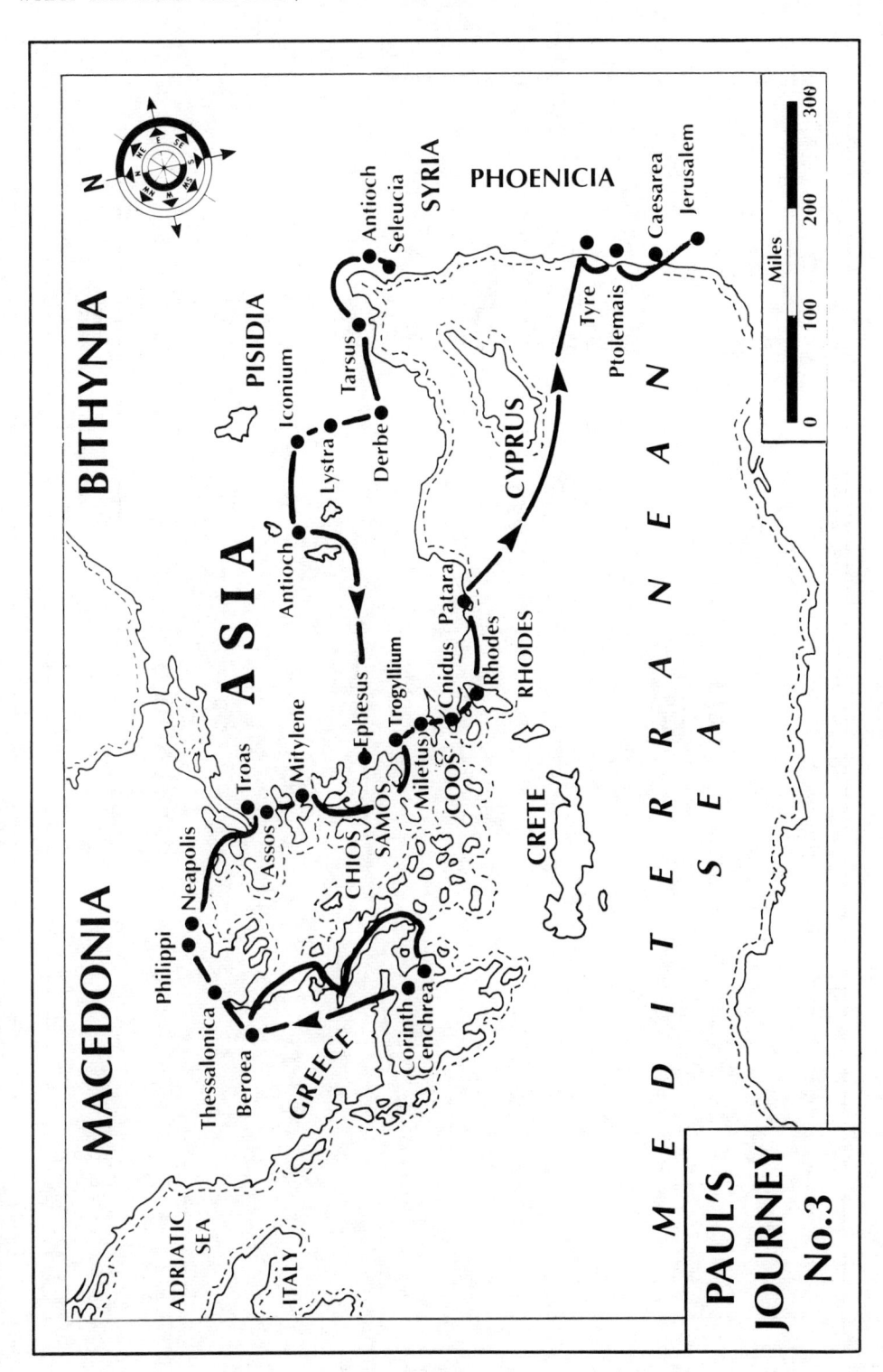

PAUL'S JOURNEY TO ROME

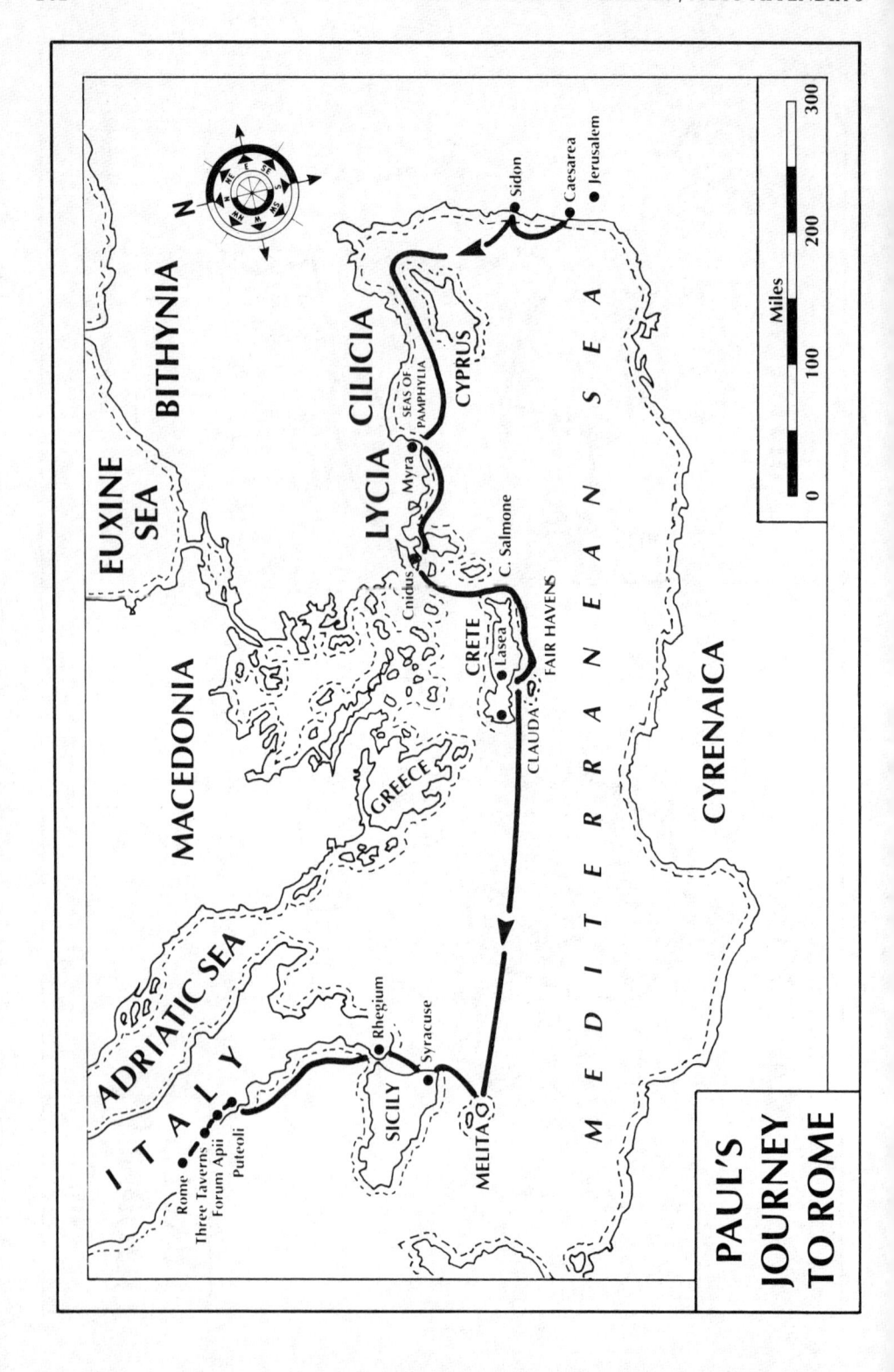

Approximate Plan of the Temple Area

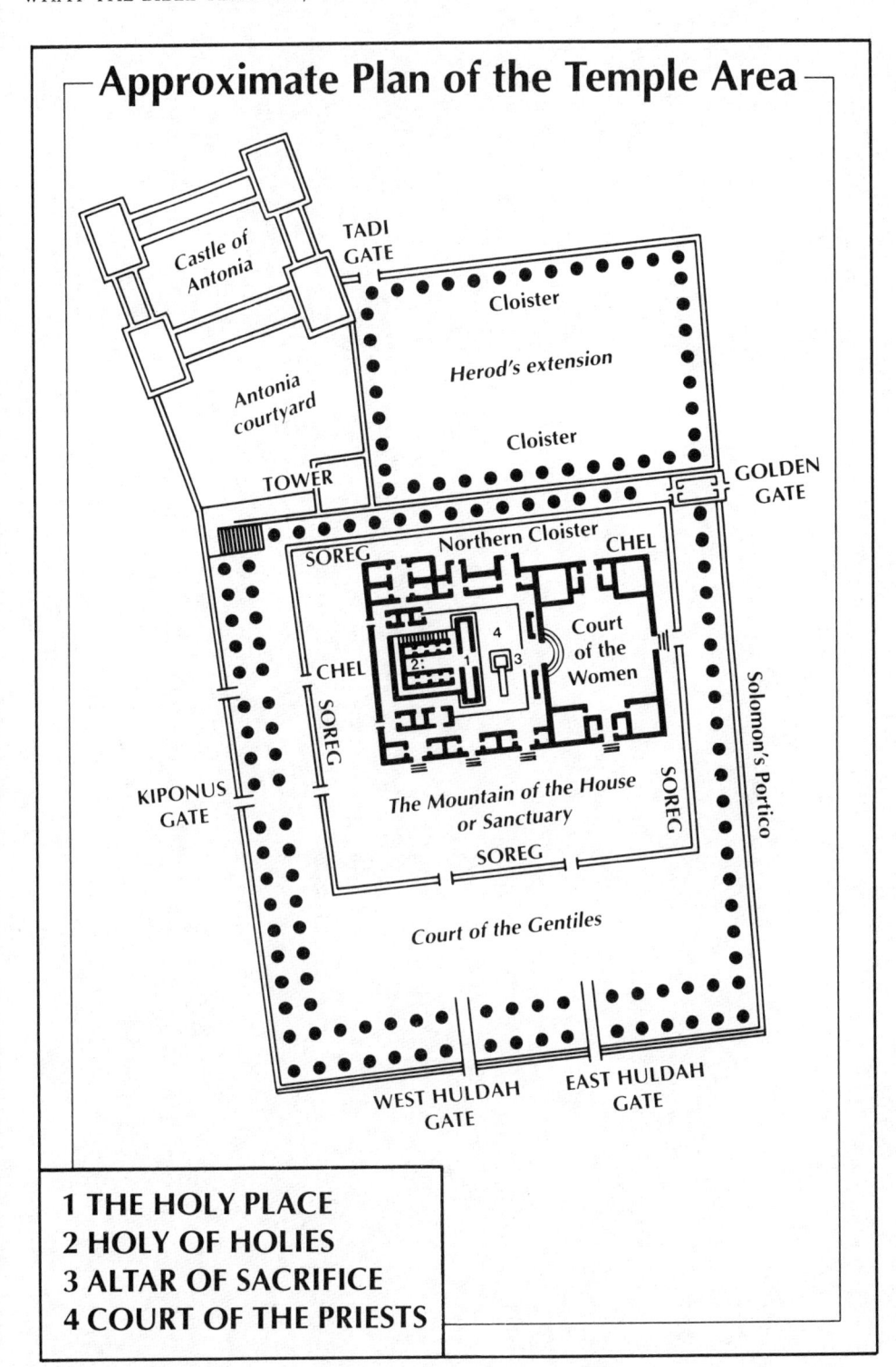

- TADI GATE
- Castle of Antonia
- Antonia courtyard
- TOWER
- Cloister
- Herod's extension
- Cloister
- GOLDEN GATE
- SOREG
- Northern Cloister
- CHEL
- CHEL
- Court of the Women
- Solomon's Portico
- KIPONUS GATE
- SOREG
- SOREG
- The Mountain of the House or Sanctuary
- SOREG
- Court of the Gentiles
- WEST HULDAH GATE
- EAST HULDAH GATE

1 THE HOLY PLACE
2 HOLY OF HOLIES
3 ALTAR OF SACRIFICE
4 COURT OF THE PRIESTS

Acts and James

Christian testimony in the first century did not lack outstanding men whose contribution to "those of the way" (Acts 9:2) was significant. Peter, Stephen, Saul (later Paul), Barnabas and James the Lord's brother – each is remembered rightly by readers of the Acts. When Paul lists men of influence in Gal 2:9 he describes James, Cephas (Peter) and John as those "who seemed to be pillars".

The contribution of Paul himself is chronicled in the Acts; that of Peter too occupies much of the earlier chapters. John's authorship of five NT books more than compensates for his lower profile within the Acts. James the Lord's brother does have a significant part to play to which Galatians refers obliquely (see Gal 1:19; 2:9), but the importance of which is recognisable in the Acts (see 1:13; 12:17; 15:13; 21:18).

Although not the apostle of the circumcision as Peter, nor the apostle to the uncircumcision as Paul (see Gal 2:7,8), the influence of James from as early as Acts 12 is discernible; even little more than ten years after his conversion James was recognised as one of the chief men among brethren. Later of course Paul describes him as an apostle in Gal 1:19; he could testify amply to the Lord's resurrection after his special interview with the risen Christ (1 Cor 15:7).

Josephus claims in his Antiquities XX.9.1 that just after the death of Festus, the high priest Ananus assembled a Sanhedrin, arraigned James and had him stoned to death. F.F. Bruce has suggested a date of c.AD 61 for James' martyrdom which would mean his influence is more or less coextensive with the period covered by the Acts of the Apostles.

In a commentary of this nature, there is no place for discussions on the canonicity of each NT book. It is a little surprising that Luther places James with Hebrews, Jude and Revelation in a supplement at the end of his 1522 edition of the NT, as R.V.G. Tasker notes, without even listing them in the contents. To some extent the place of James within the order of the books of the NT is due to Luther's influence. Both Tyndale and Calvin respected Luther's ordering without sharing his doubt about the value of James.

It was however often "the practice to place these Epistles (i.e. the catholic epistles like James) along with the Acts of the Apostles in a codex by themselves ... Such codices containing Acts plus the catholic epistles are known as Praxapostoloi" (R.V.G. Tasker). The Complutensian Polyglot published in 1522 ordered the NT as the four Gospels, the Pauline epistles, Acts, the catholic epistles and Revelation. Most orderings of the catholic epistles begin with James.

It would appear that in the minds of most of the early editors a close association existed between Acts and James. This link may have been forged by their belief that James described a more primitive testimony than is evident in the Pauline epistles or in the seven letters to the churches of Asia recorded in Rev 2,3.

In determining the linkage between Acts and James, it is essential that the dating of James is considered. One would expect it to provide evident of the moral and spiritual atmosphere James then saw and the Acts to comment upon the political factors Luke noted, perhaps in the context of the work of God then current whether through Peter or Paul. However, this commentary is not the place to evaluate the technical arguments associated with dating the epistle of James. Without such an evaluation the reader should note that two main dates are proposed for its writing: c.AD 40 and c.AD 60.

The council of Jerusalem, the record of which is given in Acts 15, occurred c.AD 49 according to scholars such as F.F. Bruce (Conybeare and Howson favour AD 50 or AD 51). Both schools of thought proposing a date for James recognise the crisis nature of that conference and agree that, had James been penned a year or two before or after that conference, it would have been likely that James would have made reference to "the Gentile problem" or at least to the encyclical letter issued by the council. The silence of James on such matters leads to the probable date of James' epistle being before AD 45 or after AD 55. The evidence may be weighed as follows:

1. Date of writing: Before AD 45

a. It is evident that James is not describing an assembly (or assemblies) long established in the faith. It would appear that the believers' association with the synagogue or at least with the language used to describe the meetings in the synagogue had not been broken. Either the believers still met in the synagogue or their language development had not enriched their vocabulary with the kind of phraseology Paul uses in 1 Cor 12-14. This may point to an early dating of the epistle.

b. The place and equipping of elders does not appear to be based upon extant Scriptures such as the Pastoral epistles of Paul or even 1 Peter. James recognises the need for elders (see 5:14) and that they like other saints will seek wisdom (see 1:5), but does not underscore the moral and spiritual qualifications Paul expects nor does he elaborate upon their role in the local church.

2. Date of writing: After AD 55

a. James is certainly not describing an assembly in its infancy. It has elders, recognised as such and available to the needy (5:14). Scant mention of other gifts such as evangelists and teachers emerges from a study of the letter; there is however evidence to suggest a degree of spiritual maturity in the church (see 3:1ff.).

b. The moral and spiritual conditions James describes do not point to his writing just after Pentecost. It would be too strong an assertion to make that decline had come in, but there is no longer a sharing of resources; there were rich and poor and they did not have "all things in common" (James 2:1-8; Acts 2:44-45).
c. The Epistle assumes rather than asserts those christian doctrines other NT writers announce, doctrines like the Lord's Person, access into the Holiest, the sanctification of all believers and the subjugation of all things to Christ.
d. James' discussions on justification may have been calculated to balance extreme views some had adopted from Paul's teaching on justification by faith.

It is the view of this writer that James was written early in the post-Pentecost era, but certainly after the first days of unparalleled devotion which Pentecost ushered in. A date of writing c.AD 40 seems probable, given the evidence of the Epistle.

What kind of conditions did James note around him? Society was settled enough to allow commercial life to flourish with all the temptations that could bring; indeed year long trips could be planned (4:13-17) and "the grace of the fashion" of the age sought by the prosperous trader (1:9-11). A Barnabas selling his land and laying the money at the apostles' feet must have seemed, as James wrote, a memory from a lost golden era (Acts 4:37). Yet only a matter of six years may have elapsed from "the son of consolation" Barnabas disposed of his estate.

But there were trials (see 1:2-4, 12-15). Among those trials were arraignments before Jewish tribunals, usually at the instigation of the rich and influential (2:6). Probably the fury of persecution unleashed by the unrestrained zeal of Saul of Tarsus and similarly-bigotted oppressors had subsided. They had enjoyed the relative calm throughout all Judaea and Galilee and Samaria; therein they had been edified and walking in the fear of the Lord and in the comfort of the Holy Spirit, they had been multiplied (Acts 9:31). Nevertheless, their confession of Christ went against the grain of public opinion and from time to time inevitably they faced trials. James offers a useful social history of that period.

Even the casual reader must have noticed that James writes in the vein of Jewish prophetic writings. Why does he address his readers as "ye adulteresses" (4:4) as Isaiah or Ezekiel or Hosea might have done (Isa 1:21; Ezek 23:43-45; Hos 7:4)? The reasons are at least two: the formative influences upon him and the perceived need around him.

James was reared where Moses and the prophets were read every Sabbath day. His Lord quoted the prophets and spoke approvingly of their testimony unto blood. James rightly detected that forthright condemnation of sin can be God's message for the day. He detected too that the standards of the Sermon on the Mount from which he draws frequently in his epistle were vital to pleasing God. (Cf. 1:14 and Matt 5:28; 1:16 and Matt 7:11; 2:5,6 and Matt 5:3 etc.) James saw that the inner life could only be strengthened as his Lord's teaching was absorbed and practised.

Some have suggested that James belonged to the strict school within the Jerusalem church or even within the apostolic band. They would point to the precedence of

James in Acts 21; Luke comments that "Paul went in with us unto James; and all the elders were present". Even after rejoicing in "what things God had wrought among the Gentiles by his (Paul's) ministry", they (probably including James) required of Paul fellowship with four men undertaking the final stages of a Nazarite vow. The conclusion is reached by a number of commentators that James was less liberal than Paul; that James was intensely devoted to Judaistic practices and James therefore was less affected by those NT truths so clearly set out in Paul's ministry, for example in his letter to Ephesus. The present writer believes such conclusions are ill-founded.

Within his letter much that James writes is uncompromising and unequivocal, but the letter does not lack warmth; it does breathe deeply the spirit of the Sermon on the Mount; indeed who could doubt the sincerity of James' family feelings as he addresses "my beloved brethren" (1:16; 2:5) or "my brethren" (2:1; 3:1; 5:12) or "brethren" (5:19)? James may be true to a good tradition, that of the prophets, but he had imbibed the spirit of the New. To assert that he who so warmly welcomed Paul in Acts 15 and 21 held anachronistic views which disrupted apostolic and church fellowship would be a travesty of James' ministry.

The epistle of James may offer, therfore, a clear impression of christian ministry around the end of the first decade from Pentecost. The oral ministry of Christ was grasped as fundamental to christian living and servants like James taught forcefully such truths, richly illustrated by reference to nature or to the Holy Scriptures.

But more particularly, James offers insight into the burdens servants carried during that period from Acts 9 to Acts 14. Stress was laid upon wisdom rather than wealth (1:5-8; 3:13-18) in a world where materialism to which so many in the twentieth century could relate was stumbling even those who confessed Christ. James' thrust was upon the ethical and, on that basis, upon the practical, so the tongue must be controlled (3:1-12) and patience (or endurance) cultivated (5:7-11) and christian virtues, the very virtues the Saviour prized and practised, were to be found glistening among the fatherless and the widows. James was writing most assuredly after Matt 23:14 *et al* and most likely after Acts 6.

We can discern too that prayer and the Word were as important then as now. The Word was to be effective in a man's experience: he was to be a doer and not just a hearer (1:19-25). James enters that caution for all who might have much to say – better to hear and, having heard, to do. The reception of the Word would reveal a man to himself and allow subsequent adjustment. And a man would pray with prayer (5:17 lit.), effectually and fervently (5:16). Great things could be expected when such righteous men pray; even the conversion of some sinner could result.

James offers that kind of insight into the *ministerial* burdens good men like James carried as routine christian duties tried those amongst whom they served.

The early chapters of Acts relate the story of conditions which have pertained only briefly and spasmodically in the last 1900 years. The power of God was present to save in large measure and a healthy fear of God together with great conviction about the resurrection of Christ developed spiritual conditions rarely seen since. However, shortly thereafter some tensions did develop between Greek-speaking Jews and

Hebrew-speaking Jews (ch.6); between Jew and Gentile (chs. 10,11); and there was the suspicion about Samaria's entrance into blessing, a potential flash-point defused by Peter.

Interestingly, although prone to prejudice on grounds of social standing, preferring rich before poor, no hint of emergent disruption on other grounds appears in James' epistle. That there should be no aftermath to the problems of chs. 6,8,10,11 is a tribute to good leadership. Both the apostles and the elders must have worked diligently among the saints as those matters were faced or else, as sadly can happen, a lingering undercurrent would have been felt for years afterwards.

The record of Acts up to ch.15 describes a world in which God still confirmed His word by miraculous signs: the lame were raised (ch.3); Aeneas was healed (9:34); Tabitha or Dorcas was raised to life from death itself (9:36-43); Peter was released from prison by an angel (ch. 12). However, although less mature Christians in Corinth were distracted by such signs and by sign gifts, James is able to write on a variety of topics without adjusting attitudes to the spectacular sign gifts. Again the value of good leadership is evident: the saints must have been taught the place and purpose of confirmatory signs.

The period of the Acts coextensive with that of James' writing provides evidence of poverty both in isolated pockets like Joppa (9:36-43) and more generally so much so that Agabus "signified by the Spirit that there should be a great dearth throughout the world" sometime before it affected Judaea. The Acts relates how Antioch responded to that word of prophecy (11:28-30).

It may be that James wrote before that "great dearth" arrived and so before Gentile relief reached Jerusalem from Antioch. Clearly James recognises there is poverty, but he shows it alongside prosperity. He commends action towards the disadvantaged, whether orphans or widows (1:26-27). The activities of Dorcas may be attributable directly to James, but certainly those widows showing on themselves the results of Dorcas' good works proved in deep pathos what James' ministry encouraged. (As the middle voice of the verb "shewing" indicates, without those garments which Dorcas continually made they would have been naked, Acts 9:39). James taught the very principles which underlie the practical Christianity of the Acts period.

Assuming the dating of James is as early as suggested in this article, James and the Acts provide an interesting cross-referencing. Despite the great advances James has seen from the moment of his conversion, he has little to say on evangelism. Despite the impact the gospel had made on the lifestyle of Luke the historian and on the many Jews and Gentiles he had seen saved, he says little in the Acts of how "our's" learned to "maintain good works for necessary uses, that they be not unfruitful" (Titus 3:14). But together James and Luke provide a three-dimensional view of Jerusalem-based Christianity. There are no spurious claims to super-spirituality, no quarter given to those who might exhibit the over-bearing attitude Paul encountered in the Judaisers who sought to bring the Corinthians into bondage, who wantonly devoured them and shamed them by physical abuse (2 Cor 11:20) and no boasting of Jerusalem over Antioch or Samaria. James the Jew might don the prophet's mantle and write sternly; Luke the Gentile might take the chronicler's pen to record accurately a second treatise to Theophilus. Together they offer our generation, as they did first their own, much of great profit in both word and deed.

T. WILSON

JAMES

Introduction

1. General Remarks
2. The Author
3. The Date of the Letter
4. Outline of the Epistle
5. Bibliography

1. General Remarks

This letter by James has divided historians and theologians throughout the centuries, many with Luther objecting to its inclusion in the canon of Scripture, others with Jerome endorsing it. Let no one underestimate its value; it is of great significance and necessary to complete the divine revelation.

In all probability it was the first book of the NT to be written. The introduction is short, simple, and straightforward. For this to have sufficed the author must have been well-known and respected by his own generation. James wastes no time identifying himself or his standing in the Church but with tremendous clarity he launches immediately into an intensely practical letter. The passing of the years has obscured these details and on-coming generations are left to wonder and speculate as to which James was the author and who the recipients of his letter were. Other questions follow: its relevance today; its applicability to Gentile believers if the recipients are uniquely described as the twelve tribes in the dispersion.

2. The Author

By common consent James is the Hellenised form of the Hebrew Jacob. It is not surprising that as many as six of our Lord's followers bore the name: James the son of Zebedee (Matt 4:21); James the son of Alphaeus (Matt 10:3); James the less, the son of Mary wife of Cleophas (Mark 15:40; John 19:25); James the Lord's brother (Gal 1:19); James the overseer of the church in Jerusalem (Acts 12:17; 15:13); James the brother of Jude (Jude 1). We may safely identify the last three as being the same person, and it is possible that James the less is James the son of Alphaeus (Cleophas and Alphaeus being different Greek forms of the Aramaic name Chalpai). Of those it is almost certain that the writer was the Lord's brother. Jerome, an early writer, is helpful on this matter. Since then much research has been undertaken and the consensus of opinion agrees. Luke gives to us the first authentic church history with his book *The Acts*. He assigns to James the place of prominent leadership in the first church Jerusalem. James is portrayed as a man of wise counsel, like a captain of a new vessel in difficult seas. Another early historian, Hegesippus, describes him as a man of moral worth, very outspoken, strong in his condemnation of corrupt practices, very blunt, forthright in his judgment, helpful and always willing to give sound and free advice. Paul refers to James the Lord's brother as a pillar, very influential in Jerusalem and of great assistance to himself (Gal 1:19). There was another letter sent out under the name of James (see Acts 15:20-29); it was encyclic, and conveyed firstly to Antioch the result of a very important meeting. That letter is short but pointed and self-explanatory. It not only dealt with the difficulty but caused rejoicing, bringing consolation to the dispersed Christians and confirming them in their faith. It is interesting to compare the letters. The epistle is given to help Jewish Christians, whereas the letter in Acts 15 is for Gentile saints. Both letters bear the same stamp and reflect a leader whose advice was workable and acceptable. The early pains of a growing church were being experienced, requiring forbearance, grit on the part of the saints, and love with wisdom from the elders. James admirably shows all these in this epistle.

However, there are other contenders for the authorship such as James the son of Zebedee and James the son of Alphaeus. The son of Zebedee has over twenty mentions in the Gospels, the son of Alphaeus some sixteen. Quite a few of the early writers suggest that the son of Alphaeus is James the Lord's brother but this involves serious difficulties, not least John's explicit statement: "neither did his brethren believe in him" (7:5).

Dante of Italy, Isodore of Seville, and until the 18th century the Spanish RC church, held that the son of Zebedee was the author. This man was martyred in AD 44 which requires too early a date for the epistle.

The writer then is probably the Lord's brother. Like others in the family he did not believe on Jesus until after the resurrection even though he was privileged to listen to the teaching and witness the acts of power. He with the others doubted, disbelieved and deserted Jesus. When Jesus rose from the dead He appeared to a number of chosen witnesses, James being one of them: "he was seen of James then of all the apostles" (1 Cor 15:7). A momentous change had taken place of which little is said in Scripture. Shortly afterwards we find him occupying a position of leadership in the church at Jerusalem, so there is no doubt that James was now a true believer. The references made to him by Luke in Acts indicate his importance: the news of Peter's release from prison is sent expressly to James (Acts 12:17); his presiding at the conference held at Jerusalem when a serious matter is discussed regarding the admission of Gentiles to equal status and privilege with the Jewish converts (15:13-21); at a meeting arranged to discuss Paul's activity in the spread of the gospel, James again presides (21:18). In Paul's letter to the Galatians, James is mentioned first then Cephas and John (2:9). They were all reputed to be pillars. The difficulties of those early days were many but James displays the wisdom of a great leader.

Other particulars of this great man can be found in writings not deemed to be inspired. Hegesippus described him as a holy man who abstained from wine and strong drink; no razor came to his head; a man of prayer who kneeled so often that his knees were hard like those of a camel.

In the end he was a target for the enemies of the gospel. They engineered his execution and he was clubbed to death. The epistle which bears his name has characteristics of a man fearless, strong and wise. Despite the local problems of the church at Jerusalem and the added burden of problems from Asia, James remains a man whose door was open to counsel the rich and poor, the illiterate and the scholar. Many of the problems James addressed are still with us today and as they recur so we return to this inspired letter. As James was authoritative in his lifetime so his epistle is today.

3. The Date of the Letter

While the letter is undoubtedly early it is difficult to be precise as to its date. In the early days the Christians used synagogues as places where they could meet for fellowship and so a Judaic Christianity was developing. Not until Paul and his distinctive teaching of the unique calling of the church was there a clear break from the deadness of Judaism. Various years between AD 49 and AD 52 have been advanced as the year of the conference in Jerusalem at which were discussed important matters occasioned by a church that was growing fast. By that time Gentiles had begun to accept the gospel; preachers were finding that the message could not be limited to Jews, hence the need for the conference chaired by James. There are features in the epistle which depict this Judaic Christianity and yet no mention is made of the problem of bringing the Gentiles into full fellowship, nor is there any hint of Paul's dispute with Peter (Gal 2). It seems likely that James was writing *before* the Jerusalem conference, given the references to the use of synagogues and the freshness of the memories of the Lord Jesus' ministry to both writer and recipients.

4. Outline of the Epistle

The epistle is intensely practical, almost informal, yet authoritative and logical. The subjects dealt with are for daily christian living and each topic, or problem, is dealt with authoritatively and sympathetically. The aim of the writer is clear to him; to strengthen the daily witness of the saints in their locality. The ethical and practical character of the five chapters is salt to preserve the saints and separate them from idolatry and the evil temptations of their new surroundings. This is not deep theology nor difficult prophecy; this is survival advice given in the power of the Spirit. An epistle of this character renders analysis difficult but since James encourages faith to grow, sections can be listed and given captions as follows:

I.	Introduction	1:1
II.	Faith and Trials	1:2-18
III.	Faith and Truth	1:19-27
IV.	Faith and Temperance	2:1-13
V.	Faith and Testing	2:14-26
VI.	Faith and the Tongue	3:1-12
VII.	Faith and the Tempter	3:13-4:12
VIII.	Faith and Tomorrow	4:13-5:9
IX.	Faith and Trust	5:10-20

5. Bibliography

Alford, H. *The Greek New Testament*. London, 1857.
Anderson, D. *Commentary On James*. Loizeaux Bros.
Elliot, C.J. *New Testament Commentary*. London, 1897.
Hiebert, D. Edmond *The Epistle of James*. Moody Press, Chicago, 1979.
Ironside, H. *Commentary On James*. Loizeaux Bros.
Lenski, R.C.H. *The Interpretation of the Epistle to the Hebrews and of the Epistle of James*. Columbus, Ohio; Lutheran Book Concern, 1938.
McShane, A. *The Power Of Faith* . John Ritchie Ltd, Kilmarnock, Scotland, 1982.
Manton, T. *An Exposition of James*. Banner of Truth.
Mayor, Joseph. *Commentary On James*. Kregel.
Mauro, P. *The Epistle of Reality*. Hamilton Bros, Boston.
Plumptre, E.H. *Cambridge Bible Series*. Cambridge, 1899.
Robertson, A.T. *Word Pictures in NT*. Harper, New York, 1933.
Stier. *The Epistle of James*. T & T Clarke, Edinburgh, 1871, Klock & Klock, Minneapolis.
Strauss, L. *Commentary on James*. Loizeaux Bros.
Tasker, R.V.G. *James*, Tyndale NT Commentaries. IVP, Leicester, 1956.
Vaughan Curtis. *James, A Study Guide*. Zondervan, Grand Rapids, 1969.
Vincent, R.V. *Word Studies in the NT*. Eerdmans, Grand Rapids.

I. Introduction (1:1)

v.1 "James, a servant of God and of the Lord Jesus Christ, to the twelve tribes which are scattered abroad, greeting."

There are three main points raised in this simple introduction:

a. The Author
b. The Recipients
c. The Greeting

a. The Author

The writer is a self-effacing individual, who in using *doulos* accepts the honour of being owned by a Master. He was a slave to God and to the Lord Jesus Christ. He refers to himself as a piece of living property, to be at the disposal of his Masters. Being owned by another, all he was as a man and all he had as possessions were his Masters'. He sees himself as equally responsible to God and to the Lord Jesus Christ. Both these Masters had equal rights and James admits this; when his colleagues refer to him they might recognise his worth as a man and the position he held among them: as a pillar of the mother church in Jerusalem; as chairman at the Jerusalem council; and as signatory of the first encyclic letter sent out to all churches (Acts 15). It was to James that Paul explained his doctrine as contained in the Galatian letter and secured his fellowship and approval to continue in his work. This is the James who became a model for all those who serve God and the Lord Jesus Christ.

The fact that he gives equality of position to God and the Lord Jesus Christ indicates he appreciates the deity of the Lord Jesus Christ. No doubt in the family home at Nazareth he would refer to Jesus and simply use the human family name. Now he has believed, now he accepts the great mystery that "God was manifest in flesh" (1 Tim 3:16), so now he gives the full title to his Lord: He is Jesus but He is Lord and Christ. These two offices equate to deity and his service and allegiance are to God and to the Lord Jesus Christ, who is equal with God. If James assumes the status of a common slave, we ought to feel challenged and to respond suitably. Paul says, "Do not think of yourself more highly than you ought to think" (see Rom 12:3). James does not use any favours which would advance himself, whether a pillar of the first mother church or son of the mother of our Lord. What an example for saints who possess educational or religious degrees and (worldly) decorations. Our highest honour must derive from our relationship with God and the Lord Jesus Christ. James said, I am a slave. This to him was of great value and makes him a man of sterling worth.

If he had a lowly estimate of self, which is in keeping with the doctrine of the NT, Paul too expected a modest assessment of self: "Do not think of yourself more highly than you ought" (Rom 12:3). But James also had a high appreciation of his Master:

"God and the Lord Jesus Christ". Some scholars suggest that these words could be translated "of Jesus Christ who is God and Lord". Thomas Manton states that these words show Jesus "as an object of equal honour with the Father; and as the Father is Lord, as well as Jesus Christ, so Jesus Christ is God as well as the Father". James ascribes to Jesus the fulness of deity and in this is on equal footing with other NT writers; to James Christ's Lordship is total and eternal. He has the rights to me, to my energy and effort: He is Owner and Master, Sovereign Lord. James is repeating the classic statement of Thomas in John 20:28 when he faced his doubts and accepted willingly the great fact that Jesus is Lord and God. Thomas initially, now James, later Jude exclaim "My Lord and my God".

b. The Recipients

James describes his readers as: "the twelve tribes which are scattered abroad", that is, they were saints of the Jewish race who found themselves in the *diaspora* or dispersion. The expression describes them as being away from the homeland, not by their own desire. They had been forced to disperse and find a home in a strange land. The twelve tribes is another way of describing Jews, for all Jews can trace their origin to Jacob through one of his twelve sons. That nation had often experienced hardship, trial and removal by forced expatriation. Probably James is thinking not of the dispersions described in the OT but of this scattering of Christians who like himself were born Jews. The christian Jews who followed the Lord Jesus Christ have suffered from the time of the martyrdom of Stephen. Many were forced to leave Jerusalem with its warm fellowship of saints. They became subject to laws of a foreign land which caused them problems as they sought to live as servants of the despised Nazarene. They needed instruction, exhortation and comfort. James in this epistle seeks to meet their need.

The authorities could separate saint from saint but could never separate them from the Lord. They would be unable to break the spiritual link that unites all Christians to Christ and to each other. What they could do was to bring the saints separated from each other to a closer fellowship with their Lord. History has given to us many occasions when under severe persecution and isolation the saints have matured personally and the church has lived on with an increasing membership.

c. The Greeting

The greeting is simple but genuine. It is in keeping with the character of James himself, ever forthright and to the point. His genuine concern for these saints is not in question as the epistle will show clearly.

II. Faith and Trials (1:2-18)

> v.2 "My brethren, count it all joy when ye fall into divers temptations;
> v.3 Knowing *this,* that the trying of your faith worketh patience.
> v.4 But let patience have *her* perfect work, that ye may be perfect and entire, wanting nothing.
> v.5 If any of you lack wisdom, let him ask of God, that giveth to all *men* liberally, and upbraideth not; and it shall be given him.
> v.6 But let him ask in faith, nothing wavering. For he that wavereth is like a wave of the sea driven with the wind and tossed.
> v.7 For let not that man think that he shall receive any thing of the Lord.
> v.8 A double minded man *is* unstable in all his ways.
> v.9 Let the brother of low degree rejoice in that he is exalted:
> v.10 But the rich, in that he is made low: because as the flower of the grass he shall pass away.
> v.11 For the sun is no sooner risen with a burning heat, but it withereth the grass, and the flower thereof falleth, and the grace of the fashion of it perisheth: so also shall the rich man fade away in his ways.
> v.12 Blessed *is* the man that endureth temptation: for when he is tried, he shall receive the crown of life, which the Lord hath promised to them that love him.
> v.13 Let no man say when he is tempted, I am tempted of God: for God cannot be tempted with evil, neither tempteth he any man:
> v.14 But every man is tempted, when he is drawn away of his own lust, and enticed.
> v.15 Then when lust hath conceived, it bringeth forth sin: and sin, when it is finished, bringeth forth death.
> v.16 Do not err, my beloved brethren.
> v.17 Every good gift and every perfect gift is from above, and cometh down from the Father of lights, with whom is no variableness, neither shadow of turning.
> v.18 Of his own will begat he us with the word of truth, that we should be a kind of firstfruits of his creatures."

"My brethren" emphasises the loving family relationship James has with every saint. This word he heard from the Lord Jesus during his earthly ministry both before and after his death at Calvary. It includes men and women who by faith in Jesus Christ are members of the same family, the family of God. It is an affectionate family expression and brings comfort to lonely saints and encouragement to downcast saints.

In this epistle it is used when closing and opening each subject, dealt with by the writer. The recipients were objects of love from a triune God and they were embraced by James the slave of God as his brethren. In such a short epistle he appeals on nineteen occasions with this family description of the saints and on three occasions strengthens the bond with the endearing word "beloved". It is the family link which cannot be severed, used by the Lord before and after his death and resurrection. This relationship goes beyond natural family or national links we may have by natural birth. This is the eternal relationship we have with all the family of God, all who have been born again by faith in our Lord Jesus Christ, irrespective of intelligence or social standing. It is entered into by faith, the faith which unites rich Zacchaeus and poor blind Bartimaeus of Jericho and in Philippi the rich business woman Lydia and the unnamed demon-possessed girl Paul's prayer liberated. James is stressing that his brethren are his, not just because of nationality but because of the relationship forged.

There is no intention to mislead the readers; Christians wherever they live will be subject to temptations. First of all we must recognise that the word for "temptation" used here could have been equally well translated testing – testing as a trial, testing as a temptation. The English word temptation almost always carries the idea of a seduction into sin but oftentimes in Scripture it suggests a means of developing and strengthening our faith. When we were infants, before we learned to walk, we tested our legs. This was part of our growing-up experience. The LXX uses the same word of the Queen of Sheba who "came to prove him (Solomon) with hard questions" (1 Kings 10:1), and again when it is recorded that "God did tempt Abraham" (Gen 22:1). Tests or temptations are designed to develop our faith and make us strong for God.

James exhorts us to adopt a healthy attitude toward testing: "count it all joy", do not be afraid of the principle of testing but approach and enter the experience positively; make it an occasion of joy and triumph. It may not be a happy *experience* but *you* can be happy by adopting a positive attitude. "Count it all joy" – make a reckoning and let it be joyful; do not adopt a defeatist attitude such as "this was sent to get me down; this has happened to destroy me and my faith"; rather count it all joy. Your joy is not affected by changing circumstances – it remains when all around has turned against you. Approach the test, reckoning that your faith is stronger than any trial because it is fixed on the triumphant Saviour.

The great example when temptation comes is that of our Lord. In Luke 22:28, after He had plainly announced to His disciples His betrayal by Judas, after the strife among them as to who should be the greatest, He lifts them with a commendation: "Ye have been and have continued with me in my temptations and there are more to follow". He turned to Peter and said "Satan desires to hurt you but I have prayed for you, that your faith does not fail altogether". He had too work for all of them to do and failure in temptation could be detrimental to them and His work. The temptation of our Lord is described in the Gospels when Satan or the devil attacked Him in His loneliness, daring to make Him offers that very few would turn down.

Victory for the Lord in that particular temptation did not mean the devil could never return again and again. He would vary the appeal of temptation and the duration of it. On every occasion when he tempted the Lord he had to withdraw from defeat. So it becomes us to study and learn from the experiences of the Lord what we must do to triumph over the tempter with his varied temptations.

Other writers in the NT are well aware of the evil intentions of Satan. Matt 6:9-15 records the exemplary prayer of the Lord. There He taught his disciples how to pray – "lead us not into temptation but deliver us from evil". On another occasion

He finished His Gethsamane prayer in a similar way. Further He enjoins His own in 26:41 to "watch and pray that ye enter not into temptation". Never put yourself into a position that gives the tempter an advantage.

Paul also adds in his advice to the younger man Timothy a similar exhortation: "But they that will be rich (like Judas) fall into temptation and the snare bringing many self-inflicted hurtful experiences which ultimately can cause defeat" (1 Tim 6:9). Paul's advice is rather to follow after righteousness. A good example of this in the OT would be Joseph who would rather flee from evil desires as he did on the approach and advance of Potiphar's wife. We should follow the example of Abraham and steadfastly say "no" to the approach of the king of Sodom (Gen 14).

Because they had been scattered abroad and would feel the pangs of separation and loss of home, friends and possessions, James would promote a positive attitude: "consider it pure joy to have the ability to overcome". Although James had not been moved from Jerusalem, he was not ignorant of such trials. Having lost a dear friend and brother like Stephen and having to endure a wave of persecutions he advises positive thinking – consider it an honour to suffer and endure such circumstances for Christ. There is a link also with Peter his colleague who writes in 1 Peter 1:6 that we should greatly rejoice though we suffer grievous trials. Both perhaps remembered the sermon on the Mount when the Lord said, "Blessed are you when they persecute you, ridicule, falsely accuse you of all kinds of evil; rejoice and be glad for if they persecute you, your Father in heaven will reward you". We discover that the source of the temptation determines the purpose of it, as when our Lord's prayer is prayed (Matt 6:13) "do not lead us into temptation but deliver us from the evil one". The evil one tempts us with a view to disgracing us by soliciting us to evil as in the temptation of the Lord. On the other hand James deals with this experience as a testing in which and out of which we can rejoice, so increasing our faith in a trustworthy God. There is a little hymn which can help us in the midst of trial: "Take the name of Jesus with you as a shield from every snare. If temptations round you gather breathe that holy name in prayer" (Baxter). In other words to withstand temptation, stand with and for God.

The word "temptation" is used for both internal and external trials, some of which might offer pleasure, others threaten with pain. The word "temptations" is found again in v.12, a related word three times in v.3 and once in v.4.

Testings or temptations will fall to every one of us. James does not say "if ye fall" but the inevitable "when ye fall" for no one escapes this experience. The nature of trial of course changes. If the same trial affected us daily we would not only find monotony but there would be no challenge to faith. Faith grows and creates within us a desire to improve our appreciation of God. The trials inevitably fall not in the same way or from the same source and they are variegated as with different colours. The black test of sad and gruesome experiences or the bright offer of sins' temptation can hit us at unexpected moments. The tense of the verb is the aorist tense indicating that the experience is singular special and complete in itself (whenever you fall into). It is not constant; rather it is temporary and most unexpected. The same verb "fall" is used by Luke in the story of the man journeying from Jerusalem down to Jericho when "he fell among thieves". He certainly did not arrange it; he fell among them. Their action in causing bodily harm and stealing his possessions is a vivid picture of manifold temptations. The word is used again by Luke in Acts 27:41 to describe the total shipwreck and the complete salvation of all the passengers and crew. In both incidents earthly possessions were lost but no lives were lost. In the story of Luke 10, the traveller experienced the healing ministry of the good stranger and the ample provision for recovery with the promise of meeting again whereas in the story of the shipwreck all the souls were saved; all safely reached the shore. To hear the story from the Samaritan or the sailors would emphasise to us that there is one who is greater than our foes and who is able to deliver us.

Our faith is tested as to its reality and its health in at least five ways:

The Validity of it	Heb 11:1-3
The Vitality of it	Heb 11:4 to 12:3
The Vigilance of it	Heb 12:1-3
The Virtues of it	2 Peter 1:8
The Victory of it	Rom 4:20

The Validity   Faith can be tested and proved to be reliable, sound and well-grounded. It is workable and useful in the spiritual sphere of life.

The Vitality   One cannot traffic successfully in divine things without faith. It is the heart and principle of spiritual life and force.

The Vigilance   Like the sentry on active duty, faith must be ever watchful and circumspect, always at the ready to respond with action appropriate to the circumstances.

The Virtues   Faith has moral excellence, is always alert and ready for action, is robust to withstand the attack of an enemy. Only faith can develop the graces of likeness to Jesus the author and finisher of faith (Heb 12:2).

The Victory   Faith is the victory that overcomes, whatever battle is being fought in a spiritual realm. Faith works to defeat the power of an enemy.

You are not struggling in the dark, says James, you have a gift of faith. This gift brings the light of knowledge. Christians are not in the darkness of ignorance but "knowing" triumphantly that the trying or proving of this reality and quality of their faith as Paul in Rom 2:5 states, "worketh patience" and that faith has her sister, "hope", to assist; so we rejoice, says Paul. James now speaks of "all joy".

We do not go out of our way to invite temptation to increase our joy, but we accept the inevitability of its arrival and we use it to develop our faith; we "fall into" it. In this development of faith within the trial we show the quality of endeavour. We stand firm and strengthen the arms of our faith by holding on to God and His promises.

The word "patience" is interesting and perhaps not strong enough to reveal its true meaning. "Patience" is strength that has withstood the batterings of trials but is also the outcome of a working faith. This is active faith responding to the onslaught of trial and converting the trial to a victory. It also gives staying power or patience to those who are being tested. We emerge much stronger and ready to face further trials.

To prove or try is really to test (*dokimion*) as for example, sterling coinage which is proved genuine and unalloyed. "Worketh" refers to the process that produces the result. It is sometimes beyond our comprehension to find valid reasons for the trial but if perseverance and patience are the results we shall develop an increasing ability to withstand pressure. This is perseverance with patience – the desirable fruit from the testing of our faith.

4 *Hupomone* is ability to withstand pressure, plus the ability to accept persecutions, to defeat them and to make the victor stronger. The result of this success makes us perfect (complete for a given purpose). It is used to describe an animal tested and proved acceptable to be a sacrifice for the pleasure of God. What surprised the heathen and religious persecutors of Christians was the attitude of the Christians to awful suffering. In the midst of it they sing and praise God.

"That ye may be perfect and entire" means entire in every part; "wanting nothing" – that there is no deficiency. James has been positive; now negatively he sets out the truth of one who never surrenders in a battle, never gives up in a fight and who is marked by continuity of faith. Such a one has every positive attribute – he is perfect and entire – and lacks none of them.

Another book in our NT addressed specially to Jews who had accepted Christ as Saviour but had not abandoned their old way of life is Hebrews. One of the major themes in that book is faith, first mentioned in 4:2 where it is looked on as an initial exercise. In chs. 10 and 11 we make acquaintance with men and women whose faith was tested. Each test was different in appeal, approach and severity. Faith is proved able to cope with every test irrespective of severity or nature. Faith holds tenaciously to God and His promises. Character is formed and the soul tested anchors itself in the risen triumphant Lord. While the trials vary in severity and nature and arise from different sources, all of them are useful in bringing victory and maturity to those under trial. Faith works and faith grows with an ability to persevere and stand firm in the face of severe trial or temptation. The greatest example of such faith is found in 12:1-3. Each of those mentioned as having endured the trial of their faith found that God's grace is ample and sufficient and God's power is made perfect is weakness.

5 James emphasises the priority to be given to wisdom in vv.5-8:

> Wisdom and its Source   v.5
> Wisdom and its Search   v.6

Wisdom and its Secret	v.7
Wisdom and its Stability	v.8

To lack wisdom might be a condition which is self-imposed. There ought, however, to be no scarcity of it; yet alas it is scarce in the world and sometimes scarce among Christians. To lack wisdom is not an excuse for being without it. To have Christ is to have the wisdom of God (1 Cor 1:24). In that section of Paul's letter Christ is made unto us wisdom and yet the question is asked by him: "where is the wise?" Not the worldly wise but the wise in the divine economy. Therefore if any lack it is not because God is not generous for He has plenty to give. The scarcity is self-imposed.

The importance of having wisdom is apparent in a world that is full of ignorance. This wisdom finds its source in God. God is described as the all-wise God. James opens this subject here but expands it in 3:13-17. Here the emphasis is on the essential need to have it. The manner of receiving is by asking. This verb "to ask" is found five times in the epistle. Here it is in the present active imperative tense. Sometimes it is translated to desire, beg, require, crave, call for. It therefore describes a penitent who is encouraged to keep on asking as he received. God is the source of wisdom and Christ is made unto us wisdom. This topic occurring again and again in this short epistle emphasises the importance and necessity of wisdom in our dealing with God and with others. When Paul writes to the Corinthian church, as already noted, he plainly states that Christ is the wisdom and the power of God. Because we belong to Christ there is no need to be short on wisdom. Yet even Corinth was questioned from Paul: "Is there not a wise man among you?" Wisdom is more than intelligence or knowledge. Too many Corinthians appeared intelligent but lacked wisdom.

At the end of v.4 we need lack nothing if we allow faith to operate and produce fruit in us. Part of that fruit includes wisdom. However v.5 shows the possibility of lacking wisdom. He is not saying we lack knowledge but we are short in the application of it. To ask God simply and sincerely to make up what we lack and what we badly need – wisdom – is a profitable exercise. It is possible to be very knowledgeable but most unwise. Solomon had tremendous knowledge but became a fool. Men can be heady with knowledge, cold as an iceberg and simply stupid.

Well might we ask what is wisdom? Both Old and New Testaments have passages shedding light on this question. Among the wisdom books of the OT many statements are found relative to the subject. Solomon discloses its source in Prov 2:6 and elaborates on its many activities: "the Lord gives wisdom and from his mouth comes knowledge and understanding". The imparting and receiving of revelation from God to us requires wisdom to accept, assimilate and then to have guidance. In the NT Paul in 1 Cor 3:19 tells us of wise men in this world who are fools before God. The message of Paul to Corinth was not enticing words of man's wisdom but was centred on Christ the wisdom and power of God. In our verse here James makes the supposition that some "lack wisdom" (not knowledge or even understanding although these activities are necessary) but how to apply truth in a correct and profitable way.

This can be readily obtained by asking from the source and fountain of wisdom. There is no unwillingness on God's part to give.

James now draws attention to the God of a full hand and to the saint with a pure mind. He reveals a God willing to give and expects the saints to see their need of receiving wisdom. Acting priests of old had no blemishes to disqualify them. Here James indicates there is no need for a deficiency of wisdom. Wisdom is not philosophy which is found only at an intellectual level. Ropes defines wisdom as the supreme and divine quality of the soul. Every priestly one needs that quality of soul.

There is no excuse for lacking wisdom, when you make yourself available for God's service. God will supply what you lack. The story of the building of the tabernacle is interesting. There was obviously a great need for skilled workmen and to their skill God would add His wisdom (Exod 31). Bezaleel and Aholiab, from different tribes and probably unknown to each other, find themselves engaged by Moses for the vast work of constructing and fitting out the tabernacle. They needed wisdom to add to their skill and this God supplied freely. God supplies in ample measure when we ask in faith, nothing wavering. Faith removes the evil of doubt and strongly rests in the simple promises of God, "Ask and ye shall receive", but the asking must be in faith.

The condition of being short of wisdom is worldwide. This is not being short of intelligence or brain power or knowledge. Many intelligent, knowledgeable persons have been most unwise in application and attitude. No one would doubt the intelligence and knowledge of Solomon, yet how unwise he was to discount the simple trust and application of faith. He dies in disgrace, though exceedingly wealthy in this world. His character is morally besmudged. The world of men and women in Old and New Testaments, and in the centuries since including our own day and generation, have many examples of high intelligence in those who were seriously short of wisdom. This in spite of the fact that God has ample supplies of wisdom and God gives liberally. Solomon who in 1 Kings 3:9 seeks help from God finds that God gives willingly and abundantly, assumes later an attitude of pleasing self and shuts out God and inevitably falls in disgrace.

6 Wisdom can be sought in faith. Care should be taken not to ask with doubt and wavering. Faith confidently asks. We do not have confidence in ourselves but in the all-wise God. It is not weakness to admit our lack; it is an act of faith to trust and rely on God. Those who waver are not fully trusting. "Nothing doubting" is in the middle voice, so reflects upon the supplicant. Firstly, this verse is describing a penitent in need and he is in the attitude and act of praying. He is not in a public gathering; he is alone with God. He is the supplicant and God is the provider. There is no assumption being made of special phrases which might excite others who listen. This person is alone with God; he is alone without vain words. He has free access to God's presence and he has a fervent need. He therefore asks as a supplicant, prompted by a felt personal need. Both the fact that he asks God and the manner of his asking insist that this is faith at work. Faith connects him to God. Indeed faith assumes great importance throughout this letter here in our approach to God. Whatever our deficiency, faith sees there is in God the sufficiency to meet our need.

In v.5 James directs the penitent saint to address his asking to God and gives good reason why he should so do. God is described as a giving God and the quality and quantity of His giving is lavish and pertinent to the request. God does not keep reminding the supplicant saint of His giving nor does God get angry and upbraid if His offer is rejected and incorrectly used. He keeps giving. Now in v.6 the supplicant is taught how to ask God, it must be with confidence in the God now being besought. To ask in faith is to have implicit confidence; it is to be free from doubt and wavering. We ought not to show a lack of confidence as we petition God nor to have an inner sense of disbelief (which may never surface for others to see) known only to ourselves and God. Our asking ought to be with simplicity and without secondary motive. Here Paul and James strike the same note; see Rom 12:8; 2 Cor 9:12, 13.

The vivid illustration of a restless wave at the mercy of a strong wind is the simple way James illustrates the to and fro of the unsettled heart. Asking in faith is putting down the anchor of faith, attached to the rock that can never move. The man of faith asks and remains rock solid in his faith in God. Others without faith are like the moving, changing tide, restless and unstable.

7   Well might we ask: why ask in faith? This explanation takes us into the inner shrine of the man and reveals his thoughts. That man, the man who is minus faith in his prayers, now finds that even when he asks God, the Lord who carries the gift of God to the saints, will not have anything for him. "That man" – such is James' emphasis – now finds that the God of infinite resource will not reward unbelief nor will the Lord carry the answer of blessing to the faithless man.

Asking from God requires faith in its exercise, otherwise the God who loves to give and the Lord the minister bringing the gift are deprived equally.

8   Instead of speaking of man in general (including both sexes) James now speaks of man (*anēr*). Usually this word makes the distinction between the sexes, and would refer only to the male.

The description, "double-minded" is interesting. It is found only in the writings of James, appearing again in 4:8. If James has coined this compound word (and he alone uses it), we must look at it immediately. It is a combination of two Greek words: *dis* meaning "twice" and *psuchē* meaning "soul". This man has a double soul, or as John Bunyan would say, he is "Mr Facing-Both-Ways". He is a person with no firm conviction. His tenor of life is then described by James as "*unstable* in all his ways". He is unreliable, unsteady, fickle and reels to and fro like a drunk man. He cannot walk a straight path; he has no firm convictions about anything. James deals with this responsible brother and totally condemns him. These are the Reuben characteristics being displayed; he is uncertain, unstable, unsuccessful. Indeed from Adam onward men have tried to serve two masters, Baal and Jehovah, God and mammon; to put their hand to the plough and look back (Luke 9:62); to be double-souled.

9 The "but" may take us back to v.2 with its advice and admonition. The joy of v.2 remains in spite of unhelpful circumstances. Now there can be differences between brothers and sisters financially, socially, intellectually, but in the Lord there ought to be no differences. The world divides people into "the haves and have-nots" but this is not entertained amongst the Lord's people. James is very practical and confronts this problem, a problem which divides and destroys the fellowship of the Lord's people.

Firstly, finance, or the lack of it, can make differences between saints. There are those who are poor and others rich in this world's goods. Both, says James, are subject to temptation. The brother of low degree (poor in the estimate of a material world) and the rich, the brother loaded with riches of this world, both face temptation.

James writes a message for each. The poor brother of low degree, can rejoice in that he has been exalted with heaven's wealth. He may be poor, yet rich in exalted graces given freely by God. God lifts him up from poverty to find new riches in Christ. He has spiritual blessings which enrich the soul and gladden his heart. He finds even if poor by the world's standard, that he is rich. Fanny Crosby wrote, "I have Christ what want I more". Good has made the poor of this world rich in faith.

"In that he is made low" is a play on the verb which is found elsewhere in our NT (Matt 11:28; Luke 1:53; Rom 12:16; 2 Cor 7:6, 10; James 4:6; 1 Peter 5:5). In v.9 one brother is of low degree; in v.10 the other is made low so both are on same level says James – there is no difference. The rich man of v.10 received salvation as a poor sinner, just like the poor man in v.9. Grace is the principle that disregards economic differences.

Jesus said, "I am meek and lowly" (Matt 11:29). This is a heart condition and not an economic worldly condition covered by a lack of worldly things.

The subject of pride is introduced by James and in vv. 9, 10 there is parallelism centring on the verb to have pride. The two positions mentioned, high and low, are equivalent to the two descriptions rich and poor. Both of these folks can have pride, so a poor man can just be as guilty as a rich man. It is important to notice that James designates the poor man as "a brother" and he easily relates to him whereas in referring to the other person described as rich there is no mention of him being a brother. He appreciates that the strangers scattered abroad would be poor in the majority and because of their economic circumstances they would require greater encouragement. Attempts to discover who this rich man is have not really been successful and James, whilst not acknowledging him as a brother, may well be thinking of a rich Jew who having moved away from Jerusalem had prospered in business. The comparison he makes is interesting. The rich man is like a wild flower that withers, fades and dies. The picture can easily fit a non-christian Jew. Similar impression is made when James again deals with a rich man in 2:6-9; 5:6. He may even possibly engage in persecuting the christian Jew with others of the community of Jews. The rich man is like a wild flower, which, subject to the hot dry wind called the sirocco, quickly withers and passes away. James may well be drawing from the wells of Isa 40:6-7; like grass that flowers, the rich quickly wither because the breath of the Lord blows on such.

While the world would divide people into the "haves" and "have-nots" this is not the standard that should be entertained among the Lord's people, for our Lord did not have lands, riches or wealth when He was here as a man. Did He not say: "the foxes have holes (by day) the birds of the air have nests (by night) but I have nowhere to lay my head"? In all this He was able to say of Himself, "I am meek and lowly" (Matt 11:29). He was neither hesitant, undecided, or easily moved. He was not like the tossing wave of the sea, He was definite in His teaching and the perfect example of His teaching. Later it would be written of Him that He who was rich, by His own choice became poor. Riches or poverty did not influence Him in His testimony and in His relationship with other people.

10 The Scriptures acquaint us of not a few rich men. We do know from Luke 16 that to die depending on your earthly riches will mean hell as your abode. This exhortation is not saying, however, that it is wrong for a Christian to be rich. This verse is seeking to have the joy of the poor man (v.9) as the enjoyed possession of the rich man. His joy of soul is not to be related to earthly possessions but to the fact that with all his worldly riches he remains humble and make his boast in the Lord.

The contrast of vv.9,10 cements a bond between the poor and deprived saints of this world's goods (v.9) and the rich who has not put his faith in riches which can fade away. The death of Christ which lifts up the poor, brings down the high. It levels humanity but it also elevates the rich and poor to be eternally rich.

In v.10 the rich brother is told that his life is as the flower of grass (not as grass) which does not last under heat and is the first property of grass to vanish. When James uses the expression here he may be borrowing from Isa 40:6 which of course was a chapter used to identify John Baptist (v.3, cf. Matt 3:2), who preached repentance to rich and poor and pointed to Jesus as the Lamb of God. Riches of earth perish like the burning grass – it is lush one day and gone the next.

Whilst James reminds the rich of the fleeting nature of this world's riches he goes further and states that the rich man like any other man will pass away. This exodus will be quick, complete and final.

11 This explanation, introduced by "for", is specially designed for the rich brother. More is said about the rich man than the poor for James understands that, whilst all expect the poor to pass away and be forgotten, the man who sets his heart on this world's goods also will pass away, or rather as our AV says "fade away" indicating a process. His journey with its travels will end. The rich man shall "fade away", "shall perish", "the light will be extinguished", his ways will end. The dry wind (called the sirocco) will burn up, dry up and wither the most beautiful flower till it is perished.

The quotation as already noted is from Isa 40:6-7. The picture is of complete dereliction. All the verbs are in the aorist tense depicting the amazing rapidity and finality of the destruction. The application is found at the end of the verse with the expression "so also shall the rich man fade away in his ways". The connection with v.8 should be noted. The double-souled is unstable in his ways and in v.11 the rich man shall fade away in his ways. We ask the question: could not this be the same typical person? The end of this rich man is graphically outlined. His departure is quick and painful. Any beauty or grace perishes quickly and his journey ends like a dying plant that has been scorched.

12 This verse seems to complete this discussion on the social differences between poor and rich. James now speaks to poor and rich together. They can be "blessed", whether rich or lacking in this world's goods. This happy man can and does endure *testing*. This blessedness is of course for the present.

From vv.2-12 we have:

The test of faith	v.3
The trial of buffeting in the storms of life	v.6
The trial of poverty	v.9
The snare of riches	vv.10,11

To this list you may add, but James has now turned to the goal of victory. The happiness of success in christian living is not dependent on changing conditions of this life on earth. These are matters which are common to all: all are subject to temptation, all can be successful despite adverse circumstances, all can know satisfaction.

Temptations change in their substance and timing but meet them we must. So to endure temptation is not to evade it or run away from it. The solid attitude of facing it and doing so with steadfast courage is enjoined by James. Success can be achieved without giving in under trial. We, whether rich or poor, must endure it as a competitor who in training accepts the most rigorous exercises; then we will be happy or blessed in ourselves. The experience of enduring without giving in or opting out produces steadfastness and a quiet feeling of success. The verse deals with the experience and attitude in the trial and the resultant experience after it. To endure it manfully is to follow the example of the Lord when personally tried. He endured such contradiction of sinners; He endured the cross, despised the shame; He emerged from the trial as the blessed Man. Many other examples of men and women who endured under severe trial and successfully emerged with the commendation "blessed" and the crown of victory or the crown of life are found in Scripture. The word "crown" (*stephanos*) is used to describe a royal crown, or the garland reserved for the victorious athlete. It is the emblem of success. The blessedness is for the man (*anēr*) who when being tried, endures and, with his heart set, his mind is stayed on the Lord who promises to be with us in the trial with His supporting love and gives His reward. The knowledge that the Lord's love is set on us gives the necessary strength to endure the fiercest fiery trial.

Peter in 1 Peter 2:20 enlarges on this verse by stating the reward for enduring is from God. There is a commendation for the victorious saint. The trial is like a race that demands endurance and the crown is for those who complete the course. The reward is the crown of life. This expression is used in a letter to one of the seven churches of Asia, Smyrna (the church that was under severe trial). The members of that church were encouraged and exhorted to be faithful until death (physical death). The crown is the emblem of success, joy and glory and is awarded for spiritual stamina and steadfastness and staying power. The faith and love for God must be wholehearted, unreserved and unchanged in the midst of unhelpful conditions. Our faith and confidence should be unshakeable saying, if necessary, like the suffering servant Job that "though he slay me yet will I trust him". The success in the trial is matched by the reward, the crown of life. The elders addressed by Peter in 1 Peter 5:10 would be encouraged in their trials and labours by the anticipation of the future reward, the crown of life. Again the confident Paul in 2 Tim 4:8 when facing the death penalty for his love for and obedience to the Lord would be the kind of example that James would set out in this verse. The genuineness of faith in the trial proves its reality and ultimately gets its reward.

13 This is advice from James when the trial is raging. Do not accuse God, either publicly or privately. To blame God can be harmful if the temptation is evil. God does prove and test; God tested Abraham often. Perhaps the greatest test was when God asked for Isaac. Abraham obeyed when no doubt he could not see the sense of it; but God never tempts to advance the cause of evil. Our attitude when adverse circumstances arrive should not be to blame God. Job's wife said to him in the midst of a fiery trial, "Curse God"; or blame Him and perish. She advised her husband to give in to the circumstances and to deny his faith in God. Job resisted the temptation and was crowned by God. Sometimes we blame God for our failures by saying God acts in His sovereignty.

Every man finds opposing forces active within his mind pushing him in different directions. In Israel these two tendencies are called the *Yetser Hatob*, which describes a good tendency, and *Yetser Hara* the opposite, evil desire; but as to the origin of the tendencies there is no help. James is now definitely stating that God is neither the source nor the operator of evil.

It is noticeable that the word "evil" is in the plural – God cannot be tempted with evils, i.e. by evil practices or schemes. Again God never uses evil practices or evil works to tempt men. It is true that He tests to prove reality, to result in a growing confidence in Him.

The evasion of responsibility began in Eden with Adam blaming "the woman". The danger of this is that in the last analysis God is blamed. Dealing with sin in himself, Paul argues in Rom 7:15-24: "It is no more I but sin that dwelleth in me". This of course he shows to be wrong, yet man would often try to attribute a wrong choice to anybody but himself. The right of choice in options is ours and ours alone.

14 James sets before us plainly the simple steps that ultimately lead to disaster and death. The origin of the temptation is in man's own lust and not in God. Every man is influenced by internal desires not so much by external powers. Within every man there is a monitor making a decision. To be drawn away by a selfish craving for good (Phil 1:23) or for evil (Rom 7:7), set before us like bait laid to catch a fish or a hunted animal, demands a decision by the tempted man. Usually the bait is beautiful to look at and enticing to possess (2 Pet 2:14-18), enjoyable at the time but fatally damaging. The catch is made but the choice was the decisive action of the man. No one is exempt from this temptation for everyone has the lust of sin:

Every man is tempted	– Common Experience
When he is drawn away	– Carnal Exertion
of his own lust	– Corrupt Exercise
and enticed	– Completely Entangled

The temptation is external and common to man, seeking to allure by strong illicit desire. Whilst this word does describe the fleshly illicit desire, and often it is to be found associated with sexual passions, it must not be held to refer only to that here. His own lust is appealed to by the temptation which is the tendency for wrongdoing. The verbs used are very forceful – like a forceful dragging in the inner man to an attractive bait. The fisher disguises the bait and makes it so attractive that the fish already having a strong desire, is unable to get away from the hook and soon it is hooked.

The fact that James says every man (and woman), shows the need to be on the watchtower and be able to say definitely, No. The individual responsibility is emphasised in the "every man". This temptation by its nature is intensely personal. The decision to succumb is usually taken in secret and is very private. Jacob's sons present us with examples of evil desires springing up from within. They hated Joseph without a cause. Saul's jealousy of David is an equally pertinent warning.

15 The sequence is clearly defined as to how the decision is made:

Step
1 The approval of lust (v.14)
2 The mother lust with the implanted seed.
3 Birth of the child sin.
4 End of sin in death.

The will leads to lust and lust to sin (definite article is used to describe *the* sin). Desire is not the act of sin but often it is the influence in the seat of decision.

Note the two time markers "then" and "when". "Then" shows the inevitable timing and sequence; "when" the vital wrong response, the motherly action of conception and bearing the seed to birth. Sin when it is finished (the child is born) bringeth forth division, death, disgrace.

The chain of events unbroken, ultimately leads to the shame of a broken testimony, for the seduction of lust in privacy becomes the scourge of open lasciviousness. It becomes full-grown sin, perhaps starting in an innocent and small way. As another has said, "Sin from its birth is big with death".

Prov 5:9 would detail the course of a sin that has brought down the mighty and blighted not only personal testimony but a good family name, sadly the church has been disgraced from time to time and the name of the Lord impugned. Many examples are within the Scriptures to warn us of the hidden rocks and the frailty of human nature.

16 This seems a fitting appeal to the message of vv.13-15. "Do not err" is probably referring to two issues:

1. Attributing blame to God for your own sin.
2. Thinking that the temptation originated with God.

It may also be a strong appeal from James with deep affection. "My brethren" would be his normal greeting but to emphasise his affection for them he describes them as "my beloved brethren".

Error can be caused by:

1. Ignorance of God's word (Matt 22:29)
2. Misjudging God and His power (Gal 6:7)
3. Accepting an enticing wave of philosophies (Col 2:4,8)
4. Accepting wrong doctrine (2 Tim 2:8)

James is here encouraging caution and giving counsel for them to receive, that they may be balanced in their thinking. He well knows it is so easy to blame others instead of searching one's own heart.

17 Instead of attributing or apportioning blame to God for the trial, there is now a statement of fact to disprove any suspicion of allegation against God. First because of His many gifts (v.17) then of His own will and its purpose as stated in v.18. The gifts are described first as "good" then as "perfect", followed by a character statement of the Father and His stated intentions for us. First let us draw attention to the two words used for "gift". The first mention strictly refers to an act of giving. Paul in Phil 4:15 thinks of it as a credit and not a debit. The active sense may well signify a giving rather than a single gift so the manner of disposition rules out any idea of wrong motive in the Giver. Essentially the "Father of lights" gives but what and how He gives is very important. The giving is good and the particular perfect gift has substance only for our benefit. The manner and the actual substantial gift come down from above as to their source.

Thereafter James indicates not the sphere from whence it came but the Person who originates and gives. He describes Him as Father, i.e. the source. "The Father of Lights" may well refer us back to the creation story when God made differences with the introduction of light or lights to creation – the sun, the moon, and the stars were different lights. They all had their purpose as lights or reflectors. Yet they all came from the same Creator; they were all associated with the manifestation of light in the heavens. They were lights (plural) and of differing strengths but all intended for good. The first recorded spoken work of God at creation was "let there be light" (Gen 1:3; Isa 45:6,9). Each gift bringing light varied but all for the good of creation and all from the source, the Father of lights. The fact that all came down not only indicates the source, but the constant giving of power from the Father. This is the only scripture which describes the Creator as the Father of lights. In the natural sphere the lights themselves might fluctuate according to the laws of creation causing movement and eclipses bringing shadow and variation. The Father of lights knows no eclipses nor shadows; the intensity and quality of His giving is eternally unchanged.

18 James now indicates there was no pressure brought to bear on the Father to give. It was "of his own wish" – the Father had absolute freedom from necessity or any other influence. "He begat us" is a reference to new birth and the Father's responsibility in it. This new birth is also a gift from the Father and is in contrast to a birth into sinnership with all its shadows and darkness. The verb used normally describes a mother's input into a birth and it seems that James is using the paternal and maternal language to emphasise in a striking way the goodness of the giving of the Father of lights. Since the verb is in the aorist tense it points to the single and complete act of regeneration.

The instrument used is the word of truth and like John, James now refers to the *logos* (the instrument) of truth. Could this be when John found the need to speak aloud? God's gift is the *logos* and God gave His Son so that new birth could be experienced. The word of truth for John was not just a doctrine to hold but a person to accept.

The purpose of being born again becomes a divine intention. "We" were probably initially James and fellow saints at Jerusalem plus the saved of the twelve tribes now scattered abroad, but of course the passage is applicable to all the saints then and now; they are to be a kind of firstfruits of His creatures. The idea of Christians as a firstfruits of a purchased creation is truth that Paul deals with in Rom 8:19-23. The verb "to bring to the birth" is used here and in Rom 8:15. In Romans the idea is of natural and spiritual birth whereas here it is spiritual birth. Other such NT occurrences are in 2 Cor 6:7; Eph 1:13; Col 1:5; 2 Tim 2:15. New birth is the sovereign act of God using the word of truth and those born again become the firstfruits of a big harvest.

Note

15 The verb *apokueō* (to bring forth) occurs in the NT only here and in v.18 where it is translated "begat".

III. Faith and Truth (1:19-27)

v.19 "Wherefore, my beloved brethren, let every man be swift to hear, slow to speak, slow to wrath:
v.20 For the wrath of man worketh not the righteousness of God.
v.21 Wherefore lay apart all filthiness and superfluity of naughtiness, and receive with meekness the engrafted word, which is able to save your souls.
v.22 But be ye doers of the word, and not hearers only, deceiving your own selves.
v.23 For if any be a hearer of the word, and not a doer, he is like unto a man beholding his natural face in a glass:
v.24 For he beholdeth himself, and goeth his way, and straightway forgetteth what manner of man he was.
v.25 But whoso looketh into the perfect law of liberty, and continueth *therein*, he being not a forgetful hearer, but a doer of the work, this man shall be blessed in his deed.
v.26 If any man among you seem to be religious, and bridleth not his tongue but deceiveth his own heart, this man's religion *is* vain.
v.27 Pure religion and undefiled before God and the Father is this, To visit the fatherless and widows in their affliction, *and* to keep himself unspotted from the world."

19 This verse begins a new sub-section which is intensely practical, beginning with an affectionate description. It has an introduction like a new beginning and is consequential to the experience of new birth with new life and a new objective. The obvious signs are practical enough for others to see the change. We leave our old ways and habits, we now display the evidence of new life with:

1. A readiness to listen
2. A reluctance to speak
3. A ruminating before wrath or making a judgment.

The writer, James, is an example of all three factors. His was a silent waiting at the Jerusalem conference (Acts 15) for all to speak. Then having listened well without interrupting, he considered the matter and gave a balanced judgment.

Samuel the prophet (1 Sam 3:10) as a boy had his ear tuned to listen to God's voice. His words have become famous; "Speak, for thy servant heareth".

It has been wisely said that what goes in then comes out but also stays in. We must therefore be swift to hear. Of the true Servant we have the words of Isaiah, "He wakeneth me morning by morning to hear as the learned".

We are given two ears to hear and one mouth to speak. Take in with both ears and have a capacity to hold what you hear. An old Scottish saying notes of some: "you hear but don't listen". We should hear and consider what we hear (Mark 4:24) and we should consider how we hear (Luke 8:18). We should cultivate the attitude of Cornelius "we are here to listen" (Acts 10:33). Our listening should be without bias and interruption. Indeed listening attentively is the first step to obedience, taken only by the one "that heareth my word".

Then says James be "slow to speak". He is not describing a difficulty in speaking but rather an exercised control of what we say. James may well have been reading Prov 10:19; 13:3; 15:2; 17:27; 18:13, 21, as he writes this verse. When words are many, sin is not absent and he who guards his tongue preserves himself. Tongue wagging in an unrestrained manner can be harmful to both speaker and hearer. When words are said they cannot be unsaid, no matter how much we would try. There is sin and folly in too many words (Eccl 12:3).

20 "For the wrath of man worketh not the righteousness of God" is an explanation for the advice of v.19 Swift to take in (hearing), slow to give out by mouth and tongue or hands and feet. The wrath (*orgē*) of man is an uncontrolled outburst of anger which has been deep-seated but now surfaces violently. The verb "to work" describes the end product of labour, the action of making and setting forth a resultant work. The wrath of man never helps forward the declaration of truth relative to the righteousness of God or the righteous character of God.

The righteousness of God may be the state into which the belligerent man can enter when he condemns sin in himself and by faith is transferred to a righteous standing before God and man. Our tongues and all our members must now be under strict control and all used to promote the rights of God and His righteous character.

21 When we understand the harm and damage to our testimony and to the testimony of the saints caused by our uncontrolled outbursts of anger we shall take appropriate action. Negative action (uprooting weeds) and positive action (implanting the word) assume great importance. We are invited to receive (i.e. to make our own) the implanted word. Here James uses horticultural expressions to explain his teaching. Unwanted weeds must be uprooted and removed, the vacant space to be filled with the good of meekness, the grace of which makes the ground good. The life-giving Word has the sustenance required for healthy growth. It can preserve us from the active or passive forms of sinful desires and positively keep our souls spiritually healthy. "The engrafted word" is given divinely, not acquired by study; it has all the potential to preserve and improve our spiritual health but if saints starve themselves of the good word of God they will deteriorate and become spiritually unhealthy. The word that brought us eternal life can keep us healthy. It is essential that Christians deeply root the good seed of the Word in their hearts and keep removing the weeds of sin to allow the Word to grow. The engrafted word is no less than a revelation sown in the heart, the good seed of that Sower who only sows good seed and should be prized as such, so James uses the imperatives "lay aside" and "receive" to insist upon ridding the soul of what is harmful and replacing it with the health promoting word.

22 "Be ye doers" is imperative aorist. The resolve is to hold the word in our hearts and let it be the monitor to guide us in every department of life, not like a sponge taking in and unless squeezed never gives out. We are expected to live out the word we have received. If not, we are like a barren fruit tree. If we be but hearers only we deceive or cheat ourselves. James would remember reports of the teaching of the Lord Jesus at various times during the days of His flesh; see Matt 7:21; Luke 6:47. First the Lord taught that His word would be received by faith and then the obedient one would accept His requests as commands. Hearing is not the end product; it is but the beginning. James is very clear that faith is first and works are necessary to a successful and happy christian life. He would agree with Paul who in Rom 10:18 states that "faith cometh by hearing and hearing by the word of God" and the initial act of faith introduces the person into a life of practising faith. To reason otherwise is to cheat yourself.

23-25   In vv. 23-25 there is a striking contrast made. Two persons are contrasted. The Word is likened to a mirror used by both men. They both hear; in this there is no difference. The Word is accepted by both; they both use the mirror and they both get a true picture of themselves. Both men get the message that refers to themselves and both know the action that they ought to take. The first man cheats: he conveniently dismisses the message of the mirror; in doing so he does himself harm. The other also looks into the mirror; James describes the mirror as "the perfect law of liberty" and looking into it as a continuing exercise. This man keeps on taking action and making adjustments. He is described not as a cheat but as a happy or blessed man. The moral of the examples chosen is surely to help us not to deceive ourselves and be miserable, rather to read the Word and allow the Word to read us and be obedient and happy. The mirror is stated to be the "perfect law of liberty". This is seemingly a contradiction; a binding law producing as it is obeyed. The feeling of being blessed is the personal experience of the second man.

The changes in the tenses of the various verbs become interesting and instructive. The first man looks (aorist) but the message he got was dismissed. He saw his natural face, or the face of his birth; he then forgot (another aorist); he goeth his way (perfect), that is, he continued to go away. His reasoning was not just suspect; it was deliberately wrong, he cheated. The second example shows a man who looks closely into the mirror; to him it is the perfect law and he keeps on looking, i.e. he continues in this exercise. In other words, this book was attractive and instructive, he became a doer, not a forgetful hearer but a man of action, a man of faith with good works. The sequel is that this man is blessed in the doing. A future tense is used in such a way as to say this man has the blessing now and will keep on enjoying the blessing forevermore. Thus the engrafted word of v.21 with saving quality is the enlightening word with the perfect rule of freedom and offers an endowment too. The doer is blessed in his deed.

James in his epistle constantly uses contrasts, eg:

    Ch.1   Two men look into the mirror

Ch.2　Two men visit the synagogue
Ch.3　Two uses of the tongue
Ch.4　Two types of men – one humble, the other proud
Ch.5　Two men, one rich, the other a labourer

26 There is a strong link with vv. 19-20 in the outworking of the righteousness of God and also with the two men of vv.22-25. The "any man" introduction of v.23 is repeated in v.26. The hypocrisy of hearing and not doing whilst feigning the opposite, shows up again in another manner. If any man thinks himself to be, or seems to be, something whilst in fact he is the opposite, he cheats himself (cf. v.22), and might be able to deceive the saints for a time. The man knows he is a fraud and it will not be long till others know too. He "seems to be religious" probably refers to how he dresses and the company he seeks. In those days it was easy to pigeonhole men and women by their clothes. This individual was given over to a sanctified order. The test of reality is when he opens his mouth; his tongue reveals his hypocrisy and the emptiness of his religion. Only James of all the NT writers uses this word "religion" (cf. 3:2). It is there in 3:2 that he elaborates on the power of the tongue. Here the man opens his mouth and destroys all the make-believe. He looks alright till he talks. His smart religious appearance and his verbal testimony are in discord. Many a good man has been deceived, like Jacob (Gen 37:33) or Isaac (Gen 27:22) but usually as time proceeds the deceiver is exposed. As soon as this man opens his mouth the vanity of his religion is exposed. Finally the only person deceived is the man himself. This test of bridling the tongue, only found in James, is also raised again in ch. 3. By opening the mouth to speak he denied the smart appearance and succeeded only in fooling himself.

27 This is where James shows the pureness of a *bona fide* religion. He states first positively and then negatively "pure and undefiled". There is no mixture and no hypocrisy. James also states it is not so much a show before men but before God. The practical proof is visiting to help the deprived and lonely. He also adds, "to keep himself unspotted from the world". The Pharisees devoured widows' houses and then showed their hypocrisy by long ineffective prayers. Godly discretion and spiritual wisdom ought to be exercised by elders who do this work of love. They must have regard to their own testimony in the world and also the good name of those visited. The ungodly world is quick to besmudge the testimony of both. The great wisdom of the Lord in sending out the disciples two by two is evident, as one considers a situation like this.

Note

21 The word "engrafted" (*emphutos*) occurs only here in the NT.

IV. Faith and Temperance (2:1-13)

v.1 "My brethren, have not the faith of our Lord Jesus Christ, *the Lord* of glory, with respect of persons.
v.2 For if there come unto your assembly a man with a gold ring, in goodly apparel, and there come in also a poor man in vile raiment;
v.3 And ye have respect to him that weareth the gay clothing, and say unto him, Sit thou here in a good place; and say to the poor, Stand thou there, or sit here under my footstool:
v.4 Are ye not then partial in yourselves, and are become judges of evil thoughts?
v.5 Hearken, my beloved brethren, Hath not God chosen the poor of this world rich in faith, and heirs of the kingdom which he hath promised to them that love him?
v.6 But ye have despised the poor. Do not rich men oppress you, and draw you before the judgment seats?
v.7 Do not they blaspheme that worthy name by the which ye are called?
v.8 If ye fulfil the royal law according to the scripture, Thou shalt love thy neighbour as thyself, ye do well:
v.9 But if ye have respect to persons, ye commit sin, and are convinced of the law as transgressors.
v.10 For whosoever shall keep the whole law, and yet offend in one *point*, he is guilty of all.
v.11 For he that said, Do not commit adultery, said also Do not kill. Now if thou commit no adultery, yet if thou kill, thou art become a transgressor of the law.
v.12 So speak ye, and so do, as they that shall be judged by the law of liberty.
v.13 For he shall have judgment without mercy, that hath shewed no mercy; and mercy rejoiceth against judgment."

James 2:1-4   Have or Hold the Faith of the Lord
       2:5-13   Heeding the Promises of an Unchanging God
       2:14-26 Harvesting the Profit of a Working Faith

In 2:1-4 we meet:
    v.1   The challenge of faith
    v.2   The contrast of visitors
    v.3   The condemnation of saints
    v.4   The conflict within

1   The affection of James permeates the epistle again and again. He describes them as his brothers. His love for them was real, and would remain real and warm, even though he would strongly chastise them and condemn their practices. The relationship of brother to brother could not be severed. It was precious, permanent, and practical. The family privilege among many others was to be the faith of our Lord, i.e. to hold all that He taught by precept and by practice. The distinctive nature of this privilege is found in the name "our Lord Jesus Christ ... the glory". This is the second time

James refers to the Lord using His full title. Among other matters James is setting us an example when we speak to men or God using His name. "Glory" is not here a qualifying adjective, it is a noun; thus James states the eternity of His Being and His equality with the God of glory (Acts 7:2). This truth concerning His person should make us careful in our witness for Him either personally or collectively, therefore do not have respect of persons. Our Lord never showed partiality in His words or works. He was ever complimenting faith wherever it was exercised by rich or poor, by Jew or Gentile. He gave the Law to Moses and in it this prohibition that there must not be a law for the rich and another for the poor. Partiality is a grave sin. The Lord who gave the law actually came down from heaven and demonstrated it in daily living as a man. He took no advantages during His time as a man under law. He never shewed partiality. What He was to the rich He was to the poor, in public or in private. He did not seek the favour of the rich nor did He despise the poor. Thus the standard is raised in v.1, have the faith of the Lord but not with respect of persons. In other words what we profess with our lips is what we should practise in life personally and collectively. This sets the standard for assembly gatherings in the matter of reception of strangers.

In 2:1-4 the standard for the elders and the doorkeepers is included in the phrase (the faith of the Lord Jesus Christ). In the faith or life of the Lord Jesus Christ excellent qualities were displayed. His faith was practised without favouritism; His gracious help and ready power were made available to all kinds of men, women and children irrespective of the material wealth they possessed. At Jericho He accepted and blessed a poor man against the wishes of the crowd and on the same visit He graced the house of the rich Zacchaeus. Many other examples would be personally known to James so he could write with firsthand knowledge of the warmth of affection shown to all kinds of people. Social, educational, financial and religious differences may divide men but these worldly distinctions did not affect the Lord in His relationships. He invited all kinds of folks from the wild untamed heathen to the solid devout religionists; all were precious in His sight. What a worthy example for doorkeepers, elders, and members of the church to follow. With such a standard James deals with the reception by the saints of two visitors.

How we receive strangers to our gatherings is very important. The welcome should be genuine and courteous to all. In the example described by James the visitors are different, one obviously rich and the other poor. Nothing is said of their spiritual state; perhaps no attempt was made to discover it. What embarrassment the poorly-dressed man suffered, not being allowed a chief seat nor guided to any other seat, perhaps finally to squat on the floor out of sight, given no attention, no word of welcome; perhaps it was difficult for him to see and hear; he must have felt unwelcome. This may be an enquiring poor stranger paying a random visit to an assembly meeting. James is not dealing with reception to the assembly membership, but simply how strangers are welcomed at the door and given a comfortable seat.

The Jewish synagogue had reserved or chief seats which the Pharisees claimed. They loved to be treated as being important, anyway most of them were rich. There are many lessons here for us today. There ought to be seats where strangers would be able to see and hear easily. Neither should they feel isolated and certainly never unwanted.

2 At the first reading we might conclude this was not an actual happening "for if" there may have come into your synagogue, but as James proceeds we discover the incident was actual. We should not be surprised about the word "synagogue" being used. The early day of church testimony when James was writing was associated with the Jewish place of meeting. The word was used in two ways at least:

1. describing the actual building, and
2. the congregation who met in the building.

Here it could be either. The door is open; people who were inside seem all to be believers. They do not seem to have the fear of the early days when the doors were shut for fear of the Jews. Two strangers arrive and are allowed inside. The responsibility of the saints is to extend a welcome to strangers. The manner of the reception must be impartial. The strangers are then described by James. It was not uncommon to have visitors in those days (cf. Paul in 1 Cor 14:24 where a visitor has arrived and takes note of the order then makes a judgment of the assembly). Here it is not the judgment by the visitors James is concerned with; it is how the assembly receives. Both visitors are welcomed but what a difference in the welcome. James describes the visitors by what they wore. Dress is important and as we gather to the various meetings of the assembly we should take account of Paul's advice in 1 Tim 2:9. There we learn that our attire is important; it should be modest, discreet, not costly, loud or shabby. Paul is not dealing with how the stranger was received but with the principles to guide the assembly at Corinth which would have an effect on the judgment made by the visitor.

James describes the visitors not by their spiritual position but by what they were wearing. They were dressed differently. The assembly makes an assessment of them from their external appearance. The one has gold rings and shining expensive clothes; the other is a poor man in vile raiment. Both are inside and welcomed. What a difference in the welcome. This is not 1 Cor 14 where the visitor judges the assembly, but here the assembly is judging the visitors. The man with the expensive dress is warmly welcomed; the other man has to find a seat or sit wherever, but obviously not in a chief seat. This is wrong, and unlike the Lord Jesus. The questions of v.4 are to provoke a reaction. There must be no distinctions allowed which are essentially standards of this world. The faith we observe cancels the standards of men and the judgment we make is based on the grace of God and the example of the faith of the Lord Jesus Christ.

5 Now James calls attention to the work and ways of God to shew the wrong of their treatment of visitors to the assembly. Having looked already at the life of the

Lord he now shows the rewarding grace of God to those who exercise faith. God rewarded faith without reference to a person's worldly possessions or lack of them. In these three verses there is,

an affectionate entreaty	v.5
an arbitrary effect	v.6
an abused evangel	v.7

James reassures the saints of his own love towards them before he proceeds to show them that their attitude to the poor man was despicable and anything but Godlike. Says James, God has displayed by clear evidence that He does not despise the poor. Look at what He does. He has chosen the socially and financially deprived; He has made them rich "in faith", but not in wordly possessions, and He has given them heirship in His kingdom. They are heirs of God and joint heirs with Christ. They have a position in the coming kingdom. They will be prominent members and be known as those who love God. Their position then in an honourable society will be easily recognised. Why then despise them now?

6   Having dealt with their treatment of the poor man he now turns to their attitude to the rich by showing the action of the rich towards them: they oppress violently; they humiliate publicly and legally. There is a progression of harassment which induced fear in the Christians and maybe this was their reason for giving the rich man a seat of honour in the synagogue. Nevertheless such partiality was wrong.

7   The real reason for the harassment and the belligerent attitude of the rich to them was the deep-seated hatred against the Christian's Lord. The elect of God would be called Christians (a worthy name) but hated by the world and specially by the masters who used the saints as slaves. The name which is "worthy" may well be "Christian" first associated with Christians at Antioch. It was intended as a reproach by the rich masters but to the persecuted Christian it was a worthy honour to have. Whilst the belligerent masters would blaspheme the worthy name, the Christians would remain true to their christian calling.

8-9   This section of the epistle deals with the gravity of the assembly's action in elevating the rich and embarrassing the poor. Does it really matter how we welcome strangers to the assembly meetings? Emphatically James says it does, and calls in the revered law of Moses. In v.4 James has stated – you did make a difference and you did act as judges. You assessed both visitors by their external appearance and not by any spiritual criteria. In this you have dishonoured the poor and paid no regard to the Scripture in such situations. This is the only place in Scripture where this law is so described (the royal law). The assembly had made a judgment based on external appearance; indeed there is no reference to their use of Scripture. This is a shameful state of affairs. Both visitors are allowed into the gathering but wherein lay the grave sin? This demands that we decide what is the royal law. Is it not the law as given to Moses, made up of ten laws? One of them has particular reference to this incident: "Thou shalt love the Lord thy God, and thy neighbour as thyself".

To bring the ten words given to Moses in a condensed form is masterly on the part of James. He is obviously stating that loving God involves obedience to His word, and love to all His people. A love for our neighbour is to be the love wherewith we love ourself. Notice that no mention is made of rich or poor. This is where the sin lay. It was in the different attitude towards the rich and the poor. The rich is accompanied to a seat of honour because he looked rich; the poorly-dressed man is treated with indifference. If the assembly had made a judgment then, the word of God through James judges them now. Firstly James refers to the royal law (its specific quality) and its implementation, and secondly to the Scriptures in general in condemnation of the way in which they acted towards both visitors.

The law is royal or kingly in quality; on it would hang all the law (the Torah) and the prophets (the whole of OT revelation). Paul reduces the law in the same way in Gal 5:14 claiming that the whole law is fulfilled in one word.

10 In v.10 by extension James emphasises the complete unity of the law so that if we fail in one part the whole is damaged. It is like a glass that is struck at one point; the whole vessel is rendered worthless.

11 V.11 is an explanation of v.10 and here the sin of favouritism is ranked with the grave sins of adultery and murder and the saints involved are termed transgressors. They are classed with the vilest of society. We thus learn at least two important matters; that every individual scripture is royal, having come from a throne, and that each tenet of the Word as found in the Lord Jesus Christ is the faith to hold. There is an obvious difference in the expressions "the royal law" and "the scripture". They are not synonymous. "The Scriptures" refer to the complete revelation, "the royal law" to a particular statement.

When Jesus was asked by the religious leaders as in Matt 22:37-40, which is the great commandment, He obliged them and summarised the Sinai code. All the law hangs on two aspects of love; (i) love God and (ii) love thy neighbour. The love is still first on a vertical scale and secondly on a horizontal scale, for the royal standard to be observed in days of law or in days of grace (vv.8-13). The law of God is royal and should be observed as should all Scripture, if not, as v.9 shows we will face its power to convict. The law has also an inbuilt unity so that if one part is not honoured the whole law is broken and totally condemns the offender.

12 V.12 helps to be positive. The law is to be kept and, if kept, it brings freedom. When we negate the law, according to v.8 we become guilty in two ways:

1. ye commit sin, i.e. you fall short of the target
2. you are transgressors, i.e. you have stepped out of line.

Speaking and doing are the two main factors to be judged at the Bema of the Lord. Our words and our works are equally important.

This section of the epistle unites the OT precepts and the teaching of the Lord Jesus. Of great moment to the Christians are:

- v.8   The royal law
- v.9   The law of Moses
- v.10   The whole law
- v.11   The law of liberty

Whilst we are not under law as given by God to Moses, we are obliged to recognise the principle of law. The fact that all our sins are forgiven should cause us to respect the good law of God and lead us in a path of pleasing God. God's amazing grace has burst out to those who were under the law, and to those who were never born under it the law is the law not of bondage but of liberty, and the law is good if we use it lawfully. James is of course dealing with the moral aspects of law. The principle is firmly and clearly stated as it affects our way of life. Now he deals with our eternal salvation that is secured for us in Christ. In Rom 8:1 the statement is clear, there is no judgment to those who are in Christ Jesus, but in our passage from James there is the way of liberty, that of simple obedience to the word of God. What we say or profess with words should harmonise with our lifestyle. James earlier has referred to our tongue and he will do so again in later chapters. Our profession with our lips and our practice should be in harmony. John exhorts us as dear children: let us not love in word (tongue) but in actions and practice (see 1 John 3:18). Here James puts both verbs "speak" and "do" in the continuous present tense. They are in harmony with each other and in practice should always be in step. We discover from his next statement that God is a righteous Judge, a title that Paul endorsed in 2 Tim 4:8. The assessment by the law of liberty is fair; our living now will also be addressed later in the day of the Bema. How can a person who has shown no mercy or consideration expect kindness? As Christians what we weave in our lifetime we shall wear afterwards.

13 In v.13 we are introduced to a person ungracious and without mercy. In the day of assessment he will be saved but so as by fire. Knowing this it surely behoves us to show mercy. In other words, we are to reflect the grace of God to others – saint and sinner alike – for mercy glories over judgment. The world describes the one who fails to manifest mercy as a harsh man.

V. Faith and Testing (2:14-26)

v.14 "What *doth it* profit, my brethren, though a man say he hath faith, and have not works? can faith save him?
v.15 If a brother or sister be naked, and destitute of daily food,
v.16 And one of you say unto them, Depart in peace, be *ye* warmed and filled; notwithstanding ye give them not those things which are needful to the body; what *doth it* profit?
v.17 Even so faith, if it hath not works, is dead, being alone.
v.18 Yea, a man may say, Thou hast faith, and I have works: shew me thy faith without thy works, and I will shew thee my faith by my works.
v.19 Thou believest that there is one God; thou doest well: the devils also believe, and tremble.
v.20 But wilt thou know, O vain man, that faith without works is dead?
v.21 Was not Abraham our father justified by works, when he had offered Isaac his son upon the altar?
v.22 Seest thou how faith wrought with his works, and by works was faith made perfect?
v.23 And the scripture was fulfilled which saith, Abraham believed God, and it was imputed unto him for righteousness: and he was called the Friend of God.
v.24 Ye see then how that by works a man is justified, and not by faith only.
v.25 Likewise also was not Rahab the harlot justified by works, when she had received the messengers, and had sent *them* out another way?
v.26 For as the body without the spirit is dead, so faith without works is dead also."

14 This verse begins a discussion on works and faith, perhaps the central and main message of this book of James and the passage that has led to it being poorly appreciated by those who misunderstand the writer. James is not dealing with justification by faith but with faith and works for if they do not harmonise, then our faith is dead; indeed as is written clearly by him "faith without works is dead". This is the section that drew from Luther the expression "a strawy epistle". He could not reconcile Paul's truth of justification by faith and the demand of James for the proof by works. They appeared to oppose each other but as we shall find, rather than oppose, they complement.

Now we move to the application after a conclusion is reached in v.13. First there is another reminder of his real association "my brethren". This is family truth. He pleads for reality in our profession evidenced in practice; faith and works must be undivided. The reality of the unseen faith is proved publicly in our behaviour. Faith of course is profitable in the exercise of tangible works and can be assessed only when evident, but there are two questions in this verse, the second "can that faith save him?" Now faith is invisible and a judgment by us on its possession by another can only be based on what we see. Faith is not barren, it works and gives evidence of its reality and its existence. We can see the evidence – a fruit tree is identifiable to us when we see the fruit so, as in 1:26, the unbridled tongue gives proof that is tangible to expose the hypocrisy of a would-be professor. In this verse by the same rule, faith is assessed as to its possession by the onlooker. If the work of our hands or the path of our feet is not in accord with the word of God then where is the evidence of faith?

15-16 Another example is cited, again dealing with tangible proof, that would be overwhelming. The brother or sister may be related naturally or spiritually, but their need is known and is desperate; they need food and clothes. What does the professor do? If he or she has faith and can assist in meeting the need but does not help, the faith professed is worthless; in fact it does not exist; it is dead. Faith without the evidence of good works is but a corpse. This is the conclusion of v.17.

18-20 Further practical examples are used by James to show how incongruous to say we have faith if we never give tangible proof. It works, it cannot but act where need exists. To profess without sharing with the needy what is yours is a denial of the profession made. If the tree is not showing leaves or fruit it is dead, it is without life. James states "my faith is event and it works". V. 19 continues the discussion. Again in the verse there are two faiths (i) a man's faith and (ii) a devil's faith. Both accept the truth of the existence of the one God, or as some theologians say, God is one. The belief of the demon causes the demon to shudder but of the representative person now described as being vain or empty in irony James says, "thou doest well"; you are just like the demons for whom the is no hope, they even acknowledged Jesus for whom he was when in the country of the Gadarenes and in the synagogue at Capernaum. That knowledge though accurate never made them possessors of saving faith. Here in v.20 the man who is a mere professor with no reality is declared empty. James pleading for reality, makes a strong appeal, Oh man realise this, that true faith shows itself by its works. The evidence of real faith is becoming like the giving God.

From v.21 to v.26 James cites two worthy examples of real faith. First he cites a man well-known, the father of the Jews, and then a woman, a Gentile, also well-known for her remarkable faith: Abraham revered as our father, and Rahab the harlot a real deep-dyed sinner. The contrast is evident yet they come together here to show that faith can be the property of a rich or poor, man or woman. God-fearing or sin-loving James gets his message to all by asking and answering relevant questions. The example of the best of men and the worst women suits admirably to cover all types and shows that the exercise of faith is available to all. Notice what he tells us of Abraham. He is not only well-known but revered by his and our succeeding generations. Jew and Gentile think of him in his fatherly role. There are those who expound the Scriptures and suggest that James exclusively addresses Jews in this letter and among other arguments they use is this expression, our father Abraham. Actually what he is doing is to strengthen the fact that Abraham had a working faith and was willing to give his best to prove the reality of his faith. James selects the occasion when he offered his only son on the altar. Paul in dealing with the same subject of faith uses other experiences of Abraham in relation to Isaac. Each trial is different in the life of Abraham, and Paul in Rom 4 thinks of the faith of Abraham relative to the birth of Isaac, and in Heb 11 to the offering of Isaac as a sacrifice. Abraham believed God could bring life out of death and God honoured him in both of these experiences.

22 The application of this working faith in the experience of Abraham is exemplary and repeatable. Faith is capable of growth and is accompanied by works. Faith and works are in harmony and must not be separated. The growth or increase of faith is accompanied by works.

23 The Scriptures or holy writings with their promises and performance were the basis of Abraham's faith. The simple but sublime statement that Abraham believed God could do the impossible and extraordinary, brought the reward he received (i) he was pronounced righteous, and (ii) he was called the friend of God. This expression "the friend of God" used of Abraham in 2 Chron 20:7 relates to what God gave to him, then in Isa 41:8 the righteous man from the east, the father of the nations, what God blessed to him. Abraham earned the title – friend of God – by his faith in, and obedience to, God. He becomes the example for saints. The proof of reality of faith was expressed by the act of obedience. This is not the initial act but one of many experiences of the active faith of Abraham.

24 The example chosen demonstrated that the works and the faith of Abraham were in accord, and Abraham experienced the liberty and love of the God he honoured. His trust and faith in God began when called by God to abandon life in Mesopotamia and walk with his God – his life was full of excitement and blessings from his first act of faith to this further proof of its reality at Moriah's mount.

25 In a similar fashion Rahab of Jericho (a wicked city) showed her faith in God by (i) receiving the messengers, and (ii) sending them out another way. In Heb 11 her faith is associated with receiving the spies but here with not only receiving by the door but with sending them out by the window, so linking her future life with the people of God.

26 The application of these two different examples is made and a conclusion for our attention given. Faith without action has no life but faith with obedience to God's word is a living joyous experience.

VI. Faith and the Tongue (3:1-12)

v.1 "My brethren, be not many masters, knowing that we shall receive the greater condemnation.
v.2 For in many things we offend all. If any man offend not in word, the same *is* a perfect man, *and* able also to bridle the whole body.
v.3 Behold, we put bits in the horses' mouths, that they may obey us; and we turn about their whole body.
v.4 Behold also the ships, which though *they be* so great, and *are* driven of fierce winds, yet are they turned about with a very small helm, whithersoever the governor listeth.
v.5 Even so the tongue is a little member, and boasteth great things. Behold, how great a matter a little fire kindleth!
v.6 And the tongue *is* a fire, a world of iniquity: so is the tongue among our members, that it defileth the whole body, and setteth on fire the course of nature; and it is set on fire of hell.
v.7 For every kind of beasts, and of birds, and of serpents, and of things in the sea, is tamed, and hath been tamed of mankind:
v.8 But the tongue can no man tame; *it is* an unruly evil, full of deadly poison.
v.9 Therewith bless we God, even the Father; and therewith curse we men, which are made after the similitude of God.
v.10 Out of the same mouth proceedeth blessing and cursing. My brethren, these things ought not so to be.
v.11 Doth a fountain send forth at the same place sweet *water* and bitter?
v.12 Can the fig tree, my brethren, bear olive berries? either a vine, figs? so *can* no fountain both yield salt water and fresh."

It is natural to connect this section with 1:19, "slow to speak" just as the previous section arises from the same verse, "swift to hear", but the more immediate connection is with the closing words of ch 2, "faith without works is dead also". Saving faith is living faith and will manifest itself in self-control, epitomised in the control of the tongue (v.2). There is ever the tendency for our lips to outrun our feet. Paul was acutely aware of this as he wrote, "lest that by any means, when I have preached to others, I myself should be a castaway" (1 Cor 9:27).

The gatherings of the saints for the various functions as practised and recorded in the book of Acts gave opportunity for brothers to address publicly the assembly. With this opportunity, and the prominence accorded to those gifted to teach, came the danger that one might assume a place for which he was not fitted. Moreover, there was the tendency among those saved out of Judaism to import into the gospel legal forms. Cf. the controversy at Antioch, instigated by "certain men which came down from Judaea" (Acts 15:1). Concerning them James would write, "to whom we gave no such commandment" or better, "to whom we gave no commandment" (Acts 15:24); it seems that they "came down" without commission and without commendation.

1 The advice, "Be not many masters (or teachers)", is not an attempt to disparage the role of the teacher but to counsel would-be aspirants to this responsible work to

weight the personal responsibility of having their work assessed and of rendering an account at the judgment seat of Christ. The review of the work of all the saints will be conducted then, and a true assessment of motive and matter will be made. The master or teacher will be scrutinised closely, more closely than those being taught. James includes himself with those who have accepted the honour of teaching the word of God and its principles for the edification and education of the saints, and personally felt his responsibility. 1 Cor 3 is a helpful chapter on this subject where the edification of the saints is paramount and the teachers are reminded of the day in which each man's work will be tried or judged. That there is a need for teachers is beyond argument and the risen Lord has given such gifts to the church (cf. Eph 4:11; 1 Cor 12:28,29), among them James. Paul was "ordained a preacher, and an apostle, ... a teacher of the Gentiles" (1 Tim 2:7); he again refers to his appointment in 2 Tim 1:11;4:3. There is a sad rebuke given in Heb 5:12, "For when for the time ye ought to be teachers, ye have need that one teach you". Immaturity was robbing the saints of teachers among the Hebrews.

James is not discouraging the saints therefore, from taking up this important office and work. He is in fact epitomising the great need of accepting with honour this service, but, because of the prominence given to those who teach, they must adorn the doctrine in daily living. The teacher must not only use goodly words; he must be in life exemplary of the doctrine ministered. True teachers with apt messages based on doctrine are of great importance. Teaching has lasting consequences, and the day of review for the teacher as well as for the taught is referred to by Paul in Rom 14:10. The teacher is like a builder: he must walk on the wall he builds.

The Lord is referred to as a teacher or master forty times in the Gospels. In those writings we learn that simplicity, sincerity and an excellent knowledge of the Scriptures marked Him. He taught the common people using language they understood, and could converse from an early age with the professional teachers, so much so that they marvelled. Later in discussing and applying the truth He had to reprimand gently an official teacher of the Jews for his lack of knowledge and understanding (John 3:10). The Lord's fame was such that even those who opposed Him recognised that He was the teacher come from God. Paul may have come from Gamaliel's school, Nicodemus may have attained the position of ruling teacher, but they all recognised that He had come from God. He was different. The teacher to imitate must be the Lord Jesus Himself.

The verses which follow, while applicable to all, have special relevance to the teacher. When James writes "the same is a perfect man" he uses the word *anēr* rather than *anthrōpos*; *anēr* describes a male in contrast to a female, whereas *anthrōpos* usually includes man and woman. "A perfect man" then, refers in a particular sense to a teacher. If we view the verses metaphorically, as the context invites us to, the tongue is the teacher among the other members of the assembly. The following commentary looks mainly, but not exclusively, in that direction.

2   The idea of judgment in v.1 is relevant because the teacher by his doctrine can stumble or offend those who hear. The responsibility involved should make him reflect whether he is gifted and competent to teach in view of the day of accountability. Teachers are akin to shepherds in that they are responsible for the well-being of their charge. This verse hints at offence not only in word but also in the manner of the teacher's life: "in many things we offend all". While failure in the believer's life is not inevitable, there is in every heart a certain proneness to stumble, a natural tendency to fall. "In many things" acknowledges the wide scope in which failure may occur, while the use of the present tense ("offend") suggests that the tendency is ever-present. The teacher must live as one with a moral right to teach others. If a church is ignorant of divine truth then the teacher is subject to greater condemnation than they, therefore what he says is very important for the church.

Stumbling in word is the teacher's special danger. If he is not at fault in what and how he teaches he "is a perfect man". The word "perfect" is evidently not used here in an absolute sense, as if he had attained to sinless perfection; rather it attributes to him full maturity of christian character.

The closing words of the verse are a bold assertion, one which he will quickly justify in vv. 3-5. It introduces the main theme of the chapter: the control of the tongue. To be in control of the tongue is a matter of great importance. More damage is said to be done by this member than by any other member of our bodies. The tongue is normally our most used member; here it is the member of communication. It is appreciated that there are other means of transmitting ministry; each of them can be included here for the general application of the advice given by James. The salient truth is that the tongue of the teacher and the life of the teacher must not be at variance. There seem to have been plenty of talkers at Corinth, not all of them teachers. The real teacher is void of offence and is a living example of the truth taught. He is never at fault in what he says; such a man has the ability "to bridle his whole body", to keep every member of it in check.

3-4   By controlling the tongue the control of the whole person is secured (cf. Prov 6:2; 18:7; 21:23). Lest that should appear an excessive or extreme claim for such a small member, James culls simple analogies from the general everyday life of the people to illustrate his point: the bit in a horse's mouth, and the helm of a large sailing ship. They have this in common: their diminutive size belies the power wielded by the one who controls them. The important factor is not the existence of the bit and the rudder, but the fact that there is a controlling hand: "that they may obey us ... whithersoever the governor listeth". A third analogy, a very small fire (we might almost say a spark) in a large forest, is introduced later to illustrate the destructive power of a small force that is uncontrolled. Each of the examples is introduced by the exclamation, "Behold". From one perspective it refutes an anticipated cavil that the claim at the close of v. 2 is an overstatement, that it is far-fetched; from another it invites our attention to a very imposing sight.

The principle of controlling a horse by bit and bridle is both well-established and general: "we put bits into the horses' mouths". The verb "put" is in the present tense, showing a recognised, accepted practice; the result is guaranteed. Whoever wishes to control a horse achieves it by this means. While the principle is of general application, James is not thinking of the patient draught horse, nor the docile trap pony, but of the scornful charger. His strength is great (Job 39:19; Ps 147:10) and his spirit indomitable (Job 39:20-25; Jer 8:6,16). It is not a desire to please on his part which motivates his submission, but the bit and bridle in the hand of the cavalryman. "Behold also" introduces the second strand of evidence; James will not rely on a single witness. The point of the analogy is emphasised by the construction "though . . . yet". A ship of enormous size, in full sail and driven by ferocious winds, presents an awe-inspiring sight. Yet even it is steered by a relatively small helm or rudder. The governor imposes his will by his control of the helm.

Some expositors have found the hint of a parable in these verses: the impulses from within which urge on the horse reflect the strength of selfwill and the restiveness of the unregenerate nature; the storms which buffet the vessel represent the storms of contrary circumstances. With wise words the individual or the assembly can be guided through safely. While the suggestion is interesting and apposite, this is not the idea that is developed.

5 In the opening sentence James begins the application. At first he simply notes that the tongue also is "very little". A warning is sounded by his use of the word "boasteth", for boasting is seldom spiritual; it is usually the fruit of pride and self-esteem. His statement is perfectly general; this is not an indictment of particular men or classes of men, but of the human tongue universally: "the tongue . . . boasteth great things". How reminiscent of the arrogance of the little horn (Dan 7:8, 25; 11:36) and the beast out of the sea (Rev 13:5) is this activity of the tongue; they are inspired by the same source (see v. 6).
In the second half of the verse he introduces his third analogy, a raging forest fire ignited by a straying spark: "Behold how small a fire! how great a wood it kindleth". It is a picture of destruction. So small a fire in a great forest can do enormous damage.

6 The picture and the consequences are frightening as the appolication is made: the tongue is a fire; it "is set" (Gk.) among our members. How quickly the evil spreads to all the other members of our bodies. The first two illustrations show how the tongue can be a power for good, the last one demonstrates how evil it can be. The control of the tongue is imperative for the teacher. His life can be pleasurable to him and helpful to others, but if his tongue with its message is destructive how great the damage to self and to others.
Curtis Vaughan writes about the tongue as follows: "It can sway men to violence, or it can move them to the noblest actions. It can instruct the ignorant, encourage the dejected, comfort the sorrowing, soothe the dying. Or it can crush the human spirit, destroy reputations, spread distrust and hate, and bring nations to war."

The comparison of the tongue to the spark in a great forest is followed by its description as the world of unrighteousness. The tongue, with such potential, is held in between two rows of teeth and two lips which can open or close. The control of the tongue is essential for the teacher. He must search out fitting words to clothe his thoughts and to minister guidance for others. John Abert Bengel observed, "As the little world of man is an image of the universe, so the tongue is an image of the little world of man."

The versatility of this member is alarming; it can encourage or corrupt, it can help or destroy. Therefore James would caution the man with the gift of teaching to be always seeking the good of men and not their destruction.

This verse tells us the potential for evil of the tongue; it is: 1. a fire; 2. a world of evil, corrupting, changing the course of life to evil and making life now what hell shall be in the future. "A fire" refers not to a domestic fire useful for heating and making comfortable the house, but rather to a fire which is out of control devouring everything that is combustible and rendering useless the incombustible. Solomon in Prov 16:27 describes the ungodly man as constantly digging up evil: he has a memory for evil things and his lips are as a burning fire, sowing strife and separating good friends. The tongue can still destroy as Solomon noted.

As the evil ingredient the tongue can also corrupt our total personality. The verb "corrupt" means to leave a stain which is indissoluble and carried by us through life, like Ahaziah, king of Israel, stained by the reputation "who did very wickedly" (2 Chron 20:35), or like Ahab known as the man who made Israel to sin (1 Kings 22:22).

The tongue sets the policy of a person's life, speaking out lies to damage the good character of others. An example of this is when lies were attributed to John Baptist claiming he had a devil (Matt 11:18) and lies levelled against the Lord Jesus (Matt 11:19).

The tongue is set on fire "by hell"; this is probably a reference to Gehenna, the valley of fire outside Jerusalem where the bodies of the undesirable sinners were burned and where the city's rubbish was burned. Gehenna is found on twelve occasions in the NT, eleven of them in the Gospels and the final reference here. The word Gehenna is used of the final place for the Devil. To be set on fire of Gehenna was (sadly) possible and the consequences of such inflaming tragic indeed.

7 James, in this verse, shows how mischievous the tongue can be. He looks at nature, at the difference between man and brute beasts. Man assumes command of the living things in creation: the beasts of the land, the birds of the air and the fish of the sea are all made subject to man. But the tongue, such a small member of his own body, he cannot control. This is a great wonder: that man has been able to subdue and tame the wild, the ferocious, of all the species whether their habitats are land, sea or air, but he cannot control the small member, his tongue. In this verse he describes its nature: unstable, uncontrollable, full of deadly poison. Although only small, and caged in by two rows of teeth, it remains uncontrollable.

While this verse presents the ability of man to control and tame every other inhabitant of his world, whether bird, beast or fish, many of them wild and ferocious, man with all this skill and power has a very little member which gets out of control at times. The statement of fact made in v.8 is condemnatory: the tongue no man can tame. Paul in his writings confirms the need to have constant vigilance. To keep his body under control meant constant vigilance and self-inflicted punishment: "I keep under my body" (1 Cor 9). To him the urge to do wrong had to be suppressed. The urge to say wrong things is a misuse of our tongue. The tongue as a physical member of our anatomy, though small, is powerful for good or ill. The Christian has two natures, one of them has a strong tendency for evil, the other for good. In this verse the evil nature is untameable. Further it will not be bound by principles which are good and, much worse, it spreads moral poison. This word "poison" is rendered "rust" in 5:3. Paul, in Rom 3:13 quoting from Ps 140:3, describes it as the deadly poison of an asp. What havoc was done to Israel at Massah and Meribah. What loss Moses sustained by misuse of his tongue.

9 In v.9 we return to the use we make of our tongue. It is capable of blessing God, of acknowledging His fatherly care and can range to the other extreme of cursing man who was made in the similitude of God. The alternative reading of this verse changes the title to "our Lord and Father" as in 1:27. This is peculiar to James and shows his appreciation of the glory of the Lord Jesus: He is equal with God.

10 In v.10 there is a strong exhortation; the cage or the mouth that houses this unruly member is used to show how versatile the tongue is. It can bless and it can curse and because of its potential James makes a strong plea. He then from nature illustrates the incongruity of this duplicity. He interrogates with questions whose answers are obvious. From nature he shows how contradictory is our behaviour. He looks at opposites: fresh and salt water issuing from the same source — impossible! a fig tree bearing olives – never! He answers in v.12, Neither can a salt spring yield fresh water. In nature this does not happen. Then "doth not nature itself teach?" How then should a Christian's tongue be bad and good? The answer is obvious: the tongue will produce according to the dictates of the old or new nature. Which nature is stronger? Obviously the one which is fed and kept healthy. It behoves us then to feed and exercise the new nature to put to death the old. The tongue will only produce from the stronger of the two sources. It has been said truly, "Thy tongue betrayeth thee".

11 A series of questions from nature are posed, the answers to which are obvious:

1. *from geology* (v.11) a cleft rock becomes a fountain – the water flows and is either sweet or bitter depending on the nature of its source. The Promised Land was described as a land of springs of water. The rock from which they sprang determined the quality of the water, such as at Elim or conversely at Marah.

2. *from horticulture* (v.12): fig, olive, vine – all trees that have differing produce; the fruit is determined by the species of the tree.

3. *from society*: so is it in human society – this is the application, albeit in question form.

From geology: The waters of Marah were bitter, unhealthy and poisonous but the water from the cleft rock was different: wholesome, sweet and plentiful. The characteristics of the water reflect the nature of the rock. By the constituents of the water a judgment can be made as to its source. The question James poses must be answered in the negative: a fountain does not send forth at the same place both sweet and bitter water.

The introduction of a rhetorical question expects a strong negative answer. It is wrong to expect sweet water and stinking water from the same source. Rhetorical questions are found in vv.11, 12. Both expect a negative answer. The examples are from nature and are well known by everybody. You cannot have salt and fresh water gushing out the same fountain or cave. Israel, who found that the water from Marah was bitter (Exod 15:23) again at Jericho found the water in its natural state was undrinkable (2 Kings 2:19-21).

Most texts omit "So can no fountain". Neither can salt yield sweet water. The Salt Sea (Dead Sea) in the deep south of the country has no life support. The water from the springs is full of sulphur, no doubt from the volcanic rocks through which the Jordan River flows, and is sour and brackish. It is not even good for washing the body, and if a drop touches the eye it stings with pain. As in horticulture so in geology, nature is consistent and abides by its natural laws.

12 *From horticulture*: The reasoning is logical and the answer is easily reached. A fig tree yields only figs, then the conclusion is obvious: no fountain yields different waters. It is either salt or fresh but not both. The examples chosen explain the principles or laws of nature. James enters the fruit garden with a question, and the answer is obvious: a fig tree bears figs, not olives; a vine does not produce figs but grapes. Israel was likened to trees in a fruit garden, tended by a good husbandsman but they did not yield the correct fruit. This simple analogy would cause us to check on what we are producing for the Master. The application from the law of nature is summarised for us: so can no fountain yield both salt and fresh water. The RV strongly emphasises the impossibility of yielding salt and fresh from the same fountain: "neither can salt water yield sweet."

VII. Faith and the Tempter (3:13-4:12)

v.13 "Who *is* a wise man and endued with knowledge among you? Let him shew out of a good conversation his works with meekness of wisdom.
v.14 But if ye have bitter envying and strife in your hearts, glory not, and lie not against the truth.
v.15 This wisdom descendeth not from above, but *is* earthly, sensual, devilish.
v.16 For where envying and strife *is*, there *is* confusion and every evil work.

	v.17	But the wisdom that is from above is first pure, then peaceable, gentle, *and* easy to be entreated, full of mercy and good fruits, without partiality, and without hypocrisy.
	v.18	And the fruit of righteousness is sown in peace of them that make peace.
4	v.1	From whence *come* wars and fightings among you? *come they* not hence *even* of your lusts that war in your members?
	v.2	Ye lust, and have not: ye kill, and desire to have, and cannot obtain: ye fight and war, yet ye have not, because ye ask not.
	v.3	Ye ask, and receive not, because ye ask amiss, that ye may consume *it* upon your lusts.
	v.4	Ye adulterers and adulteresses, know ye not that the friendship of the world is enmity with God? whosoever therefore will be a friend of the world is the enemy of God.
	v.5	Do ye think that the scripture saith in vain, The spirit that dwelleth in us lusteth to envy?
	v.6	But he giveth more grace, Wherefore he saith, God resisteth the proud, but giveth grace unto the humble.
	v.7	Submit yourselves therefore to God. Resist the devil, and he will flee from you.
	v.8	Draw nigh to God, and he will draw nigh to you. Cleanse *your* hands, *ye* sinners; and purify *your* hearts, *ye* double minded.
	v.9	Be afflicted, and mourn, and weep: let your laughter be turned to mourning, and *your* joy to heaviness.
	v.10	Humble yourselves in the sight of the Lord, and he shall lift you up.
	v.11	Speak not evil one of another, brethren. He that speaketh evil of *his* brother, and judgeth his brother, speaketh evil of the law, and judgeth the law: but if thou judge the law, thou art not a doer of the law but a judge.
	v.12	There is one lawgiver, who is able to save and to destroy: who art thou that judgest another?"

Against these examples from nature James is showing that in the natural world there are laws which are abiding and unchangeable. Nature abhors a mixture, so he makes the application in the spiritual life from vv. 13-18 with two kinds of wisdom: earthly (vv. 13-16) and heavenly (vv. 17-18).

13 *From Society:* There is the question of self-examination. The check is made by us as to our knowledge and how we express it in daily living. A teacher must not only know his subject but he must live to the standards of his knowledge. The wise and knowledgeable man will be known by his works. He will be accompanied by meekness of wisdom. Not only therefore will he have knowledge, but because he is wise he will show his knowledge in the practice of daily behaviour. This man is not just a man with natural ability but of good works. He has experience, understanding and ability and would be an acceptable teacher, rich in knowledge and good in practice. A good teacher never says, "Do as I say", rather, "Do as I do." He builds the wall as a teacher and can walk on the wall he builds. His life is in accord with his teaching. The expression James uses, "his good conversation (life)", is the affirmation of his pure mind and a demonstration in living terms of his teaching.

The application of these examples from nature is dealt with negatively in vv.14-16 and positively in vv.17-19. In v.13 there are three qualities that should be evident in a good teacher: wisdom, knowledge and works expressing meekness of wisdom.

Just as there are three items required in a teacher (wisdom, understanding and demonstration) in v.13, so in v.14 there are three undesirable and unhelpful things: envy, strife, and lies. The reason will be found in the threefold explanation of v.15. The wisdom which is not from above is characterised by three principles of evil: earthly, natural, and devilish. This latter section, ending in v.16 will depict in a threefold way the issue and the effects of an unspiritual teacher: envy and hatred; strife and division; confusion and anarchy.

From the illustrations abounding in nature, James in his application begins v.13 with a question. This matter of teaching pervades the final chapters of his book. Who is wise and knowledgeable among you, let him show this in practical terms of daily living. The Christian is not cocooned in an impenetrable shell. The community waits for his expression of wisdom and knowledge. The saint is knowledgeable and seeks ways to express these treasures of wisdom and knowledge. Paul's question to the Corinthian church, "Is there not a wise man among you?" was condemnatory. There was a lack of intelligent application of the gifts given by the Spirit of God to them. They had knowledge but lacked the wisdom to express it in practical terms. James uses the broad, inclusive word "conversation" to cover their personal and collective testimony. What they knew and what they did were at variance. The meekness of wisdom is not a soft, weak expression, but the opposite. It is the evident mark of a strong, spiritual Christian. This wisdom expressing enjoyed knowledge of God is not boastful nor aggressive but strong yet meek. An old proverb comes to mind: Foresight is better than hindsight, and insight is best of all. Therefore the teacher or master is not simply concerned by what words he uses, but the way he lives and relates personally to others. Knowledge with insight will lead to a practical exhibition and exposition of truth.

14 This verse exposes the wrong attitude and wrong approach. The bitter envying is like the bitter waters of Marah that cause spiritual diseases and is unworthy of any saint, far less of a teacher who is before the general public. The "But" which begins the verse, is in contrast to the desirable fruit of v.13, wisdom, knowledge and meekness, and against the three undesirables of envy, strifes and lies. The three undesirable products are earthly, sensual and devilish. The contrast is sharp between the spiritual and the sensual teachers. They are complete opposites. The spiritual teacher not only ministers healthy doctrine but is a living example of it, whereas the other kind of teacher has envy instead of gentleness; he is selfish instead of sharing generously and is boastful of his own ego instead of growing less and less. James writes from deep experience; he had knowledge of both kinds of teachers. The one brought joy and good fruit, the other sadness and division.

His description of envy as being bitter reminds us of the brackish, foul water that if drunk brings illness and pain. Jealousy or envy is as cruel as the grave. To have the bitter water of envy is to be bereft of spiritual health personally, but worse still is to make others drink and cause spiritual disease to spread like a plague. In Num 16 we face the awful result of envy which brought a halt to the progress of the people of God, death and destruction to the sons of Levi and Simeon. They were men of renown, well-known and very influential in their day, but full of envy and selfish ambition. James describes envy as bitter or sour to remind us of what is devilish. The characteristic of the devil is evil envy, to bring down others to push up self.

The spirit of strife, a readiness to quarrel, is generated by envy and jealousy. To fight to push up self is to put down and destroy others. On the other hand, there is a good fight described by Paul to Timothy which is:

1. to battle against the sinful and selfish desires in us which belong to the old nature;
2. to promote the new man, keeping him spiritually healthy with the good food of the word of God and the good exercise of faith.

Paul emphasises the negative and the positive when giving advice to his son in the faith Timothy. Negatively Paul said, "Refuse profane and old wives fables" (1 Tim 4:7); "Neglect not the gift that is in you" (v.14). Positively he said, "Exercise yourself unto godliness" (v.7), "meditate on these things, give thyself wholly to them".

15 The two types of wisdom are again in contrast. This verse details the so-called wisdom of this world. "Not from above" is negative; positively it is:

1. earthly: it is from beneath as to its place of origin;
2. sensual: it is unspiritual, having a bad effect; it has no food value;
3. devilish: it can be traced to its person of origin, the devil, who is the denier of truth, and is the source of lies and all evil.

The idea of being earthly relates to what is natural to this sphere called "the world". By nature and practice man is at enmity with God. His inner thoughts are devoid of divine truth, and man left to himself would miserably perish. His thought is to elevate his ego at the expense of all other earth-dwellers, thus creating instability, friction and fightings. His wisdom is earthly.

It is also sensual and instead of having a binding and uniting effect, it separates; it is the product of a fallen nature that fights and opposes what is good and godly (Jude 19).

It is devilish. The three descriptions are in descending order. This wisdom is demoniacal; it is the way the devils or demons think, totally contrary to the thoughts of God and always in opposition to God and to the good of men. Being devilish it is built on lies and deceit and will always be in opposition to God and truth and will promote evil practices intended to destroy. The source of this devilish wisdom has its signs which we ought to identify easily as in v.16. We do well to recall how our

Lord Jesus spoke of the characteristics of the one who is a liar and a murderer (see John 8).

Two wisdoms in one verse and nothing between. It is either one or the other. "Such wisdom" refers back to earthly, sensual, devilish. This is James exposing the false wisdom. He deals with its source first. It is earthly as opposed to the wisdom which is from heaven. Christ is from above and the wisdom of God and is pure, peaceable and precious. This earthly wisdom is exposed in descending order as being earthly, unspiritual and devilish: earthly in its origin in contrast to the heavenly and pure; unspiritual as to its nature – it is carnal, fleshly; devilish as to its expression – full of lies, poison and bitterness. As to its origin it comes up from a cursed earth. It is generated from beneath and carries all the despicable ingredients of the curse.

16 This is another explanatory verse helping up to identify the source of this wisdom by the effects produced by it. Where there is envy and evil – root and fruit – there will be disorder and wicked practices. Envy in the devil at the beginning of time brought man into disgrace and nature into disorder. Man, Adam, heeded the devilish suggestion and fell into grievous sin. Eve may have been deceived, but Adam deliberately accepted the suggestive poison of the devil and fell in disgrace, bringing his posterity down with him. Among the bitter fruits harvested are envy and strife. Envying proceeds open strife. Envy burns inwardly, but strife or war is open. Many examples of lustful envy are found throughout the Scriptures. The spirit of jealousy is cruel and has no regard for others. It is unseen and inward whereas its produce, strife, is open and damaging. This is not a simple difference; this is disorder and division. Our Bibles abound with examples of divisions among nations, families, assemblies and all of them can be traced to the wisdom which is devilish. The devil is still alive after all the centuries of time and will remain so until God finally judges him and all who belong to him. This is the spirit of anarchy that leads to confusion as at Babel (Gen 11) and has multiplied the wickedness that abounds in the world and sadly in christian gatherings.

17 "This wisdom" is broken down into its constituents. First and foremost it is pure. This is not first numerically but essentially; here is purity in essence and substance; all the other descriptive adjectives grow up and out from this purity of essence. You could not have the other characteristics without the basic inner purity. The purity of it cannot be defiled. It originates in heaven and descends to earth as a gift of God to be had for the asking (cf. 1:5,17). Christ is the wisdom and power of God, Paul helpfully declares (1 Cor 1:24). This wisdom is pure because God is pure and holy. It is unaffected by Eden's fall and man's disobedience. Christ is of purer eyes than to behold iniquity; with Him is purity of knowledge and intelligence; purity marked His descent to earth and His living or tabernacling amongst those who were impure. This is another statement to show the holy character of heaven's gift to the world. This wisdom was not made pure; it is eternally holy and pure. Aristotle defines this pure wisdom as that which is above law and better than justice.

This is the purity not only for social contacts with other people but provides us a standing with God, and allows us to speak with Him. The death of Christ is the sanctifying work that makes and keeps us pure. This purity is akin to the holiness which describes the nature of God and also describes the work of sanctification perfected by the Lord and transmitted to His people. Peter speaks of them as a holy nation before enjoining them to be holy in conduct. John tells us that "He is pure" (1 John 3:3). In the sermon on the mount, very familiar to James, the Lord Jesus Christ said that this purity is necessary to see God.

The offshoots from it are then detailed, like the fruit of a tree, like living water from a sweet spring or fountain:

1. It is peaceable (*eirēnikos*), i.e. "ready for peace" (Forester), always desiring and fostering peace. See Ps 120:7. So desirable is peace that we are bidden to "follow after" it (Heb 12:14), to pursue it relentlessly. This heavenly wisdom joyously responds, ever working towards the eradication of everything that impedes the enjoyment of peace, without for a moment compromising with sin.

2. It is gentle, inoffensive and considerate, mild and most reasonable, not legalistic nor hard but most considerate to others. It is unsparing in its loving care for others. It is a lover of peace, but not peace at any price; it promotes a righteous peace. Such gentleness is required in an elder (1 Tim 3:3) and is useful in settling differences (Phil 4:5).

3. It is easy to be intreated (a word found only here in the NT). The gate of this wisdom is open. This word occurs only here in the NT and is therefore rare. No one is turned away but all who contact or are touched by this wisdom feel the better of the experience. This wisdom is pliable or yielding not from the truth but in the preservation of peace.

4. It is full of mercy and good fruit. The actions of this person are now described. Wisdom is full of mercy. James is again at the mount of Matt 5:1 and recalling the teaching of his Master: "Blessed are the merciful"; "showing mercy unto thousands" (Exod 20:6). Paul says, "Christ Jesus came into the world to save sinners ... and for this cause I obtained mercy" (1 Tim 1:15, 16). The blind man cried, "Be merciful unto me" and found mercy from the fountain in great abundance. Those who came to Jesus not only found mercy that removed their guilt, but were given an abundant supply of good fruit – the fruit of the Spirit (Gal 5:20). Such pity is a pain-reliever even to those who have caused pain and suffering, as it stoops low to assist.

5. It is impartial. Again this word is used only by James in the NT. It is scarcely used either in other writings but means basically "not divided" and hence "unwavering". In other words it is always the same in attitude irrespective of the many differences in people. It is "the same"; you never find wisdom with changing moods or a changing attitude to different people. It never vascillates, and reminds us of the title describing the Lord Jesus: "the same yesterday, and

today, and forever". He is changeless, unchanging and unchangeable. This is the opposite of the doubting man (1:6). The social, moral and spiritual divisions among men are all dismissed by this wisdom. Its attitude remains unchanged whether in contact with rich or poor, good or bad, religious or otherwise.

6. It is sincere. It is absolutely true; it is not a mixture but is of one element, of truth and verity. Wisdom can arbitrate with balance; it never shows unfounded favouritism.

18 What wisdom yields is righteousness. This is the harvest and it has quality with quantity. The horticultural language of James is very expressive. We sow to reap. All the toil of sowing and the patience of waiting is for a good result. Here the result is peace for the peacemakers; a harvest worth reaping.

In 1 John 3:7 a clear statement is made of those who practise righteousness, "He that doeth righteousness is righteous, even as he (the Son of God) is righteous". This colourful language is used frequently by OT and NT writers. Isaiah in the middle section of his prophecy where he foretells the future of the nations surrounding the land of Israel often uses the analogy of whatsoever a man or nation sows that shall he or it reap. In ch. 32 he describes the near view of this King of Israel, so different from these Gentile monarchs; He sows, or governs, in righteousness and the resultant harvest is the blessing of Israel. The last verse of the chapter is very apt: "Blessed are ye that sow beside all waters, that send forth thither the feet of the ox and the ass". This tells us of the overflowing blessing of peace where even the dumb domesticated animals also are blessed. The people sow good seed and reap and the blessing extends to others.

How different the prophecy of Amos 6:12 where the sowing is with the seed of sin and injustice; not surprisingly there is a harvest of bitterness and disappointment. What we sow we shall reap. As with OT writers, so NT writers declare the principle. Cf. 2 Cor 9:10. If we want a bumper harvest of righteousness we must sow the good seed. In Heb 12:11 healthy discipline or sowing good seed produces a harvest of righteousness and peace for those exercised thereby. So now to get a good harvest of peace there is work for the saints. The work of sowing can be difficult and whilst you would watch a farmer sowing seed you would see how his whole body acts in unison – the sowing of his hands and the step of his feet are in harmony; so all the ground is covered evenly with the good seed.

The waiting time from sowing to reaping can be difficult, but the harvest surely comes. Sowing seeds of peace, love and righteousness means a harvest of righteousness. Some commentators vary the language of expressing the harvest – a harvest produced by righteousness, or a harvest consisting of righteousness and peace. The terms harvest, righteousness and peace can all be used within this context. The harvest while belonging to the sower primarily is enjoyed by others. If we wish a harvest of peace we must live righteously and godly in the present age. Whilst James uses the natural laws he is simply enforcing the principle that what we sow we reap. If we sow to the flesh we shall get a harvest of death and destruction; but if we sow to the Spirit we shall have life and peace and joy.

The work of making peace is not easy, but it is worthwhile. James enforces the principle from the laws of nature, known and appreciated by all. The peacemaker is not afraid of hard and difficult work and his eye is the eye of a good farmer, looking ahead to the bumper, good, harvest. "The work of righteousness shall be peace; and the effect of righteousness quietness and assurance forever. And my people shall dwell in a peaceable habitation, and in sure dwellings, and in quiet resting places" (Isa 32:17, 18). What we sow, we reap!

In vv. 17-18, after the exposure of the false wisdom, he now turns to the wisdom which is from above. It is heavenly as to its source and character. It is the opposite of what is earthly sensuous and devilish.

Now we have a strong positive: "The fruit of righteousness is sown in peace, by them who make peace". In all the yielding of grace there is no dilution of truth, holiness or righteousness. The seed is sown in peace, the fruit or the harvest is righteousness. The wise saint who has imbibed the spirit of the Master will sow the seed of godly living and will have the joy of a harvest of peace. It is interesting to note that the verb to sow is passive and thereby gives a beautiful picture of the peacemaker reaping with the joy of harvest.

1   James 4 may be divided as follows:

    vv 1-6   Strife – its source
    vv 7-10   Submission – its steps
    vv 11-18   Speaking or sermons

"Wars and fightings" (*polemos* and *machē*) are the evidences of strife. *Polemos* describes a state of war whereas *machē* is a battle. The problem is to determine from what source they come. There is a wisdom which is from above (3:17); its characteristics are peaceful, its fruit is peace; therefore it cannot be the source. James turns to look within. Philo, an ancient moralist, writes of "this continual war prevailing among men and turbulent as the raging sea". Its cause is identified by James as the internal desires of each saint. He could remember the early days when the believers had all things common and were of one heart and mind (Acts 4:32). These conditions were of short duration. Persecution from outside the christian society induced a spirit of unity, but internal squabbles and fights were from another source, James suggests: their own desires for selfish and carnal pleasures. Some few expositors suggest that "wars" here describe conflict other than in an assembly of saints. The author believes that James is depicting the internal conditions obtaining among saints. He is not seeking for the *reason*; what he is seeking for is the *origin* and looking inward he discovers the seat of the troubles: "Do they not come from the desires within you?"

The sinful root is found in our hearts in the form of desires (plural). These are carnal desires which disrupt the enjoyment of divine peace and spill over to disrupt assembly harmony.

So he has answered the question, Whence; the source is in our own hearts. He then proceeds to a second question, Are they not from hence; from your own lusts which constantly campaign and wage war against your fellow saints? These "lusts" seek to promote self and to demote others by foul means or fair. James having identified the hidden source, discloses the means used and the disillusionment that results: "Ye ... have not". The hidden source is within our own hearts and the sinful pleasures sought by us can be detrimental to the unity of the saints and impede the work of God.

2   This is a difficult verse to interpret. The actions are obviously not in sequence, e.g. "kill" is placed before covet ("desire to have"), but the strength of each verb is strong and frightening. To lust is to want for evil purposes; lust will employ extreme measures to obtain its objective. It is fired by our own envy and jealousy; its overpowering strength is evidenced in the murder it sanctions. If the actual deed is not committed, yet still the malignity lies within our hearts. Once the course is embarked upon anything or anyone that hinders is eliminated by us to allow the sinful personal lusts to be gratified.

The sinful craving, sometimes under a cloak of seeking to defend the truth, will not be satisfied until it achieves its goal. The assassination of others by foul means is murder. David lusted: he was not satisfied till he had actually killed the husband of the woman he wanted. The pleasure-dominated life inevitably leads to war and division; pleasurable lusts wage a constant campaign which ultimately ends in killing.

3   If in v.2 there is the lack of prayer, here there is a pseudo-asking which evokes no reply from heaven. Heaven is not only acquainted with our words but with our motives. It is not simply a matter of what we ask, but our motive in asking. It is a healthy exercise to wait in the presence of God and be searched. If what we seek in prayer is for personal gain and consumption then we ask amiss; this but adds fuel to lust. The perpetual use of the personal pronouns in prayer is not only unworthy but useless and harmful.

4   He now turns from the discussion on pseudo-prayer and its disillusionment, "Ye ask, and receive not", to their spiritual state. The relationship with God was unhealthy and we now discover other relationships are also unhealthy. The description of them by James shows how unhealthy they were. The fact that only the feminine is used, "adulteresses" (RV, JND, *et al*), does not exclude the brothers or males. This description rebukes them for what they were: unfaithful to God, to each other and to a perishing world. In the OT God accused His people of unfaithfulness. God has assumed the role of the faithful husband (cf. Jer 3; Hos 2,3,4; Isa 54:5; 62:4,5). He had cared and loved

them but they had not only rebelled, they had joined themselves to others. The question of v.4 is not addressed to the ignorant but sharply rebuked those who have chosen to forsake their God: to be friendly with a world that crucified His Son, to court that world as a matter of policy, made them enemies of God. The word "world" may include its pleasure grounds, but because of the saints' sacred relationship to God it relates primarily, though not exclusively, to its religious activities.

5   The weight of holy Scripture is emphasised. The word of God makes demands as well as revealing truth so, as in 1:26, they are invited to take stock, to stand still and review their way of life. Although the words, apparently quoted, cannot be identified with any known Scripture, yet throughout the OT there are principles stated where God jealously demands total obedience and love. The OT often reminds us that God is lover of His people and is jealous over their love and devotion (see e.g. Deut 32:16). God loves us with a burning passion according to Zech 8:2. He brooks no rival. An alternative reading views the verse as two distinct questions: "Do you think that the scripture speaketh in vain? Doth the spirit that he made to dwell in us lust to envy?" The author prefers the former view.

6   This verse reveals who gives and what is given, perhaps quoting Prov 3:34. God is again revealed as giving grace to the humble; many examples of this are found in the Scriptures and in the lives of His people today. His store is still full. Did not the Saviour say to the woman at the well, "if thou knewest the giving God … thou wouldest have asked of him, and he would have given thee" (John 4:10)? His gifts are free and worth having. It is Peter who writes about "the God of all grace" (1 Pet 5:10). Salvation is by grace (Eph 2:8-9); our standing is by grace (Rom 5:2); and "grace and truth came by Jesus Christ" (John 1:17). It was this truth that inspired Newton to write:

> "Amazing grace how sweet the sound
>   That saved a wretch like me.
> I once was lost but now am found,
>   Was blind but now I see."

The grace experienced at conversion continues in ever-rich supply to the humble and never will cease to meet each recurring need. It has no limitations. God is always on the side of the humble. On the other hand God opposes the proud. Prov 16:5 tells how He opposes. The verb "resisteth" is a military word denoting the drawing up of forces in battle formation. God freely gives to the humble and denies by force the proud. Daniel was protected and honoured by grace; the haughty proud king Nebuchadnezzar was severely disgraced. Other examples fill our history books. In Matt 18:3-4 this truth is emphasised by the Lord Jesus when He set the little child in the midst as an object lesson on humility.

7 The act of dedication at conversion is to be followed by a constant giving of our all, including ourselves, to God. The root from which we have obedience is the source from which submission springs. It is seen basically when we place our all at the service of another. In civilian life we submit to the authority and thereby become a good citizen (1 Pet 2:13); in the assembly we recognise, respect and obey the elders (1 Cor 16:16); in the home sphere wives submit to their husbands (Col 3:18); and in the business sector servants submit to or obey their masters. The saint who has submitted all to God is easily recognised and valued for his spirituality and his God-fearing attitude in all his ways. This person willingly obeys every relevant request he or she finds in the Bible. An OT character, Job, despite great difficulties obeyed God, and after many sad experiences proved the worthwhileness of submission to God's word.

Secondly we must resist the devil; this means to take a definite stand against the devil. He is real and active and is an enemy (1 Pet 5:8). We do not require to bait him and as soon as we consecrate ourselves to the Lord he attacks. Our resource is in God and His word. Just as the Lord was a marked man by the devil, so too are those who obey God. "Resist" is an active verb. The action demanded of us under the attack of the devil is to not give an inch to him. The battle is on and we stand with a sword in our hand (Eph 6), and the full panoply supplied by the successful Lord. We must never retreat from the fight.

We become proficient and professional only when we know our weapon and have developed skill in its use. The more we progress in our obedience the more severe will be the attack of the enemy, therefore there is a greater need to know the book and the God of the book. Paul as he developed said, "we are not ignorant of his devices (tactics)" (2 Cor 2:11). The outcome of our resistance is certain: he will flee from you. When this actually happens we are not told, and as and when he attacks we are not told, but we must ever be ready. This withdrawal from the fight is temporary; he is not easily defeated but he has been completely routed at Calvary. We therefore use the victory of the Lord Jesus as our victory and keep resisting. We must be vigilant for in an hour when we let down our guard he will attack. Therefore we must be vigilant if we are to be victorious. We can be more than conquerors now and as we anticipate the end of war with the enemy we take refuge in submitting to or obeying our God.

8 This verse is the prescription for victory in our conflict with the devil. In the previous verse we resist the devil, that is we distance ourselves from him, but now we draw near to God. Throughout the Scriptures there are numerous verses encouraging us to draw near to God in order that we become acquainted with His voice. The first occasion when we really got to know Him brought to us salvation. This was an introduction but now we have an exhortation to keep coming and to find that we are always welcome for He comes near to us. This is so different from what happened at Sinai when the nation of Israel (God's earthly people) had to keep their distance. The injunction is clear: "draw near". This is one of the privileges that belong to every saint of this dispensation. We do not need an earthly minister or priest or any other cleric, we have direct and immediate access to God. This is to be appreciated specially when being harrassed by the devil. The fact that God draws near to us is most comforting when we are under attack. He is a sun shield and He gives grace and glory (Ps 84). His presence also makes demands: "cleanse your hands", i.e. make them ready and usable by God. In Ps 24:4 the service of the house of God demanded purity, and so it is today, we need to have hands that are not soiled by sin. The fact that James uses the description "sinners" might suggest that actual sin had filled and soiled them, hence the need to apply the water of the Word. They needed to visit the laver of the Word if they were to be able to lift up holy hands (1 Tim 2:8). The reference to our hands is suggestive of what can be seen by others. Then he turns to the inner man and calls for purity of heart. The heart is the seat of our affections and our love must be pure. If our hearts are hard or our affections misdirected we should heed the injunction. Thirdly, our minds, the seat of intelligence, must not be carnal, but "whatsoever things are true, honest, just, pure, lovely, of good report with virtue and praise, think on these things" (Phil 4:8). Therefore we must never halt between two opinions. To enter God's presence is to move like a priest from the altar of sacrifice to the laver, and thence into the house of God's presence. Hands, heart and mind are all geared to suit God's presence: the pure heart of love inside, unseen by man but measured by God in private; the hands holy and clean after applying the water of the Word (the laver in the outer court of the tabernacle), enabling us to touch and handle holy things; and then the spiritual mind intelligent of privilege and position – single-minded for God.

9 This is a verse to bring to us a different philosophy, a philosophy that deals with the serious matters of life. It is contrary to the prodigal pursuits of the world under the domination of the devil. The verbs are active, encouraging us to face the present conditions prevailing in a world that is godless. The affliction is deep in the soul and feels the general departure from God with an urge for real repentance. This leads to the sadness in mourning; whilst deep in the heart it surfaces in visible crying and many tears, like the Lord Jesus as He rode into the city of Jerusalem and wept visibly (Luke 19:41). The Lord advises them not to shed tears for Him but for themselves. They had departed from God and they were ignorant of the day of visitation, yet they were celebrating in the open street. Soon the reality of wrath and misery would overtake them. The change would be violent. Their present need was for true repentance; instead they rushed on blindly, and ultimately suffered the cruel violence of the oppressor, and their joy was turned to sorrow. They lacked the concern for their own godless ways and were filled with pleasures which pass with the using and having nothing for God in them. These also were out of touch with God and reality. The grief (*talaipōrēsate*, used in verbal form here) is akin to Paul's feelings in Rom 7:24, "O wretched man"; it was the burden of his personal sin that made him feel thus and impressed on him the need for relief.

10 The action prescribed is self-humbling in the presence of the Lord; it is very personal and very humbling. This is a holy exercise, deeply emotional as the prodigal's remorse in returning home. His sin had brought the feeling of shame and his confession reveals his heartfelt sorrow. This is the road to recovery and only the Lord can restore the years that the locusts have devoured. Not only does the Lord graciously and righteously forgive; He also restores. The use of the aorist tense is comforting and instructive. As soon as sin is confessed it is forgiven, and the person is lifted up to start again. Communion is restored and the lesson is learned. The verse ends with the warm comforting words, "The Lord shall lift you up". The verb "humble" is in the passive voice and when translated literally would read "be humbled". The message and the power to obey it are alike from God, so that true humility is from God and the strength to be humble is also from God, so there is no boasting nor self-praise. The Lord should have all the praise. The word "lift up" (*hupsoo*) means to raise to a position of dignity. Peter says, "Humble yourselves therefore under the mighty hand of God, that he may exalt you in due time" (1 Pet 5:5). He may do it in this life; He certainly will in the hereafter.

11-12 James has something more to say about the tongue. This appears as a definite command: "Speak not evil one of another, brethren". This appears as a command, "Speak not", and denies us the right to use our tongues in this way. To slander is to talk against other people in a wicked way. This is more serious than careless talk about another person in his absence. This seems to be motivated by the desire to cause injury to character and damage to a person's testimony. Under the law of Moses the Israelites were warned against this practice (Lev 19:16). Paul had to write about this very thing to Corinth (2 Cor 12:20); Peter also adds his quota (1 Pet 2:1-2). The motives behind slander are to hurt and wound. This, alas, is one of the deadliest sins in christian circles causing untold harm and finds its instigator in the devil. One of his titles is "the accuser of the brethren" (Rev 12:10).

Then James looks more closely at this obnoxious sin. This slanderer not only demeans another but acts as the judge of his victim and sets up himself above the general law of God. By judging the law he sets himself above it and replaces it with his own law. How ridiculous a position to take, so James asks, "who art thou who judgest thy neighbour?" (JND). Notice the change from "brother" to "neighbour". This sin mars heavenly and earthly relationships. This is a sinful practice that goes on sometimes unchecked in christian circles. The person elevates himself above the law as if the law had no teeth and were not worth obeying. James also argues that this man, in setting himself above the law, makes himself equal to if not higher than God, the giver of the Law, so James is quick to defend God's authority (v.12). He makes a statement of fact; there is one and only one lawgiver; He is the originator and He reserves the right with His unique ability to take care of it. No person has the ultimate right to judge because he lacks full knowledge and information (cf. 1 Cor

4:5). Again the ability of man is severely limited, usually because of smallness of mind or impurity of motive.

Note
3:17   "Pure" (*hagnos*) is translated "chaste" three times, "clear" once and "pure" four times.

VIII. Faith and Tomorrow (4:13-5:9)

> v.13 "Go to now, ye that say, To day or to morrow we will go into such a city, and continue there a year, and buy and sell, and get gain:
> v.14 Whereas ye know not what *shall be* on the morrow. For what *is* your life? It is even a vapour, that appeareth for a little time, and then vanisheth away.
> v.15 For that ye *ought* to say, If the Lord will, we shall live, and do this, or that.
> v.16 But now ye rejoice in your boastings: all such rejoicing is evil.
> v.17 Therefore to him that knoweth to do good, and doeth *it* not, to him it is sin.
>
> 5 v.1 Go to now, *ye* rich men, weep and howl for your miseries that shall come upon *you*.
> v.2 Your riches are corrupted, and your garments are motheaten.
> v.3 Your gold and silver is cankered; and the rust of them shall be a witness against you, and shall eat your flesh as it were fire. Ye have heaped treasure together for the last days.
> v.4 Behold, the hire of the labourers who have reaped down your fields, which is of you kept back by fraud, crieth: and the cries of them which have reaped are entered into the ears of the Lord of sabaoth.
> v.5 Ye have lived in pleasure on the earth, and been wanton: ye have nourished your hearts, as in a day of slaughter.
> v.6 Ye have condemned *and* killed the just; *and* he doth, not resist you.
> v.7 Be patient therefore, brethren, unto the coming of the Lord. Behold, the husbandman waiteth for the precious fruit of the earth, and hath long patience for it, until he receive the early and latter rain.
> v.8 Be ye also patient; stablish your hearts: for the coming of the Lord draweth nigh.
> v.9 Grudge not one against another, brethren, lest ye be condemned: behold, the judge standeth before the door."

13   From dealing with the law of God, he now turns to the will of God. Time is a precious commodity and this is appreciated by the shrewd man of business, but how do we as Christians use it?

The businessman is quite arrogant and makes use of his programmer. His schedule is made to suit his plan; he maps out the details of his movements to accommodate his business objectives; he does not take God into his little plan. The will of God to him is irrelevant. Notice there is no condemnation of his business plan or his objectives; the word of God does not condemn good planning or good execution of the plan. Making money was as fashionable then as it is today but one thing was lacking: this man was planning only for this life and had made no preparation for the next life. Gold was his god and living here had no end, so he thought. Such is the materialistic man; he thinks that success is measured by profit; he has no thought of God or God's will; nor does he plan reckoning on God's will for him now.

14-17 V. 14 follows this man of business with his planning and his operations to achieve the objectives he set. "Ye know not" is the weak link. Ye know not the future, not even the immediate future. A day can alter every plan and intention. A question is to be thought of and brought into the plan: "what is your life?" The arrogant man of v.13 never for a moment thought of it. He had planned for a year, but life is like a mist which appears and vanishes. The man said "we will" as if he were independent of death. God said, "You do not have a day, far less a year; do not boast of tomorrow" (see Prov 27:1). Many such statements are made in the Old and New Testaments (cf. Job 7:6-7; 9:25; Ps 139:5; 102:3, 11). How true is the analogy of James: life is a mist. Think of the parable told by the Lord (Luke 12); a man more interested in his harvest than in heaven or hell (v.15). The acknowledgement of the Lord's will ought always to figure in our future plans. The fact that life is uncertain must affect our planning and our attitude to life now. God's sovereignty ought always to be acknowledged. Paul said in Acts 18:21, "if God will" (cf. Rom 1:10). Life's uncertainty need not prevent us making future arrangements provided we acknowledge the will of God. Another great event which must be included in our planning is the imminent return of the Lord for His church (v.17). These considerations should spur us to greater endeavour for Him; if our day of service is so short we should do good with every day we are given. There are sins of commission but in v.17 we have the sin of omission. Possibly there were those who used the uncertainties as an excuse for doing nothing; of such James says bluntly, "They are guilty of sin".

5:1 James 5 has three interesting messages to deliver:

vv.1-6	To the unconverted rich Jews
vv.7-15	To the oppressed believers
vv.16-20	To all Christians – the necessity of prayer

James has discussed in the early chapters the wrong committed by the saints in giving preferential treatment to the rich and shaming the poor, now he addresses the rich. Earlier he describes them by their dress and their attitude, now he deliberately drops the term of relationship, "brothers". They may have been religious but the reality of conversion to Christ was missed by them. The divine title used by him is an OT Jewish one, "the Lord of sabaoth", i.e. the Lord of hosts (v.4). Nevertheless saints also must take heed, for all Scripture is to profit. In the letter to the churches in Rev 2 and 3 the possession of riches is shown not to advance the spiritual life of the churches but the opposite. In the Gospels we learn that few rich find their way into the kingdom of God. Having riches can be a serious detriment to getting saved and becoming useful for God; yet God has used rich men in remarkable ways to advance His kingdom (eg. Barnabas).

James specifically deals with those who have made gold their god. Perhaps he remembered the disciples recalling the sermon given by the Lord on the mount (cf. Matt 6:19-20). To weep and to howl are expressions of violent grief; they are the results of misuse of wealth which produces soul poverty (cf. Joel 1:5).

2-3 He uses verbs in the perfect tense to intensify the irretrievable loss that has evoked such anguish. The rottenness or corruption of clothes speaks of character that has been marred. How vile they feel; how society despises them. Then what a word he chooses to refer to their riches, a word found only here in the Bible; they are "corrupted" (v.3). "Cankered", another word used only here in the NT, denotes the extreme harm of deadly poison; it eats from the inside out; rust eats in from the outside. What a totally gangrenous condition exists now. To project it into the future but compounds the total loss: miserable is the present and more miserable the future (v.4). God is interested not only in his wealth but also in how it was acquired.

4 In considering the contract first he states that the poor labourer has met his responsibility but has been denied his full wages. This denial was not an oversight on the master's part; it was his deliberate policy to short pay his workers. The amount and quality of the work performed was not in question. The labourer has met his obligations, the fields have been harvested, but the hire, the agreed wages, have not been paid in full by the rich owner. He was guilty of fraud, instead of this being the joyful occasion depicted by the Lord when at Sychar's well: "he that reapeth receiveth wages" (John 4:36). Again every servant is worthy of his hire or wages. Here we find the workers have harvested but the wages are not paid in full. The wages partially paid was not a simple mistake but a deliberate policy. Part of them was held back deliberately. The underpayment was intentional and was crying out as too did the labourers cry out. These, unheeded by the earthly master, were heard by another and higher Master, the Lord of hosts. This is another OT title, the title for an avenger who is overall and shall do right. The only other place where it is found in the NT is Rom 9:29.

5 The lifestyle of the unjust master displays that he not only hoarded but lived in sinful pleasure. His guilt lay not only in covetousness but in the insatiable lust for making gain to spend on himself. Luke in chapter 12 of his Gospel relates a parable told by the Lord of a greedy rich fool. The moral announced in the closing comment of the story is that we ought to pile up treasure in heaven where neither moth (from the outside) nor rust (from the inside) can corrupt. In Col 3:5 Paul equates greed with idolatry. James when he refers to the last days is emphasising the folly of getting rich by dishonest means when we have but a few days on earth and a long eternity. The reference to "a day of slaughter" is difficult to explain. Perhaps, having referred to the last days of life, he changes the metaphor, as he frequently does, and expresses in a religious manner the final sacrifice of service and its eternal value.

6 This is the verse of review and the final indictment of this unjust master. He had sat as judge, jury and executioner. The servant who was denied his rights displays the attitude of Abel: unresisting and prepared to trust even to death. Or it may be that James is alluding to Stephen and others who were persecuted and killed. This was also the experience of the Lord Himself, whom James seems always to have before him as he writes.

7-9 These verses speak boldly of issues James sees as important:

vv.7-9	The Need for Patience
vv.10-11	Examples of Patience
vv.12-15	The Necessity of Prayer
vv.16-18	The Example of Prayer
vv.19-20	The Recovery of the Erring

The coming of the Lord is mentioned as James summarises. In this final section there is a gathering up of the main matters dealt with in the letter and appropriate encouragements given. The return to the expression "brethren" used on four occasions, emphasises the relationship and returns the readers to family matters. His message to the rich masters outside the family circle has finished. He has thoroughly condemned them and has nothing further to say to them. He now acknowledges the common bond that binds all God's people together and will finish his message with real affection.

These is a need for patience or passionate endurance to endure the wicked outrage of the tyrannical rich masters who have been strongly condemned in the earlier verses (vv. 1-4). The end of persecution is when the Lord comes. Throughout the centuries saints in different lands have suffered; many have forfeited their goods and some have suffered martyrdom. This must end and it will at the coming of the Lord. The word used here for this event is *parousia*. It is used by other NT writers such as Matthew (24:27) when he describes the coming of the Son of man, Paul in 1 Thess 5:23, and John in 1 John 2:28; in all at least twenty four times in our NT, always denoting a personal presence with great power and accompanied with glory. Here to the suffering saints it brings relief from the unjustified punishment by the powerful rich. This event thus signals the great change. Our pain will then be over, oppression will have ended.

James, however, would emphasise the present need of patience. The illustration of the working farmer focuses not on his work but on his patience. The farmer has ploughed and prayed and now waits in patience for God to do His work. The suffering saint likewise waits with patient endurance for God to do His work; so in v.8 the patience is somewhat like that of the farmer whose work is complete. Nor does he wait just for the rain; he waits for the fruit. The harvest is the end of the rain and the reaping of the fruit. This lovely horticultural picture concludes with the joy of harvest. This too will be the joy of His coming specially for the persecuted saints. All sorrow will be over and nothing but joy will be ours at His coming.

In v.9 the simple exhortation is helpful for the present period of waiting. We must stop all moaning and groaning, not only against our oppressors but against each other. Certainly His advent is the arrival of a Saviour to remove us from the oppressor but He comes also as a legal and righteous Judge. Whilst James does not attempt to set out, like Paul, the order of all the associated events, he is giving strong incentive for presently desisting from blaming others or murmuring against God. The judge who will do right stands (ready to administer justice) before the door. The door will and must open to Him (cf. Ps 24).

IX. Faith and Trust (5:10-20)

> v.10 "Take, my brethren, the prophets, who have spoken in the name of the Lord, for an example of suffering affliction, and of patience.
> v.11 Behold, we count them happy which endure. Ye have heard of the patience of Job, and have seen the end of the Lord; that the Lord is very pitiful, and of tender mercy.
> v.12 But above all things, my brethren, swear not, neither by heaven, neither by the earth, neither by any other oath: but let your yea be yea; and *your* nay, nay; lest ye fall into condemnation.
> v.13 Is any among you afflicted? let him pray. Is any merry? let him sing psalms.
> v.14 Is any sick among you? let him call for the elders of the church; and let them pray over him, anointing him with oil in the name of the Lord;
> v.15 And the prayer of faith shall save the sick, and the Lord shall raise him up; and if he have committed sins, they shall be forgiven him.
> v.16 Confess *your* faults one to another, and pray one for another that ye may be healed. The effectual fervent prayer of a righteous man availeth much.
> v.17 Elias was a man subject to like passions as we are, and he prayed earnestly that it might not rain: and it rained not on the earth by the space of three years and six months.
> v.18 And he prayed again, and the heaven gave rain, and the earth brought forth her fruit.
> v.19 Brethren, if any of you do err from the truth, and one convert him;
> v.20 Let him know, that he which converteth the sinner from the error of his way shall save a soul from death, and shall hide a multitude of sins."

10-11 If we should need examples of the correct attitude in our day of reproach and suffering then there are many. In Matt 5:12 the Lord deals with this very subject and points to the example of the OT prophets. Even though they were the heaven-sent messengers they were not exempt from being abused and they have become examples of how to bear suffering. They did it with an enduring patience, and without complaining and murmuring, but some might argue that those prophets were extraordinary, so another example of patient, uncomplaining endurance is cited. This time it is a family man, Job, whose patient endurance fills the book of his life, and in all his many trials he did not sin; he waited patiently on his God. The next expression, "ye have seen the end of the Lord", is frequently understood as referring to the outcome of Job's trials. In His pity and tender mercy God graciously compensated Job for his piety in the extremity of his trial, so that his final state was better than his first.

The present writer believes that James, having alluded briefly to Job, now brings in his last and greatest example of patient faith displayed under the greatest test: the end of the Lord. What personal memories were his as he mentions the end of the Lord. The brave perseverance of the prophets and the exemplary witnessing of Job are helpful, but how emotional they must have felt as they remembered the closing days of the Lord. Some had listened to the piercing cries in Gethsemane, had followed Him from the garden of prayers to the palace of the wicked priests. They found the Lord was silent yet cooperative and unresisting as He made His way via a Gentile court to Calvary. Not a murmur escaped His lips but instead strong cryings and these mixed with tears as he prayed. No wonder James writes "the Lord is very pitiful and of tender mercy". Heb 5:7-9 is a fitting record of the end of the Lord and the example for all saints to follow. The quality of the compassion of the Lord for us is enhanced by His own experience. He is "very pitiful" (an adjective only found here in our Bible). Then he is "of tender mercy", a phrase used by Luke of the Father (6:36). This was His attitude to others, some of whom caused His pain. What an example to follow.

12 This is advice for those in the midst of suffering and waiting, so he appeals and enjoins them, My brethren, do not give way to outbursts of anger and do not fall into condemnation. It would be not only natural but also easy to fall so do not give way. There must be no calling for retribution, no swearing (cf. Matt 5:33-48), no calling down of God's wrath, no asking God to take revenge on your persecutors. Rather pray for them, without the urge for revenge, without swearing with an oath to get even, lest you drop to their level and into the condemned cell. This would be following the example of the Lord and even in the trial or having passed it, raise your song in triumph. The affliction referred to takes us back to v.10 and the experience of the prophets, the songs to the psalms of triumph.

13-14 The question and answer approach continues. These questions are connected in that while they relate to random experiences they often cause great exercise of heart. In the previous verse opposite conditions are dealt with and the advised attitude to each of them. In times of suffering pray, in times of joy sing appropriate

Psalms. Another circumstance is physical illness, which can prove to be a real trial; in the first century it was a much greater trial. Today in most lands there are medical facilities available, not so then. The caring group then were the elders of the church who did two things: the main part of their duty was to pray; then, there was the subordinate act of anointing with oil. This act of anointing with oil must not be associated with being anointed to an office or work as Aaron was to the priesthood. Oil was used because of its medicinal value. Notice that the word "elders" is plural and that the practice of rubbing a sick person with an healing oil was normal. All this was done in the name or by the authority of the Lord. The custom of those early days when folks were injured or sick was to pour in oil and wine (Luke 10:34). The science of medicine then was not as sophisticated as it is today.

15 The progress made and still being made is available in most lands for which we must be truly grateful to God. Nevertheless the privilege and power of prayer must not be underestimated. In this passage of Scripture the verbs are in the aorist tense. First having oiled with oil then pray. No one should think that this practice is the prerogative of special Spirit-filled religious officials. Paul on another occasion advised a little wine for Timothy's stomach disorder (1 Tim 5:23). Here in our verse we learn that elders are concerned not only about spiritual but also the physical health of the saints. This practice began in Mark 6:7-13 and continued. We in our day must make use of the various prescriptions available from the health services but we must ever engage in joint prayer for the recovery to health of the sick. James says the prayer of faith shall save the sick, that is, shall rescue the sick from the malady if the Lord wills it so. 4:15 emphasises the will of the Lord and excludes any boasting. This does not mean that every sick person will recover nor does it mean that our prayer can overrule the will of God. The NT has much to say about elders but it does not ascribe to them miraculous powers. It is the Lord who reserves this right to Himself. The elders do not command the sick person to arise. They are obliged to use the current medicine, here oil, and sometimes accompanied with wine. The natural means should not be discarded and neither should prayer; both are to be employed in the name (authority) of the Lord. If sin has been the root cause of the trouble then there is no point of using oil or prayer if the sinful practice continues; therefore a confession to condemn and a commitment to abandon its practice is necessary.

James is thought by some to be dealing with some who have succumbed to the fiery darts of the wicked one. They note that James uses two words both translated "sick" (vv. 14,15). "Sick" in v.14 means "not strong" or "weak". It occurs thirty-four times in the NT, twenty of which relate to physical weakness and fourteen to moral or spiritual weakness; those "weak in faith" in Rom 14 and 1 Cor 8 being among such usages. Clearly the context must decide whether or not James writes of physical weakness.

The second word "sick" (*kamnō*) is in v.15 and, it is claimed, really means "weary" or "exhausted". Its only other use in the NT is in Heb 12:3-4. In that celebrated passage we are to "consider him who endured such contradiction of sinners against himself least ye be weary and faint in your minds". In Heb 12 that weariness is mental rather than physical.

James may then be writing, say such interpreters, of one who is weak and weary so much so that there is the possibility that even momentarily he may have succumbed to temptation and have sinned. To such the spiritual are sent by James, much as Paul did in Gal 6:1, and they will pray over him. The mention of praying Elijah seems in keeping with the purposed recovery, they would add, for he too was involved in recovery, the recovery of a nation. The claim upon which this interpretation depends is not supported by the use of *kamnō* in writers outside of the Bible.

16 It is fitting that James should return to prayer at the end of v.16 to show its power and effect. The intelligent prayer is made possible by the open confession of sin. This confession includes the resolve by the sick person to abandon the sinful habit. This kind of prayer is effective and warm with the love of God and from a man who is not guilty of the particular sin. He is described as a righteous or a just person. Many examples are in our Bible (eg. Dan 9:18). Here in v.17 he cites another example, the prophet Elijah.

17-18 We have found in our study that living examples are often used to illustrate truth being expounded. This illustration of Elias is pertinent. He is described as a man similar to us, so his kind of prayer is within our reach. His prayer had to do, not with physical illness, but with God blessing the land with rain and then also withholding the rain. His people had grievously sinned in turning away from God and were in bondage. They also had turned to other, pagan, deities. Their sin was compounded but Elijah did not abandon them. Rain was a blessing from God and Elijah asked God to withhold His blessing knowing this would not only hurt them but also himself; he was willing to suffer with them if this would cause them to repent. His praying is described in a special way. Literally he "prayed being at prayer". The content is surprising, "Do not send the early or latter rain". He asked God to withdraw His blessing and God answered him. The loss of at least three harvests brought the nation to Elijah in humble confession of sin. At the sign of repentance he prayed again and the heaven (singular) gave rain and the earth brought forth its fruit.

19-20 Vv.19-20 contain the final word of James and conclude with an application of the history lesson from Elias. Where and when the people of God depart from the truth then act like Elias; pray earnestly, intelligently, lovingly to bring recovery from error and an abandoning of sin. To pray and suffer like Elias is to find the way of success for self and for others.

James began his letter with a ministry toward those being tried. He expected patience, but well knew the consequences upon those who failed to exercise patience. For some the trial of their faith might be in sickness and in extreme physical ailment they may fail to exercise patience or to ask for wisdom; for others the trial may bring them to the point of mental exhaustion and weary with striving against sin they too fail to show patience. Certainly the danger of sin is evident, and where some have erred, the need of conversion – the conversion of a saint! – is equally clear. The James who begins by commending the virtues which would avoid erring ends his letter by approving the restoration of those lacking these very virtues.

Even in his concluding remarks James remains practical, forthright and caring in his approach to those he has been describing as his brethren. In that he stands a lasting testimony to all who labour in the Word.

NOTES

NOTES

NOTES

NOTES

NOTES

NOTES

NOTES

NOTES

NOTES

NOTES

NOTES

NOTES

NOTES

NOTES